Cases on Open–Linked Data and Semantic Web Applications

Patricia Ordóñez de Pablos
Universidad de Oviedo, Spain

Miltiadis D. Lytras
The American College of Greece, Greece

Robert Tennyson
University of Minnesota, USA

José Emilio Labra Gayo
Universidad de Oviedo, Spain

T0320722

Information Science
REFERENCE
An Imprint of IGI Global

Managing Director:	Lindsay Johnston
Editorial Director:	Joel Gamon
Production Manager:	Jennifer Yoder
Publishing Systems Analyst:	Adrienne Freeland
Development Editor:	Myla Merkel
Assistant Acquisitions Editor:	Kayla Wolfe
Typesetter:	Christina Henning
Cover Design:	Jason Mull

Published in the United States of America by
Information Science Reference (an imprint of IGI Global)
701 E. Chocolate Avenue
Hershey PA 17033
Tel: 717-533-8845
Fax: 717-533-8661
E-mail: cust@igi-global.com
Web site: http://www.igi-global.com

Library of Congress Cataloging-in-Publication Data

Cases on open-linked data and semantic web applications / Patricia Ordonez de Pablos, Miltiadis D. Lytras, Robert Tennyson and Jose Emilio Labra Gayo, editors.
     pages cm
  Includes bibliographical references and index.
  Summary: "This book brings together new theories, research findings and case studies that cover the recent developments and approaches toward applied open linked data and semantic web in the context of information systems"--Provided by publisher.
  ISBN 978-1-4666-2827-4 -- ISBN 978-1-4666-2828-1 (ebk.) -- ISBN 978-1-4666-2829-8 (print & perpetual access) 1. Semantic Web. I. Ordsqez de Pablos, Patricia, 1975-
  TK5105.88815.C3637 2012
  025.042'7--dc23
                          2012033666

British Cataloguing in Publication Data
A Cataloguing in Publication record for this book is available from the British Library.

All work contributed to this book is new, previously-unpublished material. The views expressed in this book are those of the authors, but not necessarily of the publisher.

Editorial Advisory Board

Table of Contents

Preface..xiii

Chapter 1
Enhancing the Access to Public Procurement Notices by Promoting Product
Scheme Classifications to the Linked Open Data Initiative................................... 1
    Jose María Alvarez Rodríguez, University of Oviedo, Spain
    Luis Polo Paredes, Fundación CTIC, Spain
    Emilio Rubiera Azcona, Fundación CTIC, Spain
    Alejandro Rodríguez González, Centre for Plant Biotechnology and Genomics,
        Polytechnic University of Madrid, Spain
    José Emilio Labra Gayo, University of Oviedo, Spain
    Patricia Ordoñez de Pablos, University of Oviedo, Spain

Chapter 2
User Assisted Creation of Open-Linked Data for Training Web Information
Extraction in a Social Network 28
    Martin Necasky, Charles University, Czech Republic
    Ivo Lasek, Charles University, Czech Republic
    Dominik Fiser, Charles University, Czech Republic
    Ladislav Peska, Charles University, Czech Republic
    Peter Vojtas, Charles University, Czech Republic

Chapter 3
Providing Information from Brazilian Politicians Using Linked Data 39
    Jairo Francisco de Souza, Federal University of Juiz de Fora, Brazil
    Sean Wolfgand Matsui Siqueira, Federal University of the State of Rio de Janeiro
        (UNIRIO), Brazil
    Lucas de Ramos Araújo, Federal University of Juiz de Fora, Brazil
    Rubens Nascimento Melo, Federal University of Juiz de Fora, Brazil

Chapter 4
Extraction and Prediction of Biomedical Database Identifier Using Neural
Networks towards Data Network Construction 58
Hendrik Mehlhorn, Institute of Plant Genetics and Crop Plant Research,
Germany
Matthias Lange, Institute of Plant Genetics and Crop Plant Research, Germany
Uwe Scholz, Institute of Plant Genetics and Crop Plant Reseearch, Germany
Falk Schreiber, Institue of Plant Genetics and Crop Plant Research, Germany
& Martin Luther University, Germany

Chapter 5
Role of Vocabularies for Semantic Interoperability in Enabling the Linked
Open Data Publishing 84
Ahsan Morshed, United Nations, Italy

Chapter 6
Enabling the Matchmaking of Organizations and Public Procurement
Notices by Means of Linked Open Data 105
Jose María Alvarez Rodríguez, University of Oviedo, Spain
José Emilio Labra Gayo, University of Oviedo, Spain
Patricia Ordoñez de Pablos, University of Oviedo, Spain

Chapter 7
A Semantic Framework for Touristic Information Systems 132
Salvador Lima, Instituto Politécnico de Viana do Castelo, Portugal
José Moreira, Universidade de Aveiro, Portugal

Chapter 8
Semi-Automatic Knowledge Extraction to Enrich Open Linked Data 156
Elena Baralis, Politecnico di Torino, Italy
Giulia Bruno, Politecnico di Torino, Italy
Tania Cerquitelli, Politecnico di Torino, Italy
Silvia Chiusano, Politecnico di Torino, Italy
Alessandro Fiori, Politecnico di Torino, Italy
Alberto Grand, Politecnico di Torino, Italy

Chapter 9
Variables Performance for E-Services Acceptance: A Descriptive Statistical
Analysis.. 181
Kamaljeet Sandhu, University of New England, Australia

Chapter 10
News Trends Processing Using Open Linked Data 192
  Antonio Garrote, Universidad de Salamanca, Spain
  María N. Moreno García, Universidad de Salamanca, Spain

Chapter 11
Publishing Statistical Data following the Linked Open Data Principles: The Web
Index Project 199
  Jose María Alvarex Rodríguez, University of Oviedo, Spain
  Jules Clement, World Wide Web Foundation, Switerland
  José Emilio Labra Gayo, Univeristy of Oviedo, Spain
  Hania Farhan, World Wide Web Foundation, Switerland
  Patricia Ordoñez de Pablos, Unversity of Oviedo, Spain

Compilation of References 227

Related References 244

About the Contributors 276

Index 285

Detailed Table of Contents

Preface xiii

Chapter 1

Enhancing the Access to Public Procurement Notices by Promoting Product
Scheme Classifications to the Linked Open Data Initiative 1

Jose María Alvarez Rodríguez, University of Oviedo, Spain
Luis Polo Paredes, Fundación CTIC, Spain
Emilio Rubiera Azcona, Fundación CTIC, Spain
Alejandro Rodríguez González, Centre for Plant Biotechnology and Genomics,
*   Polytechnic University of Madrid, Spain*
José Emilio Labra Gayo, University of Oviedo, Spain
Patricia Ordoñez de Pablos, University of Oviedo, Spain

This chapter introduces the promotion of existing product scheme classifications to the Linked Open Data initiative in the context of the European Union and other official organizations such as United Nations. A common data model and an enclosed conversion method based on Semantic Web vocabularies such as SKOS are also presented to encode data and information following the W3C standards RDF and OWL. This work is applied to the e-procurement sector, more specifically, to enhance the access to the public procurement notices published in the European Union. Finally, an evaluation of the gain, in terms of expressivity, is reported with the objective of demonstrating the advantages of applying Linked Data to retrieve information resources.

Chapter 2

User Assisted Creation of Open-Linked Data for Training Web Information
Extraction in a Social Network 28

Martin Necasky, Charles University, Czech Republic
Ivo Lasek, Charles University, Czech Republic
Dominik Fiser, Charles University, Czech Republic
Ladislav Peska, Charles University, Czech Republic
Peter Vojtas, Charles University, Czech Republic

In this chapter we describe our project under development and proof of concept for creating large Open-Linked Data repositories. The main problem is twofold: (1) Who will create (annotate) Open-Linked Data and in which vocabularies? (2)What will be the usage and profit of it?

For the first problem we propose several procedures on how to create Open-Linked data, including assisted creation of annotations (serving as base line or training set for Web Information Extraction tools), employing the social network, and also specific approaches to creating Open-linked data from governmental data resources. We describe some cases where such data can be used (e.g., in e-commerce, recommending systems, and in governmental and public policy projects).

Chapter 3
Providing Information from Brazilian Politicians Using Linked Data 39
    Jairo Francisco de Souza, Federal University of Juiz de Fora, Brazil
    Sean Wolfgand Matsui Siqueira, Federal University of the State of Rio de Janeiro (UNIRIO), Brazil
    Lucas de Ramos Araújo, Federal University of Juiz de Fora, Brazil
    Rubens Nascimento Melo, Federal University of Juiz de Fora, Brazil

Since its inception, the Web has undergone continuous evolution in order to improve itself as a means of global communication and information sharing. Open Government Data are increasingly being published on the Web, contributing to the transparency and the reusability of public data. At the same time, the use of Linked Data has been increasing in recent years, enabling the development of better and smarter applications. This chapter presents a case on the publication of Open Government Data using the Linked Data practices, by creating a data set of Brazilian politicians with information collected from different sources. This is the first dataset providing Brazilian linked data.

Chapter 4
Extraction and Prediction of Biomedical Database Identifier Using Neural Networks towards Data Network Construction 58
    Hendrik Mehlhorn, Institute of Plant Genetics and Crop Plant Research, Germany
    Matthias Lange, Institute of Plant Genetics and Crop Plant Research, Germany
    Uwe Scholz, Institute of Plant Genetics and Crop Plant Reseearch, Germany
    Falk Schreiber, Institue of Plant Genetics and Crop Plant Research, Germany & Martin Luther University, Germany

Knowledge found in biomedical databases is a major bioinformatics resource. In general, this biological knowledge is represented worldwide in a network of thousands of databases, which overlap in content, but differ substantially with respect to content detail, interface, formats, and data structure. To support a functional annotation of lab data, such as protein sequences, metabolites, or DNA sequences, as well as a semi-automated data exploration in information retrieval environments, an integrated view to databases is essential. A prerequisite of supporting the concept of an integrated data view is to acquire insights into cross-references among database entities. In this work, we investigate to what extent an automated construction of an integrated data network is possible. We propose a method that predicts and extracts cross-references from multiple life science databases and possible referenced data targets. We study the retrieval quality of our method and report on first, promising results.

Chapter 5
Role of Vocabularies for Semantic Interoperability in Enabling the Linked
Open Data Publishing 84
Ahsan Morshed, United Nations, Italy

In the spite of explosive growth of the Internet, information relevant to users is often unavailable even when using the latest browsers. At the same time, there is an ever-increasing number of documents that vary widely in content, format, and quality. The documents often change in content and location because they do not belong to any kind of centralized control. On the other hand, there is a huge number of unknown users with extremely diverse needs, skills, education, and cultural and language backgrounds. One of the solutions to these problems might be to use standard terms with meaning; this can be termed as controlled vocabulary (CV). Though there is no specific notion of CV, we can define it as a set of concepts or preferred terms and existing relations among them. These vocabularies play very important roles classifying the information. In this chapter, we focus the role of CV for publishing the web of data on the Web.

Chapter 6
Enabling the Matchmaking of Organizations and Public Procurement
Notices by Means of Linked Open Data... 105
Jose María Alvarez Rodríguez, University of Oviedo, Spain
José Emilio Labra Gayo, University of Oviedo, Spain
Patricia Ordoñez de Pablos, University of Oviedo, Spain

The aim of this chapter is to present a proposal and a case study to describe the information about organizations in a standard way using the Linked Data approach. Several models and ontologies have been provided in order to formalize the data, structure and behaviour of organizations. Nevertheless, these tries have not been fully accepted due to some factors: (1) missing pieces to define the status of the organization; (2) tangled parts to specify the structure (concepts and relations) between the elements of the organization; 3) lack of text properties, and other factors. These divergences imply a set of incomplete approaches to formalize data and information about organizations. Taking into account the current trends of applying semantic web technologies and linked data to formalize, aggregate, and share domain specific information, a new model for organizations taking advantage of these initiatives is required in order to overcome existing barriers and exploit the corporate information in a standard way. This work is especially relevant in some senses to: (1) unify existing models to provide a common specification; (2) apply semantic web technologies and the Linked Data approach; (3) provide access to the information via standard protocols, and (4) offer new services that can exploit this information to trace the evolution and behaviour of the organization over time. Finally, this work is interesting to improve the clarity and transparency of some scenarios in which organizations play a key role, like e-procurement, e-health, or financial transactions.

Chapter 7
A Semantic Framework for Touristic Information Systems 132
Salvador Lima, Instituto Politécnico de Viana do Castelo, Portugal
José Moreira, Universidade de Aveiro, Portugal

The Web is a crucial means for the dissemination of touristic information. However, most touristic information resources are stored directly in Web pages or in relational databases that are accessible through ad-hoc Web applications, and the use of automated processes to search, extract and interpret information can hardly be implemented. The Semantic Web technologies, aiming at representing the background knowledge about Web resources in a computational way, can be an important contribution to the development of such automated processes. This chapter introduces the concept of touristic object, giving special attention to the representation of temporal, spatial, and thematic knowledge. It also proposes a three-layered architecture for the representation of touristic objects in the Web. The central part is the domain layer, defining a Semantic Model for Tourism (SeMoT) to describe concepts, relationships, and constraints using ontologies. The data layer supports the mapping of touristic information in relational databases into Resource Description Framework (RDF) virtual graphs following the SeMoT specification. The application layer deals with the integration of information from different data sources into a unified knowledge model, offering a common vocabulary to describe touristic information resources. Finally, we also show how to use this framework for planning touristic itineraries.

Chapter 8
Semi-Automatic Knowledge Extraction to Enrich Open Linked Data.............. 156
Elena Baralis, Politecnico di Torino, Italy
Giulia Bruno, Politecnico di Torino, Italy
Tania Cerquitelli, Politecnico di Torino, Italy
Silvia Chiusano, Politecnico di Torino, Italy
Alessandro Fiori, Politecnico di Torino, Italy
Alberto Grand, Politecnico di Torino, Italy

In this chapter we present the analysis of the Wikipedia collection by means of the ELiDa framework with the aim of enriching linked data. ELiDa is based on association rule mining, an exploratory technique to discover relevant correlations hidden in the analyzed data. To compactly store the large volume of extracted knowledge and efficiently retrieve it for further analysis, a persistent structure has been exploited. The domain expert is in charge of selecting the relevant knowledge by setting filtering parameters, assessing the quality of the extracted knowledge, and enriching the knowledge with the semantic expressiveness which cannot be automatically inferred. We consider, as representative document collections, seven datasets extracted from the Wikipedia collection. Each dataset has been analyzed from two point of views (i.e., transactions by documents, transactions by sentences) to highlight relevant knowledge at different levels of abstraction.

Chapter 9
Variables Performance for E-Services Acceptance: A Descriptive Statistical
Analysis.. 181
Kamaljeet Sandhu, University of New England, Australia

This case study examines the Web Electronic Service framework for a University in Australia. The department is in the process of developing and implementing a Web-based e-service system. The user experience to use e-services requires insight into the attributes that shape the experience variable. The descriptive data about the attributes that form the experience variable is provided in this study.

Chapter 10
News Trends Processing Using Open Linked Data 192
Antonio Garrote, Universidad de Salamanca, Spain
María N. Moreno García, Universidad de Salamanca, Spain

In this chapter we describe a news trends detection system built with the aim of detecting daily trends in a big collection of news articles extracted from the web and expose the computed trends data as open linked data that can be consumed by other components of the IT infrastructure. Due to the sheer amount of data being processed, the system relies on big data technologies to process raw news data and compute the trends that will be later exposed as open linked data. Thanks to the open linked data interface, data can be easily consumed by other components of the application, like a JavaScript front-end, or re-used by different IT systems. The case is a good example of how open linked data can be used to provide a convenient interface to big data systems.

Chapter 11
Publishing Statistical Data following the Linked Open Data Principles: The Web
Index Project 199
Jose María Alvarex Rodríguez, University of Oviedo, Spain
Jules Clement, World Wide Web Foundation, Switerland
José Emilio Labra Gayo, Univeristy of Oviedo, Spain
Hania Farhan, World Wide Web Foundation, Switerland
Patricia Ordoñez de Pablos, Unversity of Oviedo, Spain

This chapter introduces the promotion of statistical data to the Linked Open Data initiative in the context of the Web Index project. A framework for the publication of raw statistics and a method to convert them to Linked Data are also presented following the W3C standards RDF, SKOS, and OWL. This case study is focused on the Web Index project; launched by the Web Foundation, the Index is the first multi-dimensional measure of the growth, utility, and impact of the Web on people and nations. Finally, an evaluation of the advantages of using Linked Data to publish statistics is also presented in conjunction with a discussion and future steps sections.

Compilation of References 227

Related References 244

About the Contributors 276

Index 285

Preface

INTRODUCTION

Tim Berners-Lee coined the term "Linked Data" in his Linked Data Web architecture note. It refers to a way of publishing and interlinking structured data on the Web and in simple words, basically *Linked Data* aims to enable people to share structured data on the Web as easily as they can share documents today. The basic assumption behind this term is that the usefulness and value of data increases the more it is interlinked with other data. According to Tim Berners-Lee (2006), "like the web of hypertext, the web of data is constructed with documents on the web. However, unlike the web of hypertext, where links are relationships anchors in hypertext documents written in HTML, for data they links between arbitrary things described by RDF".

The book will help to communicate and disseminate relevant recent research in open linked data and Semantic Web based personalization as applied to the context of information systems.

OBJECTIVES OF THE BOOK

Linked Data literature proposes using the Web to connect related data that was not previously linked, or using the Web to lower the barriers to linking data currently linked using other methods. More specifically, the basic elements of linked data are to: (1) use the RDF data model to publish structured data on the Web; and (2) use RDF links to interlink data from different data sources. The application of both principles leads to the creation of a data commons on the Web which is often called the Web of Data or Semantic Web.

The book chapter collection covers Open Linked Data and Semantic Web approaches to information systems and ontology-based information systems research, as well as the diverse underlying database and knowledge representation aspects that impact personalization and the customization. The chapter addresses challenges for this new field of research.

Chapter 1 provides an overview on the existing product scheme classification to the Linked Open Data initiative in the context of the European Union and other official organizations such as the United Nations, and more importantly as it applied to the e-procurement sector.

Chapter 2 describes the development and concept for the creation of Open Linked Data repositories, including what will be the profit of it as well as who will create Open Linked Data and in which vocabularies. The chapter proposes several ideas in the conclusion of these issues.

Chapter 3 presents a case study on open government data that is increasingly being published on the web, which contributes to the reusability of public data. The use of linked data has increased over the years, which enables smarter applications.

Chapter 4 investigates to what extent an automated construction of an integrated data network is possible. The authors of the chapter propose a method that predicts and extracts cross-references from multiple life science databases and possible referenced data targets.

Chapter 5 focuses on the role of controlled vocabulary for publishing the web of data. Though there are no specific notions of CV (controlled vocabulary), the authors have defined it as a set of concepts or preferred terms and existing relations among them.

Chapter 6 presents a case study to describe information about organizations in a standard way using the linked data approach using models and ontologies in order to formalize the data, structure, and behaviour of organizations.

Chapter 7 introduces the concept of touristic object, giving special attention to the representation of temporal, spatial, and thematic knowledge. The chapter also proposes a three-layered architecture for the representation of touristic objects in the web.

Chapter 8 presents the analysis of the Wikipedia collection by means of the ELiDa framework with the aim of enriching linked data. The chapter considers seven databases extracted from the Wikipedia collection. Each dataset has been analyzed from two viewpoints in order to highlight relevant knowledge at different levels of abstraction.

Chapter 9 examines the web electronic service framework for a specific university in Australia. This department is in the process of developing and implementing a web-based e-service system. This study also highlights descriptive data about the attributes that form the experience.

Chapter 10 describes a news trends detection system built with the aim of detecting daily trends in a a big collection of news articles extracted from the web and exposes the computed trends data as open linked data that can be consumed by other components of the IT infrastructure.

The subject area is a combination of *Web Semantic, Open Linked Data, Business, Management, Information Technologies* and *Information Systems*.

TOPICS

The book aims to be an international platform to bring together academics, researchers, lecturers, persons in decision making positions, policy makers, and practitioners from different backgrounds; to share new theories, research findings, and case studies to enhance understanding and collaboration in open linked data in business and science; to enhance the role of information technologies and web semantics; and to analyse recent developments in theory and practice.

Finally, we would like to thank all authors for the participation in this book as well as the IGI Global staff for their continuous support during the development of the book.

Patricia Ordóñez de Pablos
University of Oviedo, Spain

Miltiadis D. Lytras
American College of Greece, Greece

Jose Emilio Labra Gayo
University of Oviedo, Spain

Chapter 1

Enhancing the Access to Public Procurement Notices by Promoting Product Scheme Classifications to the Linked Open Data Initiative

Jose María Alvarez Rodríguez
University of Oviedo, Spain

Luis Polo Paredes
Fundación CTIC, Spain

Emilio Rubiera Azcona
Fundación CTIC, Spain

Alejandro Rodríguez González
Centre for Plant Biotechnology and Genomics, Polytechnic University of Madrid, Spain

José Emilio Labra Gayo
University of Oviedo, Spain

Patricia Ordoñez de Pablos
University of Oviedo, Spain

EXECUTIVE SUMMARY

This chapter introduces the promotion of existing product scheme classifications to the Linked Open Data initiative in the context of the European Union and other official organizations such as United Nations. A common data model and an enclosed conversion method based on Semantic Web vocabularies such as SKOS are also presented to encode data and information following the W3C standards RDF and OWL. This work is applied to the e-procurement sector, more specifically, to

DOI: 10.4018/978-1-4666-2827-4.ch001

enhance the access to the public procurement notices published in the European Union. Finally, an evaluation of the gain, in terms of expressivity, is reported with the objective of demonstrating the advantages of applying Linked Data to retrieve information resources.

ORGANIZATION BACKGROUND

WESO is a multidisciplinary research group from the Department of Computer Science and the Departments of Philology at the University of Oviedo created by the Associate Professor Dr. José Emilio Labra Gayo. Since 2005 WESO is involved in semantic web research, education and technology transfer. The growth of the Internet in the last years has brought relevant changes in the way of communication. Nowadays governments, citizens, enterprises and society are more interconnected than ever and information is the key to keep the interconnection among parties. This new information society needs a step forward to exploit the new opportunities and challenges. WESO research activities try to apply semantic web technologies in order to facilitate the transition to a new web of data.

As academic research group, one of our aims is to boost the research, innovation and competitiveness of the organizations using the knowledge. WESO seeks to support research and innovation focusing on:

- Providing research services on semantics.
- Applying semantic technologies to improve existing products.
- Addressing the new-technology barriers.
- Developing and training.
- Fostering the knowledge in the scientific and industrial areas.
- Teaching to a new wave of professionals.

WESO brings together these activities for enabling and supporting people, organizations and systems to collaborate and interoperate in the new global context.

Our research lines focus on semantic web technologies with emphasis on (but not restricted to):

- **Semantic Architectures:** Designing and developing architectures based on domain knowledge.
- **Collaborative Semantic Services:** Improving existing solutions with a semantic collaborative approach.
- **Linked and Open Data:** Offering new solutions for combining RDF vocabularies and publishing data.

- **Methods and Algorithms:** Implementing methods to exploit the domain knowledge and the web of data.
- **Semantic Technologies:** Being aware of the semantic web technologies outcomes of RDF, OWL, SKOS or RIF.
- **Others:** Semantic Web Services, e-government, e-procurement, e-health, etc.

Currently we are involved in the research and development of several partnership projects in the semantic web area, more specifically in the field of e-procurement and Linking Open Data (LOD) the next project must be highlighted:

- **10ders Information Services:** This project is partially funded by the Spanish Ministry of Industry, Tourism and Trade with code TSI-020100-2010-919 and the European Regional Development Fund (EFDR) according to the National Plan of Scientific Research, Development and Technological Innovation 2008-2011, leaded by Gateway Strategic Consultancy Services (Gateway Strategic Consultancy Services, S.L, 2012) and developed in cooperation with EXIS-TI (EXIS-TI, 2012).

This project aims to apply the semantic web and LOD approaches to public procurement notices:

- Transforming government controlled vocabularies such as CPV, CPC, Eurovoc (now available in SKOS), etc. to RDF, RDF(S), SKOS (Miles & Bechhofer, 2009) or OWL.
- Modeling the information inside the public procurement notices as web information resources and enriching them with the aforementioned controlled vocabularies, geographical information (e.g. NUTS and the information now available in the linked data cloud.
- Publishing the information in a SPARQL endpoint providing a linked data node.
- Providing enhanced services (search and sort, matchmaking, georeasoning, statistics, etc.) exploiting this semantic information through ``advanced algorithms'' based on Spreading Activation (SA) techniques, rule based systems (RBS) and a mixing of them.

In the past, we participated in the development of a hybrid search engine for the BOPA (Official bulletin of Asturias). We have also experience applying semantic web technologies to other domains like processing XBRL information which enabled automatically analyze financial information of companies and developing a differential diagnosis system which could infer diseases from symptoms to help medical experts. The outcomes of our research projects are part of our technology and knowledge. Thus, we improve our semantic solutions looking for developments generic, standards, flexible and applicable to future projects.

INTRODUCTION

E-procurement is the linking and integration of inter-organizational business process and systems with the automation of the requisitioning, the approval purchase order management and accounting processes through, and Internet-based protocol (Podlogar, 2007). However, there is much more at stake than the mere changeover from paper based systems to ones using electronic communications for public procurement procedures. It should have the potential to yield important improvements in the efficiency of individual purchases, the overall administration of public procurement and the functioning of the markets for government contracts. The technology in this area may make it possible to automate the processes involved in the e-procurement context besides features for supplier management and complex auctions should be included in by means of applying new technologies and methods in order to fulfill the requirements of this new realm of electronic businesses. In the European e-procurement context there is an increasing commitment to boost the use of electronic communications and transaction processing by government institutions and other public sector organizations. The European Commission (EC) outlines the following advantages in the wider use (European Commission, 2010) of e-procurement: increased accessibility and transparency, benefits for individual procedures, benefits in terms of more efficient procurement administration and potential for integration of EU procurement markets. However several interlinked challenges to fulfill a successful transition to e-procurement are missing: overcoming inertia and fears on the part of contracting authorities and suppliers, lack of standards in e-procurement processes, no means to facilitate mutual recognition of national electronic solutions, onerous technical requirements, particularly for bidder authentication and managing multi-speed transition to e-procurement.

The first action to ease the interconnectivity and interoperability within Europe's emerging e-procurement landscape was the creation of TED ("Tenders Electronic Daily"). It is the on line version of the "Supplement to the Official Journal of the European Union", dedicated to European public procurement (1500 new procurement notices every day) but a unified information system pan-European dealing with:

1. Dispersion of the information.
2. Duplication of the same notice in more than one source.
3. Different publishing formats.

4. Problems regarding to a multilingual environment.
5. Aggregation of low-value procurement opportunities is required.

Other set of actions of the EU in the eGovernment context lies in the development of conceptual/terminological maps available in RAMON, the Eurostat's metadata server: in the Health field, the "European Schedule of Occupational Diseases" or "International Classification of Diseases"; in the Education field, thesauri as "European Education Thesaurus"; European Glossary on Education; in the Employment field, the "International Standard Classification of Occupations"; in the European Parliament activities the "Eurovoc Thesaurus", and in the e-procurement field the "Common Procurement Vocabulary", hereafter CPV, among others. The structure and features of these systems are very heterogeneous, although some common aspects can be found in all of them:

1. Hierarchical relationships between terms or concepts.
2. Multilingual character of the information.

These knowledge organization systems (KOS) enable users to annotate information, providing an agile mechanism for performing tasks such as exploration, searching, automatic classification or reasoning. Although the EC tries to encourage the creation of strategies to improve access to public procurement markets by SMEs. A question about the further steps is not yet answered:

What further steps might be taken to improve the access of all interested parties, particularly SMEs, to e-Procurement systems?

In that sense, some governments have created data catalogues under the 8 principles (*complete, primary, timely, accessible, machine processable, non-discriminatory, non-proprietary, and license-free*) of Open Government Data (OGD) initiative to make it easy for the public the access to public information. This public data enables greater transparency; delivers more efficient public services; and encourages greater public and commercial use and re-use of government information.

On the other hand, the emerging Web of Data and the sheer mass of information now available make it possible the deployment of new services and applications based on the reuse of existing vocabularies and datasets. The popular diagram of the Linked Data Cloud, generated from metadata extracted from the Comprehensive Knowledge Archive Network (CKAN) out, contains 327 datasets, with more than 25 billion RDF triples and 395 million links. In this realm, datasets coming from different sources and domains have been promoted following the principles of the Linked Data initiative to improve the access (in terms of expressivity) to large documental databases (e.g., e-government resources, scientific publications, or e-health records). In the case of KOS, such as thesauri, taxonomies or classification systems are developed by specific communities and institutions in order to organize huge collections of information objects. These vocabularies allow users to annotate (Leukel, 2004) the objects and easily retrieve them, promoting lightweight reasoning in the Semantic Web. Topic or subject indexing is an easy way to introduce machine-readable metadata for a resource's content description. Indeed, Product Scheme Classifications (also known as PSCs) such as the CPV are KOS that have been built to solve specific problems of interoperability and communication in e-commerce (Omelayenko & Fensel, 2001), especially relevant to the European e-procurement domain and related supply chain processes (Hernández, Berbís & González et al., 2010).

Obviously the public information published by governmental contracting authorities, more specifically KOS and PSCs, are a suitable candidate to apply the Linked Data principles and semantic web technologies providing a new environment in which the conjunction of these initiatives provide the building blocks for an innovative unified pan-European information system that encourages standardization of key processes and systems and gives economic operators the tools to overcome technical interoperability easing and enhancing the access and the reuse of public information.

BACKGROUND

As part of the Linked Open Data (hereafter LOD) effort other similar initiatives have also been deployed such as LinkedGeoData, GeoNames geographical database, OpenLink Data Spaces among others. More specifically in the field of LOD (Berners-Lee, 2006) and OGD there are projects trying to exploit the information of public procurement notices like LOTED (LOTED Project, 2012) ("Linked Open Tenders Electronic Daily") where they use the RSS feeds of TED. UK government (UK Government, 2011) is doing a great effort to promote its information sources using this approach. They have published datasets from different sectors: transport, defense, education, NUTS geographical information, etc. Most of the public administrations from different countries are also betting for LOD approach to make public their information: Spain-Aporta project (Spanish Government, 2011), USA (White House, 2009), etc. Currently, there is a working group defining a vocabulary and a set of instructions that ease the discovery and usage of linked datasets (Alexander, Cyganiak, Hausenblas & Zhao, 2011), the new specification of SPARQL (1.1) enables a method for discovering and vocabulary for describing SPARQL services made available via an endpoint or RDF store like OpenLink Virtuoso, OpenRDF

Sesame or OWLim. ELDA or Pubby are examples of linked data frontends that provide a configurable way to access RDF data using simple RESTful URLs that are translated into queries to a SPARQL endpoint. Other approach to consume "semantic data" consists on querying OWL models with SPARQL (Jing, Jeong & Baik, 2008) and an extension for georeasoning with SPARQL (GeoSPARQL) has been also developed.

Finally, and with regards to LOD lifecycles, there are several approaches trying to define methodologies, best practices, and recipes to promote raw data following the principles of the Linked Data and Open Data initiatives:

1. "Linked Data Design Considerations" (Heath & Bizer, 2011).
2. "Linked Data Patterns" (Dodds & Davis, 2011).
3. "Best Practices" (W3C Members, 2011), "Linked Data Cookbook" (Hyland, Villazón-Terrazas & Capadisli, 2011), "GLD Lifecyle" (Hausenblas, Villazón-Terrazas and Hyland, 2011), "Best Practice Recipes for Publishing RDF Vocabularies" (Berrueta, Phipps, Miles, Baker, & Swick, 2008) and "Publishing Open Government Data" (Bennett & Harvey, 2009) from the W3C Working Group "Government Linked Data Working Group" (W3C Members, 2011a).
4. "LOD2 Stack" from the European Project "LOD2" (LOD2 Project, 2012).
5. "Toward a Basic Profile for Linked Data" (Nally & Speicher, 2011) from IBM, it has now the status of W3C Member Submission (Nally, Speicher, Arwe & Le Hors, 2012).
6. Methodology (Cifuentes-Silva, Sifaqui, & Labra, 2011) of Library of Congress of Chile and the University of Oviedo.
7. Specific documentation and guidelines from different countries to open data.

EXISTING APPROACHES FOR CONVERTING CONTROLLED VOCABULARIES TO RDF/OWL

This section discusses existing methods to convert KOS systems. We distinguish between RDF/OWL conversions methods for thesauri and product classification systems.

THESAURI CONVERSION METHODS

A thesaurus is a controlled vocabulary, with equivalent terms explicitly identified and with ambiguous words or phrases (e.g., homographs) made unique. This set of terms also may include broader-narrower or other relationships. Usually they are considered to be the most complex of controlled vocabularies. Thesauri as a KOS system can be converted by means of different procedures. On one hand, there are methods, as the Soergel et al., that propose specific techniques for thesauri conversions into ontology. However the method does not target a specific output format and it considers the hierarchical structure of thesauri as logical is-a relationships. On the other hand, there are some generic methods for thesauri conversions, as the step-wise method defined by Miles et al. This method selects a common output data model, the SKOS vocabulary, and is comprised by the following sequenced steps:

1. Generation of the RDF encoding.
2. Error checking and validation.
3. Publishing the RDF triples on the Web.

In addition, this method has been refined adding three new sub steps for generating the RDF encoding:

1. Analyzing the vocabulary.
2. Mapping the vocabulary to SKOS properties and classes.
3. Building a conversion program.

This initial stepwise method can be considered as a previous effort to the before mentioned linked data lifecycles in which all tasks are already defined and these steps are embedded as part of the whole lifecycle.

PRODUCT CLASSIFICATION SYSTEMS CONVERSION METHODS

Product classification systems have been developed to organize the marketplace in several vertical sectors that reflect the activity (or some activities) of economy and commerce. They have been built to solve specific problems of interoperability and communication in e-commerce (Leukel, 2004) providing a structural organization of different kind of products collected together by some economic criteria. The aim of a PSC is to be used as a standard de facto by different agents for information interchange in marketplaces (Fensel, Ding & Omelayenko, 2001).

Many approaches for product classification systems adaptation to the Semantic Web, like (Hepp, 2005; 2006), present methods with the goal to convert them to domain-ontologies. The tree-based structure between product terms is interpreted then as a logical is-a hierarchy. From our point of view and following the discussion about (Hepp, 2006a; 2007), hierarchical links between the elements of each economic sector have not the semantics of subsumption relationships. The next example taken directly from CPV shows how the relationship between the element "Parts and accessories for bicycles" (34442000-7) and its direct antecessor, "Bicycles" (34440000-3), does not seem an *is-a* relation.

In this case, an ontological property for object composition like *hasPart* would be much better. Moreover, there are further remarks against the idea of using the PSCs as domain-ontologies. It is difficult to assert that the CPV element, "Tin bars, rods, profiles and wire" (27623100), represents any specific product. Rather it should be regarded as a collection of products. To correctly convert this element into a domain ontology, it should be considered as equivalent to the union of several concepts (e.g., TinBar ∪ TinRod ∪ TinProfiles ∪ TinWire).

Our approach instead will not consider PCSs as domain ontologies, but an specific kind of KOS systems. Any PSC, as well as other classification systems (i.e., product classification systems, economic activities classification systems, occupation classification systems, etc.), will be interpreted as a conceptual scheme comprised of conceptual resources. From this point of view, hierarchical relationships are not considered to be any more logical *is-a* relations, but broader/narrower ones.

The Moldeas Platform

The MOLDEAS (*Methods on Linked Data for E-Procurement Applying Semantics*) (Álvarez-Rodríguez, 2012) platform seeks to apply the LOD approach and semantic web technologies to improve and ease the access to public procurement notices addressing the principles of OGD for the e-procurement sector.

- Definition of a new formal linked data lifecycle based on previous efforts that cover the processes of producing, publishing, consuming, validating and feedbacking linked data and more specifically, linking open government data.
- Implementation of a platform to support the activities of the new linked data lifecycle reusing existing tools and technologies.
- Application of the linked data lifecycle and its implementation to the e-procurement domain. This task implies:
  - Transforming vocabularies and PSCs developed by governments such as Common Procurement Vocabulary (CPV), Combined Nomenclature (CN), Statistical Classification of Products by Activity (CPA), Standard International Trade Classification (SITC), North American Industry Classification System (NAICS), Eurovoc (now available in SKOS), etc. to RDF, RDF(S), SKOS or OWL.

- ○ Modeling the information inside the public procurement notices as web information resources and enriching them with the aforementioned controlled vocabularies, geographical information and the information now available in the linked data cloud.
- ○ Publishing the information via a SPARQL endpoint providing a linked data node based on standards.
- ○ Providing enhanced services (search and sort, matchmaking, geo reasoning, statistics, etc.) that exploit this semantic information through advanced algorithms based on Spreading Activation (SA) techniques, recommendation engines, etc.
- ○ Exploiting the enhanced services and the information of the public procurement notices using standards, easing the access to the organizations (support to multilingual and multicultural issues), lowering prices and building new business models, especially interesting for SMEs.

In this chapter, we will focus on the objective of transforming vocabularies and PSCs developed by governmental institutions to the linked data realm. Thus we demonstrate that the interoperability among product catalogues can enhance the possibilities of querying a database containing public procurement notices easing the access to information and data.

A LINKED DATA LIFECYCLE AT A GLANCE

The before mentioned approaches to define linked data lifecycles are based on performing some processes, recipes, methods or tasks using different tools to promote raw data as RDF triples. However, a formal definition of processes, methods and tasks is missing and in most of the cases are based on the author's expertise. The main consequence of this offhand mixing of approaches is the lack of a quantifiable method to measure the quality of the generated RDF data. In the MOLDEAS platform a new linked data lifecycle (three-level based) has been defined in order to define processes, methods and tasks, for instance Figure 1 shows a sketch of the processes.

This three-level lifecycle aims to specify the tasks to be combined in the execution of a semantic method to support a specific process. According to Table 1 the outcomes of a specific task are obtained using semantic web technologies and with the participation of different kind of users such as developer, domain expert, data owner and third-parties. The combination of tasks in a stepwise method enables the implementation of a semantic method to support a lifecycle's process. The formal definition of processes and semantic methods in the MOLDEAS platform enables the separation of concerns and the sustainable management of linked data. In the eGovernment area this issue must be addressed due to the implicit responsibility of

Figure 1. Sketch of linked data lifecycle

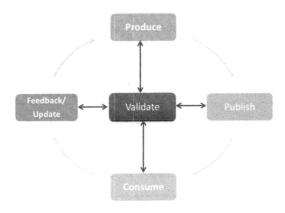

the public administrations of delivering quality services and data. Finally, the evaluation of promoting data using Semantic Web technologies and Linked Data principles is necessary to establish a method to check if the promoted data accomplish with the desired features of Open and Linked Data initiatives to ensure data quality. The method used to validate the data generated from raw sources is based on a checklist (that can be automatically check; 216 key points) created by a compilation of checkpoints, from books, W3C specifications, Open Data and Linked Data principles and know-how acquired in previous projects.

LEAST COMMON MULTIPLE OF CONTROLLED VOCABULARIES

As we have just introduced in the previous section, knowledge organizing systems are used for organizing large collections of information objects and efficient. Existing controlled vocabularies are currently represented in several formats: XML files, spreadsheets or text. However promoting them to the Semantic Web is not a merely process of RDF/OWL conversions of data. Conversions need to fulfill some requirements. Firstly, a common RDF/OWL representation is needed to ensure a) semantic compatibility between different vocabularies, b) processing vocabularies in a standard way and c) sharing vocabularies for third-parties adoption. SKOS, presented in the W3C SKOS Core Recommendation, has been selected for these purposes. Secondly, although controlled vocabularies have some specific non-shared features, in practice a distinction between them is very hard to draw. We have identified a minimum set of common features for them. The data model should be expressive enough to preserve as much as possible the original semantics of primary sources for these common features. Thirdly, a generic method is needed to ensure quality of data conversions to correct SKOS instances.

Table 1. Summary of tasks of the MOLDEAS Linked Data lifecycle

ID	Task	Outcomes
t_1	Analysis of the input dataset	Initial specification of concepts, relations, domains and ranges, etc.
t_2	Data Cleansing	Input dataset with fixed values
t_3	Vocabulary Selection	Catalog of selected vocabularies
t_4	RDF datasets Selection	Catalog of selected RDF datasets.
t_5	Model RDF data	Domain Ontology
t_6	Design of an URI Scheme	Catalog of URIs to be used in the output graph
t_7	Design of a template for RDF resources	Template for RDF resources in the output graph
t_8	Convert data to RDF	RDF dataset (output graph)
t_9	Enrich RDF resources	Enriched RDF dataset
t_{10}	Entity Reconciliation	Tuples of the RDF dataset to be mapped
t_{11}	Rank of RDF resources	Ranked tuples of the RDF dataset
t_{12}	Validate of RDF resources	Checklist of linked data principles, etc.
t_{13}	Data Consolidation	RDF dataset with extra data
t_{14}	Deploy a linked data infrastructure	Component and deployment UML diagrams.
t_{15}	Data access and format of RDF resources	Specification of output formats and query/access protocols.
t_{16}	Add metainformation to RDF	Enriched RDF dataset with metadata and provenance information
t_{17}	Add extra documentation	Documents related to all involved processes

We have carried out a refinement of the original method, covered by the MOLDEAS linked data lifecycle, for thesauri conversions, by extending it to the PSCs field and taking into account their special features commented in a previous section. These are the common features of KOS systems that have to be covered by the conversion method:

- **URI Generation:** Controlled structured vocabularies and conceptual resources are interpreted in SKOS as RDF resources: in particular, instances of *skos:ConceptScheme* and *skos:Concept*. Thus they are referenced by means of Uniform Resource Identifiers (URIs). Although namespaces are out of the scope of our analysis, one of the sub steps of the method is the generation of the rdf:IDs of *skos:Concept* and *skos:ConceptScheme* from the original source's information. Usually controlled vocabularies provide unique identifiers for their terms or concepts. The options are the following:

- ○ **Generating New Identifiers for the Concepts of the Vocabulary:** This option introduces additional management. A mapping between elements of the original source and identifiers should be maintained for updating purposes.
- ○ **Using the String of the Preferred Term:** We would like to highlight here that multilingual sources introduce a factor of complexity that it is not present in monolingual systems. In European multilingual sources, this solution implies selecting a preferred term in a given natural language, thus promoting one language over the others with a possible non-desired political impact. In addition, a control procedure has to be established to ensure URI updating if the source term changes.
- ○ **Using the Identifier Code of an Element:** This solution avoids the problem of selecting one preferred language to encode the concept URIs. Moreover, codes are usually strings composed by a serial number (legal URI characters) and it preserves the original semantics of a multilingual, where these codes identify unique terms or concepts and establish mappings between different languages. This last option has been chosen keeping in mind the desired feature of having "cool URIs" to identify RDF resources.

- **Hierarchy Formalization:** From our point of view, one of the common aspects shared by KOS is a hierarchy-based structure, at least by thesauri, taxonomies and by most of classification schemes. Hierarchical relations establish links between conceptual resources, showing that the semantics of a resource is in some way more general ("broader") than other ("narrower"). In SKOS, the properties *skos:broader* and *skos:narrower* are only used to assert hierarchical statements between two conceptual resources. By the way, these properties are currently not defined as transitive properties. Nevertheless, third-parties, if they consider valuable, can use an OWL reasoner to infer the transitive closure of the hierarchy by means of the transitive super properties of *skos:broader* and *skos:narrower*: *skos:broaderTransitive* and *skos:narrowerTransitive* properties.

From a theoretical point of view, the transitive closure of hierarchical relations of KOS is still an open issue. Transitive logical formalizations (e.g. using a Description Logics-based language, like SKOS/OWL) of broader/narrower properties have some risks. Cycles can appear in the hierarchical-based structured of controlled vocabularies. Even though, transitive closure of these properties can be useful for search applications to expand original user-queries with terms hierarchically related. In our conversion-method, we have followed the recommendation of the current SKOS specification.

- **Multilingual and Lexical Features:** Regarding European controlled vocabularies, multilinguism is a critical issue, especially in the CPV vocabulary. Thesaurus are accessible in 21 (23) official languages of the European Union (Bulgarian, Spanish, Czech, Danish, German, Estonian, Greek, English, French, Italian, Latvian, Lithuanian, Hungarian, Dutch, Polish, Portuguese, Romanian, Slovak, Slovene, Finnish and Swedish) and others such as Croatian. In SKOS conceptual resources are labeled with any number of lexical strings, in any given natural language identified by the *xml:lang* attribute, following normative RDF/XML syntax. One of these labels is selected as the *skos:prefLabel* for any given language, and the others as values of *skos:altLabel*.

CASE STUDY: PROMOTING PRODUCT SCHEME CLASSIFICATIONS TO THE LINKED DATA INITIATIVE

In this chapter, authors have summarized a linked data lifecycle to support the promotion of raw data to the Linked Data initiative. Thus, the selected PSCs (See Table 2) can be easily transformed to RDF fulfilling the requirements of promoting controlled vocabularies to the Linked Data initiative. The selection of product classifications in the e-procurement sector, more specifically in the MOLDEAS platform, has followed the next criteria:

- The use of the CPV is mandatory for all notices according to the Regulation (EC) N° 2195/2002 of the European Parliament and it is used as hub classification.
- European classifications such as CPC or CPA have direct mappings (handmade) to the CPV so they perfectly fit to the task t_8 of interlinking RDF resources (*skos:exactMatch*).
- International classifications such as ISIC, SITC or NAICS enable the interoperability with other e-procurement and e-Commerce systems as well as activities in the field of statistics.
- **GoodRelations and Product Ontology (PO):** Two of the main references in the e-Commerce sector. That is why we reuse their definitions and instances with the objective of aligning the linkage of PSCs to working efforts.
- Other classifications such as TARIC, UNSPSC, PRODCOM or NAPCS are ongoing work and they will be linked to the CPV 2008.

Following a summary of some highlighted tasks according to the Linked Data lifecycle is presented:

Table 2. Product scheme classifications

PSC	Acronym	Source
Common Procurement Vocabulary, (2003 and 2008)	CPV	European Union
Combined Nomenclature 2012	CN	"
Central Product Classification, (2008)	CPC	"
Product Classification by Activity (2008)	CPA	"
International Standard Industrial Classification of All Economic Activities, Rev.4	ISIC	United Nations Statistics Division
North American Industry Classification System 2007 y 2012	NAICS	United States
Standard International Trade Classification, Rev. 4	SITC	United Nations Statistics Division

- **Task t_1 and t_5:** There is an implicit structure in each product classification based on their structure that enables the use of graph definitions (tree and forest).
  - **Product Categories:** A PSC is divided into product categories, Cat_{psc} that group different elements according to hierarchy levels, these categories are disjointed sets of elements. Finally, each PSC element or term is defined in only one Cat^k_{psc}.
  - **Taxonomy:** Apart from categories and hierarchy division, each product sector can be considered as a tree, $T_{psc,}$ and the whole set of trees builds a forest, F_{psc}. Each t^0_{psc} element is the root of a product sector and each t_{psc} is part of only one T_{psc}. According to the forest definition, the set product sector are disjointed.

Taking into account these points and the features of the PSC, a common model using SKOS is presented in Figure 2

- **Task t_6:** One of the key points to a successful promotion of raw data consists on the URI design (Heath & Bizer, 2011). In Table 3, PSCs URIs are presented with the aim of addressing the desired features of being "Cool Uris" (Berners-Lee, 2008), meaningful, keep the namespaces under our control, etc. that easing the reuse of RDF resources in the Web of Data.

Figure 2. PSC Data Model in SKOS

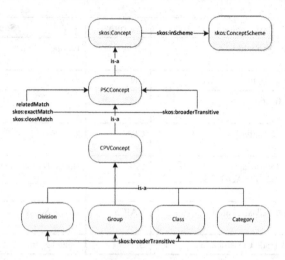

Table 3. URI patterns of the PSCs catalogue

URI Pattern	Description	Example
http://purl.org/weso/pscs/	URI base	N/A
<base_uri>/ontology	Common definitions	<base_uri>/ontology/PSCConcept
<base_uri>/resource/ds	Description of the PSCs Catalogue	<base_uri>/resource/ds
<base_uri>/{psc}/{versionlyear}	PSC Namespace (used as named graph)	<base_uri>/cpv/2008
<base_uri>/{psc}/{versionlyear}/ontology	Specific definitions	<base_uri>/cpv/2008/ontology
<base_uri>/resource/{psc}/{versionlyear}/{id}	URI for RDF resources	<base_uri>/cpv/2008/resource/55900000
<base_uri>/resource/{psc}/{versionlyear}/ds	Description of the PSC dataset	<base_uri>/cpv/2008/resource/ds

- **Task t₈:** The broad aim of this task is to enable the possibility of querying, public procurement notices from any PSC (See Figure 3) that is why there is link between any promoted PSC and the CPV 2008. The mappings can be created following two approaches: (1) *exact* mappings created by a domain expert or (2) *related*, through the execution of a custom entity reconciliation process based on Natural Language Processing techniques, these mappings are automatically discovered and generated.

Figure 3. Product Scheme Classifications Catalogue

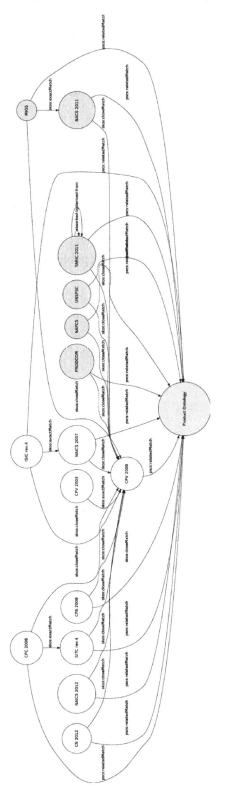

RESULTS, EXAMPLES AND EXPERIMENTATION

The result of promoting a PSCs catalogue addressing the principles of the LOD initiative can be shown in Table 4, a CPV element in N3 format is also presented in Box 1 and finally these data can be exploited making SPARQL queries that combine different PSCs, for instance if we can formulate the next query in SPARQL (See Box 2):

Give me 100 products or services related to construction in any PSC that have a mapping with products or services in CPV 2008 (descriptions in English).

On the other hand, our main objective was to enhance the access to public procurement notices linking together different controlled vocabularies. In order to accomplish this aim we have carried out the next experiment.

Let's assume the following points about the public procurement notices and PSCs used in the MOLDEAS platform:

- All notices are annotated by, at least, one CPV element.
- Each PSC is a controlled vocabulary comprised of a finite set of elements. The CPV 2008 is a controlled vocabulary, V, comprised of 10357 elements/terms/codes.

Table 4 Statistics of linking selected PSCs to CPV 2008

V_{psc}	$\#V_{psc}$	$\#V_{psc}$ (RDF tripels)	#Links to CPV 2008	%Real gain	#Links through PO	%Real gain through PO	%Max gain
CPV 2008	10357	803311	0	0	10000	96,55	100
CPV 2003	8323	546135	462	4,46	8312	80,25	80,36
CN 2012	14552	137484	2390	23,08	2390	23,08	140,50
CPC 2008	4408	100819	4402	42,50	4403	42,51	42,56
CPA 2008	5429	92749	5399	52,13	5410	52,24	52,42
ISIC V4	766	18986	765	7,39	765	7,39	7,40
NAICS 2007	2328	36292	2300	22,21	2300	22,21	22,48
NAICS 2012	2212	35390	2186	21,11	2186	21,11	21,36
SITC V4	4017	70887	3811	36,80	3820	36,88	38,79
Total	**42035**	**1842053**	**21715**	**209,66**	**29586**	**285,66**	**405,86**
			21715	209,66	39586	382,21	∞

Box 1. CPV element in N3 format

```
cpv2008-res:55900000 a gr:ProductOrServiceModel, cpv-
onto:Group;
        skos:prefLabel,
        gr:description,
        rdfs:label      "Servizi di vendita ald ettaglio"@IT,
                   "Detailhandel"@DA,
                   "Detailhandelsdiensten"@NL,
                   "Servicios comerciales al por menor"@ES,
                   "Maloobchod"@CS,
                   "Storitve trgovine na drobno"@SL,
                   "Retailtradeservices"@EN,
                   ...;
        dc:identifier   "55900000"^^xsd:string;
        dc:subject          "55900000-9"^^xsd:string;
        pscs-onto:relatedMatch
                <http://www.productontology.org/id/retail>,
                <http://www.productontology.org/id/service>,
                <http://www.productontology.org/id/trade>;
        skos:broaderTransitive
                cpv2008-res:55000000;
        skos:exactMatch
                cpv2003-res:52900000,
                cpv2003-res:52800000,
                cpv2003-res:52400000,
                cpv2003-res:52600000,
                cpv2003-res:52700000,
                cpv2003-res:52300000,
                cpv2003-res:52500000,
                cpv2003-res:52200000,
                cpv2003-res:52100000;
        skos:inScheme <http://purl.org/weso/pscs/cpv/2008/re-
source/ds>.
```

- The public procurement notices is a dataset, D, comprised of 1M of documents, already available as RDF resources. Each document, $d \in D$ is tagged, at least, using a CPV code, $v \in V$. Thus, if a query contains all elements, $v \in V$, the entire dataset of notices will be retrieved.

Box 2.

```
SELECT DISTINCT * WHERE{
        ?product pscs:relatedMatch
        <http://www.productontology.org/id/construction> .
        ?product skos:closeMatch ?cpv .
        ?product skos:prefLabel ?productLabel .
        ?cpv skos:prefLabel ?cpvLabel .
        ?product skos:inScheme ?scheme .
        FILTER (?scheme != <http://purl.org/weso/pscs/
cpv/2008/resource/ds>) .
        FILTER (lang (?cpvLabel) ="en ")
} LIMIT 100
```

Since these assumptions are fixed, the gain (in terms of percentage) of linking a new finite PSC to CPV (using Linked Data) can be calculated as follows:

- The source controlled vocabulary, V_{psc}, is comprised of $\#V_{psc}$ elements.
- The linking of terms between a source vocabulary, V_{psc}, and a target vocabulary, V can be carried out in next ways:
  - 1-1 link, there are elements $v^k_{psc} \in V_{psc}$ that are linked to only one element $v \in V$.
  - 1-n link, there are elements $v^k_{psc} \in V_{psc}$ that are linked to some elements $v \in V$ generating K links.
- The result of the previous operation generates a set of pairs: { $(v^0_{psc,} v^0)$, $(v^k_{psc,} v^k)$,..., $(v^n_{psc,} v^n)$ }. Taking into account this situation, the initial vocabulary V has been increased in all elements $v^k_{psc} \in V_{psc}$ that have a link to an element $v^k \in V$. The number of terms of V is comprised of existing terms plus the set of previous $v^k_{psc,}$ called V'_{psc}.
- The percentage of gain in terms of expressivity (number of elements to be used in queries) is related to the number of elements that enables go from V_{psc} to V: $\% = [(\#V'_{psc} +\#V)/ \#V]-1 * 100$.
- Finally, in the ongoing example, there is a specific scenario in which elements $v^k_{psc} \in V_{psc}$ are not directly mapped to elements $v^k \in V$ but assuming that there are relations r_k among elements v^j_{psc} and v^k_{psc} new links could emerge between v^j_{psc} and v^k through r_k. Nevertheless this situation should be avoided in order to prevent an infinite and recursive linking process and keep the advantages of using finite controlled vocabularies, e.g. in the ongoing example, *Product Ontology* is used as a bridge classification implying an infinite max gain (∞).

According to Table 4, the percentage of real gain, linking selected PSCs to CPV is about 209, 66% so we can use three times more elements (10357+21715) to create queries instead of the initial set of CPV elements (10357). Nevertheless, there is a drawback in this approach that lies in the type of mapping: *exact* (created by official institutions) or *related* (created automatically by applying entity reconciliation techniques). Although this last approach is widely accepted in the *Linked Data* community we have introduced a new version of the mappings using a threshold φ to indicate the goodness of the link between two elements (Figure 4).

This experiment demonstrates that the access to public procurement notices, in terms of expressivity, can be improved adding new elements (linking PSCs together) to create SPARQL queries. Besides, this objective cannot be reached without the application of Semantic Web technologies and Linked Data principles. On the other hand, the method used to promote and validate the data generated from notices is based on a checklist created by a compilation of checkpoints (216); from books, W3C specifications, Open Data and Linked Data principles and know-how acquired in previous projects that ensures the principles of the LOD initiative, easing the reuse, maintenance, governance, coverage and expressivity. Finally, these new datasets have been released to the community with more than 1 million of RDF triples have been added to "thedatahub.org" and joining in the Linking Open Data Cloud Diagram.

DISCUSSION

Following some questions to discuss are presented in order to evaluate the gain of promoting PSCs to the LOD initiative in the e-procurement context.

Figure 4. Evolution of the links from the PSCs catalogue to the CPV 2008

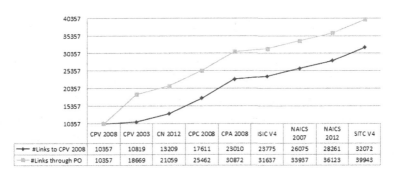

	CPV 2008	CPV 2003	CN 2012	CPC 2008	CPA 2008	ISIC V4	NAICS 2007	NAICS 2012	SITC V4
#Links to CPV 2008	10357	10819	13209	17611	23010	23775	26075	28261	32072
#Links through PO	10357	18669	21059	25462	30872	31637	33937	36123	39943

1. Which is the current expressivity, in terms of number of elements, to create queries?

    The existing CPV 2008 is comprised of 10357 elements that can be used to query a procurement notices database. Due to this vocabulary is mandatory in all European procurement processes; if all CPV 2008 elements are used in a query then all procurement notices will be retrieved. This conclusion is independent of the underlying technology. Thus the expressivity to create queries is limited to 10357 elements.

2. Which are the main advantages of using RDF as a common data model to retrieve data information extracted from the notices out?

    The use and application of RDF and LOD principles have a main consequence that lies in the standard representation of information easing the access, interoperability and integration of different data sources. More specifically and with regards to PSCs, the interlinkage of PSC elements enables the possibility of querying a database using terms coming from different classifications. Thus the expressivity is increased, queries can be formulated with an extensible and more notices can be retrieved.

3. Which is the real benefit of applying the LOD principles to PSCs?

    The real benefit lies in the representation of data and information using standards as RDF/SKOS/OWL that enables a common extensible framework to manage data. Moreover, the access is also improved due to the existence of a formal query language such as SPARQL over HTTP. Obviously, existing PSCs in MSExcel or PDF formats do not allow the complete reuse of public sector information avoiding the generation of new added-value services.

4. Is there any error, when expressivity grows, linking RDF resources?

    The data linkage has an implicit factor of ambiguity. Although this situation is a well-known and accepted in the LOD community and some tools provides a threshold value to avoid errors in entity reconciliation processes, the truth is that depending on the application the enrichment and linkage of RDF resources is better than have isolated RDF resources. Thus all promoted data can be part of the Linked Data realm. In the case study, there is a range between 6.64% and 8.65% of trusted mappings that in terms of elements implies a valuable increase of exact and new elements to make queries.

5.   How we can evaluate the conversions of PSCs to SKOS?

The evaluation of the conversions must be checked from two different levels:

- **Correctness of Conversions:** Our approach has demonstrated to produce correct SKOS for the least common multiple features of controlled vocabularies conversions: URIs generation, hierarchical relations and multilingual features.
- **Completeness of Conversions:** Our approach has demonstrated that the use of SKOS produce complete conversions of the primary sources selected. The output data model was extended with the required subclasses of *skos:Concept* to preserve the product categories hierarchy in the RDF/OWL conversion. Every product term has been interpreted as an instance of *skos:Concept* and as instance of its correspondent product category class. From a LOD point of view, the MOLDEAS platform provides a component to automatically check 216 points FIXME.

CONCLUSION AND FUTURE WORK

In this work, authors have introduce a method to transform PSCs coming from governmental organizations to the Linked Data initiative using SKOS and other semantic web vocabularies with the main objective of increasing the expressivity of SPARQL queries when an information retrieval process occurs, more specifically in the retrieving of public procurement notices from the European Union. Moreover, this work is part of the MOLDEAS platform in which a complete linked data lifecycle is also defined. The whole catalogue of PSCs has already been reported to the Linking Open Data community[1] and it has been reused by third-parties. Further steps include the application of the process (and its refinement) to other relevant PSCs, e.g. TARIC, and the reporting of results to the Office for Official Publications of the European Communities. Further steps in the field of Linked Data are aligned to current research trends such as:

- Ensure data quality (Bizer & Cyganiak, 2009), provenance (Moreau & Missier, 2012) and trust.
- Process large datasets in a cloud computing environment (Hausenblas, Grossman, Harth & Cudré-Mauroux, 2012) and others like entity reconciliation, dataset management, etc.

With regards to the results of this study, these outcomes are intended to be exploited by a commercial service like Eurolert.net (Euroalert.net, 2012) and we are also interested in report the results to The Internal Market and Services Directorate General (DG MARKT) of the EC, The Information Society and Media Directorate General (DG INFSO) of the EC, the LOD and OGD initiatives among others.

REFERENCES

Alexander, K., Cyganiak, R., Hausenblas, M., & Zhao, J. (2011). *Describing linked datasets with the VoID vocabulary*. Retrieved from http: //www.w3.org/TR/void/

Álvarez-Rodríguez, J. M. (2012). *Methods on linked data for e-procurement applying semantics*. (Unpublished doctoral dissertation). University of Oviedo, Oviedo, Spain.

Álvarez-Rodríguez, J. M., Rubiera, E., & Polo, L. (2008). Promoting government controlled vocabularies for the semantic web: The EUROVOC thesaurus and the CPV product classification system. In *Proceedings of the 1st International Workshop, Semantic Interoperability in the European Digital Library*. Tenerife, Spain: SIEDL.

Bennett, D., & Harvey, A. (2009). *Publishing open government data*. Retrieved from http://www.w3.org/TR/gov-data/

Berners-Lee, T. (2006). *Linked data*. Retrieved from http://www.w3.org/DesignIssues/LinkedData.html

Berners-Lee, T. (2008). *Cool URIs don't change*.

Berrueta, D., Phipps, J., Miles, A., Baker, T. & Swick, R. (2008). *Best practice recipes for publishing RDF vocabularies*. W3C.

Bizer, C., & Cyganiak, R. (2009). Quality-driven information filtering using the WIQA policy framework. *Web Semantics: Science. Services and Agents on the World Wide Web, 7*(1), 1–10. doi:10.1016/j.websem.2008.02.005.

Cifuentes-Silva, F.A., Sifaqui, C\. & Labra, J.E. (2011). *Towards an architecture and adoption process for linked data technologies in open government contexts: A case study for the library of congress of Chile*. I-SEMANTICS.

Dodds, L., & Davis, I. (2011). *Linked data patterns: A pattern catalogue for modelling, publishing, and consuming linked data*. Retrieved from http://patterns.dataincubator.org/book/

Euroalert.net. (2012). Retrieved from http://euroalert.net/

European Commission. (2010). *Consultation on the green paper on expanding the use of e-procurement in the EU*. Brussels, Belgium: European Commission. Retrieved from http://ec.europa.eu/internal_market/consultations/docs/2010/e-procurement/green-paper_en.pdf

Fensel, D., Ding, Y., & Omelayenko, B. (2001). Product data integration in B2B ecommerce (pp. 54-59). IEEE-Intelligent E-Business.

Gateway Strategic Consultancy Services, S.L. (2012). Retrieved from http://gateway-scs.es/en/

Hausenblas, M., Grossman, R., Harth, A., & Cudré-Mauroux, P. (2012). *Large-scale linked data processing: Cloud computing to the rescue?* Paper presented at 2nd International Conference on Cloud Computing and Services Science. Porto, Portugal.

Hausenblas, M., Villazón-Terrazas, B., & Hyland, B. (2011). *GLD life cycle*. Retrieved from http://www.w3.org/2011/gld/wiki/GLD_Life_cycle

Heath, T., & Bizer, C. (2011). *Linked data: Evolving the web into a global data space* (p. 1). San Rafael, CA: Morgan & Claypool. doi:10.2200/S00334ED1V01Y-201102WBE001.

Hepp, M. (2005). eClassOWL: A fully-fledged products and services ontology in OWL. In *Proceedings of the 4th International Semantic Web Conference*. Galway, Ireland: ISWC.

Hepp, M. (2006). A methodology for deriving OWL ontologies from products and services categorization standards. *International Journal on Semantic Web and Information Systems, 2*(1), 72–99. doi:10.4018/jswis.2006010103.

Hepp, M. (2006a). The True complexity of product representacion in the semantic web. In *Proceedings of the 14th European Conference on Information System*. Gothenburg, Sweden: ECIS

Hepp, M. (2007). Possible Ontologies. *IEEE Internet Computing, 11*(1), 90–96. doi:10.1109/MIC.2007.20.

Hernández, G. A., Berbís, J. M. G., & González, A. R. et al. (2010). HYDRA: A middleware-oriented integrated architecture for e-procurement in supply chains. *Computational Collective Intelligence, 1*, 1–20. doi:10.1007/978-3-642-15034-0_1.

Hyland, B., Villazón-Terrazas, B., & Capadisli, S. (2011). *Cookbook for open government linked data*. Retrieved from http://www.w3.org/2011/gld/wiki/Linked_Data_Cookbook

Jing, Y., Jeong, D., & Baik, D. K. (2008). SPARQL graph pattern rewriting for OWL-DL inference query. In *Proceedings of the 2008 4th International Conference on Networked Computing and Advanced Information Management* (pp. 675–680). Washington, DC: IEEE

Leukel, J. (2004). Automating product classification. In *Proceedings of the IADIS International Conference e-Society*. Avila, Spain: IADIS.

LOD2 Project. (2012). *Creating knowledge out of interlinked data.* Retrieved from http://lod2.eu/

LOTED Project. (2012). *Linked open tenders electronic daily.* Retrieved from http://loted.eu:8081/LOTED1Rep/

Miles, A., & Bechhofer, S. (2009). *SKOS simple knowledge organisation systems.* Retrieved from http://www.w3.org/TR/skos-reference/

Moreau, L., & Missier, P. (2011). *The PROV data model and abstract syntax notation.* Retrieved from http://www.w3.org/TR/2011/WD-prov-dm-20111018/

Nally, M., & Speicher, S. (2011). *Toward a basic profile for linked data.* Retrieved from http://www.ibm.com/developerworks/rational/library/ basic-profile-linked-data/index.html

Nally, M., Speicher, S., Arwe, J., & Le Hors, A. (2012). *Linked data basic profile 1.0.* Retrieved from http://www.w3.org/Submission/2012/02/

Omelayenko, B., & Fensel, D. (2001). An analysis of B2B catalogue integration problems. In *Proceedings of the International Conference on Enterprise Information Systems*. Setubal, Portugal: ICEIS

Podlogar, M. (2007). E-procurement success factors: Challenges and opportunities for a small developing country. In Pani, A. K., & Agrahari, A. (Eds.), *E-Procurement in Emerging Economies Theory and Cases*. Loveland, CO: Group Publishing. doi:10.4018/978-1-59904-153-7.ch003.

Spanish Government. (2011). *Proyecto APORTA.* Retrieved from http://www.aporta.es/

UK Government. (2011). *Opening up government.* Retrieved from http://data.gov.uk/

W3C (2011a). *Best practices discussion summary.* Retrieved from http://www.w3.org/2011/gld/wiki/Best_Practices_Discussion_Summary

W3C (2011b). *Government linked data working group charter.* Retrieved from http://www.w3.org/2011/gld/charter

WESO (Oviedo Semantic Web). (2012). Retrieved from http://www.weso.es/

White House. (2009). *Open government initiative.* Retrieved from http://www.whitehouse.gov/open

ENDNOTES

[1]   http://thedatahub.org/dataset/pscs-catalogue

Chapter 2

User Assisted Creation of Open–Linked Data for Training Web Information Extraction in a Social Network

Martin Necasky
Charles University, Czech Republic

Dominik Fiser
Charles University, Czech Republic

Ivo Lasek
Charles University, Czech Republic

Ladislav Peska
Charles University, Czech Republic

Peter Vojtas
Charles University, Czech Republic

EXECUTIVE SUMMARY

In this chapter we describe our project under development and proof of concept for creating large Open-Linked Data repositories. The main problem is twofold: (1) Who will create (annotate) Open-Linked Data and in which vocabularies? (2) What will be the usage and profit of it?

For the first problem we propose several procedures on how to create Open-Linked data, including assisted creation of annotations (serving as base line or training set for Web Information Extraction tools), employing the social network, and also specific approaches to creating Open-linked data from governmental data resources. We describe some cases where such data can be used (e.g., in e-commerce, recommending systems, and in governmental and public policy projects).

DOI: 10.4018/978-1-4666-2827-4.ch002

INTRODUCTION

Increasingthe Web size and automation of its processing is a challenge for the IT community. There are several approaches on how to tackle this problem. Most remarkable are, of course, search engines. We would like to go beyond key word search and also support web scale applications–services, based on semantics added to web pages (e.g., in a form of RDFa annotations). So that technology and standards are ready, we describe how to start the process.

We focus on two aspects of this problem. The first problem is mainly sociological. To enable machines to understand web pages like humans, an initial human effort is necessary. The problem is: who (and maybe also why, how, when, where, etc.) will create semantic content? There are several possibilities, and we will discuss some of them. One possibility is to convince publishers to annotate their web resources by some vocabulary (ontology). A big impulse for this is the schema.org and sitemaps. org initiatives of Bing, Google, and Yahoo! with aim to improve search. Large human effort is/was invested into Wikipedia and Linked data are already extracted to DBPedia. Our approach is to use a social network and a specialized tool for third party annotation of web resources. We also touch on the problem of vocabulary for annotation. Our system enables both to create its own vocabulary and to use shared vocabularies such as schema.org andGoodRelations.The second problem is assessing what will be the use and profit of such Open-Linked data. We describe several use cases.

In this chapter we describe our project under development and a proof of concept for creating large Open-Linked Data repositories and applications which use them.

For the first problem, we propose a user assisted creation of a base line of Open-Linked Data. Motivation for doing this is supported by a social network. We present a tool enabling this. Further, this base line can be used for training Web Information Extraction tools.

We describe some cases where such data can be used (e.g., in aggregated web shops, news recommendations, and in governmental and public policy projects).

HUMAN ASSISTED CREATION OF SEMANTIC CONTENT

As we already mentioned in the introduction, the main problem of Semantic Web (web of data) is a sociological problem (and only afterwards it is a managerial problem and then also a technological problem). The problem is: Who (and also why, how, when, where, etc.) will create semantic content? This is the main goal of our project of Web Semantization (Dědek, Eckhardt, & Vojtáš, 2009). Here, web semantization is understood as a process of gradual enrichment of the web by semantic content by a third party annotation. This work is based on four main ideas: (1) To have a web repository of indexes for a part of web (e.g., Czech web (.cz) in size TB's). This was based on the system Egothor, which offered full text indexing and some additional features. (2) To use web information extraction to automate the enrichment (annotation process). (3) A semantic repository, which is a crucial component for our approach. Having a third party annotation, we cannot change original pages and we have to store annotations elsewhere. (4) A "user software agent," supporting users (customers) in specific applications and making use of semantic content.

Community Efforts

Big effort and results in creating semantic content is achieved by different community efforts. If publishers themselves annotate their pages (e.g., in a process of SEO using schema.org vocabulary), it would substantially enlarge semantic content on the web (we do not go into problems of this approach–is not clear how far these annotations will be interlinked). Another impulse which can push publishers to annotate their resources acts in smaller, well-organized community forces--typically with licensed work (e.g., in medical domain). Last, but not least, are various laws pushing publisher to machine readable publishing of (mostly legal) documents.

Another big human effort is Wikipedia. From a human point of view, it contains lot of semantics, especially about named entities and their disambiguation. DBPedia is a community effort to extract structured and interlinked information from Wikipedia and make it a RDF database on the web. The main source of information for DBpedia are so called "infoboxes" (i.e., small tables on the right side of some Wikipedia articles containing basic information about a described entity). Based on hand-written mapping rules maintained by the DBpedia community, the information is extracted from the source code of particular articles and mapped to a common DBpedia ontology.

Semantic Annotator: A Tool for Third Party Annotation

It is clear that the above mentioned social forces will never cover the whole web and further human annotation is necessary. Therefore, it is useful to have a tool that would be attractive to human users providing them an easy way of doing manual semantic annotation (Fišer, D., 2011).

We store the annotations in a designated database server to be presented to other users. In the future we plan to use these annotations in a multitude of purposes, (e.g., training data, ground truth, etc.) for our other information extraction methods. A user has a plugin installed in his/her browser that enables them to annotate visited web pages by concepts and attributes from a simple vocabulary language. This vocabulary can be one of shared vocabularies like FOAF, schema.org., or GoodRelations. The system offers the possibility to create its own (simple) vocabulary (e.g., in Figure1. for concept notebook and its attributes). We have provided some experiments with different types of users with different types of IT skills.

Social Network

One possibility to get the social momentum for a community contribution in Semantization is a social network. Here we mention our project Social network of the Computer scientists in the regions of the Czech Republic (SoSIReCR[1]), funded by the European Social Fund budget and the budget of the Czech Republic, that builds a social network for people working in ICT supporting communication and cooperation among ICT professionals, universities, companies, and public sector in the country. The social network is supported by a web portal--sitIT.cz (Vojtáš, Pokorný, Nečasky, Skopal, Matoušek, & Maryška, 2011).

Portal sitIT.cz, in comparison to other existing web portals (e.g., LinkedIn, Facebook), works with more detailed social network structure specific for ICT. Persons, groups, as well as other types of entities (e.g., project teams, projects, teachers, study

Figure 1. Screen shot of Semantic annotator (Fišer, D., 2011) on a web shop with notebooks

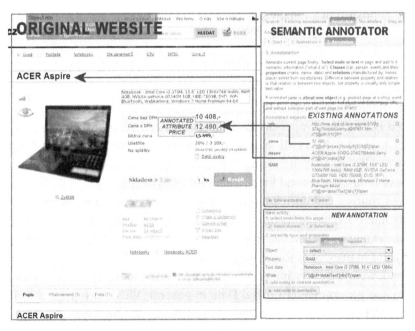

programs at universities, or even educating courses) have their corresponding home pages there. Home pages can be extended with structured (machine-readable) profile. One type is called professional profile, and it's suitable mainly for researchers and research groups. It formally express a focus and/or knowledge of a given person in terms of ICT classification (now we have chosen the ACM Classification as one of accepted standard classifications of ICT disciplines).

Portal is also suitable for our purposes of creating Open-Linked data (we have some initial experiments, providing a proof of concept for this). Our aim is to further extend the portal to achieve scalability and enable applications to use these data.

OpenData.cz

Currently, there are many Czech governmental authorities that publish their data on the Web for the public. However, the way of publication is hard to understand for common citizens. Usually, the data is published in a form of simple HTML pages which are, qualitatively, far from modern Web 2.0 applications. The form of presentation is not transparent and there are usually no analytical functions provided to the users. This has many consequences. The main problematic ones that we see in the Czech Republic are the following:

- The public does not have enough information to play the role of a natural control to the government.
- The public is not even interested in the governmental data because the data is not published in an interesting way.

OpenData.cz is a new academic initiative in the Czech Republic that puts together people from various academic institutions in Prague interested in governmental Linked Data. The aim of the initiative is twofold.

First, we build a technical infrastructure for processing governmental data such as Linked Data[2]. We scrape various data sources of Czech governmental authorities (which are mostly HTML pages), transform collected data to Linked Data and store the results inthe infrastructure. Our goal is to create quality Linked Data (i.e., we remove redundancies and inconsistencies from the data, interlink the data with other data sources and enrich the data with domain specific ontologies). We are currently interested in public procurement. We have developed ontology for public procurement and we gather data from various semi-structured data sources on public procurement in the Czech Republic.

Second, we intensively inform Czech politicians about advantages of the infrastructure and governmental Linked Data in general. We demonstrate the benefits of Linked Data for the society and government and offer them our infrastructure as a base for their activities in publishing governmental data such as Linked Data. We explain to them that opening governmental data would start an explosion of many Web applications, which would consume the data and present it to the public in many interesting ways. This would increase the interest of the public in the governmental activities and, as a consequence, the information awareness of the public. This is extremely important in the Czech Republic, which deals with corruption as one of the biggest problems perceived not only by Czech citizens, but also with foreign investors.

There are various open data initiatives in different countries which motivated us to establish a similar initiative in the Czech Republic (e.g., *data.gov.uk* in Great Britain, *data.gov* in the U.S., *digitaliser.dk* in Denmark, *data.pm.go.th* in Thailand, *opendata.go.ke* in Kenya, and many other countries). There are also various tools that support working with Linked Data in different parts of the Linked Data lifecycle (e.g., creation, linking, publishing, etc.). We use or plan to use several of these tools in our project. In particular, we experiment with tools involved in the LOD2[3] technology stack.

There are several data sources of Czech governmental authorities which are suitable candidates for annotation and semantization. Even though they publish data in a human readable HTML format, it is quite easy to get raw data from them. We therefore started our activities with these data sources. Namely, we focused on data sources related to public procurement. It is believed that most corruption happens in the area of public procurement.

There exists a central information system for publishing public contracts of public authorities in the Czech Republic. The system is called Information System for Public Procurement. It is mandatory for any public authority to publish a contract if its price exceeds a threshold given by law. Currently, the central system contains around 40.000 public contracts. Therefore, we have selected it as a primary source of data for the initial phase of the development of our infrastructure.

However, the central system contains only a part of all public contracts in the Czech Republic. There are many contracts which are below the threshold given by law and, therefore, are rarely present in the central system. These contracts are run mainly by local governments of smaller Czech cities. There are few responsible local governments and governmental organizations which publish information about all of their public contracts on the Web. However, there is no standardized form for its publishing. Therefore, each organization publishes contracts in different HTML layouts. Our goal is to get raw data from these additional HTML data sources as well. Therefore, specific scrapers for web sites of particular municipalities are a part of our infrastructure.

In addition to the data sources containing public contracts, we also consider other data sources. These include a set of public registers offered by the Czech Ministry of Finance, which provide data about economical subjects (e.g., contact information, owners, etc.) An advantage is that these registers provide machine readable data represented in XML format. A disadvantage is that each register uses its own XML format. There are some differences between the formats of various registers and, therefore, their integration was necessary.

We have developed ontology for public procurement (Klímek, Knap, Mynarz, Nečaský, Stárka, & Svátek) . It is based on Tenders Electronic Daily (TED)--an EU system for contract publishing. TED defines a set of properties of a public contract (e.g., contract kind, contact information, expected price, number of tenders, etc.). We studied these properties and enriched them with few details about organizations (e.g., who works on what position in an organization). According to the ontology, we have annotated the data from the current governmental system for public procurement which includes approximately 40.000 public contracts. We currently test the access to the data via a SPARQL endpoint and also extend the data with new data sources (e.g., Prague city public contracts, etc.).

Web Information Extraction

Our general hope is that automated and machine learning based methods for Information Extraction and Semantic Annotation can significantly reduce the amount of necessary human work. We do not develop this line here; we refer to our paper (Novotny, Vojtas, & Maruscak, 2009).

USE CASES

Availability of semantic data enables many applications. We mention here some In which we are acquainted with.

Aggregated Web Shops

A quite recent approach in e-commerce web applications development is the aggregated web shops. Such sites usually group data about the same or similar item or product from different e-shops and provide both a comparison of different items and a comparison of the same item in different e-shops.

Machine-readable data are crucial for such systems; however, current sites do not rely on the Open-linked data but rather on proprietary (mostly XML) formats. These have several disadvantages: first, the semantics of these XML descriptions is not always clear and adequately detailed. These XML descriptions mostly depend on agreement of a single shop with an aggregate shop (and this usually takes time). The challenge is to have an overview about data from an arbitrary shop which is of interest to users. Using Open-linked data as the data exchange format will improve these sites in several ways, such as to:

- Collect information about products from more sources, and employ users and their annotations, comments, or ratings.
- Collect other information related to the items (e.g., weather, climate, and destination description for tours or trips, independent product tests, etc.).

Our current experiments on the e-commerce field focuses mainly on the user preference and recommendation, leaving the data source question open (however, our methods are independent from the source of data) (Peska, Eckhardt, & Vojtas, 2011; Vojtas & Eckhardt, 2008).

News Filtering System

The availability of data on the web enables improvements not just while working with structured data such as parameters or rating of products. An example is the news domain, where mostly unstructured texts are provided. However, using information retrieval methods such as text categorization and named entity recognition, we might extract structured information from plain texts.

Popular publicly available services like OpenCalais[4], Zemanta[5], or DBpedia Spotlight[6], offer–besides the ordinary recognition of named entities and their types– the links to other web pages, where more information about such entities might be found. These links serve as identifiers of concrete entities. Often, DBpedia URIs are used. Thanks to this identification, we can find even more information about identified named entities and use it for further search and filtering of news articles.

In our case (Lašek & Vojtáš, 2011), we use the extracted information to learn a user profile. Based on ratings of articles a user reads, we identify what kind of information he or she is interested in.

We combine the named entity based representation of an article with other information as frequencies of contained terms and identification of subject-verb-object triples contained in relevant/important sentences of an article (e.g., in sentences containing named entities of interest for user).

Having such structured representation of the article content, we use various machine learning techniques to learn user preferences.

One example is association rule mining. Example rules produced by this approach may look like this:

```
type:Company ^ locatedIn:USA => ratingInteresting (confidence
0.20)
subject:Google ^ type:Company => ratingInteresting (confidence
0.80)
```

Note that we are especially interested in rules describing conditions resulting in the positive rating of an article by the user. The user profile then consists of such rules.

Another approach is clustering of articles according to their features (contained terms, named entities, properties of identified named entities and subject-verb-object triples). We monitor which articles form which clusters users read most often and then offer them another article from the same clusters. The user profile in this case is represented as a list of clusters a user is interested in.

Details on mentioned approaches are provided by Lašek (2011).

Detection of Suspicious Public Contracts

In the section *OpenData.cz*, we have described basics for potential web applications. One of them will be a system for detection of suspicious public contracts. With the necessary data collected in proper format, even the simple data aggregations (most successful tender winners in a specific region, average price per unit, average number of applicants, etc.) and metrics (e.g., difference between expected, winning, and final prices) can provide important results.

The corresponding system is in a phase of design and analysis.

CONCLUSION

We have described our project of Web Semantization with emphasis on third party human creation/annotation of RDF data on the web. These data are the base line (golden standard) for training Web Information Extraction and automatic annotation of a bigger portion of the web. For motivation and user cooperation, we will use our social network sitit.cz.

In the chapter on human assisted creation of semantic content, we discuss community efforts like annotation by website publishers, including Wikipedia.org, dbpedia.org, and OpenData.cz project. We present the tool "Semantic Annotator" designed for third party annotation of web resources. The semantic annotator allows one to create his/her own vocabularies as well as to use some shared ones. Annotated data are accessible on a server for web services for further use.

We describe some use cases where such data can be used (e.g, in aggregated web shops, news filtering and in detection of suspicious public contracts).

Future work lies mainly in integration and massive experiments.

REFERENCES

Dědek, J., Eckhardt, A., & Vojtáš, P. (2009). Web semantization - Design and principles. In *Proceedings of the 6th Atlantic Web Intelligence Conference 2009* (pp. 3018). Prague, Czech Republic: Springer Verlag.

Fišer, D. (2011). *Semantic annotation of domain dependent data.* (Master's thesis). Charles University, Prague, Czech Republic. Retrieved from http://semanticweb. projekty.ms.mff.cuni.cz/index/release/

Klímek, J., Knap, T., Mynarz, J., Nečaský, M., Stárka, J., & Svátek, V. (n.d.). *Public contracts ontology* (Vol. 1). Retrieved from purl.org/procurement/public-contracts

Lašek, I. (2011). Model for news filtering with named entities. =. *Lecture Notes in Computer Science, 7032*, 309–316. doi:10.1007/978-3-642-25093-4_23.

Lašek, I., & Vojtáš, P. (2011). News filtering with semantic web entities. In ITΛT 2011, Zborník príspevkov prezentovaných na konferencii ITAT. Terchová, Slovakia, ISBN: 978-80-89557-01-1, 2011

Novotny, Vojtas, & Maruscak. (2009). Information extraction from web pages. In *Proceedings of International Joint Conference on Web Intelligence and Intelligent Agent Technology* 2009. Washington, DC: IEEE.

Peska, L., Eckhardt, A., & Vojtas, P. (2011). UPComp - A PHP component for recommendation based on user behaviour. In *Proceedings of International Joint Conference on Web Intelligence and Intelligent Agent Technology 2011* (pp. 306-309). Lyon, France: IEEE.

Vojtas, P., & Eckhardt, A. (2008). Considering data-mining techniques in user preference learning. In *Proceedings of International Joint Conference on Web Intelligence and Intelligent Agent Technology 2008* (pp. 33-36). IEEE/WIC/ACM.

Vojtáš, P., Pokorný, J., Nečasky, M., Skopal, T., Matoušek, K., & Kubalík, J. ... Maryška M. (2011). SoSIReČR - IT professional social network. In *Proceedings of International Conference on Computational Aspects of Social Networks 2011* (pp. 108-113). Salamanca, Spain: CASoN.

KEY TERMS AND DEFINITIONS

Human Annotation: Annotation made manually by a human.

Web Content Annotation: To annotate (add metainformation about) a specific part of the website.

Web Information Extraction: To collect and store structured information from a specific website.

ENDNOTES

[1]   http://www.sosirecr.cz/
[2]   http://linkeddata.org/
[3]   LOD2 European Project http://lod2.eu
[4]   http://www.opencalais.com/
[5]   http://www.zemanta.com/?d=1
[6]   http://dbpedia.org/spotlight

Chapter 3
Providing Information from Brazilian Politicians Using Linked Data

Jairo Francisco de Souza
Federal University of Juiz de Fora, Brazil

Lucas de Ramos Araújo
Federal University of Juiz de Fora, Brazil

Sean Wolfgand Matsui Siqueira
Federal University of the State of Rio de Janeiro (UNIRIO), Brazil

Rubens Nascimento Melo
Federal University of Juiz de Fora, Brazil

EXECUTIVE SUMMARY

Since its inception, the Web has undergone continuous evolution in order to improve itself as a means of global communication and information sharing. Open Government Data are increasingly being published on the Web, contributing to the transparency and the reusability of public data. At the same time, the use of Linked Data has been increasing in recent years, enabling the development of better and smarter applications. This chapter presents a case on the publication of Open Government Data using the Linked Data practices, by creating a data set of Brazilian politicians with information collected from different sources. This is the first dataset providing Brazilian linked data.

DOI: 10.4018/978-1-4666-2827-4.ch003

INTRODUCTION

Information and Communication Technologies (ICTs) have promoted a revolution in the information sharing, building a new relationship between government and citizens. This new relationship originated the so-called Electronic Government, which allows a more accessible, efficient, democratic, and transparent government.

Within this context, the concept of Open Government Data extends this relationship by providing the availability of government information in open and accessible formats to enable reuse and interconnection between information from different sources, thus generating new knowledge (W3C Brazilian Office, 2010).

Nowadays, much government data are available on the Web, but this information is most often offered without the use of standards, in proprietary formats and structured for user interface presentation, making it difficult for third-party systems to automatically reuse it. For better exploiting the potential represented by the government information, the data must be available in standard, open and accessible formats (Agune, Filho, & Bollinger, 2009).

There are several ways to publish Open Government Data on the Web, but according to Berners-Lee (2008), the purposes expected for government data are best served by using Linked Data techniques. Within the context of the Semantic Web, the term Linked Data is used to describe a set of practices to publish, share and connect structured data on the Web in order to increase the value and usefulness of these data (Bizer et al., 2009).

There is a global movement of governments, organizations, and people publishing Open Government Data. At the same time, the use of Linked Data has been increasing in recent years, strongly supported by the W3C (World Wide Web Consortium) and Tim Berners-Lee, considered the inventor of the Web. However, several challenges must be overcome so that the Web can be used as a global database.

Brazil has a lot of government data published on the Web, but there are only a few government initiatives that give full access to these data in structured and open standards. Therefore, some initiatives are emerging in order to extract the data, make them open and give them new value through different applications.

According to the United Nations E-Government Survey 2010 (United Nations, 2010), which provides a global assessment in the field of Electronic Government, Brazil ranks 61st, losing 16 positions since 2008. Several factors are responsible for the decline, such as the lack of online services and poor telecommunications infrastructure. The report also highlights Brazilian initiatives on Open Government Data that must be followed.

Within this context, publishing Open Government Data and using Linked Data on the Web is important nowadays. Thus, the work described in this chapter aims to contribute in publishing Linked Data from Brazilian politicians on the Web with information collected from different sources, therefore contributing to the new Web of data. The implemented project aims to provide useful, open, standardized, reusable, and linked data for both human and machine. Due to the use of standard vocabularies, citizens can issue queries comparing indicators from Brazil with those of other governments. And due to the integration with external sources, users can ask a richer variety of questions including, for example, demographics, social indicators or other encyclopedic knowledge associated with their regions.The remainder of this chapter is structured as follows: Section 2 provides an overview on Open Government Data. Section 3 provides an overview on Linked Data. Section 4 presents information regarding the implemented project. Section 5 presents the conclusions and future work proposals.

OPEN GOVERNMENT DATA

According to the E-Government Interest Group (e-Gov IG, 2009), creating an Electronic Government requires openness, transparency, collaboration and knowledge. A transparent government is more than open interaction and participation; government data must be shared, discovered, accessible and manipulated by those who wish to use government information.

The aim of Open Government Data is to allow users to easily find, access, understand and use public data, bringing many benefits such as reuse, inclusion, transparency, accountability, improved search, integration, participation, collaboration, economic growth, innovation and efficiency (Agune et al., 2009). The Open Government Working Group (Opengovdata.org, 2007), developed the eight Principles of Open Government Data. They should be: (1) Complete, fully available without limitations; (2) Primary, collected at the source with the highest possible level of granularity, without aggregation or modification; (3) Timely, published as quickly as necessary to preserve its value; (4) Accessible, available to the largest possible number of users and purposes; (5) Machine processable, reasonably structured to allow automated processing; (6) Non-discriminatory, available to anyone without registration (7); Non-proprietary, available in a format over which no entity has exclusive control, (8) License-free, not subject to any copyrights, patents, intellectual property or trade secrets regulation.

Diniz (2009) describes a series of guidelines to provide Open Government Data, such as: Publish the data in its raw form in a structured way; creating an online catalog of the data with documentation so that people can discover what has been posted; using established standards and tools to allow an easy and efficient production and publication; make the data human-readable by converting them to (X)HTML; incorporate machine-readable semantic information, metadata, and identifiers; use permanently standard and/or easy to find URIs (Uniform Resource Identifiers); generate links to other URIs to help in the discovery of related resources; ensure that data are easy to recover and can be referenced as long as is necessary; do not compromise the integrity of the data only to create eye-catching interfaces; publish all the data already available in other ways; among others.

The main technologies and formats used to publish Open Government Data are: (1) CSV (Comma Separated-Values) Files, which store tabular data; (2) Atom and RSS (Really Simple Syndication) Information, which aggregate content based on XML (Extensible Markup Language); (3) REST interfaces, which link a resource to an URI using HTTP (Hypertext Transfer Protocol), allowing a site to be enriched with applications that extend the value of an available resource; (4) Semantic Web technologies, which offer a common framework where data can be shared and reused (E-Gov IG, 2009).

Open Government Data projects are emerging in different countries around the world, such as the U.S., UK, Australia, New Zealand, Norway, Holland, Sweden, Spain, Austria, Greece, Canada, and Denmark. There are also a growing number of local initiatives from states and cities (Sheridan & Tennison, 2010). Some governments have created catalogs or portals to facilitate the location and use of data for the public (Bennett & Harvey, 2009), like the portals data.gov and data.gov.uk. In addition, individuals and organizations are publishing government data on their own in various formats (Berners-Lee, 2009).

With so much government data to work with, developers are creating a wide variety of applications, mashups[1], and visualizations, especially in the U.S. and the UK, such as the projects Where Does My Money Go?[2], ITO World[3], Community Health Visualizing Data[4], FixMyStreet[5], TheyWorkForYou[6], and others. These applications offer useful information to citizens, showing the potential of reusing Open Government Data to create new knowledge.

In Brazil there are few government initiatives that give full access to the data in a structured and open language. Examples of these initiatives are the projects Governo Aberto SP[7] and LeXML[8]. While the government does not release more data in open format, initiatives are emerging in order to extract data from government sites and portals, rearrange them, make them open and/or provide new value to them through different applications, such as the projects Congresso Aberto[9], Parlamento Aberto[10], Legisdados[11], SACSP[12] and Xerifes do DF[13].

Due to the few Open Government Data projects in Brazil, there are still few projects that mix information from different sources to create new services and offer new insights about the government information. Given the growing civil interest after successful examples in other countries, more efforts should be developed.

LINKED DATA

Linked Data refers to data published on the Web in a way that they are machine readable, their meanings are explicitly defined, they are linked to other data sets, and in turn can be linked from external data sets (Bizer et al., 2009).

The basic idea was developed by Berners-Lee (2006). He defined the four principles that characterize Linked Data and should be applied to make the Web grow: (1) Using URIs for naming "things"; (2) Using HTTP URIs so that people can look up these names; (3) Providing useful information when someone looks up a URI; (4) Including links to other URIs so that people can find more related "things".

According to Berners-Lee (2009), the overall benefits of Linked Data are: they are accessible by an unlimited variety of applications because they are expressed in open formats; they can be combined through mashups with any other set of Linked Data, and no advance planning is necessary to integrate these data sources as long as they both use Linked Data standards; it is easy to add more Linked Data to the existing ones, even when the terms and definitions change over time.

URIs, HTTP, and RDF are the key technologies that support Linked Data (Bizer et al, 2008). In addition to these, other Semantic Web technologies are used to provide different types of support, such as the SPARQL language to query RDF data, the RDFS (Resource Description Framework Schema), and OWL (Web Ontology Language) languages to define vocabularies and the RDFa (RDF - in - attributes) language for publishing HTML pages with meaning.

URIs identify all items of interest on the Web, often called resources. There are two types of resources: non-informational resources and informational resources. All resources found in traditional Web, such as documents, images and other media files, are information resources. All "real-world objects" that exist outside the Web are non-informational resources, such as people, places, and others (Bizer et al., 2007).

RDF is a framework for representing information in the Web (Klyne & Carrol, 2004). The description of a resource is represented as a series of triples with a subject, a predicate, and an object. The subject is the URI that identifies the resource described. The object may be a literal value like a string, number or date, or the URI of another resource that is related to the subject. The predicate is a URI from a vocabulary that indicates the type of relationship between the subject and the object (Bizer et al., 2007).

With the HTTP protocol, a URI can be accessed so that the information about a referenced resource can be obtained. When a URI that identifies an information resource is dereferenced, the server generates a representation of the resource and sends it to the client using the response code HTTP 200 OK. Non-informational resources cannot be dereferenced directly. One of the most common approaches is to use HTTP 303 redirection, along with Content Negotiation. Clients send HTTP headers with every request to indicate what kind of representation they prefer. Servers can inspect the headers and select an appropriate response, in HTML or RDF (Bizer et al., 2007).

The most visible example of the adoption and application of the Linked Data principles is the Linking Open Data project, an open and collaborative effort supported by the W3C SWEO (Semantic Web Education and Outreach) Group[14]. Its goal is to identify existing data sets that are available under open licenses, convert them to RDF according to the principles of Linked Data, publish them on the Web, and link them with each other, generating the so called LOD Cloud (Linking Open Data Cloud) (Bizer et al., 2008), as shown in Figure 1.

With a significant volume of Linked Data being published on the Web, numerous studies and efforts are being made to build applications that explores this Web of data, for example, domain-specific applications through the mashup of data from different data sets, such as Revyu[15] and DBPedia Mobile[16]; search engines, like Falcons and indexes like Swoogle[17] crawling Linked Data from the Web and providing query capabilities over aggregated data; and Linked Data browsers that allows the navigation between different data sources by following RDF links, such as The Tabulator[18] and Disco Hyperdata Browser[19] (Bizer et al., 2009).

Figure 1. LOD cloud (Cyganiak & Jentzsch, 2010)

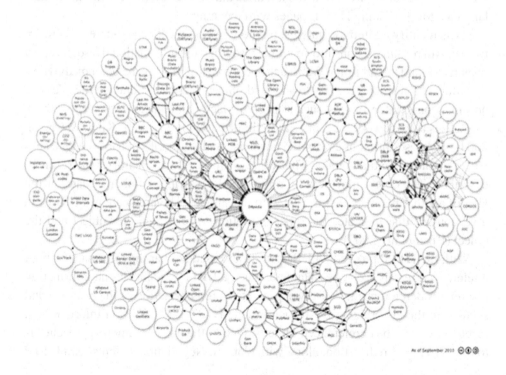

There are several ways for publishing Linked Data on the Web depending on different factors, such as the type of information, the amount of data, and how often the data changes. Several publishing tools were developed to help publishers deal with technical details and ensure that data are published in accordance with the principles and practices of Linked Data, such as D2Rserver[20], Triplify[21], Pubby[22], RDFizers[23], and others (Bizer et al., 2009).

When publishing Linked Data, simple, small, persistent and stable URIs should be chosen. Furthermore, the technical infrastructure to make them dereferenceable should be considered. Usually three URIs related to a single non-informational resource are generated: one for the resource; one for the informational resource appropriate for HTML browsers; and one for the informational resource suitable for RDF browsers (Bizer et al., 2007).

For client applications to process data more easily, it is considered a good practice to reuse terms of well known and widely used vocabularies whenever possible. New terms should only be defined if the required terms cannot be found in existing vocabularies. In this case, a file must be published with the new terms created using RDFS or OWL (Berners-Lee, 2009).

To ensure that customers can evaluate the quality of the published data and determine if they want to trust them, the data must be accompanied by various types of metadata, such as a URI that identifies the author, the creation date and the creation method (Hartig, 2009; Bizer et al., 2008). For clients to use the data in clear legal terms, each RDF document must contain the license under which the content can be used (BIZER et al., 2007).

RDF links are the foundation of Linked Data. They allow client applications to navigate between data sources and find additional data. Thus, data sources must set RDF links to relate the entities in other data sources (Bizer et al., 2009). RDF links can be set manually, but it is a common practice to use automated or semi-automated approaches to generate RDF links (Bizer et al., 2007).

In order to facilitate the discovery of data, additional mechanisms may be used, like adding the data set in the ESW Wiki[24]; creating a sitemap extension to indicate where the RDF is located and what alternative means are provided to access it; defining links from existing pages to RDF data; registering URIs with Ping The Semantic Web[25], a service for registering RDF documents on the Web; and convincing owners from related data sources to self-generate or use RDF links to the data set (Bizer et al., 2007).

After publishing information as Linked Data, it is necessary to test whether they can be handled properly. For this, one can use the Vapour Linked validation service[26]; observe if the information is displayed correctly in different Linked Data browsers and if they can follow links RDF through the data; and use the W3C RDF Validation Service[27] to make sure that valid RDF/XML documents are provided (Heath et al., 2008).

BRAZILIAN POLITICIANS DATA SET

The aim of the project is to provide a new data set with information from Brazilian politicians gathered from different sources using the Linked Data and Open Government Data practices. The name "Ligado nos Políticos" (can be translated as "keeping an eye on politicians") was used to represent the data set and the domain "http://ligadonospoliticos.com.br" was used for publishing the data. This is the first dataset providing Brazilian linked data, according to CKAN[28], followed by Portuguese DBPedia[29].

Figure 2 presents the general architecture of the project, showing the different modules and the connections between them.

Data Sources

The data sources used were the Supreme Electoral Court (TSE) website[30], the Senate website, the House of Representatives portal[31], the Non Governmental Organization (NGO) website Brazilian Politicians[32], the Clean Sheet website[33] and the Excelências project[34] from the Transparency Brazil website[35]. Personal data, election data, disclosure of assets, parliamentary data, leaderships, missions, mandates, clearances, speeches, commissions, proposals and legal occurrences were collected.

Web Crawler

With the exception of some data in CSV format, most of the listed sites offer information only in HTML format. Therefore it was necessary to create and use Web Crawlers to extract data in a methodical and automated way. The technique for extracting structured data from HTML pages is called screen scraping. There

Figure 2. General architecture of the project

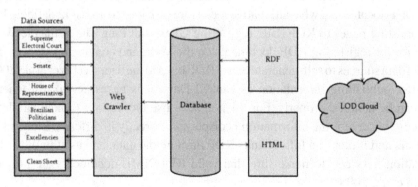

are several tools to assist in this practice, in different languages and platforms. In this project the language PHP (Hypertext Preprocessor) was used to create custom scripts to extract information from each data source.

In general, the scripts work as follows: the URLs (Uniform Resource Locators) from the pages are passed to a function that takes all the content and traverses the HTML document elements using XPath (XML Path Language), returning the content from the elements previously programmed through its attributes and positions. To traverse through all the pages, loops were created using the parameters that differed in each URL. At times, different data were presented in a single HTML element. Specific mechanisms and PHP functions were used to divide the various data before inserting them into the database and ensure their granularity. Other difficulties such as character encoding and data formats were also addressed through different functions and conversions.

Database

After extracting the data with the Web Crawler they were inserted into a relational database. As each data source uses a different approach to store and present data, it was necessary to model the new database in order to reconcile these approaches without losing or changing data, also taking into account the maintainability. Therefore, tables, fields and relationships were created to represent data from different sources in a unique way. MySQL was used as the Database Management System.

There was not a common identifier between the different data sources, due to the fact that a key is not published alongside the politics data to ensure that they are unique, like the ISBN (International Standard Book Number) for books. The task of how to best detect that two entity descriptions refer to the same real world entity is an open research problem known as duplicate record detection (Elmagarmid et al., 2007). In the case described on this book chapter, it was possible to consider different attributes from politicians, such as name, political party and date of birth to identify the data that addressed the same entity and ensure consistency and avoid duplication, using the different data at the WHERE clauses on the sources before inserting a new entry at the database. The lack of global identifiers eventually resulted in a limitation of the project, because there is not a significant key in the domain.

In some cases, a lack of pattern in the information was identified in the different data sources. For example, the Brazilian political party PC do B (Communist Party of Brazil) in some sites is presented as PCdoB; states are sometimes represented by acronyms and other times by name. Therefore, these data had to be identified and transformed to the chosen standard representation format using UPDATE clauses.

RDF Representation

After having all the structured data, the information was represented using the principles and practices of Linked Data and using the RDF model. First, the technical details were addressed, such as Content Negotiation and URIs dereferences, to ensure that the non-informational resources were generated correctly through good URIs for both HTML and RDF clients.

Simple and small HTTP URIs in the domain were chosen to represent the non-informational resources. To ensure that each URI was unique, the primary key of each politician was used. An example is "http://ligadonospoliticos.com.br/resource/1", followed by/html or/rdf, depending on the desired representation.

Then, the terms from the vocabularies that would be used to represent the resources properties were chosen. Terms from known vocabularies such as FOAF[36], BIO[37], PERSON[38], VCARD[39], DBPPROP[40], POL[41], BEING[42], TIMELINE[43], DCTERMS[44], MONEY[45], GEOSPECIES[46], EVENT[47], SKOS[48] and BIBLIO[49] were reused whenever possible. The Talis Schemacache service[50] was used to find the terms, and other data sets were also investigated, such as GovTrack.us[51]. Not all the necessary terms were found in other vocabularies. In such cases, new terms were defined under the namespace "http://ligadonospoliticos.com.br/politicobr/" represented by POLBR. Figure 3 presents a diagram with the vocabularies used in the data set, along with their respective properties.

With the vocabulary defined, the information was represented in the RDF model. The information is taken from the database and inserted dynamically into the model according to the requested resource. The subject is represented by the political URI, the predicates by the URIs from the preexisting or created terms, and the objects are described by literal values taken from the database or by URIs that represent the RDF links to other resources. Metadata were also added using terms from the DC (Dublin Core) vocabulary[52]. Control structures were inserted to ensure that blank nodes were not generated.

After that, links RDF were set to relate the resources with other data sources. For this, properties like *owl:sameAs, foaf:homepage, foaf:page, foaf:primaryTopic, rdfs:seeAlso, rdf:type* and *skos:subject* were used. In addition, some information such as occupation and geographic data are presented as links RDF for other data sources. Thus, links RDF were generated with the data sets DBpedia[53], GeoNames[54], Freebase[55], World Factbook[56], UMBEL[57] (Upper Mapping and Binding Exchange Layer) and YAGO[58]. Since there were no common identifiers between the data sets, manual and semi-automatic approaches were used to generate the links, the latter through practices similar to those used in the Web Crawler, traversing the pages of other data sources, comparing the resources properties and extracting the links.

Figure 3. Vocabulary diagram

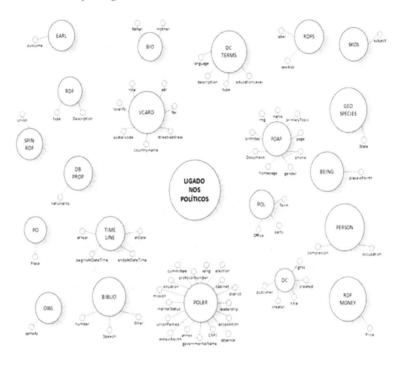

In order to facilitate the discovery of data by machines and humans, the data set was added in the ESW Wiki[59], registered in CKAN[60] and a sitemap was provided to indicate where the RDF is located. To test whether the data can be properly handled and if they can follow links RDF, The Tabulator Extension[61] was used, an extension to the Firefox browser that provides an interface for Linked Data based on The Tabulator browser. The W3C RDF Validation Service[62] was used to ensure that valid RDF/XML documents are provided.

An example of the RDF representation is provided in Figure 4, as seen with the use of The Tabulator Extension.

HTML Representation

A representation for HTML viewing and searching data was also created. The home page provides an overall description, the number of registered politicians, links to other pages on the site, and especially a search engine for users to find the desired politician according to different criteria such as name, location, status, state, political party and gender. The user can use one or more criterion to perform the search.

Figure 4. RDF representation with the tabulator extension

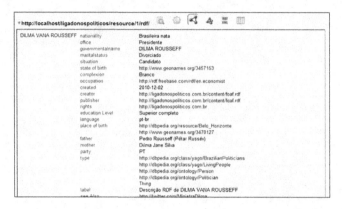

To improve the users experience and give new meaning to the collected data, different graphs are generated dynamically from different queries in the database. Pages with the main concepts of Linked Data and Open Government Data are also offered, along with a page with a more detailed description of the project and a contact page. The data are also provided in its raw format at the download page to facilitate its reuse.

After the search is performed, if there are results according to the query the politicians that correspond to the result are displayed, identified by name, location, position, status and party. Otherwise a message is displayed along with the search engine where the search can be repeated.

A link to each resource with their respective URI is generated. By selecting the politician, the proper representation is presented according to the HTTP header sent by the client. The politician data are dynamically extracted from the database and displayed on this page. To improve the navigability, certain data can be selected to search politicians with the same characteristics. A link to RDF/XML format is also presented at the beginning and at the end of the page.

An example of the HTML representation is provided on Figure 5.

In order to improve the users experience and allow for analytical insight from the collected data, different visualizations are generated dynamically from queries in the database using Fusion Charts Free[63]. We allow people to choose different parameters for personalized queries. The user can, for example, visualize a chart of the number of speeches from male senators from PSDB (Brazilian political party).

A link to RDF/XML format is also presented at the beginning and at the end of the page. To take advantage of the Web of data and the RDF links, data from other sources were also extracted and presented via SPARQL queries using ARC[64], a flexible RDF system for semantic web using PHP. An example of the HTML representation is provided on Figure 4.

Figure 5. HTML representation

Analysis

Analyzing the project according to the aspects presented over Open Government Data, we can say that the published data generally meet the basic principles that determine this practice: they are complete, as all data collected are available without restrictions of privacy, security or privileges access; they are primary, since they have the highest possible level of granularity without modifications; they are timely, as they are recent data from the Brazilian politicians; they are accessible, available to any Web user; they are machine processable, structured using the RDF model; they are not-discriminatory, because there is no need to register to access the data; they are not-proprietary, as no entity holds the exclusive control of the data, and they are license-free, as they are public data collected from different government sites.

Regarding Linked Data, the project also meets its basic principles, using HTTP URIs for naming resources, allowing people to access them, providing useful information using the RDF standard and including links to other URIs so that users can find more resources.

With the data set from Brazilian politicians online, it is possible to query the data, extract data published via RDF, link these data with data from other data sets and develop different web applications.

This work is a contribution towards narrowing the gap between citizens and politicians through open Web technologies. This has been done in four different ways:

- **Emphasizing the Impact of Each Citizen's Vote:** The collected election data establishes a link from citizens, through their location of voting, to the politicians elected by those locations. A Location Page – e.g. the page for certain town – shows a summary of topics (tag cloud) supported by politicians

51

elected by that location. We intend to use this view to catalyze on the voters a sense of responsibility for the consequences of the actions of their elected representatives.

- **Facilitating Citizen Oversight:** We allow citizens to ask questions about their representatives directly to the data. With the information available as linked data, we have the advantage to query them more flexibly and from different perspectives.
- **Empowering Citizen Opinion:** We allow politicians and citizens alike to follow online discussions that may be relevant with regard to a politician, legislation or location. A preliminary implementation of semantic annotation of citizen opinions allows us to link general public comments to the politician, legislation or location targeted by each comment.
- **Seeding an Open Government Mash-Up Ecosystem:** As a result of the integration and publication of the Brazilian politicians' data set as LOD, the project lowers the entry barrier for third-party 'citizen developers', researchers or government agencies to repurpose government data from Brazil in interesting and useful ways.

CONCLUSION

With this work it was possible to realize the importance and the benefits of publishing Open Government Data on the Web using the Linked Data practices. Government data published on the Web, by itself, have a great value, because they contribute to greater information transparency. Providing this information in accessible and open formats allows them to be reused and mixed with information from other sources to produce new conclusions about government performance.

Allying the publication of Open Government Data to Linked Data Practices is even more important, because it provides a single and standardized access mechanism, allowing data to be readable by machines, facilitating the discovery and consumption of data, allowing them to be linked to other data sets, increasing the value and utility of data and opening possibilities for smarter web applications.

The publication of Open Government Data and Linked Data has been increasing in recent years. Still, much remains to be done to evolve the Web of documents to a Web of data and ensure that these data are open and accessible to all.

Currently, the publication of Open Government Data is greater in countries like the United States and the United Kingdom. Thus, it is necessary to extend this practice to other countries and ensure that more open data are published from government initiatives. At the same time, more people and organizations must publish government data on their own.

It is important to state that the publications should go beyond the field of politicians' data, covering different government areas such as health, education, transportation and economy, among others. Then, more applications, mashups and visualizations can be created to provide useful information to citizens.

Brazil offers many government data publicly, but we need to increase the open data initiatives. Based on successful examples from other countries, catalogs or portals should be prepared to serve as a single point of access to public data. More initiatives to extract the data already available and make them open and reusable are also necessary, in addition to the creation of new applications on top of that data. Thus, the transparency of the Brazilian government would be increased, improving the country's rate at e-government surveys and bringing positive socio-economic impacts for the population.

When it comes to Linked Data, much has been done, such as disseminating their concepts and practices even further, creating and improving services to facilitate the publication of such data, building more applications and improving existing ones. There are a limited number of published data sets compared the number of (X)HTML documents available on the Web today. More governments, organizations, and individuals need to publish Linked Data in order to increase the number of interconnected data sets and the amount of useful data on the LOD Cloud.

The technical infrastructure support for publishing Linked Data must also be improved. More tools and services must be built, and publications dealing more specifically with the topic should be fostered. It is necessary to increase the number of services that assist in the generation of RDF links, especially for the cases where there are no common identifiers between the data sets.

About the project that generated the data set "Ligado nos Políticos", the published data meet the basic principles of Open Government Data and Linked Data. However, work should be done to adapt the project to all the described practices.

First, the published data needs to be useful and current. For this, the data must be constantly updated through the generated scripts for scraping data. In addition, more data can be collected, like votes, stats, and news, among others. The amount of registered politicians can also be increased by using data from candidates, senators and deputies from other years.

More RDF links related to other data sources should also be defined, through more detailed research on other data sets. It would also be interesting to publish the data in other formats, and provide a SPARQL endpoint so that queries can be performed directly on the data. To improve the user experience, it is necessary to improve the HTML representation. Moreover, new knowledge about the data collected can be generated through new graphics and individual charts for the registered politicians.

As future work, it is intended to keep the data up to date, as well as include information from candidates, senators and representatives from past years. More RDF links related to other data sources should also be created, through more detailed research on other data sets. It is also intended to provide a more flexible interface for arbitrary querying and visualization, for example through Cuebee[65], and extract entities from text through entity extraction tools, for example DBpedia Spotlight[66].

Just as the Electronic Government revolutionized the relationship between citizens and government, Open Government Data has the potential to enhance and further strengthen this relationship. And just as the Web has caused a revolution in publishing and consumption of documents, Linked Data has the potential to improve the way data is accessed and used. If the remaining challenges are properly addressed, these practices will enable an even greater evolution in the way the Web is used today.

ACKNOWLEDGMENT

The authors would like to thank PhD student Pablo Mendes, of Freie Universität Berlin, for her valuable comments, encouragement and support.

REFERENCES

Agune, R. M., Filho, A. S. G., & Bolliger, S. P. (2009). *Governo aberto SP: Disponibilização de bases de dados e informações em formato aberto*. Public Managment Congress, Panel 13/050. Retrieved from http://www.repositorio.seap.pr.go v.br/.../governo_aberto_sp_disponibilizacao_de_bases_de_dados_e_informacoes_em_formato_aberto.pdf

Bennett, D., & Harvey, A. (2009). *Publishing open government data*. W3C Working Draft. Retrieved from http://www.w3.org/TR/gov-data/

Berners-Lee, T. (2006). Linked data. *Design Issues*. Retrieved from http://www.w3.org/Desi gnIssues/LinkedData.html

Berners-Lee, T. (2009). Putting government data online. *Design Issues*. Retrieved from http://www.w3.org/DesignIssues/GovData.html

Bizer, C., et al. (2008). *Linked data on the web*. Paper presented at the 17th International World Wide Web Conference. Beijing, China. Retrieved from http://events.linkeddata.org/ldow2008/papers/00-bizer-heath-ldow2008-intro.pdf

Bizer, C., Cyganiak, R., & Heath, T. (2007). *How to publish linked data on the web*. Retrieved from http://www4.wiwiss.fu-berlin.de/bizer/pub/LinkedDataTutorial

Bizer, C., Heath, T., & Berners-Lee, T. (2009). Linked data - The story so far. *International Journal on Semantic Web and Information Systems*. Retrieved from http://tomheath.com/papers/bizer-heath-berners-lee-ijswis-linked-data.pdf

Cyganiak, R., & Jentzsch, A. (n.d.). *The linking open data cloud diagram*. Retrieved from http://richard.cyganiak.de/2007/10/lod/

Diniz, V. (n.d.). *Como conseguir dados governamentais abertos*. Public Managment Congress, Panel 13/049. Retrieved from http://www.consad.org.br/sites/1500/150 4/00001870.pdf

E-Gov IG. (2009). *Melhorando o acesso ao governo com o melhor uso da web*. Comitê Gestor da Internet no Brasil. 1a edição. São Paulo.Retrieved from http://www.w3c.br/divulgacao/pdf/gov-web.pdf

Elmagarmid, K., Panagiotis, G., & Vassilios, S. (2007). *Duplicate record detection: A survey*. Retrieved from http://www.cs.purdue.edu/homes/ake/pub/survey2.pdf

Heath, T. (2009). *An introduction to linked data*. Austin, TX:Talis Information Ltd. Retrieved from http://tomheath.com/slides/2009-02-austin-linkeddata -tutorial.pdf

Heath, T., et al. (2008). (How to publish linked data on the web. Paper presented at 7th International Semantic Web Conference. Karlsruhe, Germany: SWSA. Retrieved from http://events.linkeddata.org/iswc2 008tutorial/how-to-publish-linked-data-iswc2008-slides.pdf.

Klyne, G., & Carrol, J. (2004). *Resource description framework (RDF): Concepts and abstract syntax*. W3C. Retrieved from http://www.w3.org/TR/2 004/REC-rdf-concepts-20040210/

Opengovdata.org. (2007). *Open government data principles*. Public.Resource. Retrieved from http://resource.org/8_principles.html

Sheridan, J., & Tennison, J. (2010). *Linking UK government data*. Paper presented at Linked Date on the Web Workshop. Raleigh, NC: LDOW. Retrieved from http://events.linkeddata.org/ldow2010/papers/ldow201 0_paper14.pdf

United Nations. (2010). *United Nations e-government survey 2010*. New York: UN Publishing Section. Retrieved from http://unpan1.un.org/intradoc/groups/public/documents/un/unpan038851.pdf

W3C Brazilian Office. (2010). *O governo de inovação na copa 2014: Uso de redes sociais e dados abertos*. Paper presented at Seminar on Electronic Government Innovation. Porto Alegre, Brazil. Retrieved from http://www.procergs.rs.gov.br/uploads/1285856001W3C_Seminario_Inovacao_eGov_POA_17092010.pdf

ENDNOTES

1   Web site or application that uses or combines data, presentation or functionality from two or more sources to create new services.

2   http://wheredoesmymoneygo.org/

3   http://www.itoworld.com/

4   http://www.healthymagination.com/projects/data-visualizations/

5   http://www.fixmystreet.com/

6   http://www.theyworkforyou.com/

7   http://www.governoaberto.sp.gov.br/

8   http://www.lexml.gov.br/

9   http://www.congressoaberto.com.br/

10   http://trac.meuparlamento.org/

11   http://www.legisdados.org/

12   http://sacsp.mamulti.com/

13   http://eleicoes.mamulti.com/

14   http://www.w3.org/2001/sw/sweo/

15   http://revyu.com/

16   http://wiki.dbpedia.org/DBpediaMobile

17   http://swoogle.umbc.edu/

18   http://www.w3.org/2005/ajar/tab

19   http://www4.wiwiss.fu-berlin.de/bizer/ng4j/disco/

20   http://www4.wiwiss.fu-berlin.de/bizer/d2r-server/

21   http://triplify.org/Overview

22   http://www4.wiwiss.fu-berlin.de/pubby/

23   http://openstructs.org/resources/rdfizers

24   http://www.w3.org/wiki/TaskForces/CommunityProjects/LinkingOpenData/DataSets

25   http://pingthesemanticweb.com/

26   http://validator.linkeddata.org/vapour

27   http://www.w3.org/RDF/Validator/

28   http://ckan.net/

29   http://pt.dbpedia.org/

30   http://www.tse.gov.br/

31   http://www.senado.gov.br/

32   http://politicosbrasileiros.com.br/

33   http://www.fichalimpa.org.br/

34   http://www.excelencias.org.br/

35   http://www.transparencia.org.br/

36   http://xmlns.com/foaf/0.1/

[37] http://purl.org/vocab/bio/0.1/
[38] http://models.okkam.org/ENS-core-vocabulary
[39] http://www.w3.org/2006/vcard/ns
[10] http://dbpedia.org/property/
[41] http://www.rdfabout.com/rdf/schema/politico/
[42] http://purl.org/ontomedia/ext/common/being
[43] http://motools.sourceforge.net/timeline/timeline.html
[44] http://purl.org/dc/terms/
[45] http://www.purl.org/net/rdf-money/
[46] http://rdf.geospecies.org/ont/geospecies
[47] http://purl.org/NET/c4dm/event.owl
[48] http://www.w3.org/2004/02/skos/core
[49] http://purl.org/ontology/bibo/
[50] http://schemacache.test.talis.com/
[51] http://www.govtrack.us/
[52] http://dublincore.org/
[53] http://dbpedia.org/
[54] http://www.geonames.org/
[55] http://www.freebase.com/
[56] http://www4.wiwiss.fu-berlin.de/factbook/
[57] http://www.umbel.org/
[58] http://mpii.de/yago
[59] http://www.w3.org/wiki/TaskForces/CommunityProjects/LinkingOpenData/DataSets
[60] http://ckan.net/package/brazilian-politicians
[61] http://dig.csail.mit.edu/2007/tab/
[62] http://www.w3.org/RDF/Validator/
[63] http://www.fusioncharts.com/free/
[64] http://arc.semsol.org/
[65] http://cuebee.sourceforge.net/
[66] http://wiki.dbpedia.org/spotlight

Chapter 4

Extraction and Prediction of Biomedical Database Identifier Using Neural Networks towards Data Network Construction

Hendrik Mehlhorn
Institute of Plant Genetics and Crop Plant Research, Germany

Matthias Lange
Institute of Plant Genetics and Crop Plant Research, Germany

Uwe Scholz
Institute of Plant Genetics and Crop Plant Reseearch, Germany

Falk Schreiber
Institue of Plant Genetics and Crop Plant Research, Germany & Martin Luther University, Germany

EXECUTIVE SUMMARY

Knowledge found in biomedical databases is a major bioinformatics resource. In general, this biological knowledge is represented worldwide in a network of thousands of databases, which overlap in content, but differ substantially with respect to content detail, interface, formats, and data structure. To support a functional annotation of lab data, such as protein sequences, metabolites, or DNA sequences, as well as a semi-automated data exploration in information retrieval environments, an integrated view to databases is essential. A prerequisite of supporting the concept of an integrated data view is to acquire insights into cross-references among database entities.

DOI: 10.4018/978-1-4666-2827-4.ch004

In this work, we investigate to what extent an automated construction of an integrated data network is possible. We propose a method that predicts and extracts cross-references from multiple life science databases and possible referenced data targets. We study the retrieval quality of our method and report on first, promising results.

1. INTRODUCTION

Bioinformatics is the field of science in which biology, computer science, and in particular information retrieval merge to form a single discipline. The ultimate goal of the field is to enable the discovery of new biological insights. The first step in this direction is already done. High throughput biotechnologies, like next generation sequencing, proteomics and metabolomics techniques produce a massive amount of data (Galperin & Fernandez-Suarez, 2012). But the data gathered in biology or medicine is as manifold as the biological research areas itself. If we will narrow down in this chapter the complex areas of biomedical research to molecular biology, bioinformatics attempts to model and interprets this data pathway: *genome, gene sequence, protein sequence, protein structure, protein function, cellular pathways & networks*, and *biomedical literature*. The first consequence of this revolution is the explosion of available data that biomolecular researchers have to harness and exploit (Roos, 2001) (e.g., as of March 2012, Genbank provides access to 150,000,000 DNA sequences[1] and in PubMed there are 2,400,000 research articles listed). The number of public available databases passed currently the number of high water mark of 1,200 (Galperin & Fernandez-Suarez, 2012).

The big players in this context are on the one hand companies like pharmaceutical or plant breeders on the other hand public or private financed research institute. Their role is either a data consumer or a data producer. In consequence there is a raising need for find, extract, merge, and synthesize information from multiple, disparate sources. Convergence of biology, computer science, and information technology will accelerate this multidisciplinary endeavor. The basic needs are formulated in Lacroix & Critchlow, 2003:

1. On demand access and retrieval of the most up-to-date biological data and the ability to perform complex queries across multiple heterogeneous databases to find the most relevant information.
2. Access to the best-of-breaded analytical tools and algorithms for extraction of useful information from the massive volume and diversity of biological data.
3. A robust information integration infrastructure that connects various computational steps involving database queries, computational algorithms, and application software.

In consequence, database integration plays an important role in this context. Thus, we will subsequently briefly introduce the most popular concepts for database integration in life science. Using the World Wide Web or social networks as inspiring example, the basic idea presented in this chapter is to compute a network of biomedical knowledge by taking a set of database entries as input, analyzing the entries and their attributes and identifying potential cross-references in the same and in other databases. We propose IDPredictor, an algorithm that predicts cross-references from multiple life science databases and thus sets the basis for an enhanced information retrieval over biomedical data. We discuss to what extend IDPredictor can be used as method for an efficient and precise prediction of database cross-references.

In Section 1 we give a brief introduction to data management in life sciences. In particular approaches for data integration, information retrieval and aspects of data identifier are discussed. In Section 2 we present the underlying machine learning methods of IDPredictor. In Section 3 we discuss training methods and prediction performance measures. In Section 4 we discuss the prediction performance, preliminary results and the application to database networks.

1.1 Overview to Data Integration Approaches

With the expansion of the biological data sources available across the World Wide Web, integration is a major challenge facing researchers and institutions that wish to explore and fuse the rich deposit of information. Currently, many integration approaches exist in the field of molecular biological data. (Karp, 1995) describes different integration approaches, besides simple hyperlink navigation. These are federated databases (Sheth & Larson, 1990), mediators (Wiederhold, 1992), multi database queries (Karp, 1995), and data warehouses (Inmon, 1996). Most of the existing systems can be classified as one of these four basic types of integration. Existing implementations can be compared by means of five basic properties which are: (1) integration approach, (2) degree of integration, (3) materialization of the integration results, (4) supported data types, and (5) expressive power of the query operators.

The *degree of integration* is described as being tight or loose. A system is tightly coupled if all schemas of the integrated data sources are transformed into one common data model and a global schema exists. Whereas, an implementation is loosely integrated if a mapping into a common data model was conducted, but no global schema exists. The *materialization* distinguishes materialized and view-based solutions. A materialized approach physically transfers information of all participating data sources into one global database. In contrast, a view-based implementation generates logical views onto the integrated data. The analysis of *supported data types* distinguishes between atomic types like numbers for integer-valued identifiers or strings, and complex types (sets, lists, bags, etc.) for nucleotide and amino acids. The property *query operators* characterize the expressive power of queries sent against the integrated data stock. For example, arbitrarily complex selection predicates can be considered powerful query operators. These also include non-standard comparison in pattern matching, which are heavily required in bioinformatics. Simple single-attribute exact match queries have less expressive power and do not match the requirements of many advanced applications.

Many useful integration approaches already exist. Among the most well-known approaches are SRS (Etzold et al., 1996), the Entrez system (Tatusova et al., 1999), the TAMBIS system (Stevens et al., 2000), ISYS (Siepel et al., 2001), and DiscoveryLink (Haas et al., 2001). These systems are based on different data integration approaches (e.g., federated database systems (ISYS and DiscoveryLink), multi database systems (TAMBIS) and data warehouses (Entrez and SRS). The prerequisite for the presented methods is the approach of highly structured data. As we see in the next section, the tendency is to avoid all connected technical and organizational problems implied with this approaches. One very popular approach is to use methods from information retrieval.

1.2 Information Retrieval

Beside the classic methods of database integration, information retrieval get more and more focus in information technology research. In order to support the functional annotation to link and discover the functional context of lab data, the relationship to existing biological knowledge stored in worldwide distributed databases has to be explored. Investigations in (Stein, 2002; Stevens et al., 2001) argue that web based, in silico, research is a major challenge in life sciences. A study in Divoli et al., 2008, claims that 37% of all scientist use over 80% of their time for Web investigations. For this, the World Wide Web and all other HTTP-based services (web services, file downloads etc.) are the most popular media.

One use case is to facilitate Web information systems or desktop tools for linking wet-lab data to this world wide data cloud. Methods like sequence similarities such as BLAST (Altschul et al., 1997), text similarities queries like Entrez text queries (Schuler et al., 1996) or eTBLAST (Errami et al., 2007) are database search operations, which are commonly used in life science dry labs.

In this context, a general top-down approach is the use of biomedical search engines (Lu, 2011; Lange et al., 2010). In order to rank search results for their relevance, the most popular methods are the ranking field importance, word combinations, and term frequencies. Weighting and ranking search results on the amount (or importance) of cross-references is still an open issue for life science database integration. In order to extract the Web content, the dry lab scientists use the following workflow:

1. **Search the Most Relevant Root Data Entries:** Search databases using keyword search or match data pattern based on data similarities, e.g. sequence homology.
2. **Explore the Root Data Surrounding Knowledge:** Follow hyperlinks manually, i.e. use the HTML hyperlinks or database cross references.

Search in life science databases exhibits some fundamental differences from the way people search in the Web or in a general purpose digital library. First of all, links play a central role: not only a single article to a specific entity is of relevance, but all articles on this entity - though articles just mentioning this entity may be irrelevant. Second, life science databases are domain centric organized – usually around specific entity types (e.g. metabolomics). Here, is easy to extract all domain information related to an entity. But it is very difficult to collect information on an entity if the knowledge is spread across entities of different domains e.g. genome structure focused databases versus metabolite or pathway centric ones.

The exploitation of links across entities in different databases is impeded by the lack of an agreed-upon convention for referencing data records. Proprietary identifiers such as so called accession numbers are designed as unique combination of alphanumeric characters. For example, the proprietary identifier Q8W413 in the UniProt database (Magrane & Consortium, 2011) stands for the protein Beta-fructofuranosidase[2]. The enzyme number 3.2.1.26[3] points to the same entry, but is interpreted as standard nomenclature for enzymes classes. In "The Arabidopsis Information Resource" (TAIR) we find the locus tag At2g36190[4] as identifier for the coding gene of the same protein in the species Arabidopsis thaliana (prefix At). Furthermore, the gene synonym AtFruct6 is an example for a semantically enriched acronym of an gene: At stand for Arabidopsis thaliana and Fruct for Betafructofuranosidase.

One approach to face this is the use of graphs. The idea is to construct a graph of data records from biomedical databases. This concept is known as Data Linkage Graphs (DLG) (Lange et al., 2007). The idea is the representation of integrated databases as a network of identifiers. Colloquially, two data records are in relation if,

1. The identifiers are equal, or
2. The identifiers are 1:1 mappable to each other

Using this idea, it becomes possible to compute data networks on specific diseases, regulatory elements, protein data and gene variants. This can be supported by a multidimensional, structural analysis of integrated databases, like centrality analysis for the identification of key elements of data networks. Furthermore, quality control of public databases is an important challenge in modern bioinformatics. Using DLGs we can e. g. instance extraction all networks that include contradicting data nodes for the same schema node.

To illustrate the idea, the URL http://pgrc.ipk-gatersleben.de/dlg/can be used to download the data schema graph (GML or GraphML format), the data linkage graphs (CSV format) or examples of context specific extracted metabolic knowledge networks for plants (GML or GraphML format). Later are queried using SQL by joining the DLGs over the enzymes (EC numbers) which are present in glycolysis metabolic pathway and protein which are reported in Brassicae, Triticeae and Solanacea. Thus we extracted networks of knowledge to enzymes in barley which show catalytic activity in glycolysis. Figure 1 gives an impression of such a data network. A high resolution and comfortable version is from this figure is available, using the graph data files in a graph viewer. The files and a link to a viewer are available using the URL given previously.

Figure 1. Data network of enzymes in barley showing catalytic activity in glycolysis

1.3 Identifier Prediction

In this chapter we discuss aspects that have to be faced by scientists doing data exploration. In particular, we present methods for cross reference extraction to retrieve linked information for any kind of database entities (enzyme, gene, protein, etc.).

Efforts and strategies for the integration of life science data is the research focus in several projects. Using several methods and approaches the majority is focused on particular analytic scenarios and applications, but none of them provided a holistic, uninterpreted view to the world wide interlinked knowledge. Popular techniques, like data warehouses, multi database query languages or database mediators provided powerful query interfaces and helpful tools (Lacroix and Critchlow, 2003).

Another popular solutions for query and/or join distributed tools and databases is scripting. Dry lab scientist tend to program small pieces of scripts preferring plain popular programming languages such as PERL instead of using work flow systems like TAVERNA (Oinn et al., 2004) or Galaxy (Giardine, B. and Riemer, C. and Hardison, R. C. and Burhans, R. and Elnitski, L. and Shah, P. and Zhang, Y. and Blankenberg, D. and Albert, I. and Taylor, J. and Miller, W. and Kent, W. J. and Nekrutenko, A., 2005). Because of the original character of life science databases as highly dynamic and flexible, such scripts or workflows are difficult to keep up-to date. The nature of the knowledge stored in the WWW is a dynamic data network. Consequently, we need to provide an efficient method for the extraction of data and knowledge networks (Bry and Kröger, 2003). Systems like GoPubMed (Doms and Schroeder, 2005) or ProMiner (Hanisch et al., 2005) apply text mining methods to extract entities and other forms of relevant information (including types of interaction among entities, like "activation", "is regulated by" or phenotypic effects) in specific databases.

The navigation through and the benefits of exploiting the data networks has been motivated in graph based systems. The three systems BioDBnet (Mudunuri et al., 2009), BioNavigation (Lacroix et al., 2005) and BioGuideSRS (Cohen-Boulakia et al., 2007) support scientists in exploring the content of integrated life science databases. Here, the core idea is a graph based browsing and query building on top of integrated databases.

BioXRef (Bachmann et al., 2011) is an example of a method that extracts cross-references from multiple life science databases by combining targeted crawling, pointer chasing, sampling and information extraction. There, the authors studied the retrieval quality of the proposed method and the relationship between manually crafted relevance ranking and relevance ranking based on cross-references.

Approaches, which use regular expressions to recognize biological database identifiers (Bachmann et al., 2011), get a hard yes or no classification of input strings, but there are databases which identifiers are not discriminable in this way.

For cxample, NCBI taxonomy identifiers and NCBI gene IDs both have the shape of digits of variable digit lengths. Regular expressions assign both identifier types to both databases and are not able to, for example, factor the tendency of NCBI taxonomy identifiers to be shorter than NCBI gene IDs into the classification result, which would yield in a smooth database assignment. Summarizing, regular expression based methods show high precision but fall short in recall and flexibility in respect of supported databases.

2. METHOD

2.1 Introduction to Neural Networks

A neural network, or more precisely an artificial neural network, is a graphical model motivated by biological neural networks. Neural networks can be used as a universal approximator capable of learning patterns in a given set of data or finding complex relationships between sets of input data and output data (Oja, 1982; Galla, 2006). In the frame of this chapter we use neural networks to learn and recognize patterns in the format of identifiers from biological databases.

Neural networks consist of nodes denoted as neurons, which are organized in consecutive layers, so that exclusively neurons of successive layers are connected by interconnections (see Figure 1). The first layer is called the input layer comprising the input synapses, which receive the input of the model from a feature vector, which is a scalar vector with the same dimension as the number of input neurons. The last layer is called the output layer comprising the output synapses, which transmit the output of the model as the output vector. This output vector is being interpreted depending on the application of the neural network. The remaining layers are called hidden layers and connect the input layer with the output layer. Each neuron of the neural network receives a set of scalar values as input from the neurons of the previous layer or the feature vector and decides with the help of a given activation function how to fire a set of scalar values as output for the neurons of the subsequent layer or the output vector.

The parameters of a neural network are weights for all interconnections, which afford the adaption of the neural network to certain requirements. The general procedure of using neural networks starts with the training, where the weights of the interconnections are being adapted. Once the neural network is trained, it is ready to infer predictions.

A neural network (See Figure 2) consists of the input layer, an arbitrary number of hidden layers, and the output layer. Each layer consists of a number of neurons depicted as circles. In this case, the neurons of each layer are connected to all neurons

Figure 2. Schema of a neural network

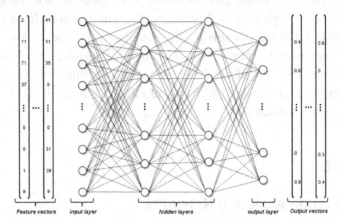

of the preceding layer and to all neurons of the successive layer. The input layer is being supplied with scalar values from feature vectors and the output layer transmits one output vector for each feature vector.

2.2 Feature Extraction in Text Token

In order to supply scalar input values for the input neurons of the neural networks, we extract features from words represented by numerical values. These numerical values constitute the elements of the feature vector. For there are different ways to represent the properties of identifiers, we test ten feature extraction strategies as summarized in Table 1.

We represent words as a vector of symbols, which each have a unique ASCII code. We denote each ASCII code value as character type. In addition, we denote the identifiers from different databases as identifier type.

Feature Extraction Focused on Positions: We apply a position specific feature extraction method in order to represent the property of many identifier types of being designed as a defined succession of symbols. For instance, TAIR identifiers such as 'At1g15850', 'AtMg01190', and 'ATCG01000' consist of the characters 'At' or 'AT' at the first two positions, a digit, 'M', or 'C' at the third position, 'g' or 'G' at the fourth position, and five digits at positions five to nine. We keep the position information by extracting the character type of the symbol of each word string position. The dimension of the feature vector is fixed, thus we limit the position specific feature extraction method to a maximum of 30 positions and choose the feature vector to a dimension of 30. If a given word is longer than 30 positions, we ignore the remaining string positions and if the given word is shorter than 30 positions, we fill the supernumerous positions of the feature vector with zeros. In

Table 1. The ten proposed feature extraction strategies. We apply the five feature extraction methods Position specific, Symbol specific, Symbol specific (partially grouped), Symbol specific (grouped), and Word statistics either to the whole word string indicated by a 'No' in the second column, or to three word substrings individually indicated by a 'Yes' in the second column. In the third column, we present the dimension of the feature extraction vector.

Feature extraction approaches	Word substrings	Feature vector dimension
Position specific	No	30
	Yes	90
Symbol specific	No	256
	Yes	768
Symbol specific (partially grouped)	No	41
	Yes	123
Symbol specific (grouped)	No	3
	Yes	9
Word statistics	No	7
	Yes	21

case of the position specific feature extraction method, neural networks have 30 input synapses, which are ordered and being supplied with the character type of the symbol of the according word position. We denote this feature extraction method as Position specific.

Feature Extraction Focused on Symbols: We apply a symbol specific feature extraction method in order to represent the property of many identifier types of comprising a specific set of characters. For instance, EC numbers such as '1.1.1.1', 'EC:3.4.24.56', and 'ec:6.4.1.-' exclusively consist of the set of characters { '.', '-', '0', '1', '2', '3', '4', '5', '6', '7', '8', '9', ':', 'C', 'E', 'c', 'e' }. We represent the symbol information by extracting the character type of all word symbols and cumulating these in three ways to test different levels of granularity.

In the first level of granularity we create one feature vector element for each of the 256 possible characters types. In this level we count the character type abundance of all possible word symbols, thus this level is the most fine graned symbol specific feature extraction method. Here, the feature vector has the dimension 256 and the neural networks have 256 input synapses. We denote this feature extraction method as Symbol specific.

In the second level of granularity we create one feature vector element per digit, one feature vector element per letter, one feature vector element for each of the character types '-', '.', ':', and 'I', and one feature vector element for all remaining character types. In this level we group all character types in one feature vector element, which are very uncommon within the identifiers of the most types to limit the feature vector dimension as well as the number of input synapses of the neural networks to 41. We denote this feature extraction method as Symbol specific (partially grouped).

In the third level of granularity we create one feature vector element for all digits, one feature vector element for all letters, and one feature vector element for all remaining character types. This is the roughest level, limiting the feature vector dimension as well as the number of input synapses of the neural networks to 3. We denote this feature extraction method as Symbol specific (grouped).

Feature Extraction Focused on Word Statistics: We apply a word statistic specific feature extraction method in order to represent the property of many identifier types of being composed of well-defined symbol proportions, symbol successions, and a fixed length. For instance, UniProt identifiers such as 'Q48HF8', 'E3E768', and 'A0MYM4' consist of two to four letters, two to four digits, and have a length of 6. We represent these word statistics by extracting the following seven features, which constitute the elements of the resulting feature vector. We extract the length of the word string (1), the proportion of letters (2), the proportion of digits (3), the proportion of whitespaces (4), the proportion of the set of symbols { '-', '.', ':', '|' } (v), the proportion of all remaining characters (5), and the number of letter-digit pairs, which stand together (6). In case of the word statistic specific feature extraction method, the feature vector has a dimension of 7 and the neural networks have 7 input synapses. We denote this feature extraction method as Word statistics.

Feature Extraction Methods Applied to Word Substrings: We apply the five presented feature extraction methods to word substrings in order to increase the position specificity of these methods. For instance, KEGG Gene identifiers such as 'ath:AT4G27720.1', 'ptm:GSPATT00025144001', and 'ani:AN2412.2' mainly consist of a prefix, a main part, and a suffix. In this case, the prefix represents a species code ('ath:', 'apn:', and 'ani:'), the main part represents the gene locus ('AT4G27720', 'GSPATT00025144001', and 'AN2412'), and the suffix represents a sequence version ('.1', '', and '.2'). We represent this identifier composition by splitting the given words in three substrings of preferably equal lengths (in case of 'ath:AT4G27720.1': 'ath:A', 'T4G27', and '720.1') and applying the five proposed feature extraction methods to each substring individually. We combine the resulting three substring feature vectors consecutively to one feature vector, which size is three times the size of each substring feature vector. The number of input neurons of the neural networks is equal to the resulting feature vector dimension.

We apply the five introduced feature extraction methods to whole word strings as well as to word substrings. We denote the resulting ten strategies for the generation of feature vectors as feature extraction strategies (See Table 1).

3. CASE STUDY

We test 960 neural network model configurations by combining the six variables number of hidden layers, number of neurons per hidden layer, type of activation function, number of identifiers per database for training, number of training cycles, and feature extraction strategy (see Table 2). Subsequently, we describe the design of the case study in detail.

3.1 Data

We extract identifiers by parsing the dumps of the KEGG database (release: 02/2011) and the UniProt database (release: 10/2011) (Kanehisa and Goto, 2000, Magrane and Consortium, 2011). From these identifiers, we select the $T = 51$ most abundant identifier types and prepare a identifier dataset with up to 1000 randomly chosen identifiers of each identifier type. The resulting data set comprises 51000 (identifier, identifier type) - pairs and is denoted as identifier data set.

We extract the vocabulary of the WordNet database and randomly choose 102.000 words (Miller, 1995). We denote this set of words as background data set.

3.2 Neural Network Design

We choose a typical design of neural networks, where all neurons of the i-th layer are connected to all neurons of the (i + 1)-th layer. We choose the number of input neurons equal to the dimension of the feature vector. We choose the number

Table 2. The six variables for the configuration of the neural network models. The variables number of hidden layers and number of neurons per hidden layer regard the neural network structure, the variable type of activation function regards the signal processing of the neural networks, the variables number of identifiers per database and number of training cycles regard the neural network training, and the variable feature extraction strategy regards the generation of the neural network input.

Variable	# of values	Set of variable values
# of hidden layers	2	{1; 2}
# of neurons per hidden layer	2	{10; 50}
Activation function	6	{gaussian, linear, log., sigmoid, sine, tanh}
# of training IDs per database	2	{100; 1000}
# of training cycles	2	{100; 500}
Feature extraction strategy	10	See Table 1

of neurons per hidden layer each equal. We choose the number of output neurons equal to the number of identifier types, so that the t-th output neuron stands for the t-th identifier type, where t $\in$ [1, T]. In this study we test various neural network structures and activation functions in order to obtain a widespread view on the applicability of different combinations of neural network properties. We choose the variable number of hidden layers as 1 or 2, the variable number of neurons per hidden layer as 10 or 1000, and the variable type of activation function as gaussian, linear, logarithmic, sigmoid, sine, or hyperbolic tangent. The combination of these three variables yields in 24 different neural network designs.

3.3 Training and Testing

We choose the well known backpropagation algorithm for the neural network training in order to adapt the neural networks to patterns within T identifier types. The backpropagation training is a supervised learning strategy, which follows an iterative approach trying to minimize the error of the neural networks output vectors for a given set of feature vectors (Werbos, 1974). We choose the variable number of training cycles as 100 or 500 in order to check for differences of the prediction quality for different training efforts.

For training and testing we select identifier sets of different sizes in order to examine the neural networks prediction quality as a function of the training set size. We choose the variable number of identifiers per database as 100 or 1000 and randomly select this many identifiers per identifier type from the identifier data set. We denote this set as positive identifiers. We randomly divide the identifiers of each identifier type from the positive identifiers set in 80% positive identifiers for training and 20% positive identifiers for testing. From the background data set we randomly select twice as many words as the size of the set positive identifiers. We denote this set as negative identifiers. We randomly divide this set in 80% negative identifiers for training and 20% negative identifiers for testing. We combine the set positive identifiers for training and the set negative identifiers for training to the training set and combine the set positive identifiers for testing and the set negative identifiers for testing to the testing set. For the training of the neural networks, we use the feature vectors from our ten feature extraction strategies applied to the identifiers from the training set. For the evaluation of the trained neural networks, we supply the identifiers of the testing set as input and compute for each identifier type the average and standard deviation of the p-value for each output neuron.

3.4 Result Evaluation

We apply a scoring function in order to rank 960 combinations of the six variables number of hidden layers, number of neurons per hidden layer, type of activation function, number of identifiers per database for training, number of training cycles, and feature extraction strategy.

We compute the evaluation score for a certain variable combination by

$$\sum_{t_1=1}^{T}\sum_{t_2=1}^{T}\begin{cases}(T-1)\,p\,(t_1,t_2) & t_1 = t_2 \\ -1p\,(t_1,t_2) & t_1 \neq t_2\end{cases}$$

where $p(t_1, t_2)$ gives the average p-value of output neuron t_2 for the identifiers of type t_1 from the testing set. By this scoring function, we intend to equally reward the average p-value of the t-th output neuron for input of the t-th identifier type and penalize the average p-value of the remaining output neurons.

According to equation (1), the variable combination with the highest score is number of hidden layers = 2, number of neurons per hidden layer = 50, type of activation function = sigmoid, number of identifiers per database = 100, number of training cycles = 500, and feature extraction strategy = Symbol specific applied to word substrings. For a detailed evaluation of this variable combination see Appendix A.3.

4. RESULTS AND DISCUSSION

4.1 Result Statistics

We compute statistics for all values of all variables (see Table 2) to get an overview. For each variable value, we compute the sum of scores of all variable combinations, where this variable value is present (see Table 3 and Table 4).

For the evaluation of different neural network structures, we vary the variables number of hidden layers and number of neurons per hidden layer. We find that the average score of neural networks comprising 1 hidden layer is higher compared to neural networks comprising 2 hidden layers, but the standard deviation is also slightly increased. This is surprising, for the recognition power of neural networks comprising 2 hidden layers should be at least as big as that of neural networks comprising 1 hidden layer. We find that the average score of neural networks comprising 50 neurons per hidden layer is significantly higher compared to neural

Table 3. Evaluation of five variables for the training and design of neural networks. In the first column, we list the five variables. In the second column, we list the applied values for each variable by quantity or lexicographically. In the third and fourth column, we present the average and standard deviation of the evaluation score of Equation (1) normalized to a sum of 1 within each variable category and rounded to two positions after the decimal point.

Feature	Feature value	Rel. Average	Rel. std dev.
# of hidden layers	1	0.62	0.55
	2	0.38	0.45
# of neurons per hidden layer	10	0.40	0.40
	50	0.60	0.60
Activation function	gaussian	0.01	0.01
	linear	0.01	0.01
	logarithmic	0.24	0.27
	sigmoid	0.45	0.37
	sine	0.01	0.02
	tanh	0.29	0.33
# of training IDs per database	100	0.50	0.54
	1000	0.50	0.46
# of training cycles	100	0.41	0.42
	500	0.59	0.58

networks comprising 10 neurons per hidden layers, but the standard deviation is increased as well. From the theory of neural networks, we expect a correlation of the recognition power with the number of neurons in the hidden layers.

The choice of the variable type of activation function is crucial for the routing of signals through the neural networks. We find that the average scores of neural networks with different activation functions partitions in three fields. Neural networks with the well established sigmoid activation function clearly outperform all neural networks with other activation functions. The second best activation functions are the hyperbolic tangent and the logarithm. The Gaussian function, the linear function, and the sine function are inferior. However, the quantities of the standard deviations are arranged in an equal order.

For the evaluation of the impact of different training procedures, we vary the variables number of identifiers per database for training and the number of training cycles. We find that the average score of neural networks trained with 100 and 1000 identifiers per database is highly comparable, but the standard deviation of neural networks trained with 1000 identifiers per database is slightly smaller. The higher

Table 4. Evaluation of the variable feature extraction strategy. In the first and second column, we list the ten feature extraction strategies introduced in section 2. In the third and fourth column, we present the average and standard deviation of the evaluation score of Equation (1) normalized to a sum of 1 and rounded to two positions after the decimal point.

Feature extraction method	Word substrings	Rel. Average	Rel. std dev.
Position specific	No	0.00	0.00
	Yes	0.00	0.00
Symbol specific	No	0.20	0.20
	Yes	0.25	0.24
Symbol specific (partially grouped)	No	0.19	0.19
	Yes	0.26	0.22
Symbol specific (grouped)	No	0.02	0.03
	Yes	0.06	0.09
Word statistics	No	0.01	0.01
	Yes	0.02	0.03

standard deviation of neural networks trained with 100 identifiers per database might be caused by the higher chance of sampling identifiers from the training set, which are not representative. We find, that the average score of neural networks trained for 500 training cycles is higher compared to neural networks trained for 100 training cycles and that the standard deviation of neural networks trained for 500 training cycles is lower compared to neural networks trained for 100 training cycles. Thus, more training cycles make the predictions of the neural networks more reliable.

The evaluation of the variable feature extraction strategy is summarized in Table 4. We find, that the feature extraction strategies Symbol specific and Symbol specific (partially grouped) both applied to whole word strings and applied to word substrings yield the best average scores and that all other feature extraction strategies are significantly inferior. In addition, the application of the feature extraction methods to word substrings increase the average scores in every case compared the same feature extraction methods applied to the whole word string.

4.2 Extraction of Cross-Reference from Biomedical Databases

As shown in section 3.3, we validated the prediction performance of IDPredictor using a set of database identifiers. In order to demonstrate the applicability of the method and to discuss possible drawbacks, we will subsequently show results of cross reference prediction in the UniProt database record CP20C_ARATH[5]. The

UniProt Knowledgebase (UniProtKB) acts as a central hub of protein knowledge by providing a unified view on protein sequences and functional information. We choose this entry because it shows a high spectrum of different types of referenced databases and therefore comprises a representative number of syntactic variations of ID tokens. In particular, we saw identifiers from more than 100 databases and because of the well structured format, it is relatively easy to manual validate the prediction quality. Nevertheless, our approach can be applied to any database record comprising plain text.

First of all, we used the best performing parameter configuration for the predictor network presented in section 3.4. This trained network was applied to the set of tokens, we extracted by decomposing the UniProt entry. Intuitively, we used for decomposition the standard whitespace definition. But programming language does not necessarily use homogeneous whitespace definition[6]. After draft inspection of the resulted token list, we saw obvious insufficiently decomposed tokens. Pattern for such problematic "super token" are key-value pairs like "MEDLINE=20083487", whereas some special characters act as "glue". Examples are ':' or '='. Those key-value pairs are very database specific and would result in too much database specific ID pattern.

In consequence, we redefined the whitespace delimiter for biomedical data records. To do so, we counted the occurrence of characters in true positive ID token in our training data. We found a high number of characters show up rarely (less than in 5%) in IDs. As shown in appendix A.2 there are 182 characters which do not show up in any ID, whereas 54 where selected in the range of frequently used 7-bit ASCII subset. Those are promising candidates for a redefinition of the so far used definition of whitespace. Using this new enhanced whitespace definition, the result was a set of 1,803 tokens.

As next step, we used the trained network to predict for each token the probability whether it is an ID and if so, to which type of database it is probably linked. In order to evaluate the prediction quality, we inspected each of the token whether it is a real ID (true positive) or a false prediction (false positive). As result of the inspection, we tagged 118 tokens as real IDs and 1,685 as non ID tokens. The complete evaluation result is included in appendix A.1. In order to test the performance of the ID token classification, we used different cut-offs for the p-value. We assume a minimal p-value of 0.5, which is a reasonable lower limit. This results in a maximum of 531 predicted identifier tokens. We end up with 184 for a cut off 1.0. The full prediction benchmark is summarized in Table 5.

We conclude that a cut-off of 0.9 for the p-value of a predicted ID token is a good tread-off between too much wrong predicted IDs and missed IDs for the use case of the construction of database networks. We see a precision of 82% with a recall of 65%. In this configuration we miss 41 out of 118 manually confirmed IDs

Table 5. Prediction performance of the IDPredictor classifier for UniProt entry CP20C ARATH. The columns cut-off, tokens, TP, TN, FP, FN, R and P are the p-value cut-off for the predicted ID tokens, the number of ID tokens has better p-value than the cut-off, the true positives, true negatives, false positives, false negatives, recall and precision.

cut-off	tokens	TP	TN	FP	FN	R	P
0.5	531	91	1154	440	27	0.72	0.72
0.6	520	88	1165	432	30	0.75	0.73
0.7	494	85	1191	409	33	0.72	0.74
0.8	425	81	1260	344	37	0.69	0.79
0.9	362	77	1323	282	41	0.65	0.82
1	184	67	1501	117	51	0.57	0.92

but predicted only 282 tokens erroneously as IDs. Practically, one would reduce those 282 false positives by query them in the predicted linked database. If the ID is not found, the token can be removed from the list of predicted IDs. In order to increase the stability of IDPredictor and to support a practical application a for cross reference extraction, we suggest subsequently further enhancements.

4.3 Enhancements for Cross-Reference Extraction

The prediction quality leads to the conclusion that the presented method is applicable in practice for an unsupervised cross reference extraction, if we consider the following enhancements:

1. **Suboptimal Tokenization:** Decompose text into tokens is the first step in presented id prediction pipeline. The result is a set of tokens. This task is error prone, especially for non-natural language text. It could lead to "super" tokens, combining a sequence of standalone words or may on the other hand fragment real tokens into sub-tokens. As consequence, the decomposition should use a smart definition of token delimiter as suggested in Section 4.2.

2. **Ambiguous Tokens:** Here we saw different semantics for similar token. The most prominent class of such tokens are numbers. Using the presented IDPredictor method it is hard to predict if a number is a numerical database ID or a measurement described in the text. For example, publication year or mol weight was matched as PubMed-ID. In general, those false positives were caused by ignoring the textual context, which could be implemented using text mining methods based on natural language processing or thesauri.

3. **Very Short Tokens:** The obvious problem of tokens with a short length is the less information content. Thus, the neural network cannot give a reliable ID prediction. Examples are abbreviations of author's first name, which result in a high number in 2 letter tokens. Thus we suggest excluding tokens with a length less than 4 from token list and defining them as stop words.

4. **Raw Data Tokens:** Raw data, like sequence fragments or geometry data of protein structure are commonly mixed with textual content. Those raw data tokens share a lot patterns with IDs, e.g. non natural language words, special characters or high frequency of digits. The challenging task of recognition if a token is a part of a raw data section or not would help to avoid a high number of false positives. One heuristic could be to check the frequency of predicted ID tokens in a sliding window. If we see in the window an accumulation of ID tokens compared to non-ID tokens, we could assume a block of raw data.

5. CONCLUSION AND OUTLOOK

We presented IDPredictor, a method that predicts and extracts cross-references from biomedical databases. We motivated this approach by discussing advantages and drawbacks of existing approaches, like database integration, ID mapping services, scripting or regular expressions.

The presented method of training a neural network as token classifier was presented and manually benchmarked using an example from the UniProt protein database. For this data set we predicted possible cross-references and mapped these to the most probable source databases. We found and discussed false negatives and false positive predictions and presented enhancements to improve the prediction quality. We suggested improvements for text tokenization as well as rules to avoid ambiguous and false positive tokens predicted in raw data sections.

This contribution is intended to give a proof-of-principle of identifier prediction in biomedical databases using neural networks as classifier. Beside the presented application of cross-reference extraction, it would be possible to support more comprehensive scenarios in information retrieval. More use cases, an increased data basis for cross-reference extraction, and applications to other domains such as social networks are on the road map.

Because of the generality of IDPredictor, it is also possible to use this algorithm for detecting cross-references in non-life sciences databases. Another option is to apply IDPredictor to database management systems, e.g. relational ones. Doing so, we could process the database schema by only tokenizing those attributes that contain cross-references. Further plans are to implement a user friendly and flexible tool and web service for link extraction over submitted datasets as well as the extraction of comprehensive data networks by tokenizing the content of datacenters like the NCBI, EBI and GenomeNet. In this context, one typical use case would be the functional annotation of sequence data, the improvement of search engines as well as the structural analysis of data networks. Finally, an interesting use case of IDPredictor is to periodically compute a network of interlinked data that could be used to connect knowledge and bridge the gap of heterogeneous databases.

The tool IDPredictor is implemented in JAVA. A command line version is freely available for download and published (DOI:10.5447/IPK/2012/4)[7].

ACKNOWLEDGMENT

We thank Thomas Münch for giving support for the execution of computation jobs at the IPK compute cluster Brocken. This work was supported by the European Commission within its 7th Framework Program, under the thematic area "Infrastructures", contract number 283496.

REFERENCES

Altschul, S. F., Madden, T. L., Schaffer, A. A., Zhang, J., Zhang, Z., & Miller, W. et al. (1997). Gapped BLAST and PSI-BLAST: A new generation of protein database search programs. *Nucleic Acids Research*, *25*(17), 3389–3402. doi:10.1093/nar/25.17.3389 PMID:9254694.

Bachmann, A., Schult, R., Lange, M., & Spiliopoulou, M. (2011). Extracting cross references from life science databases for search result ranking. In *Proceedings of the 20th ACM international conference on Information and Knowledge Management* (pp. 1253-1258). New York: ACM.

Bry, F., & Kröger, P. (2003). A computational biology database digest: Data, data analysis, and data management. *Distributed and Parallel Databases*, *13*(1), 7–42. doi:10.1023/A:1021540705916.

Cohen-Boulakia, S., Biton, O., Davidson, S., & Froidevaux, C. (2007). BioGuideSRS: Querying multiple sources with a user-centric perspective. *Bioinformatics (Oxford, England)*, *23*(10), 1301–1303. doi:10.1093/bioinformatics/btm088 PMID:17344233.

Divoli, A., Hearst, M., & Wooldridge, M. A. (2008). Evidence for showing gene/protein name suggestions in bioscience literature search interfaces. In *Pacific Symposium on Biocomputing, 13*, 568–579.

Doms, A., & Schroeder, M. (2005). GoPubMed: Exploring PubMed with the gene ontology. *Nucleic Acids Research, 33*, 783–786. doi:10.1093/nar/gki470 PMID:15980585.

Errami, M., Wren, J. D., Hicks, J. M., & Garner, H. R. (2007). eTBLAST: A web server to identify expert reviewers, appropriate journals and similar publications. *Nucleic Acids Research, 35*, W12–W15. doi:10.1093/nar/gkm221 PMID:17452348.

Etzold, T., Ulyanow, A., & Argos, P. (1996). SRS: Information retrieval system for molecular biology data banks. *Methods in Enzymology, 266*, 114–128. doi:10.1016/S0076-6879(96)66010-8 PMID:8743681.

Galla, T. (2006). Theory of neural information processing systems. *Journal of Physics. A, Mathematical and General, 39*(14), 3849. doi:10.1088/0305-4470/39/14/B01.

Galperin, M. Y., & Fernandez-Suarez, X. M. (2012). The 2012 nucleic acids research database issue and the online molecular biology database collection. *Nucleic Acids Research, 40*(D1), D1–D8. doi:10.1093/nar/gkr1196 PMID:22144685.

Giardine, B., Riemer, C., Hardison, R. C., Burhans, R., Elnitski, L., & Shah, P. et al. (2005). Galaxy: A platform for interactive large-scale genome analysis. *Genome Research, 15*(10), 1451–1455. doi:10.1101/gr.4086505 PMID:16169926.

Haas, L. M., Schwarz, P. M., Kodali, P., Kotlar, E., Rice, J. E., & Swope, W. C. (2001). DiscoveryLink: A system for integrated access to life sciences data sources. *IBM Systems Journal, 40*(2), 489–511. doi:10.1147/sj.402.0489.

Hanisch, D., Fundel, K., Mevissen, H. T., Zimmer, R., & Fluck, J. (2005). Prominer: Rule-based protein and gene entity recognition. *BMC Bioinformatics, 6*, S14. doi:10.1186/1471-2105-6-S1-S14 PMID:15960826.

Inmon, W. H. (1996). *Building the data warehouse* (2nd ed.). Hoboken, NJ: John Wiley & Sons.

Kanehisa, M., & Goto, S. (2000). KEGG: Kyoto encyclopedia of genes and genomes. *Nucleic Acids Research, 28*(1), 27–30. doi:10.1093/nar/28.1.27 PMID:10592173.

Karp, P. D. (1995). A strategy for database interoperation. *Journal of Computational Biology, 2*(4), 573–586. doi:10.1089/cmb.1995.2.573 PMID:8634909.

Lacroix, Z., & Critchlow, T. (2003). *Bioinformatics: Managing scientific data*. San Francisco, CA: Morgan Kaufmann Publishers.

Lacroix, Z., Parekh, K., Vidal, M.-E., Cardenas, M., Marquez, N., & Raschid, L. (2005). BioNavigation: Using ontologies to express meaningful navigational queries over biological resources. In *CSB Workshops* (pp. 137–138). New York: IEEE. doi:10.1109/CSBW.2005.32.

Lange, M., Himmelbach, A., Schweizer, P., & Scholz, U. (2007). Data linkage graph: Computation, querying and knowledge discovery of life science database networks. *Journal of Integrative Bioinformatics*, *4*(3), e68.

Lange, M., Spies, K., Bargsten, J., Haberhauer, G., Klapperstück, M., & Leps, M. et al. (2010). The LAILAPS search engine: Relevance ranking in life science databases. *Journal of Integrative Bioinformatics*, *7*(2), e110.

Lu, Z. (2011). PubMed and beyond: A survey of web tools for searching biomedical literature. *Database*. doi:10.1093/database/baq036 PMID:21245076.

Magrane, M., & Consortium, U. (2011). UniProt knowledgebase: A hub of integrated protein data. *Database*. doi:10.1093/database/bar009 PMID:21447597.

Miller, G. A. (1995). WordNet: A lexical database for English. *Communications of the ACM*, *38*(11), 39–41. doi:10.1145/219717.219748.

Mudunuri, U., Che, A., Yi, M., & Stephens, R. M. (2009). Biodbnet: The biological database network. *Bioinformatics (Oxford, England)*, *25*(4), 555–556. doi:10.1093/bioinformatics/btn654 PMID:19129209.

Oinn, T., Addis, M., Ferris, J., Marvin, D., Senger, M., & Greenwood, M. et al. (2004). Taverna: A tool for the composition and enactment of bioinformatics workflows. *Bioinformatics (Oxford, England)*, *20*(17), 3045–3054. doi:10.1093/bioinformatics/bth361 PMID:15201187.

Oja, E. (1982). A simplified neuron model as a principal component analyzer. *Journal of Mathematical Biology*, *15*(3), 267–273. doi:10.1007/BF00275687 PMID:7153672.

Roos, D. S. (2001). Computational biology: Bioinformatics–Trying to swim in a sea of data. *Science*, *291*(5507), 1260–1261. doi:10.1126/science.291.5507.1260 PMID:11233452.

Schuler, G. D., Epstein, J., Ohkawa, H., & Kans, J. (1996). Entrez: Molecular biology database and retrieval system. *Methods in Enzymology*, *266*, 141–161. doi:10.1016/S0076-6879(96)66012-1 PMID:8743683.

Sheth, A. P., & Larson, J. A. (1990). Federated database systems for managing distributed, heterogeneous, and autonomous databases. *ACM Computing Surveys*, *22*(3), 183–236. doi:10.1145/96602.96604.

Siepel, A., Farmer, A., Tolopko, A., Zhuang, M., & Mendes, P., Beavis, … Sobral, B. (2001). ISYS: A decentralized, component-based approach to the integration of heterogeneous bioinformatics resources. *Bioinformatics (Oxford, England)*, *17*(1), 83–94. doi:10.1093/bioinformatics/17.1.83 PMID:11222265.

Stein, L. D. (2002). Creating a bioinformatics nation. *Nature*, *417*(6885), 119–120. doi:10.1038/417119a PMID:12000935.

Stevens, R., Baker, P., Bechhofer, S., Ng, G., Jacoby, A., & Paton, N. W. et al. (2000). TAMBIS: Transparent access to multible bioinformatics information sources. *Bioinformatics (Oxford, England)*, *16*(4), 184–185. doi:10.1093/bioinformatics/16.2.184 PMID:10842744.

Stevens, R., Goble, C., Baker, P., & Brass, A. (2001). A classification of tasks in bioinformatics. *Bioinformatics (Oxford, England)*, *17*(2), 180–188. doi:10.1093/bioinformatics/17.2.180 PMID:11238075.

Tatusova, T. A., Karsch-Mizrachi, I., & Ostell, J. A. (1999). Complete genomes in WWW Entrez: Data representation and analysis. *Bioinformatics, 15*(7/8), 536–543.

Werbos, P. (1974). *Beyond regression: New tools for prediction and analysis in the behavioral sciences.* (PhD thesis). Harvard University, Cambridge, MA.

Wiederhold, G. (1992). Mediators in the architecture of future information systems. *IEEE Computer*, *25*(3), 38–49. doi:10.1109/2.121508.

ENDNOTES

1 http://www.ncbi.nlm.nih.gov/Sitemap/Summary/statistics.html
2 http://www.uniprot.org/uniprot/Q8W413
3 http://www.expasy.org/enzyme/3.2.1.26
4 http://www.arabidopsis.org/servlets/TairObject?type=locus&name=AT 2G36190
5 http://www.uniprot.org/uniprot/P34791.txt
6 http://en.wikipedia.org/wiki/Whitespace_character
7 For a direct download please use the URL: http://dx.doi.org/10.5447/IPK/2012/4

APPENDIX 1

Prediction Performance for UniProt Entry Cp20c ARATH

Table 6. Evaluation of the IDPredictor ID classifier in the UniProt entry CP20C ARATH. The columns are: extracted token, predicted database cross-reference, p-value, manual evaluation (1: true posive; 0: false positive). Overall we decomposed the entry into 1,803 tokens. The table comprise only those 531 tokens which had a minimal p-value of 0.5.

token	database	p-value	true positive
CP20C_ARATI	TREMBL	1,00	1
260	GENE_FARM	1,00	0
P34791	IN_PARANOI[	1,00	1
Q8L829	STRING	1,00	1
34366	EPO	0,90	0
UniProtKB/Sw	GENE_NAME	0,98	0
34366	EPO	0,90	0
40933	PIR	1,00	0
103.	UNI_GENE	0,92	0
CYP20-3	SMR	0,69	0
CYP20-3	SMR	0,69	0
EC	KO_NAME	1,00	0
5.2.1.8	BRENDA	0,73	1
20	GENE_FARM	0,91	0
20	PDB	0,93	0
CYP20-3	SMR	0,69	0
GN	KO_NAME	1,00	0
CYP20-3	SMR	0,69	0
ROC4	KO_NAME	1,00	0
At3g62030	TAIR	1,00	1
GN	KO_NAME	1,00	0
ORFNames	OMA	1,00	0
F21F14.200	PIR	0,63	0
OS	KO_NAME	0,98	0
NCBI_TaxID	UNIPROT	1,00	0
NCBI_TaxID	STRING	0,64	0
3702	GENE_FARM	1,00	0
RP	KO_NAME	0,98	0
NUCLEOTIDE	UNIPROT	0,77	0
SEQUENCE	UNIPROT	1,00	0
SEQUENCE	PRIDE	1,00	0
MRNA	KO_NAME	1,00	0
SUBCELLULAR	SEGUID	0,97	0
TISSUE	UNIPROT	1,00	0
RP	KO_NAME	0,98	0
STRAIN	PHYLOME_DE	0,91	0
TISSUE	UNIPROT	1,00	0
MEDLINE	UNIPROT	1,00	0
94179146	NCBI_GENE_	0,99	0
8132503	NCBI_GENE_	0,99	0
RL	KO_NAME	0,73	0
Biol.	KO_NAME	0,99	0
Chem.	KO_NAME	1,00	0
269:7863-78(	DOI	0,98	1
2	PDB	0,63	0
RP	KO_NAME	0,98	0
NUCLEOTIDE	UNIPROT	0,77	0
SEQUENCE	UNIPROT	1,00	0
SEQUENCE	PRIDE	1,00	0
STRAIN	PHYLOME_DE	0,91	0
MEDLINE	UNIPROT	1,00	0
98088013	NCBI_GENE_	0,99	0
9426607	NCBI_GENE_	1,00	0
DOI	KO_NAME	0,98	0
10.1023/A:10	DOI	1,00	1
RL	KO_NAME	0,73	0
Biol.	KO_NAME	0,99	0
35:873-892(1	DOI	0,97	1
RP	KO_NAME	0,98	0
NUCLEOTIDE	UNIPROT	0,77	0
SEQUENCE	UNIPROT	1,00	0
SEQUENCE	PRIDE	1,00	0
LARGE	STRING	0,87	0
SCALE	KO_NAME	1,00	0
STRAIN	PHYLOME_DE	0,91	0
MEDLINE	UNIPROT	1,00	0
21016720	NCBI_GENE_	1,00	0
11130713	NCBI_GENE_	0,97	0
11130713	PUB_MED	0,50	1
DOI	KO_NAME	0,98	0
10.1038/3504	DOI	0,99	1
K.	KO_NAME	0,88	0
B.	KO_NAME	1,00	0
G.	KO_NAME	0,99	0
B.	KO_NAME	1,00	0
L.A.	EC_NUMBER	0,74	0
P.	KO_NAME	0,91	0
C.	KO_NAME	1,00	0
P.	KO_NAME	0,91	0
P.	KO_NAME	0,91	0
L.	KO_NAME	0,96	0
S.	KO_NAME	0,88	0
C.	KO_NAME	1,00	0
S.	KO_NAME	0,88	0
P.	KO_NAME	0,91	0
G.	KO_NAME	0,99	0
S.	KO_NAME	0,88	0
B.	KO_NAME	1,00	0
K.	KO_NAME	0,88	0
G.	KO_NAME	0,99	0
T.-H.	BRENDA	0,90	0
G.	KO_NAME	0,99	0
O.	BRENDA	1,00	0
P.	KO_NAME	0,91	0
C.	KO_NAME	1,00	0
B.	KO_NAME	1,00	0
C.	KO_NAME	1,00	0
B.	KO_NAME	1,00	0
A.C.	EC_NUMBER	0,59	0
G.	KO_NAME	0,99	0
S.	KO_NAME	0,88	0
P.	KO_NAME	0,91	0
S.	KO_NAME	0,88	0
C.D.	KO_NAME	0,98	0
H.L.	KO_NAME	0,90	0
L.J.	EC_NUMBER	0,98	0

token	database	p-value	true positive
B.	KO_NAME	1,00	0
S.	KO_NAME	0,88	0
G.	KO_NAME	0,99	0
P.	KO_NAME	0,91	0
J.E.	EC_NUMBER	0,97	0
T.V.	EC_NUMBER	0,98	0
W.C.	KO_NAME	0,82	0
O.	BRENDA	1,00	0
J.C.	EC_NUMBER	0,93	0
Y.	KO_NAME	0,98	0
S.	KO_NAME	0,88	0
S.	KO_NAME	0,88	0
K.	KO_NAME	0,88	0
K.	KO_NAME	0,88	0
Y.	KO_NAME	0,98	0
C.	KO_NAME	1,00	0
S.	KO_NAME	0,88	0
S.	KO_NAME	0,88	0
C.	KO_NAME	1,00	0
S.	KO_NAME	0,88	0
RL	KO_NAME	0,73	0
408:820-822(	DOI	0,78	1
RP	KO_NAME	0,98	0
REANNOTATI	TREMBL	1,00	0
STRAIN	PHYLOME_DE	0,91	0
RL	KO_NAME	0,73	0
EMBL/GenBa	SEGUID	0,77	0
S	GENE_FARM	0,91	0
RP	KO_NAME	0,98	0
NUCLEOTIDE	UNIPROT	0,77	0
SEQUENCE	UNIPROT	1,00	0
SEQUENCE	PRIDE	1,00	0
LARGE	STRING	0,87	0
SCALE	KO_NAME	1,00	0
MRNA	KO_NAME	1,00	0
STRAIN	PHYLOME_DE	0,91	0
MEDLINE	UNIPROT	1,00	0
22954850	NCBI_GENE_	0,92	0
14593172	NCBI_GENE_	0,99	0
DOI	KO_NAME	0,98	0
10.1126/scie	DOI	1,00	1
K.	KO_NAME	0,88	0
P.	KO_NAME	0,91	0
C.J.	EC_NUMBER	0,93	0
A.M.	EC_NUMBER	0,97	0
A.M.	IN_PARANOI	0,90	0
H.C.	KO_NAME	0,50	0
C.J.	EC_NUMBER	0,93	0
P.K.	KO_NAME	0,94	0
G.	KO_NAME	0,99	0
B.	KO_NAME	1,00	0
G.	KO_NAME	0,99	0
H.L.	KO_NAME	0,90	0
C.H.	KO_NAME	0,50	0
C.C.	KO_NAME	0,99	0
K.	KO_NAME	0,88	0
Y.	KO_NAME	0,98	0
L.	KO_NAME	0,96	0
P.	KO_NAME	0,91	0
Q.	IN_PARANOI	1,00	0
Y.	KO_NAME	0,98	0
C.	KO_NAME	1,00	0
K.	KO_NAME	0,88	0
S.	KO_NAME	0,88	0
P.X.	KO_NAME	1,00	0
C.	KO_NAME	1,00	0
E.K.	EC_NUMBER	1,00	0
C.	KO_NAME	1,00	0
Y.	KO_NAME	0,98	0
S.	KO_NAME	0,88	0
K.	KO_NAME	0,88	0
J.R.	HOGENOM	0,71	0
J.R.	EC_NUMBER	0,99	0
RL	KO_NAME	0,73	0
302:842-846(	DOI	1,00	1
RP	KO_NAME	0,98	0
NUCLEOTIDE	UNIPROT	0,77	0
SEQUENCE	UNIPROT	1,00	0
SEQUENCE	PRIDE	1,00	0
LARGE	STRING	0,87	0
SCALE	KO_NAME	1,00	0
MRNA	KO_NAME	1,00	0
M.E.	IN_PARANOI	0,93	0
N.A.	EC_NUMBER	0,98	0
R.B.	EC_NUMBER	0,91	0
K.A.	EC_NUMBER	0,98	0
RL	KO_NAME	0,73	0
EMBL/GenBa	SEGUID	0,77	0
7	PDB	0,60	0
RP	KO_NAME	0,98	0
SEQUENCE	UNIPROT	1,00	0
SEQUENCE	PRIDE	1,00	0
OF	KO_NAME	0,68	0
117-125	NCBI_GENE_	1,00	0
131-137	NCBI_GENE_	0,52	0
183-192	NCBI_GENE_	0,94	0
242-257	NCBI_GENE_	0,99	0
RP	KO_NAME	0,98	0
MUTAGENESI	SEGUID	0,93	0
OF	KO_NAME	0,68	0
CYS-206	OMA	0,62	0
RP	KO_NAME	0,98	0
CYS-253.	KO_NAME	1,00	0
MEDLINE	UNIPROT	1,00	0
22803407	NCBI_GENE_	0,94	0
12923164	NCBI_GENE_	1,00	0

token	database	p-value	true positive
DOI	KO_NAME	0,98	0
10.1074/jbc.M	DOI	1,00	1
K.	KO_NAME	0,88	0
Y.	KO_NAME	0,98	0
RL	KO_NAME	0,73	0
Biol.	KO_NAME	0,99	0
Chem.	KO_NAME	1,00	0
278:31848-31	DOI	1,00	1
8	PDB	1,00	0
RP	KO_NAME	0,98	0
SUBCELLULAR	SEGUID	0,97	0
BY	HOGENOM	1,00	0
SPECTROMET	OMA	0,90	0
MEDLINE	UNIPROT	1,00	0
21864138	NCBI_GENE_	1,00	0
21864138	PUB_MED	0,54	1
11719511	NCBI_GENE_	1,00	0
DOI	KO_NAME	0,98	0
10.1074/jbc.M	DOI	1,00	1
U.A.	EC_NUMBER	0,79	0
B.J.	EC_NUMBER	0,64	0
C.	KO_NAME	1,00	0
W.P.	KO_NAME	0,92	0
RL	KO_NAME	0,73	0
Biol.	KO_NAME	0,99	0
Chem.	KO_NAME	1,00	0
277:8354-836	DOI	1,00	1
RP	KO_NAME	0,98	0
SUBCELLULAR	SEGUID	0,97	0
BY	HOGENOM	1,00	0
SPECTROMET	OMA	0,90	0
MEDLINE	UNIPROT	1,00	0
22819494	PUB_MED	0,88	1
12938931	PUB_MED	1,00	1
DOI	KO_NAME	0,98	0
10.1021/pr03	DOI	1,00	1
J.E.	EC_NUMBER	0,97	0
R.S.	EC_NUMBER	0,69	0
RL	KO_NAME	0,73	0
2:413-425(20	DOI	1,00	1
10	PDB	1,00	0
RP	KO_NAME	0,98	0
SUBCELLULAR	SEGUID	0,97	0
BY	HOGENOM	1,00	0
SPECTROMET	OMA	0,90	0
15322131	NCBI_GENE_	0,99	0
15322131	PUB_MED	0,70	1
DOI	KO_NAME	0,98	0
10.1074/jbc.M	DOI	1,00	1
A.J.	EC_NUMBER	0,75	0
Q.	IN_PARANOI	1,00	0
RL	KO_NAME	0,73	0
Biol.	KO_NAME	0,99	0
Chem.	KO_NAME	1,00	0
279:49367-49	DOI	0,97	1
RP	KO_NAME	0,98	0
TISSUE	UNIPROT	1,00	0
15047905	NCBI_GENE_	0,98	0
DOI	KO_NAME	0,98	0
10.1104/pp.1	DOI	1,00	1
L.	KO_NAME	0,96	0
S.	KO_NAME	0,88	0
RL	KO_NAME	0,73	0
134:1248-12(	DOI	1,00	1
RP	KO_NAME	0,98	0
GENE	UNIPROT	0,98	0
FAMILY	UNIPROT	1,00	0
FAMILY	KO_NAME	0,97	0
FAMILY	STRING	0,99	0
NOMENCLAT	TREMBL	0,78	0
15051864	NCBI_GENE_	1,00	0
DOI	KO_NAME	0,98	0
10.1104/pp.1	DOI	1,00	1
P.	KO_NAME	0,91	0
J.E.	EC_NUMBER	0,97	0
RL	KO_NAME	0,73	0
134:1268-128	DOI	1,00	1
CC	KO_NAME	0,77	0
FUNCTION:	SEGUID	0,83	0
CC	KO_NAME	0,77	0
CC	KO_NAME	0,77	0
CC	KO_NAME	0,77	0
CATALYTIC	OMA	0,84	0
ACTIVITY:	GENE_NAME	0,90	0
180)	GENE_FARM	1,00	0
180)	PDB	1,00	0
CC	KO_NAME	0,77	0
CC	KO_NAME	0,77	0
REGULATION	GENE_NAME	0,69	0
(CsA).	KO_NAME	1,00	0
CC	KO_NAME	0,77	0
PPIase.	KO_NAME	0,91	0
CC	KO_NAME	0,77	0
CC	KO_NAME	0,77	0
(TRX-M).	KO_NAME	1,00	0
CC	KO_NAME	0,77	0
CC	KO_NAME	0,77	0
IntAct	STRING	0,98	0
EBI-449385	ENA	0,64	1
CC	KO_NAME	0,77	0
SUBCELLULAR	SEGUID	0,97	0
LOCATION:	TREMBL	0,91	0
CC	KO_NAME	0,77	0
CC	KO_NAME	0,77	0
ALTERNATIVE	TREMBL	1,00	0
PRODUCTS:	GENE_NAME	1,00	0

token	database	p-value	true positive
CC	KO_NAME	0,77	0
CC	KO_NAME	0,77	0
EST	KO_NAME	1,00	0
CC	KO_NAME	0,77	0
CC	KO_NAME	0,77	0
CC	KO_NAME	0,77	0
CC	KO_NAME	0,77	0
TISSUE	UNIPROT	1,00	0
SPECIFICITY:	GENE_NAME	0,91	0
CC	KO_NAME	0,77	0
CC	KO_NAME	0,77	0
INDUCTION:	GENE_NAME	1,00	0
CC	KO_NAME	0,77	0
CC	KO_NAME	0,77	0
CC	KO_NAME	0,77	0
CC	KO_NAME	0,77	0
CC	KO_NAME	0,77	0
CC	KO_NAME	0,77	0
EMBL	STRING	0,98	0
AAA20048.1	EMBL	1,00	1
mRNA.	KO_NAME	0,96	0
EMBL	STRING	0,98	0
AAB96831.1	EMBL	0,80	1
EMBL	STRING	0,98	0
AL138642	ENA	0,96	1
CAB71910.1	EMBL	0,58	1
EMBL	STRING	0,98	0
AEE80297.1	EMBL	1,00	1
EMBL	STRING	0,98	0
mRNA.	KO_NAME	0,96	0
EMBL	STRING	0,98	0
AY059843	ENA	0,96	1
AAL24731.1	EMBL	1,00	1
mRNA.	KO_NAME	0,96	0
EMBL	STRING	0,98	0
AY093284	ENA	1,00	1
AAM13283.1	UNI_GENE	0,99	0
mRNA.	KO_NAME	0,96	0
EMBL	STRING	0,98	0
AY086899	ENA	1,00	1
AAM63944.1	EMBL	1,00	1
mRNA.	KO_NAME	0,96	0
IPI00517879	IPI	0,98	1
PIR	KO_NAME	0,75	0
B53422	STRING	0,62	1
B53422.	UNI_GENE	1,00	0
NP_191762.1	REF_SEQ	1,00	1
At.24742	UNI_GENE	1,00	1
At.48797	UNI_GENE	1,00	1
P34791	IN_PARANOI	1,00	1
SMR	KO_NAME	0,96	0
P34791	IN_PARANOI	1,00	1
97-256.	UNI_GENE	1,00	0
97-256.	NCBI_GENE_	0,72	0
DIP-32746N	ENA	0,66	0
IntAct	STRING	0,98	0
P34791	IN_PARANOI	1,00	1
P34791	IN_PARANOI	1,00	1
SWISS-2DPAG	GENE_NAME	0,83	0
P34791	IN_PARANOI	1,00	1
P34791	IN_PARANOI	1,00	1
P34791	IN_PARANOI	1,00	1
AT3G62030.1	EG_PLANTS	1,00	0
AT3G62030.1	EG_PLANTS	1,00	0
AT3G62030.	EG_PLANTS	1,00	0
825376	NCBI_GENE_	1,00	1
BA000014_GI	GENOME_RE	0,68	1
AT3G62030.	EG_PLANTS	1,00	1
KEGG	STRING	0,88	0
ath:AT3G620	GENE_NAME	1,00	1
ath:AT3G620	ENSEMBL	0,55	0
NMPDR	KO_NAME	0,99	0
fig|3702.1.pe	NCBI_GENE_	0,94	0
fig|3702.1.pe	NMPDR	1,00	1
2619	GENE_FARM	1,00	1
240.	UNI_GENE	0,93	0
At3g62030	TAIR	1,00	1
eggNOG	KO_NAME	0,77	0
HBG610621	HOGENOM	1,00	1
P34791	IN_PARANOI	1,00	1
P34791	IN_PARANOI	1,00	1
5.2.1.8	BRENDA	0,73	1
399.	UNI_GENE	0,83	0
P34791	IN_PARANOI	1,00	1
P34791	IN_PARANOI	1,00	1
AT3G62030	EG_PLANTS	0,98	1
GO	KO_NAME	0,85	0
GO:0048046	GO	1,00	1
IDA:TAIR.	SMR	0,92	0
GO	KO_NAME	0,85	0
GO:0009941	GO	1,00	1
IDA:TAIR.	SMR	0,92	0
GO	KO_NAME	0,85	0
GO:0009570	GO	1,00	1
IDA:TAIR.	SMR	0,92	0
GO	KO_NAME	0,85	0
GO:0009535	GO	1,00	1
IDA:TAIR.	SMR	0,92	0
GO	KO_NAME	0,85	0
GO:0022626	GO	1,00	1
IDA:TAIR.	SMR	0,92	0
GO	KO_NAME	0,85	0
GO:0031977	GO	1,00	1
IDA:TAIR.	SMR	0,92	0
GO	KO_NAME	0,85	0
GO:0042277	GO	1,00	1

token	database	p-value	true positive
IEA:UniProtK	GENE_NAME	1,00	0
GO	KO_NAME	0,85	0
GO:0003755	GO	1,00	1
IDA:TAIR.	SMR	0,92	0
GO	KO_NAME	0,85	0
GO:0005515	GO	1,00	1
GO	KO_NAME	0,85	0
GO:0019344	GO	1,00	1
GO	KO_NAME	0,85	0
GO:0042742	GO	1,00	1
GO	KO_NAME	0,85	0
GO:0006457	GO	1,00	1
IEA:UniProtK	GENE_NAME	1,00	0
GO	KO_NAME	0,85	0
GO:0009737	GO	1,00	1
GO	KO_NAME	0,85	0
GO:0009642	GO	1,00	1
GO	KO_NAME	0,85	0
GO:0010555	GO	1,00	1
GO	KO_NAME	0,85	0
GO:0006979	GO	1,00	1
GO	KO_NAME	0,85	0
GO:0009651	GO	1,00	1
IPR002130	INTER_PRO	1,00	1
IPR020892	INTER_PRO	0,97	1
G3DSA:2.40.1	EG_PLANTS	1,00	0
KO	KO_NAME	0,74	0
K03768	KO_ID	0,86	1
K03768	SMR	0,94	0
PF00160	PFAM	1,00	1
PRINTS	KO_NAME	0,82	0
PR00153	PRINTS	0,87	1
SSF50891	SUPFAM	0,99	1
PROSITE	STRING	0,84	0
PS00170	PROSITE	1,00	1
CSA_PPIASE_	STRING	0,99	0
PROSITE	STRING	0,84	0
PS50072	PROSITE	1,00	1
CSA_PPIASE_	STRING	1,00	0
peptide.	ARRAY_EXPRI	0,78	0
TRANSIT	TREMBL	0,73	0
78	GENE_FARM	0,95	0
79	GENE_FARM	0,95	0
260	GENE_FARM	1,00	0
CYP20-3	SMR	0,69	0
PRO_000002	ENSEMBL	0,63	0
DOMAIN	STRING	0,99	0
98	GENE_FARM	0,99	0
255	GENE_FARM	1,00	0
248	GENE_FARM	1,00	0
206	GENE_FARM	1,00	0
253	GENE_FARM	1,00	0
MUTAGEN	KO_NAME	0,60	0
C->S:	KO_NAME	0,78	0
S-248.	BRENDA	1,00	0
MUTAGEN	KO_NAME	0,60	0
206	GENE_FARM	1,00	0
206	GENE_FARM	1,00	0
C->S.	KO_NAME	0,78	0
S-253.	UNI_GENE	1,00	0
MUTAGEN	KO_NAME	0,60	0
248	GENE_FARM	1,00	0
248	GENE_FARM	1,00	0
C->E:	KO_NAME	0,78	0
S-131.	EC_NUMBER	0,94	0
MUTAGEN	KO_NAME	0,60	0
253	GENE_FARM	1,00	0
253	GENE_FARM	1,00	0
C->S:	KO_NAME	0,78	0
CONFLICT	UNIPROT	0,93	0
87	GENE_FARM	0,95	0
87	GENE_FARM	0,95	0
AAM63944).	UNI_GENE	0,82	0
CONFLICT	UNIPROT	0,93	0
202	GENE_FARM	0,99	0
202	GENE_FARM	0,99	0
5	GENE_FARM	0,91	0
SEQUENCE	UNIPROT	1,00	0
SEQUENCE	PRIDE	1,00	0
260	GENE_FARM	1,00	0
AA	PDB	1,00	0
28208	NCBI_TAXON	0,87	0
D412AECB88	GENE_NAME	0,99	0
D412AECB88	ENA	0,72	0
NRTTQSVCFG	SEGUID	0,51	0
RLHYASPIKQ	OMA	0,54	0
QRTACVKSM	TREMBL	0,94	0
AEEEEVIEPQ	UNIPROT	0,97	0
AEEEEVIEPQ	STRING	0,99	0
AKVTNKVYFD	STRING	0,99	0
VEIGGEVAGR	STRING	0,83	0
PKTVENFRAL	GENE_NAME	0,74	0
GSSFHRIIKD	OMA	0,98	0
GNGTGGISIY	GENE_NAME	0,81	0
GAKFEDENFT	STRING	0,97	0
LKHTGPGILS	SEGUID	1,00	0
MANAGPNTN	STRING	0,81	0
SQFFICTVKT	SEGUID	0,67	0
SWLDNKHVV	UNIPROT	0,69	0
SWLDNKHVV	KO_NAME	0,76	0
SWLDNKHVV	STRING	1,00	0
GQVIEGMKLV	STRING	0,97	0
RTLESQETRA	TREMBL	0,99	0
FDVPKKGCRI	GENE_NAME	0,82	0
YACGELPLDA	TREMBL	0,86	0

APPENDIX 2

Distribution of ASCII Characters In Database IDs

Table 7. Distribution of character frequency in sample of 51,000 IDs from 51 biomedical databases: The three columns show the ASCII code of the character, the printable form and the frequency of occurence. We hide the ASCII codes 128 - 255, because they never showed up in the sample IDs. Overall we see 182 characters do not show up in any ID (54 in the range of frequently used 7-bit ASCII subset).

ASCII code	Character	occurence in training IDs	ASCII code	Character	frequency in training IDs	ASCII code	Character	frequency in training IDs	ASCII code	Character	frequency in training IDs
0		0	32	' '	1	64	'@'	0	96	'`'	0
1		0	33	'!'	0	65	'A'	10642	97	'a'	1151
2		0	34	'"'	101808	66	'B'	6201	98	'b'	724
3		0	35	'#'	0	67	'C'	6217	99	'c'	801
4		0	36	'$'	0	68	'D'	3377	100	'd'	384
5		0	37	'%'	0	69	'E'	5961	101	'e'	1947
6		0	38	'&'	0	70	'F'	5346	102	'f'	1483
7		0	39	'''	0	71	'G'	7755	103	'g'	3531
8		0	40	'('	201	72	'H'	3394	104	'h'	385
9		0	41	')'	201	73	'I'	5590	105	'i'	1710
10		0	42	'*'	0	74	'J'	2087	106	'j'	621
11		0	43	'+'	435	75	'K'	3265	107	'k'	254
12		0	44	','	0	76	'L'	2759	108	'l'	561
13		0	45	'-'	1723	77	'M'	3160	109	'm'	846
14		0	46	'.'	18680	78	'N'	4251	110	'n'	691
15		0	47	'/'	1447	79	'O'	4998	111	'o'	528
16		0	48	'0'	51962	80	'P'	10741	112	'p'	1844
17		0	49	'1'	40531	81	'Q'	7965	113	'q'	188
18		0	50	'2'	26774	82	'R'	6352	114	'r'	991
19		0	51	'3'	24588	83	'S'	7686	115	's'	744
20		0	52	'4'	22828	84	'T'	4490	116	't'	1626
21		0	53	'5'	21343	85	'U'	2501	117	'u'	408
22		0	54	'6'	20201	86	'V'	2211	118	'v'	407
23		0	55	'7'	20034	87	'W'	2527	119	'w'	173
24		0	56	'8'	20666	88	'X'	2489	120	'x'	260
25		0	57	'9'	21989	89	'Y'	3007	121	'y'	242
26		0	58	':'	2363	90	'Z'	2003	122	'z'	157
27		0	59	';'	8	91	'['	0	123	'{'	0
28		0	60	'<'	18	92	'\'	0	124	'|'	1000
29		0	61	'='	0	93	']'	0	125	'}'	0
30		0	62	'>'	18	94	'^'	0	126	'~'	0
31		0	63	'?'	0	95	'_'	3231	127	''	0

APPENDIX 3

Prediction Performance for the Variable Combination with the Best Score

The detailed evaluation of the variable combination number of hidden layers = 2, number of neurons per hidden layer = 50, type of activation function = sigmoid, number of identifiers per database = 100, number of training cycles = 500, and feature extraction strategy = Symbol specific applied to word substrings can be found via the Digital Object Identifier (DOI) 10.5447/IPK/2012/0.

Chapter 5
Role of Vocabularies for Semantic Interoperability in Enabling the Linked Open Data Publishing

Ahsan Morshed
United Nations, Italy

EXECUTIVE SUMMARY

In the spite of explosive growth of the Internet, information relevant to users is often unavailable even when using the latest browsers. At the same time, there is an ever-increasing number of documents that vary widely in content, format, and quality. The documents often change in content and location because they do not belong to any kind of centralized control. On the other hand, there is a huge number of unknown users with extremely diverse needs, skills, education, and cultural and language backgrounds. One of the solutions to these problems might be to use standard terms with meaning; this can be termed as controlled vocabulary (CV). Though there is no specific notion of CV, we can define it as a set of concepts or preferred terms and existing relations among them. These vocabularies play very important roles classifying the information. In this chapter, we focus the role of CV for publishing the web of data on the Web.

DOI: 10.4018/978-1-4666-2827-4.ch005

INTRODUCTION

In the spite of explosive growth of the Internet, information relevant to users is often unavailable even when using the latest browsers. At the same time, there is an ever increasing number of documents that vary widely in content, format and quality. The documents often change in content and location because they do not belong to any kind of centralized control. On the other hand, there is a huge number of unknown users with extremely diverse needs, skills, education, and cultural and language backgrounds. One of the solutions to these problems might be to use standard terms with meaning, this can be termed as controlled vocabulary (CV) (Morshed, 2009; Morshed, 2010). Though there is no specific notion of CV, we can define it as a set of concepts or preferred terms and existing relations among them. For example, thesauri, WordNet (Miller, 1998), MeSH (MeSH, 2012), LCSH (LCSH, 2012), all kinds of ontologies, are sorts of CVs. These CVs are used to matching purpose that makes more exible for information extraction. In a semantic or controlled vocabulary (Giunchiglia, 2004), a matching operator takes two-graph like structures, for instance ontologies or classifications and produces matching relationship among them. This semantic matching system is based on two key notions. One of them is the concept of nodes and other is the concept of labels. In semantic matching, labels are written in natural language. These labels are disambiguated using a lexicon (Gale,1992). In this case, they are working as a background knowledge. In this chapter, we will see the contribution of CV for publishing the web of data purposes and review the main applications of controlled vocabularies.

CLASSIFICATION OF CONTROLLED VOCABULARY

In our case, we can classify our controlled vocabularies based on nature, construction perspective and usage. These constructions are based on regions, countries, products, services, vertical markets, clients, customer alliances, structure subsidiaries histories and cultures etc. For instance, two words "Center" and "Centre" both are having same meaning but different spelling in different regions and cultures.

We can classify controlled vocabularies in the following ways.

General Controlled Vocabulary

This class of controlled vocabulary is mainly included in usage and existing relationships among the concepts and entities. For example, the most prominent representation of these vocabularies are Thesaurus, WordNet, Classification, Directories, Lightweight Ontologies (Zhu,2006), etc. (Figure 1).

Figure 1. CVs

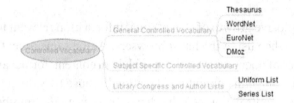

Thesaurus

A thesaurus (Gilchrist, 2006; Ibekwe-SanJuan, 2006) can be defined as "a controlled vocabulary that includes synonyms, hierarchies and associative relationships among terms to help users to find the information they need." For example, two users are looking for information "Automobile". One may use the term "Car" while the other may use "Auto". Each of them queries the same information with different terms, but these terms belong to same concept. So, the success of finding relevant documents varies based on demand and context. To address the problem, thesauri map variations in terms (synonyms, abbreviations, acronyms and altered spelling) of a single preferred term for each concept. For document indexer, the thesauri provide the index term to be used to describe each concept. This enforces consistency of document indexing. For users of a Web site, the thesauri work in the background, mapping their keywords onto single preferred terms, so they can be presented with the complete set of relevant documents.

WordNet

A human compiled electronic dictionary which is one kind of ontology that expresses meanings of bounded terms. It was developed by Prof. George Miller at Princeton University. It mainly builds up on a lexical knowledge base born out from psycholinguistic research into the human lexicon. It has applications in different fields of research, sense disambiguation, semantic tagging and information retrieval (Miller, 1998).

EuroWordNet

A European project for WordNet. The aim of this project is to develop multilingual dictionaries with WordNet for several European languages. In this project based on WordNet, each individual net is linked to a central system which is called Inter-Lingual-Index. Each net is composed of about 30,000 synsets and 50,000 entries (EuroWordNet,2012).

Dmoz

An open directory project which is most panoptic human edited directory of the Web. It is constructed and maintained by a vast, global community of volunteer editors. Web content is growing at staggering rates. Search engines are increasingly unable to provide useful results to search queries. The open directory provides a way to keep the Internet classified itself. It uses standard terms to tag the directories so that anyone can browse it (DMOZ, 2012)

Subject Specific Controlled Vocabulary (SSCV)

Construction of sentences, words, and data are most of the time used in subject specific controlled vocabularies, for example languages to express chronology, hypothesis, comparison, etc. Typically an SSCV is expressed as key words, key phrases or classification codes that describe the theme of the resource. In the library sciences, due to the ever-increasing number of records, bibliographic systems are facing difficulties. Documents in library system are heterogeneous: some of them provide a few hints, some are disparate while in others structural tags are sometimes not used properly, which results in inefficiency in extracting documents. However, controlled vocabularies which have traditionally been used in libraries, could serve as good-quality structures for subject browsing among entire documents (See Figure 2). Subject heading systems and thesauri that have traditionally been developed for subject indexing that would describe topics of the document more specifically (LCA, 2012).

Figure 2. Library of Congress online catalog

Library Congress and Authors List

The Semantic Web and library communities have both been working toward the same set of goals: naming concepts, naming entities and bringing different forms of those names together. The Semantic Web's efforts toward this end are relatively new, whereas libraries have been doing work in this area for hundreds of years. Vocabularies developed in libraries, particularly at the Library of Congress, are sophisticated and advanced in searching and representation. Libraries have a long-standing history of developing, implementing and providing tools and services that encourage the use of numerous controlled vocabularies. When the naming conventions are translated into Semantic Web technologies, they will help realize Berners-Lee's dream (LCSH, 2012). Furthermore, the roles of libraries in the Semantic Web are as follows:

- Exposing collections by using Semantic Web technologies to make content available
- Web'ifying
- Thesaurus/Mappings/Services
- Sharing Learned
- Persistence

As all of the previous roles are equally important, the intuition to move controlled vocabularies into a standard to which web services can gain easy access to information management. By Conforming all these vocabularies to Semantic Web standards such as controlled vocabularies will provide limitless opportunities to use them in different ways. This can make possible searching and browsing diverse records, verifying and identifying particular authors and browsing sets of topics related to a particular concept (LCA,2012). Authors List (Figure 3) can be categorized into two ways.

Uniform List

This category (Gilchrist, 2006) includes all universal names, for example, the "Bible", the "Gita", the "Quran", the "Tripod" and the "Lake of Garda", etc. This kind of series list of controlled vocabularies is included in different consecutive names. From a unique list it is easier to match the concepts they represent.

Series List

This category includes the series of same name with the different themes such as "Terminator-1", "Terminator-2", and "Terminator-3".

Figure 3. Library Congress author list

APPLICATIONS

Applications for Managing Controlled Vocabularies

Traditional Controlled Vocabulary Tools

The vocabulary which is used in legacy systems is called the traditional vocabulary. For example, the AGROVOC (Agrovoc, 2012), a thesaurus, is mainly in relational database format and is published on the website for browsing and navigating concepts and their relations. It was previously available only in four languages. Now it is available in 22 languages. Major drawbacks of traditional controlled vocabularies are that they were not well structured, they were only text format or SQL format, their relationships were not well defined, there was no semantics between the concepts and there was no Unified Resource Identifier (URI) for locating the concepts.

A Modern Controlled Vocabulary Collaborative Management System

Modern controlled vocabularies (Vocbench, 2012) are one kind of lightweight ontologies with well defined multiple formats (SKOS, RDF, OWL, etc.). In this vocabulary, each concept is assigned a URL. Using this URI, one can populate concept information and use this information for further research. One example of modern controlled vocabulary is AGROVOC VocBench (Figure 4). In VocBench, one can add or modify the concepts in disturbing manner.

Figure 4. AGROVOC VocBench

Applications for Exploiting Controlled Vocabularies

Background Knowledge

Controlled vocabularies are used in subject indexing schemes, subject headings, thesauri and taxonomies to provide a way to organize knowledge for subsequent retrieval (Faatz, 2000; Shvaiko, 2006).The Controlled vocabulary strategy assigns the use of predefined, authorized terms that have been preselected by the designer of the vocabulary. For easy accessing to the digital information and library catalogs, tags are carefully selected from the words and phrases in a controlled vocabulary. CV controls the use of synonyms (and near-synonyms) by establishing a single form of the term. This ensures that indexers apply the same terms to describe the same or similar concepts, thus reducing the probability that relevant resources will be missed during a user search. The biggest advantage to controlled vocabularies is that once you find the correct term, most of the information you need is grouped together in one place, saving you the time of having to search under all of the other synonyms for that term. In large organizations, controlled vocabularies may be introduced to improve inter-departmental communication. The use of controlled vocabularies ensures that everyone is using the same word to mean the same thing. This consistency of terms is one of the most important concepts in technical writing and knowledge management, where effort is expended to use the same word throughout a document organization instead of slightly different ones refers to the same thing.

Document Annotation

The objective of document annotation is to use appropriate terms so that machines can easily understand and correctly classify the documents, allowing the user easily access while searching or browsing. For example, Clusty (2012), Vivisimo (2012), Swoogle (2012), and others, are classified documents under pre-defined keywords or terms so that one can go to specific locations to find the needed information (Daphne, 1997). Furthermore, document annotation is needed for building knowledge bases that will be used in the future Web and existing large sets of corporas. However, existing information retrieval systems use string matching techniques for full-text search or key phrase search. Thus, a major problem with these systems is overlapping the matching terms or matching results. To overcome these difficulties, more semantic information should be added to matching techniques. The present NLP (natural language processing) techniques cannot provide the complete solution. There is more work to be done. In additional, document annotation can help to improve the performance of information extraction.

Information Retrieval and Extraction

WordNet has been used as a comprehensive semantic lexicon in a module for full text message retrieval as a communication aid, in which queries are expanded through keyword design. In (Gilchris, 2006), automatic construction of thesauri, based on the occurrences determined by the automatic statistical identification of semantic relations is used for text categorization. English words can have different meanings or the same meaning with different structures or descriptions. For example, "center" and "centre" have the same meaning but different spelling for American and British English. Conversely, the same words can have different meanings, for example "bank" means "river side" or "financial institution". It is hard to classify documents or satisfy user queries according to the meaning of words. Text categorization is the process of categorizing the document under a specific class. WordNet lexical information builds a relation between sentences and coherent categories. Sebastiani (2002) describes an algorithm for text categorization using WordNet.

Audio and Video Retrieval

In the digital age, the most challenge is to handle the huge amount of hyper-media or non-textual information on the Web. For example, on YouTube (YouTube, 2012), over 150,000 videos are uploaded and 100,000,000 queries are performed every day (Figure 5). In order to control these high volumes of hyper-media information, information must be used and used in the right way. For instance, the multimedia miner (OVP, 2011) is a prototype to extract multimedia information and knowledge from the web to generate conceptual hierarchies for interactive information retrieval and build multi-dimensional cubes for multimedia data. Finally, WordNet or Thesaurus are used in query expansion for TV or radio programs to index the news automatically. It has some drawbacks; for instance, it is not domain specific and it is not possible to find relationships between terms with different parts of speech.

Semantic Interoperability, Data Exchange, and Integration

Controlled vocabularies are used in resolving semantic heterogeneity among data sources for data exchange and integration in different domain.

In bioinformatics domain (SEMEDA, 2003), controlled vocabulary is used in ingrating molecular biological data for resolving different terms of the same thing and accessing data without know the structure and technical issues. In medical domain (Merabti, 2003), different ontology alignment through controlled vocabularies is used in semantic ingration of medical data. In geology and mining (Xoagang, 2010), controlled vocabulary is used for semantic interoperability of geodata from mining projects. For this purpose, concepts and their relationships are proposed in knowledge domain of mineral exploration for mining projects. In developing controlled vocabulary, the used national standard of geosciences taxonomies and terminologies. Further, controlled vocabulary is used resolving heterogeneity among data sources from mining projects in integrating databases. Sharing data in hydrological domain (Cuahsi, 2012), controlled vocabulary is also used. In Srinubabu (2011), to annotate and integrate biological datasets, controlled vocabulary is used.

Figure 5. Video indexing

Managing Information in a Social Network

The endlessly growth of information resources on the web demands better classification. This classification is needed to browse web pages more smoothly. Previous orthodox information resources were not consistent because of changing static to dynamic pages on the Web. After changing those information resources to modern information resources, a more consistent to categorization is needed. However, the problem was not only browsing the pages but also consisting of qualities of Web sites content. To overcome this problem, a change to apply online vocabulary resources is needed to help end users to find what they are looking for. Furthermore, social networking, linking data, Flickr (Flickr, 2012), Google Maps (Map, 2012) and intercompany collaboration, have a common ground which further necessitates a controlled vocabulary (Figure 6).

Controlled Vocabulary in Web Intelligence and Recommender Systems

In personalized recommender system (Liang, 2009), controlled vocabulary is used in tagging of items. The item taxonomy is a set of controlled vocabulary terms.

SEMANTIC INTEROPERABILITY OF CONTROLLED VOCABULARIES FOR PUBLISHING LINKED OPEN DATA

People are breaking their legacy data silos and uploading the data on the web. To get the real value from these uploaded data, it is needed to connect them. It occurs

Figure 6. Controlled vocabulary used as tagging in Flickr

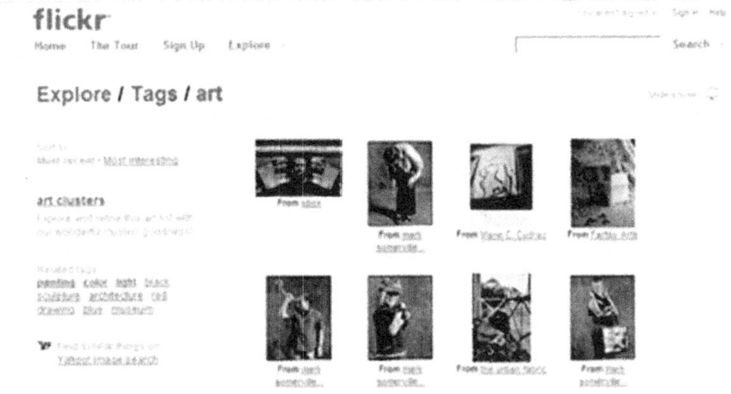

the heterogenous issue. The Matching is the main factor for linking the data in distributed environment. According to Tim Berners-Lee, linking resource get the highest start for Linked Open Data principle's (LOD, 2012).

Matching Problem

The semantic heterogeneity is a big problem of matching the controlled vocabularies. In order to clarify our problem statement, let us proceed to match CVs. The CV stores concepts and relationships between these concepts. We write C_{cv} to denote the set of concepts stored in the CV database. We write c^i to denote a concept with ID i in the CV database (i.e., $c^i \in C_{cv}$). The stored relations are specificity($c^i \subseteq$ cj) and disjoint relationship($c^i \cap$ cj). We write Ro to represent the ($\subseteq$ or $\perp$) that holds between concept c^i and cj. The set Ro can be used to compute all the other possible relations that hold between concepts in CV. The set of concepts and the set of original relation in the CV can be represented in the form of a graph, whose nodes are concepts and which has two kind of edges. The first kind represent the specificity and it is shown as a directed edge. An edge directed from node i (concept c^i) and node j (concept cj) means that cj $\subseteq c^i$. The second kind of relation is disjoint relation. Let a mapping element be a 4-tuple $\langle ID_{ij}, c_i, c_j, R \rangle$, where $ID_{ij} =$ is unique identifier of the given element $c^i =$ a set of concepts in CV_1, cj = a set of concepts of concept CV_2 (Figure 7), R=relation which holds between concepts of vocabularies. The possible semantic relations are: equivalence ($\equiv$), more general ($\supseteq$), less general ($\subseteq$), and mismatch ($\perp$).

For instance, we consider two concepts from CV1 and CV2. The two concepts respectively C_{car} and $C_{automobile}$ which represent concept label car and concept label automobile that mean car is a entity or thing in the real world, similarly automobile mean an entity in the real word. As we know that

$$C_{car} \equiv C_{automobile} \text{ if } C^I_{car} = C^I_{automobile}$$

Figure 7. CV_1 and CV_2

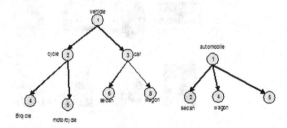

Since there is no similarity between two concepts label then we cannot say that they are equivalent. Now, we check their synonym to find out if there is any similarity existing or not.

Synset of C_{car}: <car, auto, machine and>

Synset of $C_{automobile}$:< auto, automobile, motorcar>

Since they have common word "auto" then we can assume they have an existing relationship. However, it is not enough to draw the conclusion about similarity between two concepts only using synonym. We go through less general ($\subseteq$) and more general ($\supseteq$) relationship of concepts. For example, car is having two children

$C_{sedan} \subseteq C_{car}$

$C_{wagon} \subseteq C_{car}$

and automobile is having three children

$C_{sedan} \subseteq C_{automobile}$

$C_{wagon} \subseteq C_{automobile}$

$C_{taxi} \subseteq C_{automobile}$

Since they have two common children, we can assume they might same concept. For these reason we need to find out the parent of car and parent of automobile. For instance, these two concepts are having same parent vehicle. So, we can say that they are siblings.

$C_{vehicle} \supseteq C_{car}$

$C_{vehicle} \supseteq C_{automobile}$

The following assumption we know from CV database (Moshed,2009, Morshed,2010) that a word cannot exist in the database without at least one synset associated with it a synset cannot exist in the database without at least one word associated with it.

According to this assume, we can say, a concept can represent one word or multiple words.

For instance, C_{car} can be represented word "car" and similarly, $C_{automobile}$ can be represented word "automobile":

$$W_{car}^{CV1} \neq W_{automobile}^{CV2}.$$

These two words can compare only by syntactically [0,1]. Therefore, we can only use equivalent relation ($\equiv$) on it. The problem occurs due to different word form stores in different controlled vocabularies and there is no standard file or authenticate file to describe for forming of words. For instance, if we have two words network and networking:

$$W_{netork}^{CV1} \qquad W_{networking}^{CV2}$$

This case, we can see that both words have a common 6 literals. In our case, we consider equivalent relation between words by given threshold in order to solve the problem. More precisely, we will give equivalent relation ($\equiv$) between words if their three literals are common. As result:

$$W_{netork}^{CV1} \equiv W_{networking}^{CV2}$$

Therefore, the only the equivalence relation could be used for words and synonyms. Furthermore, concepts are equivalent if they have the same concept label, i.e., they carry the same meaning in the real world for example if we say concept of car, it means a set of document which tell about the car [11]; otherwise, they are mismatched. Hence, equivalence is the stronwgest binding relation as the second entity is exactly the same as the first. On the other hand, "more general" and "less general" relations give us containment information with respect to the first entity, while the mismatch relation provides containment information with respect to the extension of the complement of the first entity.

There are some restrictions in case of mapping control vocabularies.

If $\langle c_i, c_j, \perp \rangle \in Ro(c_i, c_j \in C_{cv}, i \neq j)$ then $c^i \not\sqsubseteq c_j$ and $c_j \not\sqsubseteq ci$

If $\langle c_i, c_j, \perp \rangle \in Ro(c_i, c_j \in C_{cv}, i \neq j)$ then $\nexists c_k \left(k \neq i, k \neq j \right)$ s.t. $c_k \subseteq c_i$ and $c_k \subseteq c_j$;

The first restriction specifies that there cannot be a "disjoint" relation between two concepts if one is more specific than other, the second restriction specifies that "mismatch" concept cannot have common descendent. Apart from these restrictions, we do not consider the "more general" or "less general" relation between words and synonyms.

Matching Methods

String Matching

These techniques are often used to match between two words from given entities. They consider strings as sequences of letters in an alphabet. They are typically based on the following intuition: the more similar the strings, the more likely they denote the same concepts. Some examples of string-based techniques which are extensively used in matching systems are *prefix*, *suffix*, *edit distance*, and *n-gram* (Cohen, 2003; Volz, 2009). For example, we can consider a match between the words the "Hot" and "Hotel" *according the prefix matching.*

Semantic Matching

Semantic Matching is introduced in(Giunchiglia, 2003; Giunchiglia, 2004; Euzenate, 2007) and it does not consider straight string matching techniques for matching purpose. It takes two classification and produces matches. This matching system based on two key notation; one is concept of node, concept of label. However, background knowledge is major factor for its functionalities. WordNet plays vital role for this purpose.

Vocabulary Matching Tools

There are several tools for matching purposes. We describe some of them in here.

FALCON-AO

Falcon(Gong Chengingsheng, 2005), is a platform for Semantic Web applications that provides fundamental technology for finding, aligning and learning ontologies. Falcon-AO, is an automatic ontology matching system that aids interoperability between ontologies. The Falcon-AO tool takes RDF/OWL as input and produces RDF as output. Furthermore, this tool includes LMO (linguistic matching for ontologies), GMO (graph matching for ontologies) and PBM (a partition-based matcher for large ontologies).

CTXMatch, S-Match

Context Match (CTXmatch) and Semantic Matcher (S-match) (Giunchiglia, 2003; Bouquet, 2003) is developed by the University of Trento. CtxMatch presents an approach to derive semantic relations between classes of two classification schemas, which are extracted from databases or ontologies. Based on the labels the system identifies equivalent entities. For this, it also makes use of synonyms defined in WordNet. Other element level matchers are also included. Through an SAT-solver the system identifies additional relations between the two schemas. The SAT-solver takes the structure of the schemas into account, especially the taxonomy and its inferred implications, e.g., the fact that any object in a class is also an element of all the superclasses there of. As a result, the system returns equivalence, subsumption, or mismatch between two classes. A recent version S-Match also provides explanations of the alignments.

Silk Framework

The Silk frame work is a tool for matching the data from different Linked Open data source. It takes two RDF files (Resource Description Framework) as input and generate the similarity matrics among the links by using the string matching techniques. It uses the concept-to-concept matching approach (Volz,2009).

Controlled Facilitating the Linked Open Data

The key factor of semantic web is a web of data. These data need to be Linked for the broader usages of semantic web community. "Linked Data is about using the Web to connect related data that wasn't previously linked, or using the Web to lower the barriers to linking data currently linked using other methods". More specifically, Wikipedia defines Linked Data (LOD,2012) as "a term used to describe a recommended best practice for exposing, sharing, and connecting pieces of data, information, and knowledge on the Semantic Web using URIs and RDF." The controlled vocabularies play important role for this new dimension of data sharing arena. The most challenges are the data formats (i.e., XML, CVS, txt, etc) and licence policy. In order to publish the data, we need to make the data sources in RDF/XML format and the free licence policy so that anybody can use the published data in their applications.

For example, "AGROVOC thesaurus"(Morshed, 2011; Agrovoc LOD, 2012) is aligned with thirteen vocabularies, thesauri and ontologies in areas related to the domains it covers for joining the LOD. The Six of the linked resources are general in scope: the Library of Congress Subject Headings (LCSH), NAL Thesaurus,

RAMEAU Répertoire d'autorité-matière encyclopedique et alphabetique unifie, Eurovoc, DBpedia, and an experimental Linked Data version of the Dewey Decimal Classification. The remaining seven resources are specific to various domains: GEMET on the environment, STW for Economics, TheSoz is about social science and both GeoNames and the FAO Geopolitical Ontology cover countries and political regions. ASFA covers all aquatic science and the aptly named Biotechnology glossary covers biotechnology. These linked resources are mostly available as RDF/XML resources.

The thesauri were considered in their entirety barring RAMEAU, for which only agriculture related concepts were considered (amounting to some 10% of its 150 000 concepts). Candidate mappings were found by applying string similarity matching algorithms to pairs of preferred labels and by using the Ontology Alignment API for managing the produced matches. The common analysis language used was English in all cases except the AGROVOC - RAMEAU alignment for which French was used. Table 1 shows, for each resource linked to AGROVOC (column 1), its area of coverage (column 2), the language considered for mapping with AGROVOC (column 3), and the number of matches resulting from the evaluation (column 4).

Candidate links were presented to a domain expert for evaluation in the form of a spread sheet. Once validated the mappings were loaded in the same triple store where the linked data version of AGROVOC is stored. All resulting validated candidate matches were considered to be skos:exactMatch.

Table 1. Resources linked to AGROVOC

Vocabulary	Coverage	Lang used for link discovery	#matches
EUROVOC	General	EN	1,297
DDC	General	EN	409
LCSH	General	EN	1,093
NALT	Agriculture	EN	13,390
RAMEAU	General (cut on Agri.)	FR	686
DBpedia	General	EN	1,099
TheSoz	Social science	EN	846
STW	Economy	EN	1,136
FAO Geopol. Ontology	Geopolitical	EN	253
GEMET	Environment	EN	1,191
ASFA	Aquatic sciences	EN	1,812
Biotech	Biotechnology	EN	812
GeoNames	Gazeteer	EN	212

The objective when linking AGROVOC to other resources was to provide only main anchors, privileging accuracy over recall. This is why it only used exactMatch, found by means of string-similarity techniques as opposed to more sophisticated context-based approaches. Also, the One Sense per Domain hypothesis (Stoilos, 2005; David, 2011) supports the claim that in the case similar strings correspond to equivalent meanings. The use of more sophisticated approaches might have contributed to filtering out potential results more than widening their number (thus incrementing precision over recall), however this potential loss of precision was well compensated by the manual validation of candidate links by a domain expert (Morshed,2011).

In addition, these secure links from the AGROVOC LOD (Figure 8) are used to facilitate the AGRIS (Agris,2012) which is "a global public domain Database with 2830342 structured bibliographical records on agricultural science and technology. 79.78% of records are citations from scientific journals. The bibliographic references contain either links to the full text of the publication or additional information retrieved from related Internet resources" to network to join the LOD. The Agris Linked Open Data version is called the "OpenAgris" (OpenAgris, 2012). The OpenAgris uses the AGROVOC links to connect the Dbpedia and extract the information. All the process happens on the fly.

Figure 8. AGROVOC links use for the extracting the information

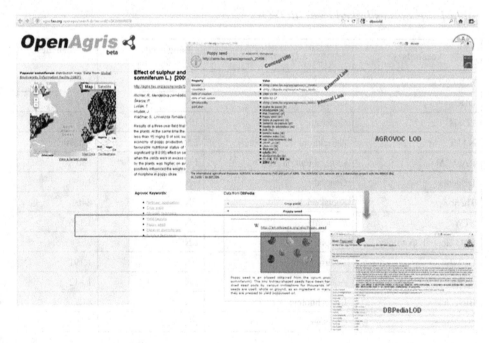

Finally, we learn a couple of lessons

- The AGROVOC can be a hub of linking data sources and use these links for extracting the information from different data providers.
- The most important things that we can classify the information and search them easily by using the CVS.

CONCLUSION

Controlled vocabularies are playing vital role for information integration and information retrieval.It can be more useful as linking information, discovery knowledge, knowledge base in the web. However, a complete universal controlled vocabulary is not yet to be done by any research. It is extremely necessary in the filed of information science, earth science, biological science, cyber science and medical science for common ground of vocabularies so that anyone can access information even he or she does not understand full of language. We have discussed pros and cons different kind of controlled vocabularies and mentioned some on going work on this domain.

REFERENCES

Agris. (2012). Retrieved May, 2012, from http://agris.fao.org/knowledge-and-information-sharing-through-agris-network

AGROVOC. (2012). *AGROVOC thesaurus*. Retrieved Jan, 2012, from http://aims.fao.org/standards/agrovoc/functionalities/search

AgrovocLOD. (2012). Retrived May, 2012 from http://aims.fao.org/agrovoc/lod

Bouquet, P., Serafini, L., & Zanobini, S. (2003). Semantic coordination: A new approach and an application. In *Proceedings of the 2nd International Semantic Web Conference (ISWO'03)*. Sanibel Islands, FL: ISWO.

Clusty. (2012). *MetaSearch engine*. Retrieved March, 2012, from http://clusty.com/

Cohen, W. W., Ravikumar, P., & Fienberg, S. E. (2003). *A comparison of string distance metrics for name-matching tasks*. IJCAI.

Cuahsi. (2012). Retrieved 5 June, 2012 http://his.cuahsi.org/mastercvdata.html

Daphne, K., & Sahami, M. (1997). Hierarchically classifying documents using very few words. In D. H. Fisher (Ed.), *Proceedings of ICML-97, 14th International Conference on Machine Learning*, (pp. 170–178). Nashville, TN: Morgan Kaufmann Publishers.

DMOZ. (2012). *Open directory project*. Retrieved Jan, 2012, from http://www.dmoz.org/

EuroWordNet. (2012). Retrieved Jan, 2012, from http://www.illc.uva.nl/EuroWordNet/

Euzenate, J., & Shaviko, P. (Eds.). (2007). *Ontology matching*. Berlin: Springer.

Faatz, T., Kamps, A., & Steinmetz, R. (2000). Background knowledge, indexing and matching interdependencies of document management and ontology maintenance. In *Proceedings of the First Workshop on Ontology Learning* (OL-2000). OL.

Flickr (2012). Retrieved March, 2012, from http://www.flickr.com/

Gale, W., Church, K., & Yarowsky, D. (1992). A method for disambiguating word senses in a large corpus. *Computers and the Humanities, 26*, 415–439. doi:10.1007/BF00136984.

Gilchrist, A., Aitchison, J., & Bawden. (2006). *Thesaurus construction and use: A practical manual* (4th ed). London: Aslib.

Giunchiglia, F., &Shvaiko, P. (2003). Semantic matching. *International Journal of Computer and Artificial Intelligence*.

Giunchiglia, F., Shvaiko, P., & Yatskevich, M. (2004). S-match: An algorithm and an implementation of semantic matching. In *Proceedings of ESWS'04*. ESWS.

Ibekwe-San Juan, F. (2006). *Construction and maintaining knowledge organization tools a symbolic appraoch*.

Jérôme, D., Euzenat, J., Scharffe, F., & dos Santos, C. T. (2011). The alignment API 4.0. *Semantic Web Journal, 2*(1), 3–10.

Jian, G. C. I., Hu, W., & Qu, Y. (2005). Falcon-ao: Aligning ontologies with falcon. In *Proceedings of the International and Interdisciplinary Conference on Modeling and Using Context (CONTEXT)*, (pp. 85-91). CONTEXT.

LCA. (2012). *Library congress author list*. Retrieved Feb, 2012 http://www.loc.gov/bookfest/2009/authors/

LCSH. (2012). *The library of congress classification system*. Retrieved from http://www.loc.gov/catdir/cpso/lcco/lcco.html/

Liang, H., Xu, Y., & Nayak, R. (2009). Personalized recommender systems integrating social tags and item taxonomy. In *Proceedings of the 2009 IEEE/WIC/ACM International Conference on Web Intelligence and Intelligent Agent Technology Workshops*. Milano, Italy: IEEE/WIC/ACM.

LOD. (2012). *Linked open data*. Retrieved June, 2012, from http://linkeddata.org/

Ma, X., Wu, C., Carranza, E. J. M., Schetselaar, E. M., van der Meer, F. D., & Liu, G. etal. (2010). Development of a controlled vocabulary for semantic interoperability of mineral exploration geodata for mining projects. *Computers & Geosciences, 36*(12), 1512–1522. doi:10.1016/j.cageo.2010.05.014.

Map. (2012). *GoogleMaps*. Retrieved June, 2012, from https://maps.google.com.au/

McCulloch, E. (2005). *Digital direction thesauri: Practical guidance for construction.*

McGuinness, D. L., Shvaiko, P., Giunchiglia, F., & Pinheiro da Silva, P. (2004). Towards explaining semantic matching. In *Proceedings of the International Workshop on Description Logics at KR'04*. KR.

Merabti, T., Soualmia, L. F., Grosjean, J., Joubert, M., & Darmoni, S. J. (2003). Aligning biomedical terminologies in French: Towards semantic interoperability in medical applications. In *Medical Informatics* (pp. 41–68). InTech.

MeSH. (2012). *The national library of medicine's controlled vocabulary thesaurus*. Retrieved April, 2012, from http://www.nlm.nih.gov/mesh/

Miller, G. (1998). *WordNet: An electronic lexical database*. Boston: MIT Press.

Morshed, A. (2009). Controlled vocabulary matching in distributed system. In *Proceedings of the 26th British National Conference on Databases*. London, UK: Databases.

Morshed, A. (2010). *Aligning controlled vocabularies for enabling semantic matching in a distributed knowledge management system. (Unpublished doctoral disseration)*. Trento, Italy: University of Trento.

Morshed, A., Caracciolo, C., Johannsen, G., & Keizer, J. (2011). Thesaurus alignment for linked data publishing. In *Proceedings of the DCMI International Conference on Dublin Core and Metadata Applications*. DC.

OpenAgris. (2012). Retrieved May, 2012, from http://agris.fao.org/news/openagris-journals-rdf-visual-reader

OVP. (2011). *Open video project*. Retrieved December, 2011, from http://www.open-video.org/

Sebastiani, F. (2002). Machine learning in automated text categorization. *ACM Computing Surveys, 34*(1), 1–47. doi:10.1145/505282.505283.

SEMEDA. (2003). *Ontology based semantic integration of biological databases..*

Shvaiko, P., Giunchiglia, F., & Yatskevich, M. (2006). Discovering missing background knowledge in onology matching. In *Proceedings of the 17th European Conference on Artificial Intelligence (ECAI 2006)*, (vol. 141, pp. 382-386). ECAI.

Srinubabu, G. (2011). *Integration, warehousing, and analysis strategies of omics data, methods in molecular biology.*

Stoilos, G., Stamou, G., & Kollias, S. (2005). A string metric for ontology alignment. In *Proceedings of the 4th International Semantic Web Conference*, (pp. 624–637). Berlin: Springer-Verlag.

Swoogle. (2012). *Semantic search engine.* Retrieved March, 2012, from http://swoogle.umbc.edu/

Vivisimo. (2012). *MetaSearch engine.* Retrieved March,2012, from http://vivisimo.com/

VocBench. (2012). Retrieved June, 2012, from http://aims.fao.org/tools/vocbench-2

Volz, J., Bizer, C., Gaedke, M., & Kobilarov, G. (2009). *Silk – A link discovery framework for the web of data.* Paper presetned at the 2nd Workshop about Linked Data on the Web (LDOW2009). Madrid, Spain.

YouTube. (2012). Retrieved May, 2012, from http://www.youtube.com/

Zhu, H., & Madnick, S. (2006). *A lightweight ontology approach to scalable interoperability.* Working paper CISL. Cambridge, MA: The Massachusetts Institute of Technology.

Chapter 6

Enabling the Matchmaking of Organizations and Public Procurement Notices by Means of Linked Open Data

Jose María Alvarez Rodríguez
University of Oviedo, Spain

José Emilio Labra Gayo
University of Oviedo, Spain

Patricia Ordoñez de Pablos
University of Oviedo, Spain

EXECUTIVE SUMMARY

The aim of this chapter is to present a proposal and a case study to describe the information about organizations in a standard way using the Linked Data approach. Several models and ontologies have been provided in order to formalize the data, structure and behaviour of organizations. Nevertheless, these tries have not been fully accepted due to some factors: (1) missing pieces to define the status of the organization; (2) tangled parts to specify the structure (concepts and relations) between the elements of the organization; 3) lack of text properties, and other factors. These divergences imply a set of incomplete approaches to formalize data and information about organizations. Taking into account the current trends of applying

DOI: 10.4018/978-1-4666-2827-4.ch006

semantic web technologies and linked data to formalize, aggregate, and share domain specific information, a new model for organizations taking advantage of these initiatives is required in order to overcome existing barriers and exploit the corporate information in a standard way. This work is especially relevant in some senses to: (1) unify existing models to provide a common specification; (2) apply semantic web technologies and the Linked Data approach; (3) provide access to the information via standard protocols, and (4) offer new services that can exploit this information to trace the evolution and behaviour of the organization over time. Finally, this work is interesting to improve the clarity and transparency of some scenarios in which organizations play a key role, like e-procurement, e-health, or financial transactions.

ORGANIZATION BACKGROUND

WESO is a multidisciplinary research group from the Department of Computer Science and the Departments of Philology at the University of Oviedo created by the Associate Professor Dr. José Emilio Labra Gayo. Since 2005 WESO is involved in semantic web research, education and technology transfer. The growth of the Internet in the last years has brought relevant changes in the way of communication. Nowadays governments, citizens, enterprises and society are more interconnected than ever and information is the key to keep the interconnection among parties. This new information society needs a step forward to exploit the new opportunities and challenges. WESO research activities try to apply semantic web technologies in order to facilitate the transition to a new web of data.

As academic research group, one of our aims is to boost the research, innovation and competitiveness of the organizations using the knowledge. WESO seeks to support research and innovation focusing on:

- Providing research services on semantics
- Applying semantic technologies to improve existing products
- Addressing the new-technology barriers
- Developing and training
- Fostering the knowledge in the scientific and industrial areas
- Teaching to a new wave of professionals

WESO brings together these activities for enabling and supporting people, organizations and systems to collaborate and interoperate in the new global context.

Our research lines focus on semantic web technologies with emphasis on (but not restricted to):

- **Semantic Architectures:** Designing and developing architectures based on domain knowledge.
- **Collaborative Semantic Services:** Improving existing solutions with a semantic collaborative approach.
- **Linked and Open Data:** Offering new solutions for combining RDF vocabularies and publishing data.
- **Methods and Algorithms:** Implementing methods to exploit the domain knowledge and the web of data.
- **Semantic Technologies:** Being aware of the semantic web technologies outcomes of RDF, OWL, SKOS or RIF.
- **Others:** Semantic Web Services, e-government, e-procurement, e-health, etc.

Currently we are involved in the research and development of several partnership projects in the semantic web area, more specifically in the field of e-procurement and Linking Open Data (LOD) the next project must be highlighted:

- **10ders Information Services:** This project is partially funded by the Spanish Ministry of Industry, Tourism and Trade with code TSI-020100-2010-919 and the European Regional Development Fund (EFDR) according to the National Plan of Scientific Research, Development and Technological Innovation 2008-2011, leaded by Gateway Strategic Consultancy Services (Gateway Strategic Consultancy Services, S.L, 2012) and developed in cooperation with EXIS-TI (EXIS-TI, 2012).

This project aims to apply the semantic web and LOD approaches to public procurement notices:

- Transforming government controlled vocabularies such as CPV, CPC, Eurovoc (now available in SKOS), etc. to RDF, RDF(S), SKOS or OWL.
- Modeling the information inside the public procurement notices as web information resources and enriching them with the aforementioned controlled vocabularies, geographical information (e.g., NUTS and the information now available in the linked data cloud.
- Publishing the information in a SPARQL endpoint providing a linked data node.
- Providing enhanced services (search and sort, matchmaking, georeasoning, statistics, etc.) exploiting this semantic information through ``advanced algorithms'' based on Spreading Activation (SA) techniques, rule based systems (RBS) and a mixing of them.

In the past, we participated in the development of a hybrid search engine for the BOPA (Official bulletin of Asturias). We have also experience applying semantic web technologies to other domains like processing XBRL information which enabled automatically analyze financial information of companies and developing a differential diagnosis system which could infer diseases from symptoms to help medical experts. The outcomes of our research projects are part of our technology and knowledge. Thus, we improve our semantic solutions looking for developments generic, standards, flexible and applicable to future projects

INTRODUCTION

An organization is considered to be a set of constraints on the activities performed by agents. This approach was presented by Weber (1987), who viewed the process of bureaucratization as a shift from management. Previously, Mintzberg provided an analysis of organization structure distinguishing among five basic parts of an organization and five distinct organization configurations. This vision put together some mechanisms to achieve coordination with the objective of modeling goals, business processes and rules, authority, positions and communication. In this context, some works have emerged (Fox, Barbuceanu & Gruninger, 1995) trying to create ontologies and models that specify the realm of organizations but different problems are arisen due to some factors: (1) missing pieces to define the status of the organization; (2) tangled parts to specify the structure (concepts and relations) between the elements of the organization; (3) lack of text properties, etc. Currently the application of semantic technologies and Linked Data (Berners-Lee, 2006) and Linked Open Data (LOD) in several fields like Open Government Data (OGD) try to improve the knowledge about a specific area providing common data models and formats to share information and data between agents. In this context the information about organizations (structure, human resources, name mismatches, purposes, products and services, activities with others, etc.) is a new field in which semantic web technologies and the Linked Data approach (Heath & Bizer, 2011) can be applied to exploit this valuable information.

On the other hand, in the European e-procurement context (European Commission, 2011) there is an increasing commitment to boost the use of electronic communications and transaction processing by government institutions and other public sector organizations. The European Commission (EC) outlines (European Commission, 2010) the following advantages in the wider use of e-procurement: increased accessibility and transparency, benefits for individual procedures, benefits in terms of more efficient procurement administration, and potential for integration of EU procurement markets. However, several interlinked challenges to fulfill a successful transition to e-procurement are missing (European Commission, 2010a): overcoming inertia and fears on the part of contracting authorities and suppliers, lack of standards in e-procurement processes, no means to facilitate mutual recognition of national electronic solutions, onerous technical requirements, particularly for bidder authentication and managing multi-speed transition to e-Procurement.

Thus public information published by governmental contracting authorities are a suitable candidate to apply the LOD approach, more specifically data about organizations, and the semantic web technologies providing a framework to develop advanced algorithms and deal new enhanced services oriented to SMEs.

BACKGROUND

The state of the art of this chapter is summarized according to three points of views: (1) LOD and OGD approaches to model, enrich and publish data included in public procurement notices. (2) Semantic methods to exploit the new structured information providing enhanced services and (3) modeling organization purposes and structure through the LOD principles.

In the scope of LOD and OGD there are projects trying to exploit the information of public procurement notices like LOTED-"Linked Open Tenders Electronic Daily" (LOTED Project, 2012) where they use the RSS feeds published by the European Union or the LOD2 Project (LOD2 Project, 2012) that tries to develop a complete suite and platform for Linked Data. UK government is doing a great effort to promote its information sources using the LOD approach. They have published datasets from different sectors: transport, defense, NUTS geographical information, etc. Most of the public administrations in the different countries are also betting for OGD approach to make public their information: Spain (Aporta project), New Zealand, Australia, USA, and others. Regarding the use of LOD and organizations there is a new ontology for modeling the information about organizations (Reynolds, 2010; Reynolds, 2012; Joinup & European Commission, 2012) and recently it has been released as "The Open Database Of The Corporate World" (Taggart & McKinnon, 2010).

In the field of the semantic web technologies and for modeling the domain knowledge there are several options: RDF (W3C Recommendation 10 February 2004), RDF(S) (W3C Recommendation 10 February 2004), OWL 2 (W3C Recommendation, 2009b) or SKOS (W3C Recommendation, 2009a) among others. They provide a common format and data model for sharing and linking knowledge organization systems via the web. This information can be retrieved using SPARQL (W3C Recommendation, 2008), a query language and a protocol to retrieve the information of datasets published via an endpoint. Currently, there is a working group defining a vocabulary and a set of instructions that ease the discovery and usage of linked datasets (Alexander, Cyganiak, Hausenblas & Zhao, 2011), the new specification of SPARQL (1.1) enables a method for discovering and vocabulary for describing SPARQL services made available via an endpoint and ELDA an implementation of *linked-data-api* that provides a configurable way to access RDF data using simple RESTful URLs that are translated into queries to a SPARQL endpoint.

On the other hand, the use of semantic methods to exploit the data from the semantic web like Spreading Activation (SA) techniques and Rule Based Systems (RBSs) is widely used. The main application of SA techniques is focus on Document (Labra, Ordoñez-de Pablos, & Cueva, 2007) and Information Retrieval (Collins & Loftus, 1975; Preece, 1981). These techniques have been also used in semantic search based on hybrid approaches (Rocha & Schwabe, 2004; Berrueta, Polo, & Labra, 2006) and user query expansion (Qiu & Frei,1993; Nie, 2003; Gao, Yan, & Liu, 2008) combining metadata (Schumacher, Sintek, & Sauermann, 2008) and user information (Gouws, Van Rooyen, & Engelbrecht, 2010) to improve web data annotations (Gelgi, Vadrevu, & Davulcu, 2005). RBSs have been used a long time to decision support, diagnosis, etc. in different fields. In the semantic web area and due to the apparition of OWL 2-RL, SPARQL Rules and RIF (Rule Interchange Format-W3C Recommendation 22 June 2010), these systems are growing in their use to deal with the web of data but a clear approach to mix datasets and RBSs is missing. They can also be applied to SA techniques to handle the activation and propagation of the concepts. Moreover, they are several algorithms (like MapReduce) and approaches available to process a huge amount of data in searching and reasoning systems which are based on incremental indices, sync/async parallel search and semantic search (Hogan, Umbrich, Kinsella, Polleres, & Decker, 2011).

Finally, in the case of organizations this is quite a hard search to do because a *lot* of ontologies need some notion of organization to point to (e.g., FOAF is about people but needs to mention the organizations of which a person is a member; Inference Web is about distributed inference but covers trust and provenance which, in turn, requires a notion of organizations that are in a trust relationship). In each of these cases the representation of organization is minimal. Following the evaluation in this web report (Reynolds, 2010) several approaches can be found. Firstly, in previous works there are a number of similar upper ontologies (Proton, Sumo, SmartWeb) that include some notion of organization. These models have a lot of other intentions that are not match with the specific requirement of a small and reusable model to describe organizations but they should be reviewed. Secondly, if search engines are used to look for the concept of Organization the next results will be found: Swoogle 3,990 matches, Falcons gives 15,881 hits for Organization concept from 15 highlighted vocabularies and Google turns up: 1) the "Organization Ontology 1.0" written in SHOE, giving a basic hierarchy of organization, industries and employee roles; 2) an "Organization Ontology for Enterprise Modelling" which is focused on supply chain and 3) "Enterprise Ontology", an ontology to represent the activity of business enterprises expressed in Ontolingua. *Jeni Tennison* has also pointed to an ontology developed by TSO for the London Gazette RDFa markup: Gazette Organization and Gazette Person. According to the authors of this survey the approaches are presented in Boxes 1 through 8.

Moreover other specific organizations like School of ECS (University of Southampton) have another ontology[1] used to publish their internal data. In this sense, Academic Institution Internal Structure Ontology (AIISO)[2] is another vocabulary to describe the internal organizational structure of an academic institution.

From this excellent survey and previous work, the authors have detected some questions to resolve:

- How rich a set of Organization classification should we hard-wire into the core ontology? Should be restrict ourselves to a minimalist notion of organization and organizational unit or have a top level classification of types of organization. A lot of existing ontologies embed some basic division between

Box 1. AKT Portal Ontology

```
Temporal-Thing
  Generic-Agent
    Legal-Agent
      Organization      props: organization-part-of, affiliated-
person,
                          has-sub-unit -> Organization-Unit
                            has-academic-unit -> Academic-
Unit
                            has-support-unit -> Academic-
Support-Unit
                          headed-by -> Affiliated-Person
                          has-size -> Organization-Size
                          subsidiary-of -> Profit-Organiza-
tion
          Political-Organization
          Non-Profit-Organization
            Government-Organization
              Government
              Civil-Service
```

continued on following page

Box 1. Continued

```
        Profit-Organization
        Partnership
        Company
            Private-Company
            Public-Company
        Industrial-Organization
    Learning-Centered-Organization
     R-And-D-Institute
        R-And-D-Institute-Within-Larger-Institute
     Educational-Organization
        Higher-Educational-Organization
            University              props: has-faculty, has-
vice-chancellor
              Distance-Teaching-University
        School
     Publishing-House
     Organization-Unit      props: sub-unit-of-organization-
unit, unit-of-Organization
        Education-Organization-Unit
          Academic-Unit
          University-Faculty
          Academic-Support-Unit
Organization-Size  oneOf{very-large-size, large-size, medium-
size, small-size, micro-size}
```

Government, Corporate, NotForProfit, Religious organizations. Yet some of the divisions are not clear cut and are dependent on legislative (e.g. precise not of not-for-profit).

- How do we model the role someone plays in an organization (or indeed the role an organizational unit plays in relation to other units or the overall organization)? This in an n-ary relationship between an agent (e.g. person) and the organization or unit, including notions of scope, authority, responsibility, contract (including salary). Yet one of our requirements is maximal ease of query and a preference for avoiding reified n-ary relationships.

The outcome of this work was the Organizations Ontology (Reynolds, 2012), a core ontology for organizational structures aimed at supporting linked-data publishing of organizational information across a number of domains. It is designed to allow

Box 2. Proton top

```
Happening
  Situation
    JobPosition    props: withinOrganization -> Organization
    Role           props: roleHolder -> Entity, roleIn -> Happen-
ing
Agent              props: controls, owns, partiallyControls, par-
tiallyOwns, involvedIn, isLegalEntity
  Group            props: hasMember -> Agent
    Organization props: childOrganizationOf, doingBusinessAs,
establishedIn, establishmentDate,
                        registeredIn, parentOrganizationOf,
numberOfEmployees Person          props: isBossOf -> Person, ha-
sPosition -> JobPosition
Product            props: producedBy -> Agent
Service            props: operatedBy -> Agent
```

Box 3. GoodRelations

```
BusinessEntity    props: hasDUNS, hasGlobalLocationNumber, ha-
sISICv4,
                        hasNAICS, hasPOS, legalName
BusinessEntityType
  instances:  Business, Enduser, PublicInstitution, Reseller
BusinessFunction
  instances: ConstructionInstallation, Dispose, LeaseOut, Main-
tain,
ProvideService, Repair, Sell, Buy
```

Box 4. FOAF (Friend Of A Friend)

```
Agent
  Group            props: member -> Agent
  Organization
```

Box 5. SIOC (Semantically-Interlinked Online Communities)

```
Community         props: dct:hasPart
UserGroup         props: has_member, usergroup_of
```

Box 6. Enterprise Modelling Ontology

```
organization   props: has_goal -> organisational-goal, consists_
of -> division
organizational-goal
sub_goal       props: decomposition_of -> organizational-goal
role           props:  has_goal -> sub_goal
                       requires_skill -> skill
                       has_authority -> authority
organization-agent  props: member_of -> division/team, per-
forms -> activity
                          has_communication_link -> communi-
cation-link
                          has_supervisor, has_supervisee
activity            props: constrained_by -> constraint, con-
sumes -> resource
role                props: subordinate_of
                           specialized_role, generalized_role
communication-link
   communication-with-authority
```

domain-specific extensions to add classification of organizations and roles, as well as extensions to support neighboring information such as organizational activities. This ontology fits perfectly to the aim of modeling organizations in a standard and reusable way with semantic technologies. Nevertheless some issues have not yet resolved, like tracking of activities or the representation of the financial information (maybe XBRL could be used to address this intention).

THE MOLDEAS PLATFORM

The MOLDEAS (*Methods on Linked Data for E-Procurement Applying Semantics*) (Álvarez-Rodríguez, 2012) platform seeks to apply the LOD approach and semantic web technologies to improve and ease the access to public procurement notices addressing the principles of OGD for the e-Procurement sector. The functional architecture, See Figure 1, illustrates the processes for retrieving the information about public procurement notices and implementing the semantic methods to produce, publish, consume and validate linked data. Following, the building blocks and basic processes of the architecture are summarized:

Box 7. Enterprise Ontology

```
Legal-Entity
  Corporation
  Customer
    Reseller
  Partnership
  Person        props:  Employer -> Legal-Entity, Works-For-Ou ->
Organisational-Unit
    Partner
  Shareholder
  Vendor
    Competitor
Potential-ActorPotential-Actor
  Organisational-Unit  props:  Managed-By -> Organisational-
Unit
Role-Class
Qua-Entity
  Purpose
    Goal, Mission, Objective, Strategic-Purpose, Vision, Criti-
cal-Success-Factor
Employment-Contract  props: Employee -> Person
```

Box 8. Gazette organization and person ontologies

```
Organisation  (subClassOf foaf:Organization)
            props: hasDepartment -> Department, hasPrevious-
Name -> Organisation,
                isBasedAt -> geo:Feature, hasLocation ->
geo:Feature,
                natureOfBusiness, name, status,
  ForProfitOrganisation       props: isTradingAs
    LimitedCompany            props: registeredCountries,
hasITCTradeClassification,
                                hasRegisteredOffice -> Of-
fice, companyNumber,
                                sitcTradeClassification
      PublicLimitedCompany
```

continued on following page

Box 8. Continued

```
    SoleTrader
    Partnership                 props: alsoKnownAs, defindAs,
partnershipNumber
      GeneralPartnership
      LimitedPartnership
      LimitedLiabilityPartnership
  PublicInstitution
    PublicCorporation
    RegionalAdminstration
      Council...
      GovernmentOfficeRegionCouncil
    GovernmentDepartment...
    ExecutiveAgency...
Department    props: -> isPartOfOrganisation, departmentName
Office        props: officeName, hasOfficeAddress ->
vcard:Address
Person    (subClassOf foaf:Person)  props: hasRole -> Role, em-
ployedAs -> Role InsolvencyPractitioner  props: hasIPnum
Position props: isMemberOfDepartment, isMemberOfOrganisation,
isBasedAt -> geo:Feature
  Role        props: roleName, assignedBy
    Receiver
    Petitioner
    Member
    Liquidator
    Solicitor
    Director
  Employment  props: jobTitle
```

- **Public Procurement Notices:** Source of documents published by official European organisms about public contracts. They are extracted out from all online available sources in European (e.g., TED- European public procurement journal), national (e.g., BOE-Official State Gazzete of Spain) and regional scopes (e.g., BOPA- Autonomous Community's Official Newspaper, Principality of Asturias-Spain).
- **Public Procurement Notices Database:** Local database containing the retrieved information from different sources, including data about organizations. The format of this information is available in XML as intermediate language.

Figure 1. Functional architecture overview

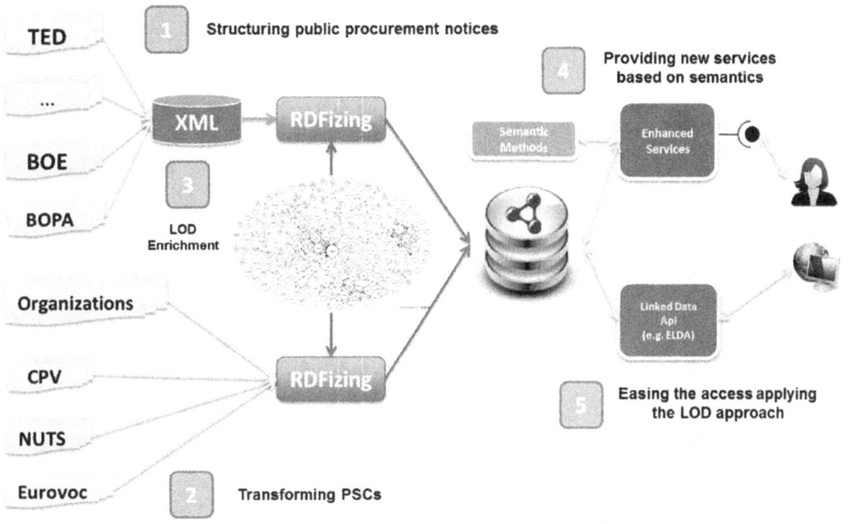

- **Product Scheme Classifications:** Set of classifications used to classify the public procurement notices. Currently, they are available in different formats: MSExcel, PDF, and others. They are coded using RDF/OWL.
- **RDFizing:** It is the production process to convert the data available in the databases to generate a RDF view. This process link together all the information, enrich with the existing vocabularies and store it in a triple store.
- **RDF Store:** It is a triple store such as OpenLink Virtuoso in which the RDF data is stored and published via the SPARQL endpoint.
- **Semantic Consume Methods:** (See Figure 2) It is the application of the libraries such as ONTOSPREAD (Álvarez-Rodríguez, Polo, Abella, Jimenez & Labra, 2011) to exploit the information and provide enhanced services to the clients.
- **Linking Open Data:** It is the set of existing linked data vocabularies to be used in the enrichment of the information.
- **Linked Data API:** (e.g. Pubby or ELDA) It is an API to publish information about datasets, URI scheme specification, etc.

The combination of these building blocks seeks for creating a new innovative way (Álvarez-Rodríguez, Labra, Calmeau, Marín, & Marín, 2011) to exploit the information included in public procurement notices in the context of the semantic web and LOD initiatives reusing the existing technologies, vocabularies, etc. In

117

Figure 2. Query expansion methods in the MOLDEAS platform

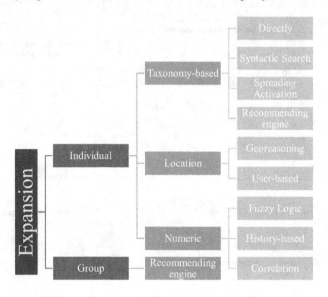

this chapter, we will focus on the objective of modeling organizations as part of e-Procurement processes and in the development of advanced services to match notices according to company profiles.

The MOLDEAS platform, with the aforementioned features, is able to answer questions like the next one:

Which public procurement notices are relevant to Dutch companies (only SMEs) that want to tender for contracts announced by local authorities with a total value lower than 170K € to procure "Road bridge construction work" and a two year duration in the Dutch-speaking region of Flanders (Belgium)?

This work aims to apply the LOD approach and semantic web technologies to improve and ease the access to organization's information addressing the principles of OGD. Following, the main contributions are highlighted: (1) unify existing models to provide a common specification; (2) apply semantic web technologies and the Linked Data approach; (3) provide access to the information via standard protocols and 4) offer new services that can exploit this information to trace the evolution and behavior of the organization over time.

SPECIFICATION OF ORGANIZATIONS WITHIN LINKED OPEN DATA INITIATIVE

The main objective of this specification is to promote the information about organizations using semantic technologies and the linked data approach. To get this broad objective the aforementioned Organizations Ontology represents a first step but some issues should be resolved to spread the scope of this specification. For instance the financial transactions of an organization should be covered as well as the mismatching of organization's name. In that sense it should be addressed these kinds of issues:

- Structure
- Human resources
- Name mismatches
- Purposes and intentions
- Cataloging products, services and activities
- Multilingual and multicultural problems
- Inter/Intra relationships…among others

Taking into account some of these requirements the use of ontologies, taxonomies and vocabularies coming from the Linked Data initiative can provide the next benefits[3]:

- Via the RDF model, equal applicability to unstructured, semi-structured, and structured data and content.
- Elimination of internal data 'silos'.
- Integration of internal and external data.
- Easy interlinkage of enterprise, industry-standard, open public and public subscription data.
- Complete data modeling of any legacy schema.
- Flexible and easy updates and changes to existing schema.
- Report creation and data display based on templates and queries, not requiring manual crafting.
- Data access, analysis and manipulation pushed out to the user level.
- The ability of internal linked data stores to be maintained by existing DBA procedures and assets.

However, it is not enough to publish data using standards, services should be provided exploiting this data to generate new business models as Euroalert.net (Euroalert.net, 2012) does. For example, a service for tracking the activity of an organization (opinion mining or sentimental analysis) could be provided with a high accuracy.

OPEN CORPORATES

In the next code listing, an example of an organization (in N3 format) using the Open Corporates approach is presented. This information is potentially relevant due to the large database that Open Corporates provides with high-valuable information like the company ID. These data follow a mixed approach between Open and Linked Data but a formal model describing the organizations is missing. That is why the use of a common ontology could improve the information sharing and the exploitation of the information in a standard way generating new value-added services of *five stars* like activity tracking. First step to get this purpose should be the publishing of the information following a common data model (e.g., RDF) and specification (e.g., Organizations Ontology++). After that this information should be stored in a RDF triplestore with the capability of accessing the information via SPARQL (language, endpoint & protocol). Finally, a linked data API should be used to ease the access to the SPARQL endpoint (Box 9).

The process of publishing data of Open Corporates following this approach should not be intrusive with the current database. Some ETL tools have emerged to transform existing data in the scope of Linked Data easing the use of new specifications to model the data and information.

CASE STUDY: MATCHMAKING OF ORGANIZATIONS AND PUBLIC PROCUREMENT NOTICES

In the e-procurement information domain, one of the targeted services to be improved is the "search of public procurement notices according to a profile." In the context of searching, matchmaking refers to the procedure of retrieving a relevant list of results that matches with the intentions of an organization that wants to tender in a specific activity sector. Other interesting service on e-procurement is the extraction of statistics to generate reports about the history of some place, organization or contracting authority. They can be exploited through temporal series, weighted aggregation operators (Grabisch, Marichal, Mesiar, & Pap, 2009; Torra & Narukawa, 2007) or statistical inference, specifically predictive inference.

Box 9. Information about an "Open Corporates" organization in N3.

```
http://opencorporates.com/companies/nl/37136346.html?id=5828504
            a <http://purl.org/dc/dcmitype/Text>,
        foaf:Document;
        dct:format "text/html";
        dct:isFormatOf
<http://opencorporates.com/companies/nl/37136346?id=5828504>;
        dct:title "Data in HTML format for Benuma";
        foaf:primaryTopic
<http://opencorporates.com/id/companies/nl/37136346>.
            a <http://purl.org/dc/dcmitype/Text>,
        foaf:Document;
        dct:format "application/json";
        dct:isFormatOf <http://opencorporates.com/companies/
nl/37136346?id=5828504>;
        dct:title "Data in JSON format for Benuma";
        foaf:primaryTopic
<http://opencorporates.com/id/companies/nl/37136346>.
<http://opencorporates.com/companies/nl/37136346.
rdf?id=5828504>
            a <http://purl.org/dc/dcmitype/Text>,
        foaf:Document;
        dct:format "application/rdf+xml";
        dct:isFormatOf
<http://opencorporates.com/companies/nl/37136346?id=5828504>;
        dct:title "Linked Data in RDF format for Benuma";
        foaf:primaryTopic
<http://opencorporates.com/id/companies/nl/37136346>.
<http://opencorporates.com/companies/nl/37136346.
xml?id=5828504>
            a <http://purl.org/dc/dcmitype/Text>,
        foaf:Document;
        dct:format "application/xml";
        dct:isFormatOf
<http://opencorporates.com/companies/nl/37136346?id=5828504>;
        dct:title "Data in XML format for Benuma";
        foaf:primaryTopic <http://opencorporates.com/id/compa-
nies/nl/37136346>.
```

continued on following page

Box 9. Continued

```
<http://opencorporates.com/companies/nl/37136346?id=5828504>
a <http://purl.org/dc/dcmitype/Text>,
        foaf:Document;
        dct:created "2011-01-13 12:35:27 UTC"^^xsd:dateTime;
        dct:hasFormat <http://opencorporates.com/companies/
nl/37136346.html?id=5828504>,
<http://opencorporates.com/companies/nl/37136346.
json?id=5828504>,
<http://opencorporates.com/companies/nl/37136346.
rdf?id=5828504>,
<http://opencorporates.com/companies/nl/37136346.
xml?id=5828504>;
        dct:modified "2011-01-13 12:35:27 UTC"^^xsd:dateTime;
        dct:title "Information about Benuma";
        foaf:primaryTopic <http://opencorporates.com/id/compa-
nies/nl/37136346>.
<http://opencorporates.com/id/companies/nl/37136346>
            a <http://s.opencalais.com/1/type/er/Company>;
        :label "Benuma".
```

The first example shows the process to enhance the search service (See Figure 2) from a simple query according to the profile of an organization and the CPV codes of the public procurement notices. In the second example, the query is extended to get results more relevant for this organization in the target sector. Finally, a system with features of georeasoning and fuzzy logic on public procurement notices is presented to get a more accurate query according to the information available about the public procurement notices, the previous history (statistics of the participation in public procurement processes) and the preferences of the organization. The URI prefixes of this example come from the "Prefix.cc", a service to look up prefixes for RDF developers. Also, *muo* (Measurement Units Ontology by Fundación CTIC) and *ppn** (namespace for public procurement notices and associated datasets) prefixes are also added to do a more human-readable example.

Let be *E* an organization that wants to tender in a public procurement process, the representation using N3, this information is provided by the process of *RDFizing* according to the information extracted out of the public procurement notices and other sources, is in Box 10 and Table 1.

The process to provide an enhanced service of searching notices is the next one: (1) the system builds directly a query, See Table 1, according to the profile (intentions that are turned to filters in the query) of an organization (CPV Codes, location,

Box 10. Information about an organization in N3

```
<http://mydutchcompany.com/> a v:VCard ;
     v:fn "Dutch Company Inc." ;
     v:org [   v:organisation-name "Dutch Company Inc." ;
             v:organisation-unit "Corporate Division" ] ;
     v:adr [ rdf:type v:Work ;
             v:country-name "Netherlands" ;
             v:locality "Amsterdam" ;
             v:postal-code "1016 XJ" ;
             v:street-address "Lijnbaansgracht 215" ] ;
     v:geo [ v:latitude "52.36764" ;
             v:longitude "4.87934" ] ;
     v:tel [ rdf:type v:Fax, v:Work ;
             rdf:value " +31 (10) 400 48 00"] ;
     v:email <mailto:company@mydutchcompany> ;
     v:logo <http://mydutchcompany.com/logo.png>.
ppn-def:euro a muo:UnitOfMeasurement;
     muo:measuresQuality <http://purl.org/weso/physicalQuality/
Money>.
     muo:altSymbol "€" ;
     muo:prefSymbol "€".
ppn-def:budget  a muo:QualityValue;
     muo:numericalValue "170.000";
     muo:inTime "2011-01-12" ;
     muo:measuredIn ppn-def:euro,
ppn-def:year a muo:UnitOfMeasurement;
     muo:measuresQuality <http://purl.org/weso/physicalQuality/
Time>.
     muo:altSymbol "year" ;
     muo:prefSymbol "year".
ppn-def:duration a muo:QualityValue;
     muo:numericalValue "2";
     muo:inTime "2011-01-12" ;
     muo:measuredIn ppn-def:year.
ppn-orgs-def:dutchOrganization a org:FormalOrganization;
     org:purpose cpv2008-res:45221111 ;
     org:purpose cpv2008-res:45221113 ;
     org:purpose  ppn-def:budget ;
     org:purpose  ppn-def:duration;
```

continued on following page

123

Box 10. Conrinued

```
org:purpose <http://sws.geonames.org/50.85_43.49/> ;
skos:prefLabel "Dutch organization" ;
org:classification ppn-orgs-def:SME;
org:hasSite <http://mydutchcompany.com/> ;
org:siteAddress <http://mydutchcompany.com/> ;
```

Table 1. List of public procurement notices. Let N be a set of public procurement notices with the next features (all of them are Active).

ID (dct:identifier)	Description (CPV 2008 code)	Budget (€)	Located in (lat/ lon) NUTS-id (level)	Duration (years)	Type of company
PPN-1	cpv2008-res:45221111 Road bridge construction work	160,000	lat "50.85" lon "43.49" NUTS-NL326 (3) 13860 Groot-Amsterdam	2	SME
PPN-2	cpv2008-res:45221113 Footbridge construction work	180,000	NUTS-BE2 (3) 290 VLAAMS GEWEST	3	SME
PPN-3	cpv2008-res:45221110 Bridge construction work	100,000	lat "50.85" lon "43.49"	2	SME
PPN-4	cpv2008-res:45221111	80,000	NUTS-BE2	2	SME
PPN-5	cpv2008-res:45221100 Construction work for bridges	190,000	NUTS-B3 (3) 300 RÉGION WALLONNE	4	SME
PPN-6	cpv2008-res:452211137	300,000	lat "50.85" lon "43.49"	3	SME
PPN-7	cpv2008-res:45221000 Construction work for bridges and tunnels, shafts and subways	200,000	NUTS-1025 (2) NL NEDERLAND	3	SME
PPN-8	cpv2008-res:45221113	150,000	lat "50.85" lon "43.49"	2	SME
PPN-9	cpv2008-res:45221111	100,000	NUTS-BE2	2	Large Company
PPN-10	cpv2008-res:45221114 Construction work for iron bridges	200,000	NUTS-275 (2) BE BELGIQUE-BELGIË	2	SME

amount and duration) to be executed via the SPARQL endpoint, and 2) the query returns a result set with the public procurement notices matching the purposes of the client (organization, etc.)

The results of this request (See Box 11), are similar to a search process based on a classical relational database query (e.g., using SQL) and it does not suppose neither advance in the state of the art nor an enhanced service for searching. It only matches the profile of the company with the characteristics of the public procurement notices, if there is an exact match then the public procurement notice is selected in the result set.

In the second example, the system builds a SPARQL query but previously the Spreading Activation techniques are performed on CPV with the purpose codes as input parameters and a value for each relation in the CPV (*skos:broader, skos:narrower,*

Box 11. Basic SPARQL query

```
SELECT ?id ?description ?budget ?duration WHERE{
  ?notice rdf:type ppn-def:PublicProcurementNotice.
  ?notice dct:identifier ?id.
  ?notice dct:description ?description.
  ?notice hasStatus ppn:Active.
  ?notice org:classification ppn-def:SME.
  ?notice wgs84_pos:lat ?lat.
  ?notice wgs84_pos:lon ?long.
  ?notice ppn:budget ?budget.
  ?amount muo:measuredIn ppn-def:euro.
  ?notice ppn:duration ?duration.
  ?duration muo:measuredIn ppn-def:year.
 FILTER (
((?notice ref-cpv-code cpv2008-res:45221111)
   OR (?notice ref-cpv-code cpv2008-res::45221113))
 and (?lat == "50.85") and (?long == "43.49")
 and (?budget <= 170,000^xsd:double) and (?duration <= 2))}
```

Table 2. Result set of the first SPARQL query

ID (dct:identifier)	Description (CPV 2008 code)	Budget (€)	Duration (years)
PPN-1	cpv2008-res:45221111	160,000	2
PPN-8	cpv:45221113-7	150,000	2

etc.) to get a list of most representative concepts according to the input ones (Table 2). This new query uses this rank list of concepts (CPV codes) to build an extended SPARQL query that finally is executed via the endpoint.

Currently, the SPARQL language does not allow specifying that a triple match has more relevance to sort the results than other triple match as existing syntactic search engines do like Apache Lucene (boosting terms). This situation implies that a query for each CPV code must be performed (Table 3). Finally, a merge process must gather the results and sort them according to the relevance of the specific CPV code. That is why a query is built for each CPV code.

The results of this request (Box 12) are different from the first ones (a new public procurement notice is added) because the search has been spread using new CPV codes not presented in the input parameters but representative to the preferences of the organization.

Finally, the third improvement consists in the application of georeasoning (like the *findNearby* service of GeoNames) and fuzzy logic techniques (e.g., aggregation operators) to evaluate the history (statistics) of the company in its previous participations in public procurement processes to establish an extended margin on the total value and duration of the contract announced in the public procurement notices. These two processes generates the specific values to build an extended semantic query in SPARQL (Table 4) keeping the use of the Spreading Activation to

Table 3. Ranking of concepts after Spreading Activation

CPV Code	Product Description	Activation Value (normalized)
cpv:45221110-6	Bridge construction work	0,95
cpv:45221113-7	Footbridge construction work	0,65
cpv:45221111-3	Road bridge construction work	0,65
...	...	...
cpv:45221114-4	Construction work for iron bridges	0,25

Box 12. One of the enhanced SPARQL queries

```
SELECT ?id ?description ?amount ?duration WHERE{
    ...
    ?notice ref-cpv-code cpv2008-res:45221110.
 FILTER ((?lat == "50.85") and (?long == "43.49")
            and (?budget <= 170,000^xsd:double) and (?duration
<= 2))}
```

Table 4. Result set of the second SPARQL query

ID (dct:identifier)	Description (CPV 2008 code)	Budget (€)	Duration (years)
PPN-3	cpv:45221110-6	100,000	2

previously create a ranking of most representative concepts. The formal mathematical models of these functions are out of the scope of this paper and they will be reported to the appropriate logical/mathematical venue.

The final results of this request (Box 13), taking into account the aforementioned situation with SPARQL queries, are the next ones in Table 5 (results from first and second queries are skipped).

The public procurement notices PPN-5, PPN-6, PPN-9 and PPN-10 are never retrieved due to: (1) and (2) the duration and the total value of the public contract are out of the permitted limit, (3) the public contract requires a large company and (4) the geographical scope of PPN-10 is Belgium and it cannot be ensured that this public procurement notice matches with the geographical area desired by the company.

Box 13. One of the enhanced SPARQL queries with georeasoning and fuzzy logic

```
SELECT ?id ?description ?amount ?duration WHERE{
    ...
    ?notice nuts:containedBy ?place.
    ?notice ref-cpv-code cpv2008-res:45221113-7.
FILTER ((((?place nuts:containedBy nuts:NUTS-NL326) or
            (?place nuts:containedBy nuts:NUTS-1025) or
            (?place nuts:containedBy nuts:NUTS-B3) or
            (?place nuts:containedBy nuts:NUTS-BE2) or
        ) and (?duration <= 3) and (?budget <=
200,000^xsd:double))}
```

Table 5. Result set of the third SPARQL query

ID (dct:identifier)	Description (CPV 2008 code)	Budget (€)	Duration (years)
PPN-2	cpv:45221113-7	180,000	3
PPN-4	cpv:45221111-3	80,000	2
PPN-7	cpv:45221000-2	200,000	3

CONCLUSION AND FUTURE WORK

According to the EC, e-procurement may, by its nature, be more compatible or facilitate the use of procurement budgets in support of EU 2020 objectives. Some countries have adopted the recommendations of the EU introducing strategies to encourage SMEs participation in the procurement processes but the intended participation of the SMEs is still far from the EU expectations. The MOLDEAS platform tries to enable the access to the public procurement notices using LOD and semantic methods. Following the advantages of this approach are presented: decreasing of the information's dispersion, unification of the data models and formats, implicit support to multilingual and multicultural issues, enrichment of the public procurement notices, alignment with the Digital Agenda for Europe, raising awareness on public procurement opportunities among SMEs and deployment of innovative and enhanced services (such as matchmaking) on public procurement notices based on standards.

On the other hand, the information about organizations is considered to be a key factor for the transparency and the improvement of corporate image of companies. In that sense, public administrations are very interested in the publication of their data following the Linked Data approach and the *Organizations Ontology* (it was original motivated by a need to publish information relating to government organizational structure as part of the *data.gov.uk* initiative) is a first step to reach this broad objective. That is why a specification to model organizations can change the current approach to discover, track and search organizations in a specific domain. For instance in the e-Procurement sector an organization can be followed making possible the extraction of statistics about their public contracts (type, region, etc.).

Finally, the availability of government data enables greater transparency; delivers more efficient public services; and encourages stronger public and commercial use and re-use of government information. Moreover, the Open Data Strategy (European Commission, 2011a) for Europe, led by Vice President *Neelie Kroes* and presented in December 2011 outlines three types of measures that will help to unleash potential of data held by governments in Europe. The strategy is strongly focused on the commercial value of the re-use of public sector information, by which the Commission expects to deliver a €40 billion boost to the EU's economy each year.

REFERENCES

Alexander, K., Cyganiak, R., Hausenblas, M., & Zhao, J. (2011). *Describing linked datasets with the VoID vocabulary*. W3C Interest Group Note. Retrieved from http://www.w3.org/TR/void/

Álvarez-Rodríguez, J. M. (2012). *Methods on linked data for e-procurement applying semantics*. (PhD Dissertation,) University of Oviedo, Oviedo, Spain.

Álvarez-Rodríguez, J. M., Labra, J. E., Calmeau, R., Marín, A., & Marín, J. L. (2011). Innovative services to ease the access to the public procurement notices using linking open data and advanced methods based on semantics. In *Proceedings of the 5th International Conference on Methodologies and Tools Enabling e-Government*. Camerino, Italy: MeTTeG.

Álvarez-Rodríguez, J. M., Polo, L., Abella, P., Jimenez, W., & Labra, J. E. (2011). Application of the spreading activation technique for recommending concepts of well-known ontologies in medical systems. *In Proceedings of First International Workshop on Semantic Applied Technologies on Biomedical Informatics*. Chicago, IL: ACM-BCB

Berners-Lee, T. (2006). *Linked data*. Retrieved from http://www.w3.org/DesignIssues/LinkedData.html

Berrueta, D., Labra, J. E., & Polo, L. (2006). *Searching over public administration legal documents using ontologies*. Paper presented at Conference on Knowledge-Based Software Engineering. Tallinn, Estonia.

Collins, A. M., & Loftus, E. F. (1975). A spreading activation theory of semantic processing. *Psychological Review, 82*(6), 407–428. doi:10.1037/0033-295X.82.6.407.

Euroalert.net. (2012). Retrieved from http://euroalert.net/

European Commission. (2010a). *Consultation on the green paper on expanding the use of e-procurement in the EU*. Retrieved from http://ec.europa.eu/internal_market/consultations/docs/2010/e-procurement/green-paper_en.pdf

European Commission. (2010b). *Public procurement indicators 2009*. Retrieved from http://ec.europa.eu/internal_market/publicprocurement/docs/indicators2010_en.pdf

European Commission. (2011a). *Modernising European public procurement to support growth and employment*. Press Release. Brussels, Belgium: European Commission. Retrieved from http://europa.eu/rapid/pressReleasesAction.do?reference=IP/11/1580

European Commission. (2011b). *Digital agenda*: *Turning government data into gold*. Press Release. Brussels, Belgium: European Commission. Retrieved from http://europa.eu/rapid/pressReleasesAction.do?reference=IP/11/1524

EXIS-TI. (2012). Retrieved from http://www.exis-ti.com/

Fox, M. S., Barbuceanu, M., & Gruninger, M. (1995). An organisation ontology for enterprise modelling: Preliminary concepts for linking structure and behaviour. In *Proceedings of the 4th Workshop on Enabling Technologies: Infrastructure for Collaborative Enterprises* (p. 71). Washington, DC: IEEE.

Gao, Q., Yan, J., & Liu, M. (2008). A Semantic approach to recommendation system based on user ontology and spreading activation model. In *Proceedingsof the 2008 IFIP* (pp. 488–492). Washington, DC: IEEE. doi:10.1109/NPC.2008.74.

Gateway Strategic Consultancy Services, S.L. (2012). Retrieved from http://gateway-scs.es/en/

Gelgi, F., Vadrevu, S., & Davulcu, H. (2005). Improving web data annotations with spreading activation. In WISE.

Gouws, S., Van Rooyen, G.-J., & Engelbrecht, H. E. (2010). Measuring conceptual similarity by spreading activation over Wikipedia's hyperlink structure. In *Proceedings of the 2nd Workshop on The People's Web Meets NLP: Collaboratively Constructed Semantic Resources* (pp. 46–54). Beijing, China: IEEE.

Grabisch, M., Marichal, J. L., Mesiar, R., & Pap, E. (2009). *Aggregation functions*. New York: Elsevier. doi:10.1017/CBO9781139644150.

Heath, T., & Bizer, C. (2011). *Linked data: Evolving the web into a global data space*. San Rafael, CA: Morgan & Claypool. doi:10.2200/S00334ED1V01Y-201102WBE001.

Hogan, A., Harth, A., Umbrich, J., Kinsella, S., Polleres, A., & Decker, S. (2011). Searching and browsing linked data with SWSE: The semantic web search engine. *Journal of Web Semantics*. doi:10.1016/j.websem.2011.06.004 PMID:21918645.

Joinup and European Commission. (2012). *Share and reuse open source software, semantic assets and other interoperability solutions for public administrations*. Retrieved on http://joinup.ec.europa.eu/

Labra, J. E., Ordoñez-de Pablos, P., & Cueva, J. M. (2007). Combining collaborative tagging and ontologies in image retrieval systems. In *Proceedings of 2nd International Conference on Metadata and Greece Semantic Web Research*. Corfu Island, Greece: Electronic Library.

LOD2 Project. (2012). *Creating knowledge out of interlinked data*. Retrieved from http://lod2.eu/

LOTED Project. (2012). *Linked open tenders electronic daily*. Retrieved from http://loted.eu:8081/LOTED1Rep/

Nie, J.-Y. (2003). Query expansion and query translation as logical inference. *Journal of the American Society for Information Science and Technology, 54*(4), 335–346. doi:10.1002/asi.10214.

Preece, S. E. (1981). *A spreading activation network model for information retrieval.* (PhD Dissertation). University of Illinois, Urbana, IL.

Qiu, Y., & Frei, H. P. (1993). Concept-based query expansion. In *Proceedings of the 16th Annual Internation ACM-SIGIR Conference on Research and Development in Information Retrieval* (pp. 160-169). Pittsburgh, PA: ACM.

Reynolds, D. (2010). *An organization ontology.* Epimorphics Ltd. Retrieved from http://www.epimorphics.com/web/category/category/developers/organization-ontology

Reynolds, D. (2012). *An organization ontology.* W3C. Retrieved from http://www.w3.org/TR/vocab-org/

Rocha, C., Schwabe, D., et al. (2004). A hybrid approach for searching in the semantic Web. In *Proceedings of the 13th International Conference on World Wide Web* (pp. 374–383). New York: ACM.

Schumacher, K., Sintek, M., & Sauermann, L. (2008). Combining metadata and document search with spreading activation for Semantic desktop search. In S. Bechhofer, M. Hauswirth, J. Hoffmann, & M. Koubarakis (Eds.), *Proceedings of 5th European Semantic Web Conference* (pp. 569–583). Berlin, Germany: Springer.

Taggart, C., & McKinnon, R. (2010). *The open database of the corporate world.* Retrieved on http://opencorporates.com/

Torra, V., & Narukawa, Y. (2007). *Modeling decisions. Information Fusion and Aggregation Operators.* Berlin, Germany: Springer.

Weber, M. (1987). *Economy and society.* Berkeley, CA: University of California Press.

WESO (Oviedo Semantic Web). (2012). Retrieved from http://www.weso.es/

ENDNOTES

[1]   http://rdf.ecs.soton.ac.uk/ontology/ecs
[2]   http://vocab.org/aiiso/schema
[3]   http://structureddynamics.com/linked_data.html

Chapter 7
A Semantic Framework for Touristic Information Systems

Salvador Lima
Instituto Politécnico de Viana do Castelo, Portugal

José Moreira
Universidade de Aveiro, Portugal

EXECUTIVE SUMMARY

The Web is a crucial means for the dissemination of touristic information. However, most touristic information resources are stored directly in Web pages or in relational databases that are accessible through ad-hoc Web applications, and the use of automated processes to search, extract and interpret information can hardly be implemented. The Semantic Web technologies, aiming at representing the background knowledge about Web resources in a computational way, can be an important contribution to the development of such automated processes. This chapter introduces the concept of touristic object, giving special attention to the representation of temporal, spatial, and thematic knowledge. It also proposes a three-layered architecture for the representation of touristic objects in the Web. The central part is the domain layer, defining a Semantic Model for Tourism (SeMoT) to describe concepts, relationships, and constraints using ontologies. The data layer supports the mapping of touristic information in relational databases into Resource Description Framework (RDF) virtual graphs following the SeMoT specification. The application layer deals with the integration of information from different data sources into a unified knowledge model, offering a common vocabulary to describe touristic information resources. Finally, we also show how to use this framework for planning touristic itineraries.

DOI: 10.4018/978-1-4666-2827-4.ch007

1. INTRODUCTION

The touristic communities, the suppliers of touristic information, and other groups of interest, namely the consumers of touristic information, rely on the Web for exchanging ideas, information and knowledge. In this sense, the touristic information resources made available by these communities have increased exponentially. These resources about recommended or advertised touristic objects, are mostly specified in a syntactic manner, complying with the grammatical rules of the language in use and guided towards the structuring of the content. Thus, the current structure of the Web, which discloses touristic phenomenon using mainly syntactic and structured, semi-structured and non-structured resources, is short on the schematisation of data and is not able to ensure effective and comprehensible information retrieval, transfer, search and automated processing. Hence, the role of the Semantic Web emerges to contribute to the organisation of knowledge through significance (or meaning), purpose and context of use. In other words, the Semantic Web can establish a bridge or a mapping of meanings, through specific (thematic) areas of speech associated with the touristic phenomenon. These meanings enable computational agents to filter, aggregate and transform knowledge autonomously.

This chapter highlights the role of the integration of information for each (sub) domain involved in the touristic phenomenon, and puts in evidence the importance of the availability of semantically enriched information to the agents involved in the touristic phenomenon, in particular, to the touristic web-users (tourists). These users look for singularities and recreational aspects on available and recommended touristic objects, according to their preferential, motivational and restrictive patterns. The quality of the data retrieved to answer user queries depends on the schematisation of the data sources (particularly, relational databases schemas), as well as on the methods of integration or mapping to be used to resolve the heterogeneity of the touristic data at different levels: the syntactic level, the schematic level and the semantic level. The challenge is to integrate touristic information from different data sources at the schematic level (here we try to use unified data representation schemas to map different concepts from several areas of knowledge) and the semantic level (with the additional use of vocabularies (ontologies) in the integration of data).

This chapter is organised as follows. Section 2 presents an overview on the main semantic information systems proposed for the touristic domain. Section 3 introduces the concept of touristic object and presents a semantic model for tourism based on three main dimensions: thematic, spatial and temporal. Section 4 presents an ontological architecture to handle the semantic interoperability among distinct data sets. Section 5 deals with the mapping of relational data sources into RDF data models and the integration of RDF data models. Section 6 gives some examples that use the concepts proposed in this chapter in the planning of touristic itineraries. Finally, Section 7 puts in evidence the main contributions of this work and proposes some guidelines for future research.

2. SEMANTIC SYSTEMS FOR THE TOURISTIC DOMAIN

The complexity of the touristic phenomenon makes the "processing" of knowledge more difficult and complex on traditional or non-semantic systems, rather than on semantic systems, as the latter are able to deal with heterogeneous associations of explicit knowledge and the inference of implicit knowledge. The success of the semantic systems is closely related with the use of ontologies. In addition, ontologies can also be used to improve the interoperability of touristic content's stored in relational and non-relational databases. Such ontologies are consensual vocabularies that unify the universe of concepts represented in the touristic domain and consist in the sets of abstract concepts that unify distinct modes of representing similar touristic concepts.

The *OpenTravel Alliance* (OpenTravel Alliance (OTA) 2001; OTA 2007) is a non-profit organisation composed by airlines companies, hotel chains, car rental companies, sea and railway trips promoters, global distribution systems, software service providers for the touristic industry and consultants. This organisation draws up specifications (common terminology vocabulary for the "tourism industries," represented in the *eXtensible Markup Language* (XML) format) since 2001, to promote the efficiency, performance and competitiveness of the global sales of touristic products and services, through communication channels where a wide range of transactional, informative and descriptive content is available in the XML format. These specifications are called OTA Specifications, which encourage the development of systems for the "tourism industries."

In 2001, the European Commission, promoted and financed the *Harmonise* project (Dell'Erba, Fodor, Ricci, & Werthner 2002) through the *Information Society Technologies Program* (IST Program), in order to create a "harmonisation space" to support interoperability using reconciliation semantics (mediator-standard) for unconnected information systems and technologically heterogeneous environments, where different proprietary data formats and ontological schemes may coexist. The ontological schemes proposed by this project, describe subdomains related with the context of travelling, geographical locations, touristic activities, means of transportation, political and touristic institutions and temporal references.

There are also other proposals for tourism that stimulate the interaction between the potential tourists and travel agents, where the potential tourists look for suggestions or destination packages for their vacations. In other words, travel agencies offer recommendations tailored to the preferences and to the behaviour of each individual customer (tourist) or collective customer (tourist groups). Such proposals aim at guiding the web-users through a chain of stages in the decision making process without any type of human intervention. The entire knowledge of the travel agents is coded in a database and will be used to help web-users throughout the decision making chain: (1) *Intelligent Travel Recommender* (Ricci, Arslan, Mirzadeh, & Venturini, 2002), as a system of touristic recommendation, developed at the *eCommerce and Tourism Research Laboratory* (eCTRL) of the *Istituto Trentino di Cultura - Istituto per la Ricerca Scientifica e Tecnológica* (ITC - irst), (2) *VacationCoach* (Vacation-Coach Inc., 2002), and (3) *TripleHop Technologies* (Delgado & Davidson, 2002).

The *GraniteNights* project developed at the Department of Computing Science of the University of Aberdeen, proposes a multi-agent application, based on the Semantic Web standards and on the *Foundation for Intelligent Physical Agents* (FIPA) specifications, which creates specific after-hours entertainment plans for the Scottish city of Aberdeen according to the preferences of the web-users (Grimnes, Chalmers, Edwards, & Preece, 2003).

Agentcities is an international initiative aiming at highlighting the commercial value of research on applications based on agents, and consists in an open and distributed network of interconnected platforms accessible through the Internet, where each platform appends one or more agents with the capacity to interact with external environments (agents and services), using standard communication mechanisms (interaction protocols, agent languages, ontologies, communication protocols, among other mechanisms) based on FIPA specifications (Zou, Finin, Ding, Chen, & Pan, 2003). One of the achievements of this alliance - *Agentcities* infrastructure and FIPA technology--is the *Travel Agent Game in Agentcities* (TAGA), which is an agent-framework for simulating the global travel market on the Web. For instance, a Portuguese customer may want to search for a recreational visit to the *Radisson Plaza Resort* in Tahiti, and also needs an airplane round trip ticket and the respective accommodation at the hotel. The TAGA simulations use ontologies covering basic and superficial travel concepts, such as the customers, travel services, booking of services, auctions, among others.

Mondeca's Intelligent Topic Manager (Mondeca's ITM) (Le Grand, 2005) is a technological solution based on standards set by the *World Wide Web Consortium* (W3C), which allows to represent and manage ontologies, to classify and record content, taxonomies and thesaurus, and to manage knowledge databases. The French company Mondeca has used this technological solution to create a cross-language portal of touristic resources, touristic packages and multimedia contents for a French region. The indexing, association and description of these resources, packages and contents are maintained and managed by a travel ontology specified with concepts or terms based on *World Tourism Organization's thesaurus* (WTO's thesaurus), and covers some subdomains, such as accommodation, transportation and cultural events.

The *DARPA Agent Markup Language Repository* (The DARPA Agent Markup Language (DAML), 2003; DAML 2004) contains "minimalist" and non-W3C ontologies for the touristic domain and for the travel domain. One of them is a very simple ontology used to represent touristic itineraries that reuses other ontologies to represent terms such as *Airfare, Aircraft, Date, Amount, Flight*.

Some of the proposals presented prior (*Harmonise, GraniteNights* and *Mondeca's Intelligent Topic Manager*) use the Semantic Web as a technological platform according to the standards set by the W3C, while the remaining proposals either do not follow the current W3C standards (*DARPA Agent Markup Language Repository*), employ hybrid paradigms (*Intelligent Travel Recommender, VacationCoach, TripleHop Technologies* and *Travel Agent Game in Agentcities*) or adopt the XML format for the touristic vocabulary (*OpenTravel Alliance*). In the following, we present a thematic, temporal and spatial formulation for touristic objects, allowing the application of automated mechanisms for inferential knowledge, focused on the integration of touristic information resources and on the planning of customised touristic itineraries.

3. SEMANTIC MODEL FOR THE TOURISTIC DOMAIN

Conceptualisation of the Touristic Object

Ethno-religious articles, restaurants, beaches or gastronomy are objects not constructed naturally, but socially (Bourdieu, Chamboredon, & Passeron, 1991) and scientifically (Bachelard, 2006) created for tourism, since they embed their touristic value (thematic or business component), the location (geographical component) and, where appropriate, the restriction of availability (temporal component).

So, the touristic objects combine and contextualise their speech on three domains: (1) the thematic domain, where both the intrinsic and extrinsic values of the touristic attractions and other descriptors associated with these attractions are extracted; (2) the temporal domain, which reveals the temporal scale of the touristic attractions, for instance, their opening hours; and (3) the spatial domain, referring to the location and the typology of the touristic attraction's location. Consequently, our conceptualisation of touristic objects adopts three out of the five semantic dimensions proposed by Truong, Abowd and Brotherton (2001): (1) *what*, which touristic objects comply with the preferential spectrum of the tourists or which objects may be an alternative when the first choices are not available; (2) *when*, the touristic objects may be "consumed" according to previously defined schedules; and (3) *where*, the touristic objects, being immovable, have their geographical location and typologies well-defined, allowing the tourists to move into their direction. The remaining semantic dimensions–*who* and *how*–being relevant, were not the object of study in this work.

In the context of the Semantic Web, the search and retrieval of touristic objects matching the motivational and preferential criteria, the temporal and the spatial restrictions of the touristic web-users, will enable the creation of customisable touristic itineraries. We can say that a touristic object comprises a syntactic and semantic object, enriched with a certain pragmatic intention, that the tourism promoters (agents related with economy, politics, culture, etc.) create multiple statements regulated by conventions (web-pages or portals), and that their intelligent agents decode or interpret, using appropriate hermeneutical codes or strategies.

Semantic Model for Tourism

We have developed an ontological framework based on the three semantic domains referred previously, which we called *Semantic Model for Tourism* (SeMoT) (Figure 1). It consists in a semantic model for the touristic domain, which describes concepts, relations and restrictions of the touristic objects in their semantic dimensions, using ontologies as a mechanism for modelling, reuse and integration of knowledge.

Thus, the ontologies contextualised for tourism and which comprise the SeMoT ontological framework (Lima, & Moreira, 2009) are classified into three domains:

- **Temporal Domain:** The temporal measures have a decisive importance in the organisation and planning of recreational and leisure activities, in particular, the schedules of operation (opening hours, interruption or holiday period) for accommodation, catering, transportation services, etc., the schedules of events (start time of parades and ethnographic festivals), or the dates of liturgical and ethnographic events (certain popular festivities take place on fixed dates and some take place at mobile dates); the ontological model of the proposed time (time ontology), is based mainly on the work of Hobbs and Pan (2004), with new conceptual definitions planned for the touristic context, such as the Catholic liturgical calendar and the Portuguese ethnographic calendar;

- **Spatial Domain:** Towns, historical villages, museums and restaurants can be georeferenced in their positions (longitude and latitude) in relation to the land surface on one point; the beaches and the river courses for nautical sports may, in turn, be spatially represented by a line and the wildlife parks by an area. We have developed a spatial model (*space ontology*) based on the works

Figure 1 Semantic model for tourism (Lima & Moreira, 2009)

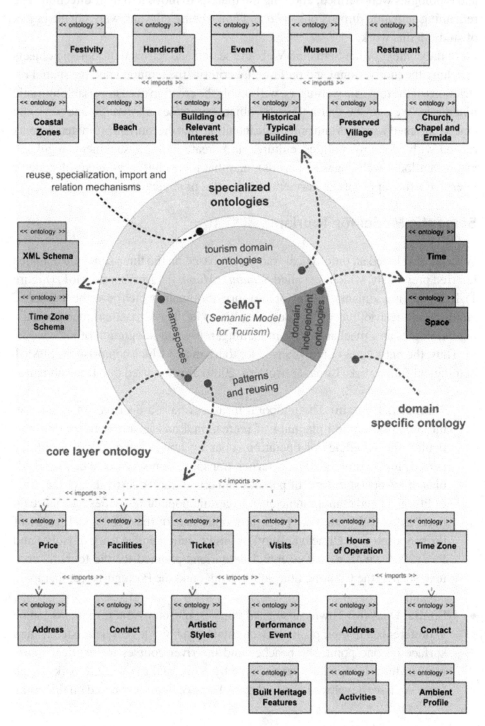

of Jones, Alani, and Tudhope (2001), and Perry, Sheth, and Arpinar (2006), and we have proposed new definitions for sub-types of locations, such as fluvial beaches, ocean beaches, figurative ceramics handicraft and festivities;

- **Thematic Domain:** The tourists' preferential network is very complex, for instance, some tourists are interested in popular festivities for an active social participation with the locals, others are interested in museums as multipliers of new knowledge on the country or region, or other tourists may choose gastronomy as the means of socialising with other people; to model tourism thematically, several ontologies proposals were developed: (1) *handicraft ontology*, which is an ontology based on the triangle *craft artefact, craftsman* and *craft production unit*; (2) *museum ontology*, to classify the museum objects in permanent or temporary thematic collections, as well as to specify the type of visits, the opening hours and the services; (*3*) *restaurant ontology*, reuses some restaurant related concepts, proposed on the ontology based on DAML (Semantic Web Search and Metadata Engine, 2004) and introduced new definitions, such as the classification of the restaurants, the recommendation, the need to make a reservation, the opening hours, including the staff's days of rest, etc.; (*4*) *festivity ontology*, to classify festivities as *cyclic festivities, civic festivities and laic popular festivities*, and their respective temporal restrictions (duration of celebrations, mobility of celebrations, etc.); and (*5*) *event ontology*, to classify events (*religious events, sportive events, leisure and recreation events, artistic and entertainment events*, etc.) and the plan for the events (*performance event*), which may include ethnographic groups and their respective artistic styles and schedules of performance.

Some of these ontologies rely on other vocabularies that we also have developed for the touristic domain, in particular: (1) *hours of operation ontology* (ontology about the hours of operation which includes the definition of the opening hour, the closing hour, the staff's days of rest, etc.); (2) *facilities ontology* (this is an ontology that classifies the types of facilities or resources, such as *disabled facilities, information facilities* and *interpretive facilities*); and (3) *ticket ontology* (ontology about the ticket for the events and entrances in museums and other points of interest).

This ontological framework (Figure 1) is supported by specifications standardised by the W3C for the syntactic, structural, semantic and logical representations of the concepts, as well as for the thematic, temporal and spatial restrictions usually applied in the touristic domain.

4. SOURCES FOR TOURISTIC DATA

The Web has a large amount of unconnected touristic data sources through pages on the surface Web (Bergman, 2001) or the indexable Web (Baeza-Yates, 2004), assembled in different databases on the deep Web (Bergman, 2001) or on the hidden Web (Baeza-Yates, 2004). With the new formalism of semantic reference (vocabularies, ontologies and inferential logic) there was an attempt to maximise and enable other scientifically and technologically proven formalisms. Hence, it is worthy to take advantage of the touristic information residing in databases to build ontologies to create new knowledge. Notice that the relational database schemas do not provide a formal semantics and are not reusable in similar contexts or in contexts designed by domain experts.

This work focuses on the mapping of relational database models into ontological models in the domain of tourism.

The ontologies that compose the core of SeMoT constitute a conceptual framework of semantic reference (ontological framework), so that it is possible to extend them with new semantic descriptions for specific domains in a given touristic context. This means that we can reuse concepts, relations and common properties, and also include additional semantics to create a new and more specific ontology with a smaller ontological spectral overlay, which encourages the free movement of different visions (perspectives) of the specific domain (context). This imposes a limited number of standardised ontologies for tourism.

However, this ability to extend specific ontologies from core and standard ontologies raises a new issue related with the implementation of semantic interoperability between different datasets. Thus, we propose a three layered ontological architecture: (1) application layer (application ontology); (2) domain layer (SeMoT and extended ontologies); and (3) data layer (data quasi-ontology).

We show that this ontological architecture proposal is suitable for the integration of datasets from different touristic contexts and that it allows obtaining an unified ontology (which contains or refers to ontological vocabularies of the considered domains and rules of inference) at the application layer (domain ontologies and data quasi-ontologies) for querying those distinct datasets as if they were a single one.

The first issue was finding a solution to attach an ontology (domain layer) into a database through a mechanism of mapping (Hu, & Qu, 2007). One of the mapping paradigms referenced in the scientific bibliography (Bizer & Seaborne, 2004; Laborda, & Conrad, 2005; Laborda, 2007), is the creation of virtual data repositories over the physical repository for storage of data in relational databases. In other words, the mapping mechanism will create an (total or partial) image of the relational database (non-RDF database) in a virtual RDF graph (Figure 2).

Figure 2. Mapping non-RDF database to virtual RDF

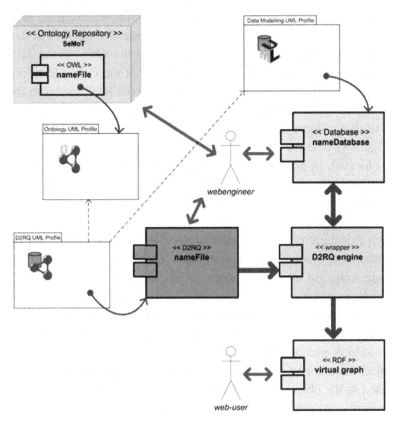

The main advantages of this solution are: (1) avoiding unnecessary replication of data, since the data in the database is accessed virtually through a RDF graph; (2) ensuring the interoperability of the database on the Web by adding semantic expressiveness into the relational schema, as it is converted into another schematic description semantically enriched as a primitive data ontology (data quasi-ontology layer); (3) allowing the *webware*[1] (Lima, 2003; Lima & Moreira, 2009) to query the database using the domain vocabulary (domain layer); (4) the Web engineers may focus on the details of the data mapping process rather than to the details of the data domain residing in the databases (construction or creation of the schematic description of the mapping process that we call quasi-ontology); and (5) the mapping between the databases' data models into ontological models, helps to solve syntactic differences (for example, we can have conflicts when the data types are heterogeneous), schematic or structural issues (for example, to access heterogeneous data sources), and semantic (synonymic, homonymic or even orthographic variation conflicts in the names (entities in the databases and concepts in the ontologies)).

This process aims at generating a virtual RDF graph for the data in the databases to carry out semantic queries: each table in the database is considered as an entity of interest (ontological class), the attributes of the table as properties of data types, and the foreign keys defining relationships between the tables in the database as properties of an object. It is important to mention that the virtual RDF repository does not contains any specification on how to map the RDF model to the corresponding objects in the database (tables, columns, and values).

To fulfil this task we have used the *Database to RDF Query* tool, or simply D2RQ (Figure 3), to carry out the RDF mapping of the relational databases where the data is located, by associating each subject to an *Uniform Resource Identifier* (URI) and developing mapping connections called *"property bridges"* (Bizer & Seaborne, 2004; Bizer & Cyganiak, 2007; Bizer, Cyganiak, Garbers, Maresch, & Becker, 2009).

D2RQ is a declarative language that allows the mapping of relational structures from databases into ontologies, using *Structured Query Language* (SQL) statements to define the mapping rules and it does not implies any modification to the relational databases schemas (Bizer, Cyganiak, Garbers, Maresch, & Becker, 2009). In other words, the content of a database is mapped into RDF through a parameterised mapping (non-automatic) that specifies how the content of a table shall be converted into subject-predicate-object triplets. The primary key of a table is identified as the subject of the triplet, the name of the column is the predicate and the column-value is used as the object of the triplet. Figure 4 shows an example of a mapping where the Festivities domain in intentionally simplified.

Notice that the two colours in the figure allow distinguishing a cluster (group) of darker elements around the element that identifies the database, comprising the "data layer" (quasi-ontology), and another cluster of lighter elements, on the top of the previous ones, which contributes to the "domain layer" (SeMoT ontologies and extended ontologies).

In any case, the mapping process of the touristic relational databases schemas into D2RQ schemas, allows establishing an infrastructure for querying heterogeneous touristic data residing on unconnected databases, using a single RDF dataset. On the other hand, the ontologies of the SeMoT model and the D2RQ schemas (D2RQ maps) provide a platform on which the *webware* applications from different areas of the touristic context can be developed or constructed.

Once the virtual RDF graph is finalized, we can query the RDF repository using SPARQL *Protocol and RDF Query Language* (SPARQL) semantic queries together with *Jena Rules* (Knublauch, 2006; Reynolds, 2010) or *Semantic Web Rule Language* (SWRL).

Figure 3. UML profiles

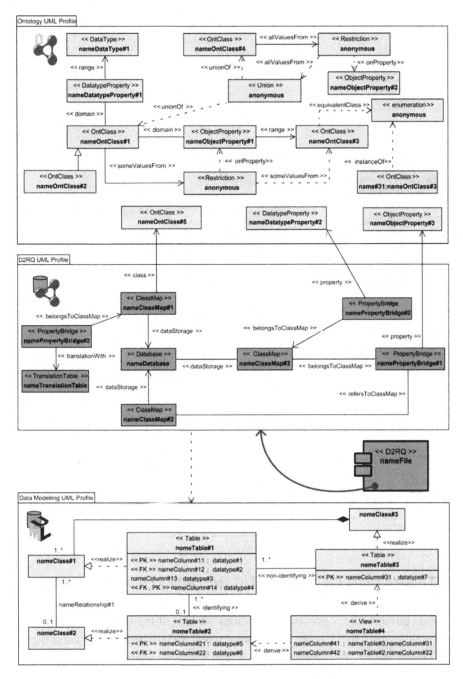

Figure 4. Festivities domain

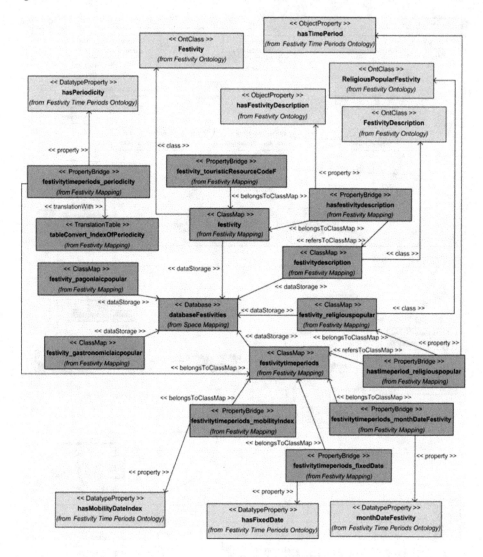

5. INTEGRATION OF TOURISTIC INFORMATION SOURCES

Up to this point we have presented solutions for two of the three layers of the proposed architecture: the domain layer (ontological SeMoT framework) and the data layer (D2RQ maps). The focus of this section is on the application layer.

We have used the D2RQ technology to perform the mapping of relational data sources into unique RDF data models (virtual RDF graphs). Now we must investigate "how to integrate the different virtual RDF graphs (individual datasets) into a single and common virtual RDF graph (single dataset)".

The solution that we propose is based on insertion rules (*Jena Rules* or SWRL) (Figure 5). This means that when the data from the external data sources is available as RDF graphs, we need to design the connections between the different models of knowledge using rules. Moreover, the unified virtual RDF model may also, when integrated with the data recorded by the ontologies, result in a richer and broader data model, which we can query with SPARQL queries.

In the previous section, we have seen that the D2RQ technology generates maps of relational databases (D2RQ maps) schemas, and that it allows to query transparently the instances obtained directly (explicitly) from those data quasi-ontologies or from instances obtained implicitly by inference. Yet, we propose the generation of parameterised D2RQ maps, in which the semantic enrichment is achieved by the "alignment" of the ontology concepts (domain layer) with the entities of the real world represented in the databases (data layer).

The touristic agents benefit from offering their touristic data in formats recognisable by computational agents. These touristic data will be even more valuable if they are easily accessible to the agents (human and computational), and if they can

Figure 5. Data integration

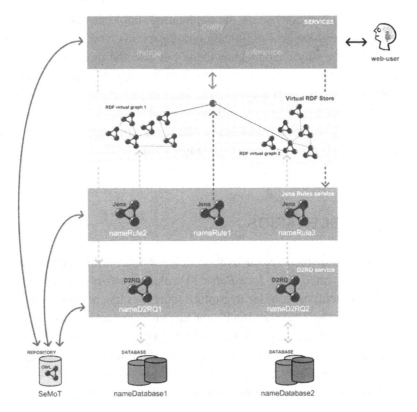

be reused when integrated with other data. So, the storage and retrieval of touristic information must be transparent regardless of the databases (data sources) where the information was obtained. But that transparency, as we have seen previously, implies the management of the differences in technological aspects (software and hardware) and informational aspects (representation of the information) between source databases. Notice that such differences do exist and arise from the craftsman abilities of the software engineers in designing and creating databases based on their own conceptual visions of the domains considered, as well as with their project's vision about such databases. Therefore, the mapping that translates a schema of a relational database with a low semantic level (or without semantics) into a semantically enriched schematic description, provides enriched schemas comprehensible both for human agents and for computational agents, and ensures the interoperability of the databases on the Web.

Figure 6 shows a transversal view of the ontological architecture in layers for a simplified scenario of a touristic itinerary that includes the spatial, temporal, and festivities domains.

The first level (data layer) defines the mapping of the databases data on concepts defined by the domain ontologies at the second level (domain layer). We have also called the first level, consisting in D2RQ maps, by quasi-ontologies. The third level (application layer) consists in the application ontologies obtained from the ontological integration process of domain ontologies involved in a given scenario, in order to infer not only explicit knowledge but also the desired "hidden" (implicit) knowledge. With this approach, the D2RQ wrapper is used to define the relationships between the data sources (relational databases) and the D2RQ maps, to obtain RDF virtual graphs which will be "merged" through bridging rules (Golbreich, 2004), into a single RDF dataset (without implying the physical creation of that dataset). The web-users will query the single virtual RDF graph using SPARQL semantic queries.

6. TOURISTIC SCENARIOS

We have developed distinct scenarios to validate the feasibility of our approach, which were implemented using *Jena Rules*: (1) rules to restrict a geographical area of interest for the tourists in order to capture touristic objects contained within a certain region; (2) rules to determine Easter Sunday (day and month associated to a given year or to the current year) (Reingold & Dershowitz, 2001); (3) rules that define the dates associated with the liturgical periods of the Catholic calendar; (4) bridging rules "for reasoning across distinct domains" (Golbreich, 2004); (5) rules determining any beginning of the week on any month; and others.

Figure 6. Ontological layers

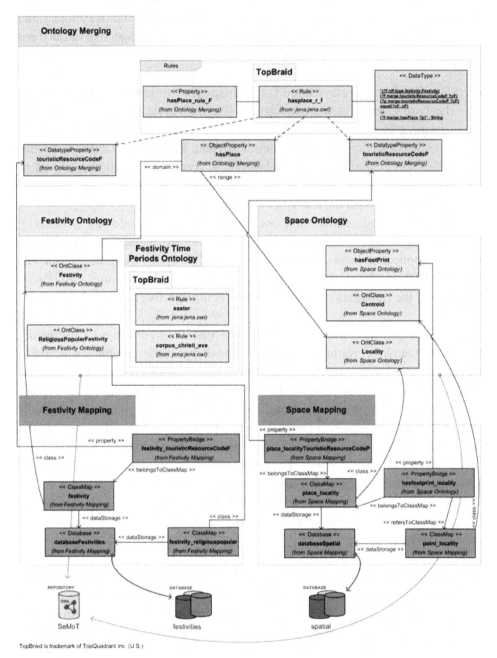

As an example we present the scenario in which a group of tourists wants to participate in a gastronomic itinerary between the third weekend of February and the second weekend of May. Figure 7 shows a transversal perspective of the three layers for the "Gastronomy" scenario, where:

- The data layer displays three D2RQ maps (one to transform the relational database schema "restaurant_Database" into a virtual RDF graph about restaurants ("Restaurant Mapping"), another to convert the relational database schema "festivity_Database" into a virtual RDF graph about festivities ("Festivity Mapping"), and the last one to convert the relational schema of the database "space_Database" into a virtual RDF graph about the location of the restaurants and the festivities ("Space Mapping")).
- The domain layer shows three ontologies, "Restaurant Ontology", "Festivity Ontology" and "Space Ontology", from the SeMoT ontological framework.
- The application layer displays the merging ("Ontology Merging") of the virtual RDF graphs using the "Has Place Rule" rule, which ensures the connection of the restaurants and festivities to their respective geographic location.

The Alto Minho (northwest region of Portugal) gastronomy ontology ("Gastronomy Alto Minho Ontology") promotes the associations between the restaurants adhering to the gastronomic festivities of Alto Minho through the "hasAdherent:GastronomyAlto Minho Ontology" relation between the individuals of the "GastronomicLaicPopular Festivity:GastronomyAltoMinhoOntology" class (domain-class), the individuals of the "Restaurant:Restaurant Ontology" class (*range-class*) (in this case, only the individuals-restaurants considered as adhering to the gastronomic weekends initiative in Alto Minho) and the tourist ontology ("Tourist Ontology") that defines the temporal criteria (the actual date and the weekend of the festivity).

The application layer allows entering SPARQL queries. The following query examples for building itineraries associated with gastronomy summarize some of the main features of this work:

1. Find a gastronomic festivity (*GastronomicLaicPopularFestivity class subclass Festivity class*) for the third weekend of February: (*1*) in certain places there are fixed dates for gastronomic events while on other places the gastronomic events occur occasionally; (*2*) the "Weekend Rule" determines the third Saturday (beginning of the third weekend) for the month of February in relation to the current date; (*3*) not all the restaurants consider their participation in gastronomic events as an added value for the promotion of their services, the gastronomic festivity will feature a range of adhering restaurants that will

Figure 7. Scenario "gastronomy"

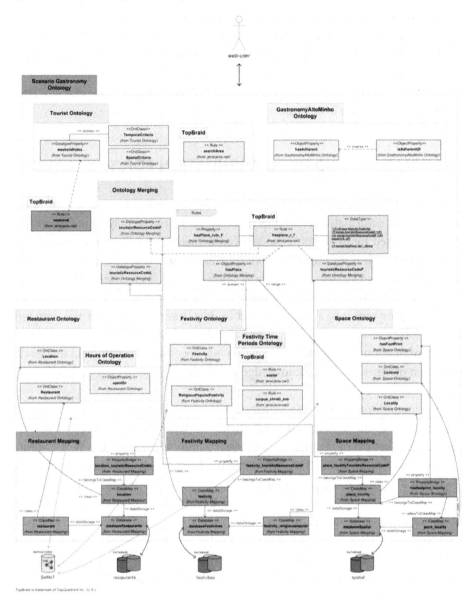

present their gastronomic dishes (*Festivity class* hasAdherent *Restaurant class*); and (*4*) the festivities are associated to a location (*Festivity class* hasPlace *Place class*) through the "Has Place Rule" rule.

2. Find a restaurant (*Restaurant class*) within a certain distance from a place of reference, opened on Fridays and with "kid meat" as gastronomic speciality: (*1*) the "Search Area Rule" restricts the search to a region within the distance from

a place of reference (place where we are at the time); (*2*) the restaurants have their operating hours (*Restaurant class* hasHoursOfOperation *OperatingHours class*), including the days of the week when they are open (*Friday* instanceOf *DayOfWeek class*); (*3*) not all the restaurants have "kid meat" as gastronomic speciality (*Restaurant class* hasSpecialities *MeatSpecialities class*); and (*4*) the restaurants have a location (*Restaurant class* hasPlace *Place class*) defined by the "Has Place Rule" rule.

7. CONCLUSION AND RECOMMENDATION FOR THE FUTURE

The Web is currently an essential tool for tourism agencies, tourists and travelers, but the touristic information resources made available by the players in this area are not well-prepared for efficient retrieval of information and sharing of knowledge. The Semantic Web is an important tool for the organization and dissemination of information and knowledge, and the application of semantic technologies in tourism information systems keeps on as an interesting field of research.

This chapter presents a three-layered architecture to deal with the semantic interoperability of touristic information. The data layer is designed to support the mapping of relational databases information into specialized ontological models for the domain of tourism. These knowledge models are implemented by RDF virtual graphs.

The domain layer defines the Semantic Model for Tourism (SeMoT) for the description of touristic objects in three dimensions (temporal, spatial and thematic). This is an ontological model that follows the recommendations of the W3C. SeMoT is designed for reutilization, integration and modular development of vocabularies. It provides a set of ontologies designed to cope with the requirements of a wide range of applications, which are modular and prepared to be extended, and semantic interoperability is guaranteed by two requirements: (1) specifications (they identify the mechanisms that describe the structure and the semantics of the touristic objects) and (2) interpretations (they identify the mechanisms that interprets the semantics assigned to the touristic objects). These requirements support the mechanisms of inference and the search and retrieval of touristic information.

Finally, the application layer deals with the transformation and migration of data issuing from different external data sources into a single repository of semantically enriched information. The integration of the RDF virtual models is performed by the implementation of rules that define the connections between the different knowledge models. The result is a unified knowledge model with the description of touristic resources using a known vocabulary.

Notice that D2RQ provides general rules for automatic mapping of relational database schemas (tables, attributes, constraints and relationships) into RDF virtual models. So, the additional connection rules introduced in our work are driven to the creation of specialized D2RQ maps for the touristic domain that can be reused for a large spectrum of touristic scenarios.

Even though, this approach has some issues requiring attention in future research, namely: (1) it does not have any automated support to the development of new connection rules meeting the requirements of expert scenarios and (2) when the database schema changes, the update of the D2RQ maps is a manual process, which may be difficult to control.

REFERENCES

Bachelard, G. (2006). *The formation of the scientific mind*. Lisboa: Dinalivro. (In Portuguese).

Baeza-Yates, R. (2004). Excavating the web. *El Profesional de la Información*, *13*(1), 4–10. doi:10.1076/epri.13.1.4.29026.

Bergman, M. (2001). The deep web: Surfacing hidden value. *Journal of Electronic Publishing*, *7*(1). doi:10.3998/3336451.0007.104.

Bizer, C., & Cyganiak, R. (2007). D2RQ – Lessons learned. *W3C Workshop on RDF Access to Relational Databases*. Retrieved May 2010, from http://www.w3.org/2007/03/RdfRDB/papers/d2rq-positionpaper/

Bizer, C., Cyganiak, R., Garbers, J., Maresch, O., & Becker, C. (2009). *The D2RQ Platform v0.7 – Treating non-RDF relational databases as virtual RDF graphs (user manual and language specification)*. Retrieved May 2010, from http://www4.wiwiss.fu-berlin.de/bizer/d2rq/spec/

Bizer, C., & Seaborne, A. (2004). *D2RQ - Treating non-RDF databases as virtual RDF graphs*. Poster presented at the 4th International Semantic Web Conference. Retrieved May 2010, from http://sites.wiwiss.fu-berlin.de/suhl/bizer/pub/Bizer-D2RQ-ISWC2004.pdf

Bourdieu, P., Chamboredon, J.-C., & Passeron, J.-C. (1991). *The craft of sociology: Epistemological preliminaries*. Berlin, Germany: Walter de Gruyter & Co. doi:10.1515/9783110856460.

Delgado, J., & Davidson, R. (2002). Knowledge bases and user profiling in travel and hospitality recommender systems. In K. Wöber, A. Frew, & M. Hitz (Eds.), *Proceedings of the 9th International Conference Information and Communications Technologies in Tourism* (pp. 1-16). Wien: Springer.

Dell'Erba, M., Fodor, O., Ricci, F., & Werthner, H. (2002). Harmonise: A solution for data interoperability. In J. Monteiro, P. Swatman, & L. Tavares (Eds.), *Proceedings of the 2nd IFIP Conference on E-Commerce, E-Business and E-Government* (pp. 433-445). Dordrecht: Kluwer.

Golbreich, C. (2004). Combining rule and ontology reasoners for the semantic web. In G. Antoniou & H. Boley (Eds.), *Proceedings of the Third International Workshop-* (LNCS), (Vol. 3323, pp. 6-22). Berlin, Germany: Springer.

Grimnes, G., Chalmers, S., Edwards, P., & Preece, A. (2003). GraniteNights - A multi-agent visit scheduler utilising semantic web technology. In M. Klusch, S. Ossowski, A. Omicini, & H. Laamanen (Eds.), *Proceedings of the 7th International Workshop on Cooperative Information Agents* (LNCS), (Vol. 2782, pp. 137-151). Berlin, Germany: Springer.

Hobbs, J., & Pan, F. (2004). An ontology of time for the semantic web. *ACM Transactions on Asian Language Information Processing, 3*(1), 66–85. doi:10.1145/1017068.1017073.

Hu, W., & Qu, Y. (2007). Discovering simple mappings between relational database schemas and ontologies. In K. Aberer, K.-S. Choi, N. Noy, D. Allemang, K.-I. Lee, L. Nixon… P. Cudré-Mauroux (Eds.), *Proceedings of the 6th International Semantic Web Conference, 2nd Asian Semantic Web Conference* (LNCS), (Vol. 4825, pp. 225-238). Berlin, Germany: Springer.

Jones, C., Alani, H., & Tudhope, D. (2001). Geographical information retrieval with ontologies of place. In D. Montello (Ed.), *Proceedings of the International Conference Spatial Information Theory, Foundations of Geographic Information Science (COSIT 2001)* (LNCS), (Vol. 2205, pp. 323-335). Berlin: Springer.

Knublauch, H. (2006). Semantic web rules: Tools and languages. *Tutorial Bridging Research and Practice - Making Real-World Application of Ontologies and Rules at the Second International Conference on Rules and Rule Markup Languages for the Semantic Web.* Retrieved May 2010, from http://2006.ruleml.org/slides/tutorial-holger.pdf

Laborda, C. (2007). *Incorporating relational data into the semantic web – From databases to RDF using relational.OWL.* Saarbrücken: VDM Verlag.

Laborda, C., & Conrad, S. (2005). Relational OWL: A data and schema representation format based on OWL. In S. Hartmann & M. Stumptner (Eds.), *Proceedings of the 2nd Asia-Pacific Conference on Conceptual Modelling*: *Conferences in Research and Practice in Information Technology* (Vol. 43, pp. 89-96). Sydney, Australia: Australian Computer Society.

Le Grand, B. (2005). *Semantic web methodologies and tools for intra-European sustainable tourism*. Retrieved May 2005, from http://www.mondeca.com/article-JITT-hitouch-legrand.pdf

Leiper, N. (2004). *Tourism management*. Frenchs Forest: Pearson Education Australia.

Lima, S. (2003). *Webware crisis? The new werewolves are also slaughtered*. Viana do Castelo: Escola Superior de Tecnologia e Gestão.

Lima, S., & Moreira, J. (2009). The semantic web in tourism. In Cunha, M., Oliveira, E., Tavares, A., & Ferreira, L. (Eds.), *Handbook of Research on Social Dimensions of Semantic Technologies and Web Services* (pp. 675–703). Hershey, PA: IGI Global. doi:10.4018/978-1-60566-650-1.ch033.

OpenTravel Alliance. (2001). *OpenTravel alliance 2001A specification*. Retrieved April 2010, from http://www.opentravel.org/Specifications/DownloadZip.ashx?spec=2001A

OpenTravel Alliance. (2007). *OpenTravel alliance 2007A specification*. Retrieved April 2010, from http://www.opentravel.org/Specifications/DownloadZip.ashx?spec=2007A

Perry, M., Sheth, A., & Arpinar, I. (2006). Geospatial and temporal semantic analytics. *Large scale distributed information systems (LSDIS) technical report*. Retrieved March 2010, from http://lsdis.cs.uga.edu/library/download/encyclopedia_geoinformatics_uga_tech_report.pdf

Reingold, E., & Dershowitz, N. (2001). *Calendrical calculations: The millennium edition*. Cambridge, MA: Cambridge University Press.

Reynolds, D. (2010). *Jena 2 inference support*. Retrieved March 2010, from http://jena.sourceforge.net/inference/

Ricci, F., Arslan, B., Mirzadeh, N., & Venturini, A. (2002). ITR: A case-based travel advisory system. In S. Craw & A. Preece (Eds.), *Proceedings of the 6th European Conference Advanced in Case-Based Reasoning* (LNCS),(Vol. 2416, pp. 613-627). Berlin, Germany: Springer.

Semantic Web Search and Metadata Engine. (2004). *Restaurant ontology*. Retrieved May 2005, from http://www-agentcities.doc.ic.ac.uk/ontology/restaurant.daml

The DARPA Agent Markup Language. (2003). *DAML time ontology*. Retrieved January 2005, from http://www.cs.rochester.edu/~ferguson/daml/daml-time-20020728.daml

The DARPA Agent Markup Language. (2004). *DAML ontology library*. Retrieved April 2010, from http://www.daml.org/ontologies/

Truong, K., Abowd, G., & Brotherton, J. (2001). Who, what, when, where, how – Design issues of capture & access applications. In G. Abowd, B. Brumitt, & S. Shafer (Eds.), *Proceedings of the International Conference on Ubiquitous Computing* (LNCS), (Vol. 2201, pp. 209-224). Berlin, Germany: Springer.

VacationCoach Inc. (2002). *Using knowledge personalization to sell complex products*. Retrieved May 2010, from http://www.sourceit-travel.com/documents/pdf/vacationcoach_knowle dge_personalisation.pdf

Zou, Y., Finin, T., Ding, L., Chen, H., & Pan, R. (2003). Using semantic web technology in multi-agent systems: A case Study in the TAGA trading agent environment. In N. Sadeh (Ed.), *Proceedings of the 5th International Conference on Electronic Commerce: ACM International Conference Proceeding Séries* (Vol. 50, pp. 95-101). New York: ACM.

KEY TERMS AND DEFINITIONS

Tourism: "Can be defined as the theories and practices for being a tourist. This involves travelling and visiting places for leisure-related purposes. Tourism comprises the ideas and opinions people hold which shape their decisions about going on trips, about where to go (and where not to go) and what to do or not do, about how to relate to other tourists, locals and service personnel. And it is all the behavioural manifestations of those ideas" (Leiper, 2004, p. 44).

Tourist: "Can be defined as a person who travels away from their normal residential region for a temporary period of at least one night, to the extent that their behaviour involves a search for leisure experiences from interactions with features or characteristics of places he chooses to visit" (Leiper, 2004, p. 35).

Webware: Is an "artefact with a set of functionalities and components which are adequate to the Web context" (Lima, 2003, p. 10); that is, it is software with specific proprieties which are inseparable from the Web environment and that we do not find in traditional software products. Therefore, it may be considered an information system in which a great amount of volatile data–highly semi-structured and structured, semantically enriched and located in web-servers–are consulted, processed and updated by information navigators which are designed according to patterns of usability, adaptability, ergonomics, accessibility and autonomy.

ENDNOTES

[1]   Concept developed by Salvador Lima in the monograph "Webware Crisis? The New Werewolves Are Also Slaughtered" (Lima, 2003).

Chapter 8
Semi–Automatic Knowledge Extraction to Enrich Open Linked Data

Elena Baralis
Politecnico di Torino, Italy

Silvia Chiusano
Politecnico di Torino, Italy

Giulia Bruno
Politecnico di Torino, Italy

Alessandro Fiori
Politecnico di Torino, Italy

Tania Cerquitelli
Politecnico di Torino, Italy

Alberto Grand
Politecnico di Torino, Italy

EXECUTIVE SUMMARY

In this chapter we present the analysis of the Wikipedia collection by means of the ELiDa framework with the aim of enriching linked data. ELiDa is based on association rule mining, an exploratory technique to discover relevant correlations hidden in the analyzed data. To compactly store the large volume of extracted knowledge and efficiently retrieve it for further analysis, a persistent structure has been exploited. The domain expert is in charge of selecting the relevant knowledge by setting filtering parameters, assessing the quality of the extracted knowledge, and enriching the knowledge with the semantic expressiveness which cannot be automatically inferred. We consider, as representative document collections, seven datasets extracted from the Wikipedia collection. Each dataset has been analyzed from two point of views (i.e., transactions by documents, transactions by sentences) to highlight relevant knowledge at different levels of abstraction.

DOI: 10.4018/978-1-4666-2827-4.ch008

ORGANIZATION BACKGROUND

The Politecnico di Torino offers excellence in technology and acknowledges its historical context. It promotes the ability to carry out theoretical or applied research. Engineers and Architects are the main professional figures at the Politecnico di Torino. Both have strategic planning and a common interdisciplinary approach. The range of studies is broad and ever-widening: it spans space, environment and land, telecommunications, information, energy, mechanics, electronics, chemistry, automation, electrical engineering, industrial design, architecture and building, and many others. The Politecnico has 30.000 students studying on 120 courses (28 Bachelor's degree courses; 32 Master of Science courses; 23 Doctorates and 37 specialization courses). 12 of them are held in English. In the academic year 2011/2012 the Politecnico had around 5,600 students in the first year; in 2010 around 4,500 students graduated with a Master of Science or a Bachelor's Degree. Each year, between lectures, laboratories and practical exercises there are 170,000 hours of teaching. There is a staff of over 890 lecturers and researchers, and around 800 administration staff. There are 5 Schools, 1 Graduate School, 1 Post-graduate specialization, and 11 Departments.

SETTING THE STAGE

The case study exploits data mining techniques to support the semi-automatic inference of interesting knowledge to enrich open linked data. As representative example we consider the Wikipedia dataset, the world's largest online encyclopedia. Authors, affiliated to the Dipartimento di Automatica e Informatica (DAUIN) or to the Dipartimento di Ingegneria Gestionale e della Produzione of Politecnico di Torino, have been active for a long time in the research area of data mining and database systems management. The research activity is mainly devoted to the design and development of innovative efficient techniques for data analysis applied to different domains, including algorithms and data structures to mine large databases, classification algorithms for structured and unstructured (textual) data, algorithms for sequential patterns analysis, algorithms for extracting high level abstraction of the mined knowledge, sensor data analysis, network data analysis, and context-aware applications. Authors have published several papers in both international journals and conference proceedings. They have also been for a long time either teachers or teaching assistants in different databases and data mining courses at the Politecnico di Torino.

INTRODUCTION

Open linked data are collections of interlinked structured data available on the web. Like web data, linked data are constructed with documents on the web (Berners-Lee, 2006). However, unlike web data, where links are relationship anchors in hypertext documents written in HTML, links between objects are represented in RDF format (Manola & Miller, 2004).

Linked data allow data sources to be more easily crawled by search engines, accessed using generic data browsers, and connect data from different sources. Working on linked data, search engines can provide sophisticated query capabilities, similar to those provided by conventional relational databases, thus enabling a new class of applications (Bizer et al., 2007). Since a significant number of individuals and organizations have adopted linked data to publish their data, a giant global graph is being constructed consisting of billions of RDF statements from numerous sources covering all sorts of topics (Heath & Bizer, 2011). The prototypical example of cross-domain linked data is DBpedia (Bizer et al., 2009), generated from publicly available Wikipedia dumps. RDF statements in DBPedia are generated by extracting information from various parts of Wikipedia articles, in particular from the infoboxes, usually located on the right hand side of Wikipedia articles. Other major sources of cross-domain linked data are Freebase (Bollacker et al., 2008) and YAGO (Suchanek et al., 2007), both of which are linked to DBpedia.

While the number of tools for publishing linked data on the Web grows steadily, there is still a significant lack of solutions to efficiently discover links between data (Ngomo & Auer, 2011). RDF links among data can be set manually, automatically, or semi-automatically. Manual interlinking is typically employed for small static datasets, while larger datasets generally require an automated or semi-automated approach. Automatic linking approaches include simple key-based methods exploiting a common naming schema of data sources, and more complex similarity-based methods comparing data items and linking them if their similarity is above a given threshold (Heath & Bizer, 2011). Semi-automatic linking approaches rely on the support of a domain expert to filter relevant links from those automatically extracted from the dataset.

In this chapter, we exploited the ELiDa (Enriching Linked Data) framework to efficiently discover interesting and relevant linked data from large document collections. ELiDa has been designed to effectively support domain experts in constructing meaningful and previously hidden linked data. Its *flexible* architecture covers all main steps in the knowledge discovery process, including data pre-processing, information extraction, and knowledge filtering driven by the support of a domain expert. In addition, ELiDa provides high flexibility in enriching linked data by allowing the integration of any data mining algorithm suitable to extract interesting knowledge from document collections. To extract frequent and hidden correlations among "terms", including words and linked-words (i.e,. words associated with a hyperlink), ELiDa currently exploits association rule mining, a well-founded data mining technique. Although these correlations do not have the semantic expressiveness of formal ontological statements, they can support domain experts in identifying interlinked data and characterize it. The domain expert is in charge of analyzing the extracted knowledge, by defining different filtering parameters (e.g., support constraint) to significantly reduce the volume of extracted knowledge and identify only the relevant one. He/she is also responsible for assessing the quality of the extracted knowledge and enriching the knowledge with the semantic expressiveness which cannot be automatically inferred.

Data mining is the process of automatically discovering useful information hidden in large data collections. A critical issue, when dealing with large data collections such as document collections, is that a huge set of frequent itemsets is often generated. Consequently, the extraction process becomes computationally intensive, and the analysis of the extracted knowledge a complex task. To address this issue the ELiDa framework exploits a persistent data structure, called Array-Tree (Baralis et al., 2010), to compactly materialize on disk the extracted itemsets and efficiently perform itemset and association rule retrieval. Using the Array-Tree, the set of itemsets can be efficiently queried many times, by enforcing user-defined constraints.

As a case study, we exploit the ELiDa framework to efficiently analyze the 2009 dump of the English Wikipedia dataset. We focus on extracting meaningful correlations among Wikipedia words and hyperlinks, to help the human analyst in identifying interesting relationships that can be exploited to derive and enrich Semantic Web data. We consider seven datasets extracted from the Wikipedia collection. Each dataset has been analyzed from two points of view to highlight different levels of relevant knowledge. Case 1 considers all sentences in a given document as a single transaction, while Case 2 considers a single sentence as a transaction. The amount of extracted knowledge from each dataset is often very large, but the Array-Tree structure allows compactly storing frequent itemsets, reducing their size from 25% to 90% with respect to the flat file storage. Its compactness significantly reduces the time required to retrieve interesting itemsets for further analysis. Experimental results show that interesting correlations can be found by using the ELiDa framework. These correlations do not have the semantic expressiveness of full-fledged RDF statements, yet they can be used to effectively support experts in identifying interlinked data, enriching an existing ontology, and understanding how existing resources can be interlinked with new predicates.

The chapter is organized as follows. First, the overall ELiDa framework is presented. Then, the instance of the framework on the case study considered in this chapter is described. Finally, conclusions and possible future directions are presented and discussed.

THE ELiDa FRAMEWORK

The ELiDa (Enriching Linked Data) framework allows the efficient discovery of interesting and relevant linked data from a document collection by means of association rule mining techniques. The ELiDa framework is based on a two-phase mining process, entailing (i) knowledge discovery and (ii) data analysis refinement. The first phase allows automatically discovering the frequent co-occurrences of terms in a given document collection, while the second one supports the domain experts in identifying and semantically enriching the most relevant interlinked data. Figure 1 shows the ELiDa blocks involved in each phase.

The first analysis phase mainly performs the following two activities.

- **Data Pre-Processing:** Given a document collection, the *Data pre-processing* block performs different evaluation steps to model unstructured text data in a format suitable for the data mining and knowledge discovery process.

Figure 1. The ELiDa framework

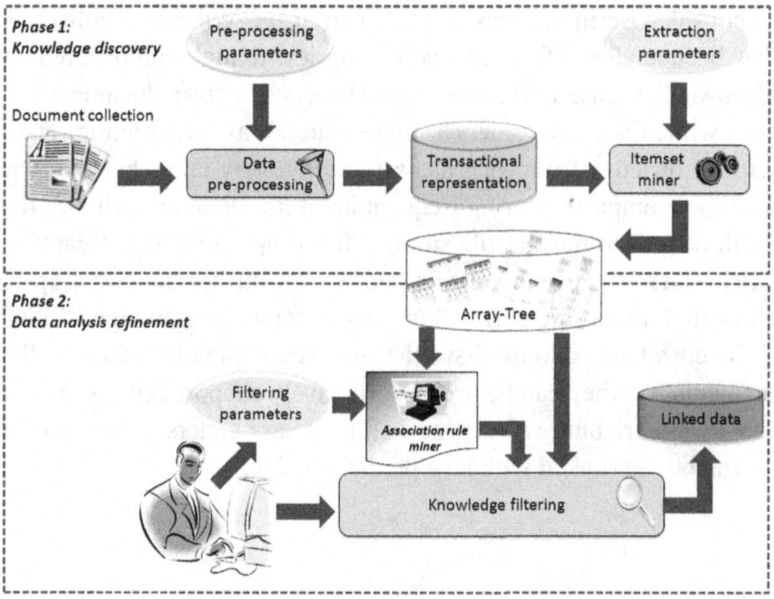

Documents are transformed in a transactional representation based on the stemmed terms (i.e., the root form of the term). In particular, each document can be represented at two abstraction levels: (1) document and (2) sentence level. Moreover, different kinds of information can be associated with each stemmed term according to various information retrieval and natural language analyses performed in the block. For instance, each term can be characterized by using a weight (e.g., term frequency, based on its document frequency) and a tag describing its part-of-speech (e.g., verb, noun, adjective). The subsequent blocks in the ELiDa framework use this information to discover hidden correlations among document terms, based on the context of each document and/or sentence.

- **Itemset Mining:** The *Itemset miner* block extracts frequent itemsets from the transactional representation of the document collection. This mining task is usually driven by some input extraction parameters, corresponding to quality indices (e.g., support) used to reduce the knowledge space and select a subset of relevant knowledge. Different algorithms for itemset mining might be easily integrated into ELiDa. Since the itemset extraction task often discovers a huge amount of knowledge, which needs to be efficiently queried to support in-depth analysis, we store the extracted itemsets in a persistent disk-based data structure named Array-Tree (Baralis et al., 2010). It is an array-based structure which exploits both prefix-path and subtree sharing to reduce data replication in the tree, thus increasing its compactness. The Array-Tree can be profitably exploited to efficiently query extracted itemsets by enforcing filtering parameters.

The data analysis refinement phase supports the domain expert in validating the extracted knowledge and exploiting this knowledge to semantically enrich open linked data. The following activities are performed.

- **Association Rule Mining:** The *Association rule miner* block extracts the association rules by exploiting the frequent itemsets stored in the Array-Tree, and based on the evaluation of the filtering parameters (e.g., confidence, lift (Tan et al., 2002)). Different algorithms for association rule mining might be easily integrated into the framework.
- **Knowledge Filtering:** The *Knowledge filtering* block, through the evaluation of the filtering parameters, allows selecting only the most relevant and interesting knowledge. The domain expert is involved in defining filtering parameters and assessing the quality of the extracted knowledge. In addition, the domain expert can exploit this knowledge to enrich open linked data.

For example, she/he can analyze the selected knowledge to enrich it with the semantic expressiveness which cannot be automatically inferred (e.g., definition of the semantic link).

A more detailed description of the functionalities of each ELiDa architectural block exploited in our case study follows.

Exploitation of the ELiDa Framework to Discover Linked Data in Wikipedia Datasets

As a case study, we exploited the Wikipedia dataset, the world's largest online encyclopedia. Wikipedia is a very large, well-known and widely exploited knowledge repository, where people can freely contribute. We considered a 2009 dump of the English version of the online encyclopedia, including 3,038,075 articles. Due to its large data volume and its rich content, useful knowledge to augment open link data can potentially be extracted.

In our case study, we focus on extracting meaningful correlations among Wikipedia words and hyperlinks, to help the human analyst identify interesting relationships that can be exploited to derive and enrich Semantic Web data. Wikipedia content is characterized by a highly heterogeneous nature, spanning topics as diverse as science, geography or cinema. For this reason, to increase the relevance of the discovered correlations, the analysis should be conducted on smaller subsets of this huge collection sharing the same subject. To this aim, the DBpedia knowledge base was exploited. In DBpedia, "things" are classified according to three different schemata. Based on the WordNet Synset Links classification schema, several groups of semantically coherent objects (i.e., language, monument, newspaper, scientist, song, website, and location) were selected. The Wikipedia articles belonging to each group were then used to build separate datasets, named after the corresponding WordNet Synset. We report experiments on 7 such datasets, extracted from the Wikipedia collection. In Table 1, the number of documents included in the collection, terms (i.e., distinct words) and L-terms (i.e., distinct words with hyperlink) cardinality, and its size are shown for each dataset. Let us note that, although the availability of semantically coherent document collections can dramatically alleviate the subsequent analysis task for the domain expert and increase the likelihood of discovering interesting relationships, the approach proposed in this paper is general and can be applied to any document collection. However, further preliminary analysis might be necessary in the latter case (e.g., topic detection, classification).

All experiments have been performed on an Intel(R) Core(TM) i5-2500K CPU @ 3.30GHz processor with 16 GByte main memory running Linux kernel v. 3.0.0-17-generic.

Table 1. Dataset characteristics

Dataset	# documents	# sentences	# distinct items	# distinct L-items	Size (kB)
Language	2,335	69,661	57,727	23,130	15,928
Monument	920	54,387	46,481	31,087	9,900
Newspaper	2,105	41,281	35,266	18,998	11,180
Scientist	4,583	132,635	71,794	57,011	30,624
Song	1,042	16,091	16,597	9,130	4,764
Web_site	993	30,650	25,904	12,014	6,308
Location	25,964	574,264	141,237	153,763	147,172

Data Pre-Processing

The ELiDa framework allows modeling a document collection at different abstraction levels, by means of a transactional representation exploiting the bag-of-word (BOW) representation. The Data pre-processing block extracts the most relevant information from raw textual data and models it using a representation suitable for the data mining and knowledge discovery process. This block has been developed in the Python programming language.

Let $D=\{d_1, \ldots, d_n\}$ be a set of textual documents stored in electronic form (e.g., Wikipedia articles). Each document d_q in D consists of a set of sentences $S_q=\{s_{1q}, \ldots, s_{nq}\}$. Let S be the union of all the S_q sets over the whole document collection D. Set X, where $X=D$ or $X=S$, can be generally named as the abstraction level used to represent the document collection. The BOW representation of an arbitrary element x_i of X (i.e., either a document d_q or a sentence s_{jq}) is the set of all terms (called word stems) occurring in it. To define the transactional representation of a document collection at the abstraction level X, the following transformation steps are performed. First, to avoid noisy information, stopwords and numbers are removed from X, and the Wordnet stemming algorithm (Bird et al., 2009) is applied to reduce words to their base or root form (i.e., the stem). Then, let x_i be an arbitrary element of the abstraction level X and $y_i=\{w_1, \ldots, w_M\}$ the subset of distinct terms occurring in the BOW representation of element x_i, i.e., $y_i \subseteq x_i$ and $w_p \neq w_r$ for any $p \neq r$. Moreover, let $L_{x(i)}=\{l_1, \ldots, l_v\}$ be the set of hyperlinks, named in the following L-items, included into the abstraction element x_i. The transactional representation of element x_i is the transaction t_i whose items are the union of the distinct terms taken from the BOW representation and the L-items belonging to $L_{x(i)}$. These items can be further characterized by diverse features (e.g, frequency, POS tag). The transactional representation T_X of the document collection is the union of all transactions t_i corresponding to each element x_i in X.

Currently, the ELiDa framework allows enriching the items belonging to the transactional representation by means of the following features.

- To distinguish item relevance, weights can be assigned to each item in the transactional representation. These weights can be computed based on statistical or information retrieval analyses. Many different approaches for weight evaluation can be included in ELiDa. In the case study presented in this paper, we exploited a statistical analysis based on the document frequency. The document frequency tf_{iq} associated with an item w_i belonging to the document d_q is computed as follows (Tan et al., 2006):

$$tf_{iq} = \frac{n_{iq}}{\sum_r n_{rq}}$$

  where n_{iq} is the number of occurrences of i-th item w_i in the q-th document d_q and $\sum_r n_{rq}$ is the sum of the number of occurrences of all items in the q-th document d_q.

- Moreover, the transactional representation can be enriched by distinguishing the role of each item according to the context. In the natural language processing field, a typical analysis is the part-of-speech (POS) tagging. This process marks up a word in a text as corresponding to a particular part of speech, based on both the word definition and the word context (i.e., relationship with adjacent and related words in a phrase, sentence, or paragraph). Thus, by using the POS method we can distinguish the role (e.g., noun, verb) of a term based on its context.

In the following, we detail the data pre-processing steps for the case study considered in this chapter.

Case 1: Transactions by documents. In this case study, we considered the abstraction level X as the set of textual documents (i.e., $X=D$). Each element x_i in X represents a document. In the transactional representation of X, each transaction is the set of distinct terms occurring in the BOW representation of each document x_i in X. Each term has been characterized by distinguishing its role (e.g., noun, verb) based on the context and by weighting it according to its document frequency. Terms with an hyperlink are marked as L-terms. Table 2 reports the main characteristics for the considered datasets after the data pre-processing phase. Since each transaction contains all relevant terms in a document, the average transaction length ranges from 100 to 400. It follows that some datasets contain short documents (i.e., about 100 terms) while others include longer documents (i.e., about 400 terms).

Table 2. Case 1: Transactions by documents - dataset characteristics

Dataset	# transactions	Avg trans. length	Size (kB)
Language	2,335	153.0	2,744
Monument	920	343.3	2,422
Newspaper	2,105	126.9	2,036
Scientist	4,583	196.6	7,164
Song	1,042	108.7	839
Web_site	993	184.7	1,383
Location	25,964	136.1	29,662

Case 2: Transactions by sentences. In this case study, we considered the abstraction level X as the set of all sentences in the document collections (i.e., $X=S$). Thus, each element x_i in X represents a sentence. In the transactional representation of X, each transaction is the set of distinct terms occurring in the BOW representation of each sentence x_i in X. Each term has been characterized by distinguishing its role (e.g., noun, verb) based on the context. Terms with an hyperlink are marked as L-terms. Table 3 reports the main characteristics for the considered datasets after the data pre-processing phase. Since we have split a document in its sentences, the number of transactions in each dataset in Case 2 is always larger than in the corresponding dataset in Case 1. Since each transaction contains only terms appearing in a given sentence, the average transaction length is very small and ranges from 8 to 10.

Table 3. Case 2: Transactions by sentences - dataset characteristics

Dataset	# transactions	Avg trans. length	Size (kB)
Language	69,661	8.4	4,491
Monument	54,387	9.9	4,123
Newspaper	41,281	9.8	3,066
Scientist	132,635	10.2	10,763
Song	16,091	9.6	1,146
Web_site	30,650	9.5	2,206
Location	574,264	9.4	45,418

Itemset Miner

The Data pre-processing block provides the transactional representation of a set of documents. In the considered case studies, documents belong to the Wikipedia collection. Within the transactional representation, each transaction is a set of terms. Each term can be either a simple word or a word including a hyperlink to an article on the word subject. In the following, *item* will denote a word and *L-item* (i.e., Linked-item) a word including a hyperlinkl. An itemset is a set of items and/or L-items. An itemset with k objects (including both items and L-items) is also called k-itemset. Each itemset is usually characterized by the support quality index, representing the itemset frequency observed in the transactional dataset. Given a minimum support threshold *MinSup*, an itemset is frequent when its support is greater than or equal to *MinSup* (Agrawal & Srikant, 1994).

Given the transactional representation of a document collection and a *MinSup* threshold, the *Itemset miner* block extracts all frequent itemsets including both items and/or L-items. The shortest itemset that can be extracted contains a single item (or L-item), while the longest one contains all items and L-items appearing in the longest transaction. Currently, we integrated in the *Itemset miner* block the LCM v.2 algorithm (Uno et al., 2004). LCM v.2 is a very efficient state-of-the-art algorithm for frequent itemset extraction.

Frequent itemset mining usually discovers a huge amount of knowledge which is hard to process and analyze. In addition, itemset support is often not a good estimate of quality, because low support itemsets can provide high quality knowledge (Brin et al., 1997). Considering low support thresholds further increases the number of extracted itemsets. To overcome this limitation, the ELiDa framework exploits an adapted version of the Array-Tree data structure (Baralis et al., 2010) to store on disk the extracted itemsets. This structures it extremely compact and supports an effective itemset retrieval. The Array-Tree structure is detailed in the next section.

Frequent Itemset Extraction on Cases 1 and 2: Tables 6 and 7 show the number of frequent itemsets generated in the analyzed case studies for the lowest considered support thresholds. A huge set of itemsets is extracted from each dataset. In Case 2 (See Table 7) the number of frequent itemsets ranges from few thousands to hundreds of thousands, while in Case 1 (See Table 6) the set is significantly larger. Case 1 is characterized by a high average transaction length (i.e., on average each transaction contains a large number of items and/or L-items, See Table 2). Consequently, many combinations of items/L-items satisfy the support constraint.

The Array-Tree Data Structure

The Array-Tree (Baralis et al., 2010) compactly represents the set of frequent itemsets extracted from a transactional dataset according to a given minimum support threshold (*MinSup*). The Array-Tree also supports an effective retrieval of the subset of interesting itemsets satisfying user-defined parameters (e.g., support and item constraints).

The former version of the Array-Tree proposed in Baralis et al. (2010) was only able to manage items. In this chapter we extended the Array-Tree structure to also represent L-items, as well as all additional features characterizing items and L-Items such as weight and part-of-speech (POS) tag. To reduce the Array-Tree size, items and L-items are represented in the Array-Tree by using an identifier. A data dictionary has been introduced storing all available information for each item and L-item, together with their identifiers. The number of entries in the data dictionary is equal to the total number of items and L-items. Currently, two primitives, written in C++, have been integrated in the ELiDa framework, to create the Array-Tree on disk and efficiently query it by enforcing different filtering parameters.

Table 4 reports a small dataset, used as an example to describe the main characteristics of the Array-Tree. For the sake of simplicity, items and L-Items have been replaced in the dataset with their identifier. Table 5 shows the complete set of frequent itemsets extracted from the dataset when no support threshold is enforced (i.e., *MinSup* = 1). Figure 2 reports the disk-based Array-Tree representation for the frequent itemsets in Table 2.

The Array-Tree is a prefix-tree like structure. Each itemset is represented by a single path, but a prefix-path may represent the common prefix of multiple itemsets.

Each node in the Array-Tree is a variable length array. Each entry of the array corresponds to a different item. All entries in a node are siblings, (i.e., direct descendants of the same entry in the parent node). A subpath from the tree root to an arbitrary tree node *N* represents a set of itemsets. These itemsets include all items found along the direct subpath reaching the node (i.e., disregarding sibling items along the path), together with one of the items in node *N*.

Table 4. Example dataset

TID	Items	TID	Items
T1	A,D,E	T7	B,C,E
T2	A,B,D	T8	A,B,D,E
T3	B,C,E	T9	C
T4	B,C	T10	B,C,E
T5	A	T11	B,C
T6	A,C,D	T12	B,C,D,E

Table 5. Frequent itemsets extracted from the example dataset (MinSup = 1)

Itemset (support)	Itemset (support)	Itemset (support)	Itemset (support)
C (8)	D (5)	D,E,B,C (1)	A,D,C (1)
B (8)	D,C (2)	A (5)	A,D,B (2)
B,C (6)	D,B (3)	A,C (1)	A,D,E (2)
E (6)	D,B,C (1)	A,B (2)	A,D,E,B (1)
E,C (4)	D,E (3)	A,E (2)	
E,B (5)	D,E,C (1)	A,E,B (1)	
E,B,C (4)	D,E,B (2)	A,D (4)	

Figure 2. The Array-Tree data structure

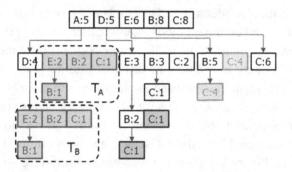

Within the node, each entry is a pair < *item: local item support* >. Each item is thus associated with a *local item support* value, representing the support of the itemset which contains (without any different interleaved items) all the items in the prefix path reaching the item. Refer to Figure 2. Local supports of items in node N_3 are 2 for e and b, and 1 for c. Itemsets {a, d, e} and {a, d, b} (generated by the subpath from the tree root to node N_3) have support equal to 2, given by the local support of items e and b in node N_3. For itemset {a, d, c} (generated similarly) the support is 1, given by the local support of item c in node N_3. Items in each node are sorted by increasing value of their global support (i.e., computed over the entire dataset). In the Array-Tree paths, items are sorted according to the same order.

Performance in itemset retrieval is significantly affected by the number of blocks that are read from disk to access the Array-Tree portion relevant for the search. To reduce the Array-Tree size we exploited *prefix path sharing* (i.e., a prefix path may represent the common prefix of multiple itemsets) and *subtree sharing* to limit the replication of the identical subtrees in the Array-Tree (Baralis et al., 2010). For example, subtrees T_A and T_B in Figure 2 have the same structure that is written on disk only once. To support top-down tree traversal each entry in the node is connected to its child node through a pointer. This pointer stores the physical location of the corresponding node and allows selective loading the block including it.

The Array-Tree can be profitably exploited to retrieve a subset of itemsets satisfying user-defined parameters.

By querying the Array-Tree with the support constraint as a filtering parameter, all itemsets with support larger than or equal to the user-defined support threshold are retrieved. These itemsets are collected by navigating the Array-Tree through a top-down depth-first visit. Each visited subpath represents an itemset including all items in the subpath, and with support equal to the local support of the last item in the subpath. The Array-Tree visit ends when an entry with local support below the support threshold is reached. Then, the search restarts from the last visited node including at least one entry whose local support satisfies the support constraint.

By querying the Array-Tree with item constraint as a filtering parameter, all itemsets including at least the items available in a user-specified set C are retrieved. These itemsets are represented in the Array-Tree paths including all items in C. These paths are retrieved through a top-down depth-first visit of the Array-Tree. To speed up the search process, items in set C are sorted according to the same order used along the paths. Hence, the visit of a path can be interrupted when an item that follows the next item in set C to be found is encountered. Since this path does not contain all items in C, it is not relevant for the search.

For example, from the Array-Tree shown in Figure 2, we retrieve all itemsets including at least items e and b (i.e., C={e,b}) and having support no less than 2. First, in the subtree of entry $< a: 5 >$ in node N_1, subpath from N_1 to node N_4 is visited. Itemsets $\{a, d, e, b\}$ and $\{a, e, b\}$ satisfy the item constraint but not the support constraint, since they have support equal to 1. Thus, they are discarded. Then, from the subtree of entry $< d: 5>$ in node N_1, subpath from N_1 to node N_6 is read. Itemset $\{d, e, b\}$ is retrieved which satisfies both constraints (its support is 2). Finally, from the subtree of entry $< e: 6 >$ in node N_1, itemsets $\{e, b\}$ and $\{e, b, c\}$ are retrieved, with support 5 and 4 respectively.

The Array-Tree characteristics on Cases 1 and 2. Different experiments on both case studies have been performed to analyze the performance of the Array-Tree data structure. Tables 7 and 8 report the main characteristics of the Array-Tree data structures which store the frequent itemsets extracted by the *Itemset miner* block. To evaluate the compactness of the Array-Tree data structure we compared the Array-Tree size with the size of a flat file storing the frequent itemsets. The compression factor achieved by the Array-Tree has been computed as

Table 6. Case 1: Transactions by documents – characteristics of the Array-Tree data structure

Dataset	Lowest MinSup (%)	# distinct frequent items	# distinct frequent L-items	# frequent itemsets	Flat file size (kB)	Array-Tree size (kB)	CF (%)
Language	0.75	238	1	1,959,032	102,456	7,556	92.63
Monument	0.75	254	2	607,579	32,706	4,100	87.46
Newspaper	0.75	385	5	713,960	32,080	6,404	80.04
Scientist	0.75	399	3	347,257	15,275	3,332	78,19
Song	0.75	299	8	90,905	3,502	708	79.79
Web_site	0.75	356	1	84,011	4,078	836	79.50
Location	0.75	338	6	493,116	23,789	6,020	74.69

Table 7. Case 2: Transactions by sentences – characteristics of the Array-Tree data structure

Dataset	Lowest MinSup (%)	# distinct frequent items	# distinct frequent L-items	# frequent itemsets	Flat file size (kB)	Array-Tree size (kB)	CF (%)
Language	0.05	1,927	170	8,122	193	148	23.15
Monument	0.05	2,673	67	8,577	210	152	27.45
Newspaper	0.05	2,344	97	12,470	325	148	54.49
Scientist	0.05	2,678	143	8,805	212	152	28.25
Song	0.05	2,760	245	23,285	674	280	58.49
Web_site	0.05	2,732	108	9,239	204	152	25.31
Location	0.07	1,797	85	200,401	12,451	208	98.33

Table 8. Example itemset filtering parameters

Filter name	Value
Support	≥ 0.05%
Length	≥ 3 and ≤ 5
Number of verbs	≥ 1
Number of L-items	≥ 1
Items do not include	be (verb), have (verb)

$$CF = \left(1 - \frac{size\left(\text{Array} - \text{Tree}\right)}{size\left(\text{flat file}\right)}\right)\%$$

Experimental results show that, for all considered datasets, the CF is always larger than 23.15% and increases when the number of frequent itemsets increases. Hence, the Array-Tree data structure can effectively represent large sets of itemsets, by significantly reducing the required disk space. Thanks to this compact representation, the I/O cost to retrieve the interesting itemsets from the Array-Tree is reduced.

Association Rule Miner

Association rules (Agrawal & Srikant, 1994) are usually represented as implications $X \rightarrow Y$, where X and Y are arbitrary itemsets such that $X \cap Y = \emptyset$. The rule length is the length of $X \cup Y$. The quality of the rule is typically measured in terms of support and confidence quality indices. The support of rule $X \rightarrow Y$ is equal to the support of itemset $X \cup Y$ in the source dataset. The confidence of rule $X \rightarrow Y$ is the conditional probability of finding Y having found X and is given by $\sup(X \cup Y)/\sup(X)$ where $\sup(X \cup Y)$ and $\sup(X)$ denote, respectively, the support of itemsets $X \cup Y$ and X.

The Association rule miner block receives as input the Array-Tree data structure, storing all frequent itemsets, and some parameters (e.g., minimum confidence threshold) to filters the subset of relevant rules. The block retrieves from the Array-Tree the association rule set satisfying the enforced constraints. Currently, the block integrates our implementation of a traditional association rule mining algorithm (Agrawal & Srikant, 1994), developed in C++.

Knowledge Filtering

As a result of the itemset mining process, a large quantity of itemsets are extracted from the transactional representation of the Wikipedia documents, and stored in the Array-Tree. The domain expert is in charge of discriminating among relevant co-occurrences of both items and L-items, encoded in the itemsets, and pruning uninteresting ones. However, the volume of data makes this task a rather cumbersome one.

To address these issues and effectively support the domain expert throughout the selection process, the *Knowledge filtering* block can enforce different filtering conditions on the set of extracted itemsets and association rules, based on various parameters listed next. Currently, the knowledge filtering algorithm integrated in the ELiDa framework has been developed in Python.

- **Itemset Support:** The support filter selects all itemsets stored in the Array-Tree satisfying a given support threshold, or in a given support range. A high support represents a strong co-occurrence and can thus indicate a meaningful relationship among two or more terms. On the other hand, relationships suggested by high-support itemsets might turn out too general or too obvious. In such cases, analyzing less frequent co-occurrences may offer interesting insights on rare but meaningful relationships.

- **Itemset Length:** The length filter selects all itemsets whose length is in a given range. Indeed, while offering a high degree of flexibility–because they can capture interesting co-occurrences among any number of terms–itemsets may sometimes be too short (i.e., too general) or too long (i.e., too specific) to convey any useful information. Thus, the length of the itemsets should be carefully considered in the knowledge filtering process.

- **Item Filtering:** The POS (part-of-speech) tags associated with each term provide useful information that can be exploited in the itemset filtering process. The item filter can thus be used to enforce constraints on the type of items included in the itemsets, such as nouns, verbs or L-items. For example, a given subject (i.e., a term representing a noun, or an L-term) could be characterized by the fact that it is often associated, throughout the document collection, with a given action (i.e., a term representing a verb) performed on, or in the context of, a given object (i.e., another term representing a noun, or another L-term). If such a co-occurrence is found to be frequent, then a relationship could be inferred that the analyst might choose to formalize into an RDF statement. In addition, relationships containing one or more L-items may be especially meaningful, because L-items represent key concepts for which a possibly dedicated document exists (e.g., a Wikipedia article). Hence, L-items might be regarded as candidate resources to be included in an ontology. Other kinds of constraints may be defined as needed on the items included in the itemsets. For example, it might be useful to discard itemsets containing specific terms (nouns or verbs) that are overly frequent (e.g., verbs such as "to have", "to be").

- **Rule Filtering:** Using the most interesting frequent itemsets, association rules are generated. The confidence and lift indices have been exploited to assess rule quality, but other metrics can be adopted and easily included in the *Knowledge filtering* block. For example, given an itemset, the highest-confidence rule is chosen as representative.

Knowledge filtering on Cases 1 and 2. Based on the filtering conditions described previously, several potentially interesting itemsets have been identified on the considered cases. For instance, the filtering parameters in Table 8 were enforced on

Monument and Scientist collections obtained in Case 2 (Transactions by sentences). Some interesting itemsets identified after enforcing these filtering conditions are reported in Table 9, while the corresponding association rules are shown in Table 10.

The first two itemsets (which can be considered as a whole, since they involve the same terms taken first as a link and then as single words) suggest the idea that "Unesco designates world heritage sites", which could lead to an RDF statement where "Unesco" and "world heritage site" are respectively the subject and the object, and "designate" is the verb. This is somehow confirmed by the corresponding association rule, stating that "it is *world heritage sites* (rule head) that are often *designated* by *Unesco* (rule body)". Similarly, it can be inferred from the third itemset that "it is usually from a *university* that a *doctor of philosophy* title is *received*". Although such sentences do not represent full-fledged RDF statements, they can help the human analyst enrich an existing ontology or understand how existing resources can be interlinked with new predicates.

Related Works

Traditional data mining tasks attempt to find patterns from a collection of independent instances of a single relation. 'Link mining' (Getoor & Diehl, 2005) is instead a recent key challenge problem which focuses on mining richly structured and heterogeneous datasets where instances are linked either by an explicit (e.g., a URL) or a constructed link (e.g., a join operation between two database tables). Relevant tasks in 'Link mining' include, for example, predicting the number or the type of links between two objects, inferring the existence of a link or the identity of an object, finding co-references, and discovering subgraph patterns.

Table 9. Example itemsets extracted from the monument and scientist datasets

Dataset	Itemset	Support
Monument	{designate (V), unesco (L-item), world_heritage_site (L-item)}	0.11%
Monument	{designate (V), unesco (L-item), site (N), heritage (N), world (N)}	0.12%
Scientist	{doctor_of_philosophy (L-item), receive (V), university (N)}	0.06%

Table 10. Association rules generated from the example itemsets

Rule	Confidence
{unesco (L-item), designate (V)} ⇒ {world_heritage_site (L-item)}	86.57%
{doctor_of_philosophy (L-item), receive (V)} ⇒ {university (N)}	64.54%

Data mining algorithms were applied to the analysis of Wikipedia and DBPedia content, to extract a variety of information. For example, clustering techniques have been used to organize a large set of documents retrieved from a search engine, such that they can be interactively browsed by the user. To consider the important information on the semantic relationships between key terms, Hu et al. (2008), coupled the bag-of-words (BOW) representation with a concept thesaurus based on the semantic relations (synonym, hypernym, and associative relation) extracted from Wikipedia. In Szczuka et al. (2011), documents are clustered based on their content and with the assistance of the DBpedia knowledge base. Text classification has also been widely used to assist users in discovering useful information from Wikipedia. Wang et al.(2009), expanded the BOW representation with semantic relations constructed from Wikipedia. Yun et al. (2012), represented text data with syntactic and semantic information based on the Wikipedia concepts related to terms.

Frequent itemset and association rule mining focuses on studying efficient algorithms to discover correlation among data items in a transactional dataset (Agrawal & Srikant 1994; Han et al., 2010; Uno et al., 2004). Since the capabilities of generating and collecting data have been rapidly increasing, the interest in itemset mining is continuously growing.

Association rules have been exploited to support the generation of ontologies from folksonomies (Jaschke et al., 2008) and semantic annotations in text documents (Kuittinen et al., 2008). Jiang & Tan (2006) computed association rules from RDF data, while Nebot & Berlanga (2010) use association rules to discover causal relations in RDF-based medical data. Association rules have also been applied for ontology matching as in the AROMA system (David et al., 2006). Most recently, (Parundekar et al. (2010) studied containment relationships among sets of class instantiations to generate alignments among several linked data repositories, including DBpedia. Volker & Niepert (2011) proposed an approach based on association rule mining to extract expressive schemas from large RDF repositories as DBpedia.

In the context of pattern extraction, an approach was proposed in Ruiz-Casado et al. (2005) to enrich the WordNet lexical semantic network (containing classical relations such as synonyms, hyponyms, etc.) with new relationships extracted from Wikipedia. Shnarch et al. (2009) addressed the extraction of lexical inference rules from Wikipedia. The lexical reference relation between two terms may be viewed as a lexical inference rule, where the left-hand-side (LHS) term would generate a reference, in some texts, to a possible meaning of the right-hand-side (RHS) term. By considering only titles of Wikipedia articles as LHS of rules, this approach is less suitable for the detection of new semantics among entities. (Nguyen et al. (2008) proposed an approach to extracting entities and relations among entities from Wikipedia data. Articles are processed to first remove HTML tags, extract hyperlinks to other Wikipedia's articles, and then they are split in sentences. In each article all the occurrences of the principal entity (the subject of the article) are anchored to the secondary entities (the link to other subjects). Then, sentences including at least one pair of principal entity and secondary entity are extracted, and the summary sections of the articles are analyzed to mine ground true relations. Since the approach proposed in this chapter does not differentiate between principal and secondary entities, the extracted relations are not limited to Wikipedia subjects.

Previous approaches on frequent itemset and association rule mining focused on extraction algorithms, without addressing how mined knowledge can be compactly stored and efficiently retrieved. Hence, the efficient management of the typically huge mined knowledge is a critical, still open, research issue. Currently, three persistent data structures have been proposed to compactly store and efficiently query a collection of itemsets. In Liu et. al. (2003), frequent closed itemsets are stored in a disk-based structure, named CFP-tree, and algorithms have been proposed to retrieve patterns from it. Since frequent closed itemsets provide a compact representation of frequent itemsets, a decompressing technique needs to be exploited to derive all frequent itemsets from the CFP-tree. An extension of the CFP-tree, named CFP-tree-all, has been proposed in (Liu et al. (2007) to store frequent itemsets. However, the CFP-tree-all size is still too large to compactly represent a huge set of itemsets. The Array-Tree data structure has been proposed in Baralis et. al (2010) to compactly represent frequent itemsets on disk as well as to support an effective retrieval of itemsets satisfying user-defined item and support constraints. Baralis et. al (2010) showed that the Array-Tree is a significantly more compact data structure than CFP-tree-all. Since performance in itemset retrieval is mainly affected by the number of disk access needed to read the Array-Tree relevant for the search, different strategies have been adopted to reduce the I/O costs. In this chapter, the Array-Tree data structure has been extended to represent all information used to characterize a set of documents from a Wikipedia collection.

SOLUTIONS AND RECOMMENDATIONS

This chapter presented and discussed the analysis performed on several datasets extracted from the Wikipedia collection. The focus of the analysis was on discovering interesting correlations among terms to enrich open linked data. Experimental validation, performed on two different abstraction levels (i.e., document and sentence), demonstrated that a large amount of knowledge can be automatically extracted. By means of the data analysis refinement, the domain expert can select only a subset of knowledge by setting appropriate filtering parameters. We have experimentally verified that interesting and relevant correlations exist among items and L-Items which can be used, for example, to enrich open linked data, or to discover new links.

This work can be extended in different research directions: (1) Integration in the ELiDa framework of different data mining algorithms able to extract either more compact itemsets (e.g., closed itemsets (Wang et al., 2003)) or sequence patterns (Pei et al., 2004). (2) Design and development of different persistent structures to compactly represent the new types of knowledge (e.g., closed itemsets and sequence patterns). (3) Exploitation of the devised approach to analyze user-generated content coming from different application contexts (e.g., social media, online communities).

REFERENCES

Agrawal, R., & Srikant, R. (1994) Fast algorithms for mining association rules in large data-bases. In *Proceedings of International Conference on Very Large Data Bases* (pp. 487-499). IEEE.

Baralis, E., Cerquitelli, T., Chiusano, S., & Grand, A. (2010). Array-tree: A persistent data structure to compactly store frequent itemsets. In *Proceedings of IEEE Conference of Intelligent Systems* (pp. 108-113). IEEE.

Berners-Lee, T. (2006). *Linked data*. Retrieved from http://www.w3.org/DesignIssues/LinkedData.html

Bird, S., Klein, E., & Loper, E. (2009). *Natural language processing with Python*. O'Reilly Media.

Bizer, C., Cyganiak, R., & Heath, T. (2007). *How to publish linked data on the web*. Retrieved from http://sites.wiwiss.fu-berlin.de/suhl/bizer/pub/LinkedDataTutorial/20070727/

Bizer, C., Lehmann, J., Kobilarov, G., Auer, S., Becker, C., Cyganiak, R., & Hellmann, S. (2009). DBpedia – A crystallization point for the web of data. *Journal of Web Semantics: Science. Services and Agents on the World Wide Web, 7*, 154–165. doi:10.1016/j.websem.2009.07.002.

Bollacker, K., Evans, C., Paritosh, P., Sturge, T., & Taylor, J. (2008). Freebase: A collaboratively created graph database for structuring human knowledge. In *Proceedings of ACM SIGMOD International Conference on Management of Data* (pp. 1247-1250). ACM.

Brin, S., Motwani, R., & Silverstein, C. (1997) Beyond market baskets: Generalizing association rules to correlations. In *Proceedings of ACM SIGMOD International Conference on Management of Data* (pp. 265–276). ACM.

David, J., Guillet, F., & Briand, H. (2007). Association rule ontology matching approach. *International Journal on Semantic Web and Information Systems*, *3*(2), 27–49. doi:10.4018/jswis.2007040102.

Getoor, L., & Diehl, C. P. (2005). Link mining: A survey. *SIGKDD Explorations*, *7*(2), 3–13. doi:10.1145/1117454.1117456.

Han, J., Pei, J., & Yin, Y. (2010). Mining frequent patterns without candidate generation. In*Proceedings of the 2000 ACM SIGMOD International Conference on MANAGEMENT of Data* (pp. 1-12). ACM.

Heath, T., & Bizer, C. (2011). Linked data: Evolving the web into a global data space. In Synthesis Lectures on the Semantic Web: Theory and Technology. Morgan & Claypool.

Hu, J., Fang, L., Cao, Y., Zeng, H.-J., Li, H., Yang, Q., & Chen, Z. (2008). Enhancing text clustering by leveraging Wikipedia semantics. In *Proceedings of ACM SIGIR Conference on Research and Development in Information Retrieval* (pp. 179-186). ACM.

Jaschke, R., Hotho, A., Schmitz, C., Ganter, B., & Stumme, G. (2008). Discovering shared conceptualizations in folksonomies. *Journal of Web Semantics*, *6*(1), 38–53. doi:10.1016/j.websem.2007.11.004.

Jiang, T., & Tan, A.-H. (2006). Mining RDF metadata for generalized association rules. *Lecture Notes in Computer Science*, *4080*, 223–233. doi:10.1007/11827405_22.

Kuittinen, H., Tuominen, J., & Hyvonen, E. (2008). Extending an ontology by analyzing annotation co-occurrences in a semantic cultural heritage portal. *Workshop on Collective Intelligence*.

Lin, D. (1998). Dependency-based evaluation of minipar. In *Proceedings of International Conference on Language Resources and Evaluation*. IEEE.

Lin, H. T., Koul, N., & Honavar, V. (2011). Learning relational bayesian classifiers from RDF data. *Lecture Notes in Computer Science*, *7031*, 389–404. doi:10.1007/978-3-642-25073-6_25.

Liu, G., Lu, H., Lou, W., & Xu Yu, J. (2003). On computing, storing and querying frequent patterns. In *Proceedings of the 9th ACM SIGKDD International Conference on Knowledge Discovery and Data Mining* (pp. 607-612). ACM.

Liu, G., Lu, H., & Xu Yu, J. (2007). CFP-tree: A compact disk-based structure for storing and querying frequent itemsets. *Information Systems, 32*(2), 295–319. doi:10.1016/j.is.2005.11.004.

Manola, F., & Miller, E. (2004). *Resource description framework (RDF) primer*. W3C. Retrieved from http://www.w3.org/TR/rdf-primer/

Narasimha, N., Kappara, P., Ichise, R., & Vyas, O. P. (2011). LiDDM: A data mining system for linked data. *Workshop on Linked Data on the Web*.

Nebot, V., & Berlanga, R. (2010). Mining association rules from Semantic Web data. *Lecture Notes in Computer Science, 6097*, 504–513. doi:10.1007/978-3-642-13025-0_52.

Ngomo, A.-C. N. & Auer, S. (2011). LIMES - A time-efficient approach for large-scale link discovery on the Web of data. *Framework, 15*(3).

Nguyen, D. P. T., Matsuo, Y., & Ishizuka, M. (2008). Exploiting syntactic and semantic information for relation extraction from Wikipedia. *Workshop on Text-Mining & Link-Analysis*.

Parundekar, R., Knoblock, C. A., & Ambite, J. L. (2010). Linking and building ontologies of linked data. *Lecture Notes in Computer Science, 6496*, 598–614. doi:10.1007/978-3-642-17746-0_38.

Pei, J., Han, J., Mortazavi-Asl, B., Wang, J., Pinto, H., & Chen, Q. et al. (2004). Mining sequential patterns by pattern-growth: The PrefixSpan approach. *IEEE Transactions on Knowledge and Data Engineering, 16*(10).

Ruiz-Casado, M., Alfonseca, E., & Castells, P. (2005). Automatic extraction of semantic relationships for WordNet by means of pattern learning from Wikipedia. *Lecture Notes in Computer Science, 3513*, 67–79. doi:10.1007/11428817_7.

Shnarch, E., Barak, L., & Dagan, I. (2009). Extracting lexical reference rules from Wikipedia. In *Proceedings of the Annual Meeting of the ACL*. ACL.

Suchanek, F. M., Kasneci, G., & Weikum, G. (2007). Yago: A core of semantic knowledge. In *Proceedings of the International Conference on World Wide Web* (pp. 697–706). IEEE.

Szczuka, M. S., Janusz, A., & Herba, K. (2011). Clustering of rough set related documents with use of knowledge from DBpedia. *Lecture Notes in Computer Science, 6954*, 394–403. doi:10.1007/978-3-642-24425-4_52.

Tan, P., Steinbach, M., & Kumar, V. (2006). *Introduction to data mining*. Boston, MA: Addison-Wesley.

Tan, P.-N., Kumar, V., & Srivastava, J. (2002). Selecting the right interestingness measure for association patterns. In *Proceedings of ACM SIGKDD International Conference on Knowledge Discovery and Data Mining* (pp. 32–41). ACM.

Uno, T., Kiyomi, M., & Arimura, H. (2004). LCM ver. 2: Efficient mining algorithms for frequent/closed/maximal itemsets. *Workshop on Frequent Itemset Mining Implementations*.

Volker, J., & Niepert, M. (2011). Statistical schema induction. *Lecture Notes in Computer Science, 6643*, 124–138. doi:10.1007/978-3-642-21034-1_9.

Wang, J., Han, J., & Pei, J. (2003). Closet+: Searching for the best strategies for mining frequent closed itemsets. In *Proceedings of ACM SIGKDD International Conference on Knowledge Discovery and Data Mining* (pp. 236–245). New York: ACM.

Wang, P., Hu, J., Zeng, H. J., & Chen, Z. (2009). Using Wikipedia knowledge to improve text classification. *Knowledge and Information Systems, 19*, 265–281. doi:10.1007/s10115-008-0152-4.

Yun, J., Jing, L., Yu, J., & Huang, H. (2012). A multi-layer text classification framework based on two-level representation model. *Expert Systems with Applications, 39*(2), 2035–2046. doi:10.1016/j.eswa.2011.08.027.

KEY TERMS AND DEFINITIONS

Association Rule: An implication between two sets of elements (antecedent and consequent) which measures, by means of the support and confidence values, how much the antecedent and the consequent are dependent.

Bag-of-Words (BOW): A natural language processing and information retrieval representation of a text (document or sentence) as an unordered collection of words, disregarding the structure of the text.

Data Mining: The process of extracting hidden information from datasets, which includes algorithms for classification, clustering, association rules and sequence extraction.

Frequent Itemset: A set of items jointly appearing in a number of transactions which is higher or equal to a minimum support threshold.

Part-of-Speech (POS) Tagging: The process of assigning a word a common linguistic category (e.g., noun, verb), which is defined by the syntactic behavior of the word.

Persistent Structure: A data structure materialized on secondary memory. It is often stored in a binary file.

Term Frequency: A statistical measure to evaluate how important a word is with respect to a document in a collection. The higher this value, the more representative the word.

Chapter 9
Variables Performance for E–Services Acceptance:
A Descriptive Statistical Analysis

Kamaljeet Sandhu
University of New England, Australia

EXECUTIVE SUMMARY

This case study examines the Web Electronic Service framework for a University in Australia. The department is in the process of developing and implementing a Web-based e-service system. The user experience to use e-services requires insight into the attributes that shape the experience variable. The descriptive data about the attributes that form the experience variable is provided in this study.

INTRODUCTION

Descriptive statistics can offer powerful insights into the factors involved in e-Services system acceptance by analysing students' responses from the survey. A large volume of descriptive data can highlight the role of these factors in influencing the international student's use of the e-services system on the University of Australia (not the real name) website. Analysing descriptive statistics is particularly effective for illuminating the inner workings of the constructs and ascertaining the strength of their effects in the international student's e-services acceptance process. The international students were from first, second, and third year degree courses including commerce, arts, science, and nursing. They were studying full time. Both male and female international students participated in the survey.

DOI: 10.4018/978-1-4666-2827-4.ch009

Data Collection

The data for the survey was collected from the university's international student population. An invitation to the international students to participate in the survey was sent to them by an e-mail. In addition the researcher also visited computer laboratories and distributed leaflets to international students requesting them to participate in the survey. This approach is believed to have been effective as the international students who were in the computer laboratories and in front of the computers responded immediately. An invitation was also sent in the international student's fortnightly newsletter email which is sent by the international students union. Participants could complete the survey online at anytime. The total numbers of responses received was 403. All responses received electronically were complete and without any errors. This resulted in eliminating incomplete survey responses which has its limitations in a paper-based survey.

Research Project Background

This chapter is part of a larger study investigating the critical success factors in e-service user acceptance. The aim of the case study is to investigate the acceptance and use of e-services system amongst student users. The case study examines the Web Electronic Service framework of the University of Australia (not the real name). The department is in the process of developing and implementing Web-based e-service system. International students have the option to lodge the admission application through either of any: web-based e-service system on the World Wide Web, phone, fax, or in person. On receiving the application a decision is made by the staff on the admission status. The department is implementing the electronic delivery of its services on the website. The Web electronic service is believed to be in use for approximately last two and half years. The e-service process involves students making the application and the staff processing application on the website.

The items that are measured in this study are adopted for building and testing the user experience variable for studying the user acceptance of e-services. The items are also tested for effectiveness and performance for the measurement of the variables.

THE INTERNATIONAL STUDENT EXPERIENCE WITH USING THE E-SERVICES SYSTEM

The international students were asked to respond to seven category items about the extent of their experience with the e-services system. The seven items that measured international students experience were: (1) their skills; (2) finding information on the e-services system; (3) knowing about using the e-services system; (4) finding the e-services system; (5) movement within the e-services system; (6) awareness when interacting with the e-services system; and (7) confidence in using the e-services system.

Skills

Taylor and Todd (1995) and Yaobin and Tao (2007) argue that the user's experience and skills influence IT usage. In this study, 51% of international students agreed that they had become skilled at using the university's e-services system. A further 28.8% strongly agreed with the same statement. Nine percent of international students disagreed and another 11% were unsure. The data suggests that international students' skills had improved, and that they strongly believed that the e-services system had assisted them in their university work. The descriptive data is shown in Table 1.

The connection between improved skills and using the university's e-services system may explain the role of the international student's experience in enhancing their acceptance of e-services system.

Finding Information on the E-Services System

Ramaswami et al. (2001) demonstrated that user adoption of on-line services takes a path of gaining familiarity and comfort before people use them for other purposes. Traditional consumer behaviour literature suggests that high involvement of users on e-services system generates intense efforts by the user to attend to and search out sources of information (Ramaswami et al., 2001; Huang et al., 2007). In this study the international students agreed (53.6%) that they knew where to find information on the university e-services system. A further 20.8% strongly agreed. The data is shown in Table 2. Given that 75% of the international students indicated they knew

Table 1. Students skills in using the e-services system

		Frequency	Percent	Valid Percent	Cumulative Percent
Valid	Strongly Disagree	8	2.0	2.0	2.0
	Disagree	40	9.9	9.9	11.9
	Not Sure	55	13.6	13.6	25.6
	Agree	216	53.6	53.6	79.2
	Strongly Agree	84	20.8	20.8	100.0
	Total	403	100	100	

Table 2. Students' ability to find information on the e-services system

		Frequency	Percent	Valid Percent	Cumulative Percent
Valid	Strongly Disagree	2	.5	.5	.5
	Disagree	35	8.7	8.7	9.2
	Not Sure	44	10.9	10.9	20.1
	Agree	205	50.9	51.0	71.1
	Strongly Agree	116	28.8	28.9	100
	Total	102	99.8	100	
Missing	Not Applicable	1	.2		
Total		403	100		

where to find what they wanted on the university e-Services system, it follows that they probably had a clear idea of the purpose of their activity within the e-Services system. International students who were not sure of where to find what they wanted on the university e-services system accounted for 13.6%. Nearly 10% (9.9%) of international students disagreed with the statement.

Understanding about Using the E-Services System

D'Ambra and Rice (2001) argue that technology usage is dependent on a user's perceptions of the impact of the e-services system on their tasks, as well as on a host of social and contextual factors. A total of 50.9% of the international students reported that they were not sure if they knew more about using the university e-services system than most other international students. These international students may not have discussed their experience with others, or may have felt either apprehensive or hesitant about the consequences of disclosing such information.

The self-evaluation of their use of the e-services system by international students may require a specific understanding of the student-specific experiences that may drive the use of e-services across different student groups. Twenty-two percent of the international students agreed that they knew more about using the university e-services system than most other international students (Table 3). These international students responded that they had from intermediate to advanced experience in using the university's e-services system. Fifteen percent of international students disagreed about knowing more about using the university e-services system than most other international students.

Table 3. A student knowing more about using the e-Services system than most other students

		Frequency	Percent	Valid Percent	Cumulative Percent
Valid	Strongly Disagree	10	2.5	2.5	2.5
	Disagree	62	15.4	15.4	17.9
	Not Sure	205	50.9	51.0	68.9
	Agree	89	22.1	22.1	91.0
	Strongly Agree	36	8.9	9.0	100.0
	Total	402	99.8	100.0	
Missing	Not Applicable	1	.2		
Total		403	100		

Finding the E-Services System

Cockburn and McKenzie (2000) show that e-services system revisiting is a prevalent activity amongst most users. Forty-eight percent of the international students in this study agreed that the university e-services system was easy to locate as it was on the homepage on all university computers. Sometimes international students had difficulty in relocating previously visited websites or sub-websites on the e-services system that required remembering a website address or other information that would assist the international students in returning to that website.

If relocating the e-services system is made easy, it is reasonable to expect an increase in continued use of e-services by international students. This prediction is based on the understanding that international students relocating the e-services system may display enhanced experience on continued visits. The evidence is made stronger by the finding that another 38% of international students strongly agreed that the e-services system was easy to locate (Table 4). The ever-increasing number of websites on the e-services system will influence an international student's experience in terms of finding website addresses that are difficult to remember.

The e-services system website address often marks the starting point of an international student's evaluation of using e-services.

Movement within the E-Services System

Hoffman and Novak (1995), Heijden (2000), and Koufaris (2002) demonstrate that a user's experience improves with sustained movement within the e-services system website. E-services system websites that are difficult to navigate may have low us-

Table 4. E-Services system is easy to locate by students

		Frequency	Percent	Valid Percent	Cumulative Percent
Valid	Strongly Disagree	4	1.0	1.0	1.0
	Disagree	15	3.7	3.8	4.8
	Not Sure	31	7.7	7.8	12.5
	Agree	195	48.4	48.9	61.4
	Strongly Agree	154	38.2	38.6	100.0
	Total	399	99.0	100.0	
Missing	Not Applicable	4	1.0		
Total		403	100		

age (Heijden, 2000). The majority of international students in this study (50.6%) agreed that it was easy to move between different sections of the university e-services system. If the international student's navigation between different sections of the e-Services system is straightforward, it will probably influence e-services usage.

The role of flow in a user's experience in moving from one section to another is important in understanding use of different features of the e-services system (Zeithaml et al., 2000; Chea & Lou, 2008; Chellappan, 2008). In this study, the evidence is made stronger with a further 23.6% of international students strongly agreeing that it was easy to move within the university e-services system (Table 5). The level of e-services delivered to international students then, it can be argued, had a degree of easy accessibility and reach. Students indicated that they could reach the points of each of the e-services without difficulty.

Table 5. Students ease of movement within the e-services system

		Frequency	Percent	Valid Percent	Cumulative Percent
Valid	Strongly Disagree	7	1.7	1.7	1.7
	Disagree	46	11.4	11.5	13.2
	Not Sure	49	12.2	12.2	25.4
	Agree	204	50.6	50.9	76.3
	Strongly Agree	95	23.6	23.7	100.0
	Total	401	9935	100.0	
Missing	Not Applicable	2	.5		
Total		403	100		

Awareness when Interacting with the E-Services System

Webster et al. (1993) argue that users enter a state of intense focus when interacting with e-services system websites and thus merge their actions with awareness. Hoffman and Novak (1995) argue further that the user's experience consists of skills and challenges, and that their focused attention must be present in e-services system interaction for successful use. In this study, only 28.8% of the international students reported that they were unaware of potential distractions around them when interacting with the e-services system. The evidence subjectively points to very intense student concentration when in that state of focus and a decreased awareness of other things happening around them. Another 21.8% of international students agreed that they were less aware of other things when interacting with the university e-services system.

A significant percentage of international students (38% in Table 6) disagreed that they were less aware of other things around them when interacting with e-services. The students would have had some degree of awareness of what was happening in their surroundings, and it may be expected that there would be a decreased focus on their work and a lower level of experience as their attention was being drawn elsewhere (Webster et al., 1993).

E-services flow then may require complete user attention while interacting with a e-services system. Distractions could potentially affect their experience and acceptance process (Csikszentmihalyi, 1990).

Table 6. Students awareness when interacting with the e-services system

		Frequency	Percent	Valid Percent	Cumulative Percent
Valid	Strongly Disagree	22	5.5	5.5	5.5
	Disagree	150	37.2	37.6	43.1
	Not Sure	116	28.8	29.1	72.2
	Agree	88	21.8	22.1	94.2
	Strongly Agree	23	5.7	5.8	100.0
	Total	399	99.0	100.0	
Missing	Not Applicable	4	1.0		
Total		403	100		

Confidence in Using the E-Services System

Ramaswami et al. (2001) and Morris and Turner (2001) argue that users who use the on-line channel for information search have a greater tendency to use it for other transactions. Obtaining information gives users an opportunity to experience the range of e-services and obtain a certain level of comfort before they are ready to use it for other purposes (Ramaswami et al., 2001 and Chellappan, 2008). This analysis anticipates that the international student's confidence level is expected to increase with every e-services based activity in which they are successful. A study by Gardner et al. (1993) shows that the more people use computers, the more their self-confidence with respect to computer increases.

The majority of international students in this study (51.6%) believed that when they were successful in using the e-services system for one task, they felt confident about using it for other tasks. The evidence is strengthened by a further 17% of international students strongly agreeing to the item. The data shows that a high number of international students were willing to try to test the use of e-services in more than one e-services activity. This suggests that in this case international student usage grows with increased experience.

Hoffman and Novak (1995) and Zeithaml et al. (2000) argue that users experience a number of positive consequences of flow such as: increased learning, increased perceived behavioural control, and increased exploratory and participatory behaviour, when interacting with e-services system websites. Wanting to continue to use an e-services system then may stem from the interactivity involved, which may positively or negatively influence client's perceptions, and such perceptions favourably

Table 7. When successful in a task, students feel confident using e-Services for other tasks

		Frequency	Percent	Valid Percent	Cumulative Percent
Valid	Strongly Disagree	4	1.0	1.0	2.5
	Disagree	22	5.5	5.6	6.6
	Not Sure	95	23.6	24.0	30.6
	Agree	208	51.6	52.5	83.1
	Strongly Agree	67	16.6	16.9	100.0
	Total	396	98.3	100.0	
Missing	Not Applicable	7	1.7		
Total		403	100		

affect the use of different types of e-services. In this study, 24% of the international students in this study were not sure whether, if successful in one type of task, they would feel confident using the e-services system for other tasks (Table 7).

The international student's experience involves direct interaction with the university e-services system. User's skills should provide them with experience in using different e-services features that may facilitate their interaction with a system (Koufaris, 2002; Chea & Lou, 2008; Chellappan, 2008). Van Riel et al. (2001) and Chea and Lou (2008) found information on an e-services system should provide a clear understanding to the user about where to look for that information rather than wasting time and effort in searching for information in the wrong place. However, some users may not have a very clear perception of knowing more compared to other users which has been demonstrated in studies by Taylor and Todd (1995) and Morris and Turner (2001). It may be that every user's experience is unique and may differ from that of another user (Morris & Turner, 2001). In this study, 68% of international students had confidence in using and then re-using the e-services system.

CONCLUSION

The descriptive statistical data shows that student user experience was an important factor in deciding the acceptance, use, and continued use of the e-services System. The empirical evidence shows the importance of their skills, ability to find information on the e-services system, ease of movement within the e-services system, and confidence in using the e-services system in accepting and using the system.

The initial acceptance of e-services is the starting point where the international students evaluate the different features and functions of e-services based on individual experiences. The international student's assessment of the e-services application is formed on the basis of whether it is easy to follow the c-Services, whether the application is used in their work, and whether information is quicker to find. Such aspects of e-services form an underlying measurement related to how international students form their beliefs about using e-services. After initial acceptance the international student makes careful consideration about using e-services on a continuous basis in their work.

REFERENCES

Chea, S., & Lou, M. (2008). Post-adoption behaviors of e-service customers: The interplay of cognition and emotion. *International Journal of Electronic Commerce*, *12*(3), 29–56. doi:10.2753/JEC1086-4415120303.

Chellappan, C. (2008). *E-services: The need for higher levels of trust by populace*. Chennai, India: Anna University.

Cockburn, A., & McKenzie, B. (2000). What do web users do? An empirical analysis of web use. *International Journal of Human-Computer Studies*, *54*(6), 903–922. doi:10.1006/ijhc.2001.0459.

D'Ambra, J., & Rice, R. E. (2001). Emerging factors in user evaluation of the world wide web. *Information & Management*, *38*, 373–384. doi:10.1016/S0378-7206(00)00077-X.

Heijden, H. (2000). *Using the technology acceptance model to predict website usage: Extension and empirical test*. Amsterdam, The Netherlands: Vrije Universiteit.

Hoffman, D. L., & Novak, T. P. (1995). *Marketing in hypermedia computer-mediated environments: Conceptual foundations*. Working Paper No. 1 (Revised July 11,1995). Project 2000: Research Program on Marketing in Computer-Mediated Environments: 1-36.

Huang, C.-Y., Shen, Y.-C., Chiang, I.-P., & Lin, C.-S. (2007). Concentration of web users' online information behaviour. *Information Research*, *12*(4). Retrieved from http://InformationR.net/ir/12-4/paper324.html

Koufaris, M. (2002). Applying the technology acceptance model and flow theory to online consumer behaviour. *Information Systems Research*, *13*(2), 205–223. doi:10.1287/isre.13.2.205.83.

Morris, M. G., & Turner, J. M. (2001). Assessing users' subjective quality of experience with the world wide web: An exploratory examination of temporal changes in technology acceptance. *International Journal of Human-Computer Studies*, *54*, 877–901. doi:10.1006/ijhc.2001.0460.

Ramaswami, S. N., Strader, T. J., & Brett, K. (2000-2001). Determinants of on-line channel use for purchasing financial products. *International Journal of Electronic Commerce*, *5*(2), 95–118.

Taylor, S., & Todd, P. A. (1995). Understanding information technology usage: A test of competing models. *Information Systems Research*, *6*(2), 144–176. doi:10.1287/isre.6.2.144.

van Riel, A. C. R., Liljander, V., & Jurriëns, P. (2001). Exploring consumer evaluations of e-services: A portal site. *International Journal of Service Industry Management*, *12*(40), 359–377. doi:10.1108/09564230110405280.

Webster, J., Trevino, L. K., & Ryan, L. (1993). The dimensionality and correlates of flow in human computer interactions. *Computers in Human Behavior*, *9*(4), 411–426. doi:10.1016/0747-5632(93)90032-N.

Yaobin, L., & Tao, Z. (2007). A research of consumers' initial trust in online stores in China. *Journal of Research and Practice in Information Technology*, *39*(3). Retrieved from http://www.jrpit.acs.org.au/jrpit/JRPITVolumes/JRPIT39/JRPIT39.3.167.pdf.

Zeithaml, V. A., Parasuraman, A., & Malhotra, A. (2000). *A conceptual framework for understanding e-service quality: Implications for future research and managerial practice*. Marketing Science Institute.

Chapter 10
News Trends Processing Using Open Linked Data

Antonio Garrote
Universidad de Salamanca, Spain

María N. Moreno García
Universidad de Salamanca, Spain

EXECUTIVE SUMMARY

In this chapter we describe a news trends detection system built with the aim of detecting daily trends in a big collection of news articles extracted from the web and expose the computed trends data as open linked data that can be consumed by other components of the IT infrastructure. Due to the sheer amount of data being processed, the system relies on big data technologies to process raw news data and compute the trends that will be later exposed as open linked data. Thanks to the open linked data interface, data can be easily consumed by other components of the application, like a JavaScript front-end, or re-used by different IT systems. The case is a good example of how open linked data can be used to provide a convenient interface to big data systems.

ORGANIZATION BACKGROUND

The organization involved in the project is an Internet company providing data analysis services for different kinds of web data. Integration of different data sources capable of generating more useful insights on clients' data is an essential task in the company strategy.

DOI: 10.4018/978-1-4666-2827-4.ch010

From the organizational point of view, the software development process is accomplished by small and highly autonomous engineering teams responsible for different projects and relying on services provided by other teams. Use of big data technologies means that many times resources like computer clusters must be shared by different teams. This practice demands a high degree of cooperation between teams.

Within this context of small teams building a network of services that are used and combined by other teams, the use of open linked data makes it possible for the easy inter-operability between data resources as well as provides a shared vocabulary for the outcome data, processed by big data systems like Apache Hadoop.

Data management in big data systems is a hard problem. The organization undergoing the development project described in this case generates and processes tera bytes of data on a daily basis. Most of these data have been so far stored as plain tab-separated files in the Hadoop Distributed File System (HDFS) (Shvachko et al., 2010).

Re-using and cataloging the available data sources have been traditionally an important issue, due to the distributed nature of the development teams in the organization. As a consequence, problems like finding if the right information is already available in some part of the cluster file system or if some particular data generation process is still in use have been hard to solve, usually involving a lot of communication overhead between members of different teams.

This situation was slightly improved when a more structured data storage technology like Apache Hive started to be used instead of direct access to plain HDFS files. Hive provides a data abstraction layer in the form of data tables with a certain data schema and a relation SQL-like data retrieval language that can be used on top of the map-reduce platform offered by Hadoop. The use of a schema and an easy interface to query the stored data made it easier for non technical users to retrieve information from the cluster as well as provided a better definition of the available data. However, the problem of finding available data in the cluster remained a problem.

When making available structured information about news trends started to be considered as development project, linked data appeared as a possible alternative to provide a more open interface to the available data stored in the cluster, as well as a mechanism to interlink isolated data sets using well known web technologies like URIs and hyper-links.

CASE DESCRIPTION

The main goal of the project was to make available daily news trends as a structured data source that could be used as an additional input in any data analysis task being performed in the organization. Computation of the news trends was to be achieved in a series of steps involving:

- Crawling of news raw data from web sources.
- Classification of the news data by country, language, and topic.
- Extraction of trends using natural language processing techniques.
- Storage of the processed trends in the data cluster in a structured format compatible with Apache Hive.
- Building a data interface for the data available as a collection of web services that could be re-used by other applications without accessing directly the data stored in HDFS.
- Providing a web application exposing the news trend data through a user interface that could be used by non technical users.

The team assigned to the project consisted of two developers with a good knowledge of the statistical techniques for natural language processing as well as experience with the underlying Hadoop platform and web development skills.

The decision of using open linked data affected the later goals of the projects, like providing a web interface for the computed trends. A combination of linked data standards for data modeling like the Resource Description Language (RDF) embedded inside Java Script documents using the JSON-LD standard that could be made available through a series of simple RESTful (Fielding, 2000) web services was the intended solution for the web data interface.

Technology Concerns

From a technical point of view, the project showed important challenges. Crawling of web data is an error prone task, especially when no stable web APIs are available and techniques like web scrapping must be used.

Statistical analysis of the crawled data can also be problematic in particular when multiple languages must be processed in order to produce meaningful trend data.

Finally, the decision of using open linked data technologies as the primary web interface was also problematic. RDF is not a popular data format between web developers used to working with unstructured and schema-less JSON objects. This lack of familiarity can also be extended to other Semantic Web technologies traditionally used in combination with open linked data, like the SPARQL query language for RDF. Traditional encoding of RDF data as verbose XML documents was also highly unpopular among developers in the organization. Successful deployment of open linked data interfaces for the generated trends data required a solution for this particular issues and concerns.

Technology Components

The final solution consisted on a series of loosely coupled components solving the different sub-problems detected in the project.

A crawling component was developed using the Clojure programming language in order to retrieve raw news data from the web. Different news sources were evaluated, looking for suitable interfaces that could make the crawling task easier. Finally, Google News service was chosen as a convenient provider of an aggregated stream of news articles from different countries, topics and languages. Google News does not provide a data API properly, but gives access to the raw HTML for the news articles through a stable set of URIs that can be easily processed by an user agent.

News data retrieved by this component are processed using standard HTML parsing techniques and then stored in a temporary location in the HDFS file system using a conventional directory structure including the information about the date, country, and topic for the news article. Clojure support for distributed systems made it easy to build a distributed crawling application capable of processing in parallel different data sources from Google News as well as dealing with the regular scheduling of the crawling process.

Trends analysis of the crawled data was achieved combining the output of two different techniques. The first kind of analysis is performed using natural language processing techniques. The Apache OpenNLP Java framework is used as the main resource in the analysis since it includes many useful tools and models like part of speech (POS) taggers, tokenizers, and others, readily available for different natural languages. The analysis process was implemented as a single Hadoop map-reduce job that was capable of processing the already crawled raw news data. The resulting output of the process is a collection of tab separated value files including the most relevant fragments of the news data with an associated quality score.

The second analysis process of crawled news data involves the use of linked data technology to perform semantic analysis of the news articles. The Apache Stanbol project makes it possible to accomplish named entity detection on arbitrary text fragments and documents using different semantic data engines as the sources for the annotations. Named entities that can be extracted include countries, people, organizations, and companies. Stanbol performs the annotation of documents through a RESTful interface were a simple HTTP request is enough to trigger the analysis process. Another advantage of using Apache Stanbol is its modular design. New semantic engines can be added making it possible for Stanbol to generate richer annotations. In this project, Reuters Open Calais project was used as an additional engine for Apache Stanbol, improving dramatically the quality of the annotations.

The named entities retrieved from Stanbol were finally stored in additional tab separated value files in HDFS linked to the original news data by the path used to store the files.

The final processing step in the cluster consisted in an additional Hadoop map-reduce job that merges the output of both analysis to create the final set documents including a brief description of the news article, like URI, summary, date, media where the article was published, among others, and the collection of relevant text fragment and extracted named entities. The three kind of documents are linked by a uniquely generated identifier that makes it possible to relate annotations and text fragments to the article information. All these documents are then loaded as Hive partitions data can be used in structured queries over the news information.

The final part of the project involved exposing the generated trends data through some kind of web API. Due to the amount of data generated in the analysis process, no all data were suitable to be offered through the web interface, but a representative subset was chosen. The presence of a quality metric in all fragment and named entities generated by the analysis process made it easy to select only the most relevant results per hour, country and news topic from HDFS using a simple Hive query.

These queries are run periodically and then stored in a MongoDB database as plain JSON documents with property names mirroring the schema of the Hive tables.

A small ruby web application was built to expose these documents as linked data using the JSON-LD standard. JSON-LD makes it possible to embed the RDF data model inside plain JSON objects. The main advantage of this encoding is that JSON-LD documents can be consumed as any other JSON document by API clients not willing to take full advantage of RDF features, but still delivering these details for semantic enabled clients. Transformation of plain JSON documents into JSON-LD objects is also an straightforward process requiring only the selection of the right ontology or vocabulary for the properties and the addition of a couple of additional properties with information about the mapping from JSON property names into RDF properties. In our case an ontology based on the Dublin Core ontology extended with some custom properties was the main vocabulary used to expose the computed news trends data.

Finally, a web interface consisting of a rich JavaScript application consuming the JSON-LD API was built using a couple of libraries developed at the Universidad de Salamanca: RDFStore-JS (Garrote and Moreno, 2012), a triple store that can be embedded inside a JavaScript application running on a web browser; and SemanticKO, a front-end library that can be used to built user interfaces for JavaScript web applications binding visual components to RDF data stored in RDFStore-JS.

CURRENT CHALLENGES FACING THE ORGANIZATION

The implementation of the project was a success, finishing its execution in the scheduled three weeks period. The news trend data generated by the project have already been used by different projects in the organization and has become a valuable asset in data analysis tasks.

However, the Hive interface for the computed data is still the preferred data access mechanism over the semantic API. Only a couple of applications are currently using the web API and they are using the offered data as plain JSON objects without taking advantage of the RDF data model. As we have noticed in the initial sections of this chapter, the development mentality and concerns around the perceived complexity of RDF are important handicaps for taking advantage of RDF, especially for simple use cases.

Nevertheless, the web front-end built as part of the project, showing particular examples of how to make use of RDF in order to build useful features in a JavaScript applications that are hard to achieve with plain JSON data, like running custom SPARQL queries over the data stored in the application, has boosted the interest of different teams in the potential use of the RDF data exposed by the projects web data interface. It is also a good example of how the developers of a particular API can become the first clients of the services there exposed, making it easier to design and polish the interface.

Another important future challenge is to increase the value of the web data API adding incoming and outgoing links to the exposed data set. Exposing additional data sets available throughout the organization, using a shared vocabulary, and inter-linking those datasets can multiply the value of the already exposed data, like the interface built in this project. It also has the potential to solve the data storage and curation issues mentioned before. RDF provides the ideal data model and support for vocabularies that can be used to achieve these goals. The use of a simple encoding like JSON-LD also offers a suitable mechanism for delivering RDF data, aligned with the engineering culture of the organization and lowering the adoption barrier for other developers.

SOLUTIONS AND RECOMMENDATIONS

Based on our experience building this project, we think the use of linked data technologies, particularly the RDF data model, can be part of the answer to data exchange problems in data intensive organizations. Features like the powerful data model and support for the use of ontologies providing semantic content for the raw data available in different information silos are important and useful assets when trying to re-use and merge heterogeneous data catalogues. This is a special concern in organizations like the one briefly described in this case, composed of distributed and autonomous teams that need to collaborate and provide data for other team projects. However, the use of RDF at this moment can be regarded as controversial. It is not a very well known technology stack and many developers find it too complex and over-engineered. The open linked data approach to semantic technologies, with a focus on pragmatism, can be a necessary answer to these concerns in actual deployments. The use of JSON-LD to wrap RDF data, making it possible for development teams to decide how much of the semantic stack want to use, is an example of this pragmatic approach.

REFERENCES

Fielding, R. (2000). Principled design of modern web architecture. In *Proceedings of the 22nd International Conference on Software Engineering* (pp. 407-416). New York: ACM.

Garrote, A., & Moreno García, M. N. (2012). *A JavaScript RDF store and application library for linked data client applications.* Paper presented at W3C 2012 Web Conference. New York, NY.

Shvachko, K., Kuang, H., Radia, S., & Chansler, R. (2010). *The Hadoop distributed file system.* Paper presented at IEEE 26th Symposium on Mass Storage Systems and Technologies (MSST). New York, NY.

Chapter 11
Publishing Statistical Data following the Linked Open Data Principles:
The Web Index Project

Jose María Alvarez Rodríguez
University of Oviedo, Spain

Jules Clement
World Wide Web Foundation, Switzerland

José Emilio Labra Gayo
University of Oviedo, Spain

Hania Farhan
World Wide Web Foundation, Switzerland

Patricia Ordoñez de Pablos
University of Oviedo, Spain

EXECUTIVE SUMMARY

This chapter introduces the promotion of statistical data to the Linked Open Data initiative in the context of the Web Index project. A framework for the publication of raw statistics and a method to convert them to Linked Data are also presented following the W3C standards RDF, SKOS, and OWL. This case study is focused on the Web Index project; launched by the Web Foundation, the Index is the first multidimensional measure of the growth, utility, and impact of the Web on people and nations. Finally, an evaluation of the advantages of using Linked Data to publish statistics is also presented in conjunction with a discussion and future steps sections.

DOI: 10.4018/978-1-4666-2827-4.ch011

ORGANIZATION BACKGROUND

WESO is a multidisciplinary research group from the Department of Computer Science and the Departments of Philology at the University of Oviedo leaded by the Associate Professor Dr. José Emilio Labra Gayo. Since 2005 WESO is involved in semantic Web research, education and technology transfer. The growth of the Internet in the last years has brought relevant changes in the way of communication. Nowadays governments, citizens, enterprises and society are more interconnected than ever and information is the key to keep the interconnection among parties. This new information society needs a step forward to exploit the new opportunities and challenges. WESO research activities try to apply semantic Web technologies in order to facilitate the transition to a new Web of data.

As academic research group, one of our aims is to boost the research, innovation and competitiveness of the organizations using the knowledge. WESO seeks to support research and innovation focusing on:

- Providing research services on semantics by applying semantic technologies to improve existing products
- Addressing the new-technology barriers and developing and training
- Fostering the knowledge in the scientific and industrial areas
- Teaching to a new wave of professionals

WESO brings together these activities for enabling and supporting people, organizations and systems to collaborate and interoperate in the new global context. Our research lines focus on semantic Web technologies with emphasis on (but not restricted to):

- **Semantic Architectures:** Designing and developing architectures based on domain knowledge.
- **Collaborative Semantic Services:** Improving existing solutions with a semantic collaborative approach.
- **Linked and Open Data:** Offering new solutions for combining RDF vocabularies and publishing data.
- **Methods and Algorithms:** Implementing methods to exploit the domain knowledge and the Web of data.
- **Semantic Technologies:** Being aware of the semantic Web technologies outcomes of RDF, OWL, SKOS or RIF.
- **Others:** Semantic Web Services, e-government, e-procurement, e-health, etc.

Web Foundation

The World Wide Web Foundation was established in 2009 by Web inventor Sir Tim Berners-Lee to tackle the fundamental obstacles to realizing his vision of an open Web available, usable, and valuable for everyone.

The Web is the most powerful tool for communication in the history of humanity, creating the potential for all people to participate in building a more peaceful and equitable world.

However, only a small minority of people – mainly urban, male, and affluent – are part of the Web's global conversation. Despite the recent surge in mobile Internet access, nearly two-thirds of the world's people (mostly in the developing world) are still not connected at all. And once connected, what people are able to do on and with the Web is increasingly threatened by government controls, as well as by certain commercial practices.

We seek to establish the open Web as a global public good and a basic right, ensuring that everyone can access and use it freely. The foundation is unendowed and relies on charitable donations and partnerships to carry out its work. A registered charity in Switzerland and the USA, we have offices in Boston, Geneva, and Cape Town.

INTRODUCTION

Every day public bodies, organizations and people in general are generating data about different situations such as financial information, legislation updates, weather forecast, news or user behaviour in social networks that can be accessed through the Web. This sheer mass of data and information is, most of the times, referring statistical data that can be reused to be processed and analysed with the objective of generating new services or assessing the status of a specific indicator. Thus companies can make decisions according to the exploitation of data in a sector or new marketing campaigns can take advantage of the user behaviour to offer ad-hoc services and goods. Therefore the proper exploitation of statistical data is one of the most important information sources relevant to multiple and distinct stakeholders. Domains such as e-Government, e-Health or e-Tourism are currently publishing valuable data for final users and practitioners but the reuse of this information is not always adequate: different formats, models, access methods among others prevent the proper reuse of the digital ecosystem converting this valuable data realm in a tangled environment of numbers, methods and specifications in which the access, understanding and exploitation is not a mere issue.

In this context the Semantic Web initiative tries to elevate the meaning of Web information resources through common and shared data models with the aim of improving the interoperability and integration in service oriented architectures. In this sense two major efforts are being carried out:

1. The Linked Data initiative (Berners-Lee, 2006) that proposes a set of principles for publishing data and information using the Resource Description Framework (RDF) to ease the creation of the new Web of Data realm. Thus data can be easily identified, shared, exchanged and linked to other datasets through Uniform Resource Identifiers (URIs). Existing works are focused on publishing and consuming data via the SPARQL language that offers a formal language and a protocol to query RDF repositories, commonly called endpoints. The main objective of this effort lies in the creation of a new data-based environment in which added-value services can be deployed taken advantage of the vast amount of data available via Internet protocols encouraging and improving B2B (Business to Business), B2C (Business to Client) or A2A (Administration to Administration) relationships. Moreover, the emerging Web of Data and the sheer mass of information now available make it possible the deployment of new applications based on the reuse of existing vocabularies and datasets. In this sense the popular diagram of the Linked Data Cloud, generated from metadata extracted from the Comprehensive Knowledge Archive Network (CKAN) out, contains 337 datasets, with more than 25 billion RDF triples and 395 million links. In this context, data coming from different sources and domains have been promoted following the principles of the Linked (Open) Data (LOD) initiative to improve the access to large documental databases, e.g. e-Government resources, scientific publications or e-Health records.
2. The design and development of logic formalisms and knowledge-based systems using ontologies in OWL (the Ontology Web Language). In this sense new expert systems are arisen to tackle existing problems in medical reasoning, analysis of social media, etc. in which data heterogeneities, lack of standard knowledge representation and interoperability problems are common factors.

On the other hand, since its invention by Tim Berners-Lee in 1989, the World Wide Web (the Web) has had a deep impact on humanity. The creation of new contents, services, software and infrastructures is continuously facing challenges to integrate data and information for delivering intelligent services. From social, economic or political points of view the Web has changed the perception of well-grounded activities and habits whether these changes are positive or negative the fact is that some countries have moved faster and more effectively than other to harness the Web as a new accelerator of development. Nevertheless the lack of an effective way to assess the impact of the Web in countries is preventing the proper development of a new economy in which the Web can play a key-role. The Web Index project emerges in this context to bridge the gap between the Web as a tool and the real impact of its use in social, economic and political issues. According to (Farhan & D'Agostino, 2012) to address this gap, the Web Foundation has created an index, hereafter The Web Index, that combines existing secondary indicators and data coming from institutions such as the United Nations, the World Bank or the International Telecommunication Union (ITU) among others with new primary data to rank countries assessing their progress and use of the Web. This index is both an analytical tool for researchers and a resource for policy makers in distinct sectors. One of the key points of this project lies in the full transparency in the construction, data and methodology to produce it and all is open and publicly available to be reused by others easing the undertake of own research.

Obviously the public data and information published by the Web Foundation, more specifically by the Web Index project, is a suitable candidate to apply the Linked Open Data (LOD) principles and semantic Web technologies providing a new environment in which the conjunction of these initiatives can provide the building blocks for an innovative unified view of statistical data that encourages standardization of key decision processes and systems and gives economic and political operators tools to overcome technical interoperability easing and enhancing the access and the reuse of public information.

The chapter is structured as follows. Next section reviews the relevant literature and background concepts. Afterwards the promotion of raw statistics to the Linked Data initiative is depicted to continue in the next section with the case of study: the Web Index project. Results and examples of the Web Index as Linked Data are also presented. Finally, the chapter ends with some discussion about existing limitations of the current approach and other concluding remarks and future actions are also outlined.

BACKGROUND

As part of the LOD effort other similar initiatives have also been deployed such as the Linked Geo Data effort, the GeoNames service, the Linked Open Drug Data initiative or the OpenLink Data Spaces network among others. More specifically in the field of Open Government Data (OGD) there are projects trying to exploit the information of public procurement notices like the "Linked Open Tenders Electronic Daily" project (LOTED Project, 2012) or the MOLDEAS project (Álvarez-Rodríguez, 2012). In the context of European projects the LOD2 (LOD2 Project, 2012), LATC (LATC Project, 2012) and PlanetData (PlanetData, 2012) projects are also increasing the awareness of LOD across Europe delivering specific research and dissemination activities such as the "European Data Forum". Besides legal aspects of public sector information are being reviewed in the LAPSI project (LAPSI Project, 2012) creating the proper digital ecosystem from both legal and technical points of view.

In the case of national actions, the United Kingdom government (UK Government, 2012) is doing a great effort to promote its information sources applying the principles of the LOD initiative. They have published vocabularies and datasets to be used in the transport, financial, economical, or educational domains, as an example the Nomenclature of territorial units for statistics (NUTS) have been promoted to the LOD initiative. Furthermore, they have also funded the Open Data Institute to boost the deployment of this effort in conjunction with Linked Data. Most of the public administrations from different countries are also supporting the LOD approach to make publicly available their information: Spain (Spanish Government, 2012), USA (White House, 2009), etc. In the case of research works, new vocabularies and datasets are being released as well as foundational concepts such as the execution of federated SPARQL (Buil-Aranda, Arenas & Corcho, 2011) queries or tools for testing the quality, usage and features of those datasets (Alexander, Cyganiak, Hausenblas & Zhao, 2011). In the particular case of publishing linked data, the Linked Media Framework, PoolParty, ELDA or Pubby provide a configurable way to access RDF data using simple RESTful URLs that are translated into queries to a SPARQL endpoint. Other approaches to consume "semantic data" consists on querying OWL models with SPARQL (Jing, Jeong & Baik, 2008) or the emerging C-SPARQL (Barbieri, Braga, Ceri et al., 2010) and EP-SPARQL (Anicic, Fodor, Rudolph et al., 2011) to support stream reasoning and complex event processing in this data realm.

In the particular case of statistical data, the RDF Data Cube Vocabulary (Cyganiak & Reynolds, 2012), a W3C Working Draft document, is a shared effort to represent statistical data in RDF reusing parts (the cube model) of the Statistical Data and Metadata Exchange Vocabulary (SDMX) (SDMX initiative, 2005), an ISO standard for exchanging and sharing statistical data and metadata among organizations. The Data Cube vocabulary is a core foundation which supports extension vocabularies to enable publication of other aspects of statistical data flows or other multi-dimensional data sets. Previously, the Statistical Core Vocabulary (SCOVO, 2009), published by DERI, was the standard in fact to describe statistical information in the Web of Data. Some works are also emerging to publish statistical data following the concepts of the LOD initiative such as (Bosch, Cyganiak, Wackerow et al., 2012), (Zapilko & Mathiak, 2012) or (Rivera-Salas, Martin, Maia Da Mota, Auer, S. et al., 2012) among others.

Finally and with regards to the promotion of raw data to RDF, some LOD life-cycles aim to define methodologies, best practices and recipes such as the "Linked Data Design Considerations" (Heath & Bizer, 2011), the "Linked Data Patterns" book (Dodds & Davis, 2011), the W3C "Best Practices" (W3C Members, 2011), the "Linked Data Cookbook" (Hyland, Villazón-Terrazas & Capadisli, 2011), the "Government Linked Data Lifecyle" (Hausenblas, Villazón-Terrazas and Hyland, 2011), the W3C notes on "Best Practice Recipes for Publishing RDF Vocabularies" (Berrueta, Phipps, Miles, Baker, & Swick, 2008) and "Publishing Open Government Data" (Bennett & Harvey, 2009), the "LOD2 Stack" (LOD2 Project, 2012), the technical report entitled "Toward a Basic Profile for Linked Data" (Nally,& Speicher, 2011) from IBM that has now the status of W3C Member Submission (Nally, Speicher, Arwe & Le Hors, 2012) or other specific documentation and guidelines from different countries and people.

PROMOTION OF RAW STATISTICS TO THE LINKED OPEN DATA INITIATIVE

The promotion of raw data to the Linked Data initiative usually follows a common process in which some tasks must be carried out in order to ease and control the data coded as RDF. As the previous section has reviewed existing methodologies, best practices and recipes try to unify the steps and processes to get a successful transformation. Nevertheless each data promotion or transformation has its own particularities that must be taken into account to boost the generation process. Following a summary of the common tasks to promote raw data to RDF is outlined:

- Analysis of the input dataset identifying entities and relationships.
- Data cleansing.
- Vocabulary selection to code data as RDF.
- Creation of RDF data models to represent the domain knowledge and validate the generated data.
- Datasets selection to link our data with existing and major community efforts.
- Design of an URI scheme.
- Transformation of raw data to RDF.
- Creation of metadata to ease the reuse of the new RDF dataset.
- Validation of the generated RDF data.
- Deployment of a Linked Data infrastructure to make the RDF data publicly available.

According to the aforementioned points there is no such special thing in the case of transforming statistical data with regards to other kind of data. However, the use of the RDF Data Cube vocabulary implies the necessity of paying attention in the design of RDF Data Cube datasets, measurements, dimensions, slices or views that are particular in the statistics domain. Thus some tasks such as the analysis of the input dataset, the design of an URI scheme or the whole transformation must cover these particular features to provide a proper publication of data for both practitioners and final users.

On the other hand, albeit the existence of several ways, see Background section, for promoting data to RDF, a formal definition of processes, methods and tasks is missing and, in most of the cases, they are based on the author's expertise. The main consequence of this offhand mixing of approaches is the lack of a quantifiable method to measure the quality of the generated RDF. That is why we have selected and applied the lifecycle proposed in the MOLDEAS project (Álvarez-Rodríguez, 2012; Alvarez-Rodríguez, Labra-Gayo, Cifuentes-Silva et al., 2012) that perfectly defines which the steps to produce, publish, consume and validate linked open data are. Figure 1 summarizes several tasks to be performed in order to get the transition from raw information to linked data. The formal definition of processes, methods and tasks in this lifecycle enables separation of concerns and the sustainable management of linked data. In public bodies or non-profit organizations this issue must be addressed due to the implicit responsibility of delivering high-quality services and data.

CASE STUDY: THE WEB INDEX PROJECT

Authors have hitherto outlined which tasks of the linked data lifecycle can be applied to the promotion of raw data to linked data and they have also highlighted some issues that must be evaluated before transforming statistical data. According to the MOLDEAS lifecycle (Álvarez-Rodríguez, 2012) the most prominent tasks are presented. For the sake of a better reader understanding, this report is not intended to focus on the design of the index from a mathematical point of view but rather explain the experience and findings during the transformation process.

1. Task t_1. The structure of the Web Index, see Figure 2, is relatively intuitive and based on the own Web infrastructure with the objective of identifying and assessing the impact of the Web in social, economic and political aspects. Thus, the Web Index, as a composite index, is comprised of three major sub-indexes *Communications and Institutional Infrastructure*, *Web Content and Web use* and *Political, Economic and Social Impact*. These sub-indexes are not necessarily proportional so in order to aggregate their values in the final index each one has its own weight. This situation is repeated in the next levels: 7 component and 85 indicators. Indicators are aggregated to calculate the value of a component and those are also aggregated to establish a value for

Figure 1. Summary of tasks of the MOLDEAS linked data lifecycle

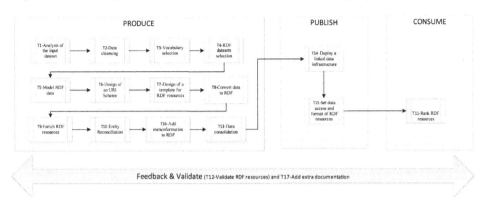

a sub-index. From a bottom-up point of view there are observations which refer to an indicator. Each observation consists in distinct metadata, in most of the cases, provider, country, year and value. Once observation values are cleaned (missing values) and aggregated applying different statistical methods such as normalization the value of the component can be calculated and so on taking into account their corresponding weights. Summarizing next data and information is available for the Web Index entities:

- **Observation:** Measured value provided by an organization that corresponds to an indicator in a certain country and year.
- **Indicator:** Description of the measurement provided by an organization. There are three types of indicators: (a) primary indicators: data gathered by the Web Foundation through different techniques such as personal surveys and expert opinion; (b) secondary indicators: data extracted out from public and private bodies that annually generate statistics about the use of Internet and (c) external indicators, it is a special kind of secondary indicator that is used to enrich information but not for the calculation of the Web Index. An indicator is part of one and only one component.
- **Component:** Aggregation of indicators to calculate a value. A component is part of one and only one sub-index.
- **Sub-Indexes:** Aggregation of components to calculate a value. The final aggregation of sub index values generates the Web Index.
- **Geographical Information:** All data gathered by the Web Index project is geo-located. Depending on the type of indicator, data refers to a country, a region or a continent. The identification of these areas can be found in different forms: (1) names (textual descriptions) or (2) codes in different schemes such

Figure 2. The web index structure

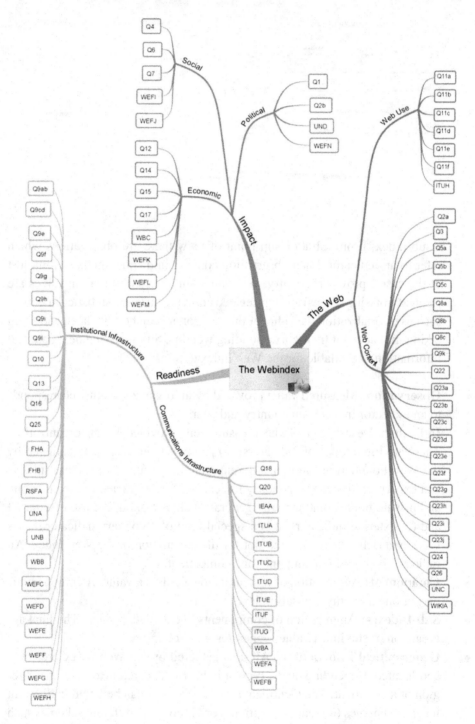

as ISO 3166 version 2 and 3. In the case of names there is a lack of unification depending on the institution so it is necessary to perform an entity reconciliation process to unify the nomenclature of countries, regions and continents.

- **Providers:** It is the metadata about the public and private bodies that have compiled statistics in a certain field. It is comprised of two major blocks of data: (1) metadata about indicators (data, source URL, description, etc.) and (2) the own identification of the provider covering postal address and contact person.

According to this analysis, some typical requirements in the promotion of raw data to RDF can be found: necessity of a common and shared data model to represent geo-located data coming from different data sources. Finally, it is necessary to emphasize that all data is available as MSExcel files with the next structure for each tuple of data: country, indicator, type, year and value, more specifically the variable type refers to the kind of value that can be "Raw," "Imputed," or "Normalised."

2. Following the lifecycle's tasks, the most important action to accomplish in task t_2 (clean data) lies in the unification of float values, more specifically decimal separators and geographical names in order to ensure that values are comparable and the index can be computed from the RDF version.

3. Task t_3. This task aims to select the appropriate vocabularies and ontologies for representing the information and statistical data with a common and shared data model. Thus the reuse of existing definitions, classes and properties, enables a wider impact in the community when someone is looking for reusing the Web Index data for performing some task such as reasoning, validation or visualization. Table 1 summarizes the selected vocabularies and their use and applicability.

4. Task t_4. In the same way as the previous task, this action seeks for providing the appropriate mappings and links to existing datasets in order to create a real linked data environment and enrich the Web Index data. According to the information and data available in the Web Index project the next external datasets have been selected, see Table 2. The selection of these datasets have been carried out due to the own authors experience in the promotion of raw data to RDF and checking the most valuable and used datasets in the Linked Data realm that fits to the Web Index data. In this case, the consultation of Prefix.cc and datahub.io among others data catalogues gives us the right tool to select existing datasets.

5. Task t_5. Since task t_1 helps to identify the entities and relationships that emerge from data this task is in charge of capturing the previous analysis to create a common data model in which all information and data can be defined using the

Table 1. Task t_3-selected vocabularies for representing the web index information and data

Vocabulary	Use
W3C-Simple Knowledge Organization System (SKOS)	Definition of concepts (Index, Component, Indicator, etc.) and their relationships to represent the Web Index structure and data.
W3C-RDF Data Cube Vocabulary	Publication of statistical data about indicators including SDMX concepts and properties.
W3C-Organizations Ontology (Reynolds, 2012)	Publication of metadata about information providers.
The Friend of a Friend (FOAF) project	Publication of metadata about people involved in the project and description of datasets.
W3C-Time Ontology	Modelling time intervals and dates.
Vocabulary of Interlinked Datasets (VoID)	Description of RDF datasets metadata
Dublin Core Metadata Initiative (DCMI)- Metadata Terms	Addition of extra metadata in RDF resources, etc.
Linked Geo Data Ontology	Reuse of country and region definitions.
Semantic Web stack vocabularies and ontologies	RDFS, OWL2, XML-Schema, etc. for defining own classes and properties as extension of existing ones.

Table 2. Task t_4-selected existing datasets for linking and enriching the web index information and data

Dataset	Use
DBPedia Ontology and Data	Link to countries and other concepts for describing Web Index entities.
World Bank Data	Reuse of some indicators and values (This data is previously transformed to RDF as well as other native Web Index indicators).
FAO Geopolitical Ontology and Data	Link to geographical data.
NUTS	Link to geographical data in the European Union.

selected vocabularies from task t_3. Obviously new concepts and properties must be added as an extension of existing definitions but keeping always in mind that the major objective of reusing common definitions. In this sense, Figure 3 depicts the formalization of concepts and properties that can be extracted from the Web Index data out. As a direct consequence of the defined hierarchy new statistics can be easily added including new sub-indexes, components or indicators without modifying the previous structure. Moreover, the particular representation of RDF Data Cube datasets is completely covered enabling the creation of new slices over the same data.

Figure 3. Partial view of the RDF data model for the web index

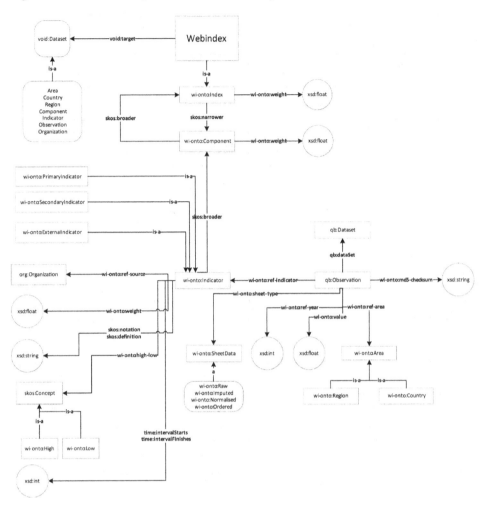

6. Task t$_6$. The main objective of this task is naming the Web Index entities with URIs, see Table 3, with the aim of easing people and machines the consultation of information and data. There are several reference documents (Berners-Lee, 2006) (Berners-Lee, 2008) (UK Government, 2012a) in which some recipes are presented in order to create a good scheme that makes it easy to tie data about things. Taking into the account the Web Index features some different kinds of URIs can be identified:

    a. URIs for naming things such as ontology concepts and properties, sub-indexes, components, indicators, datasets or slices, in this case human-readable URIs are generated for each entity.

Table 3. URI scheme for the web index entities and data

URI Pattern	Example and notes
http://data.Webfoundation.org/Webindex/	N/A
<base_uri>/ontology/{name}	http://data.Webfoundation.org/Webindex/ontology/value
<base_uri>/index/{name}	http://data.Webfoundation.org/Webindex/index/Readiness
<base_uri>/component/{name}	http://data.Webfoundation.org/Webindex/component/InstitutionalInfrastructure
<base_uri>/indicator/{name} and <base_uri>/indicator/external/{id}	• http://data.Webfoundation.org/Webindex/indicator/ITUA •http://data.Webfoundation.org/Webindex/indicator/external/AG.LND.TOTL.K2
<base_uri>/dataset/{indicator}-{dataset}	http://data.Webfoundation.org/Webindex/dataset/ITUA-Normalised
<base_uri>/slice/{indicator}-{dataset }/{year}	http://data.Webfoundation.org/Webindex/slice/ITUA-Normalised/2010
<base_uri>/observation/{indicator}-{ type }/obs{id}	http://data.Webfoundation.org/Webindex/observation/ITUA-Normalised/obs24
<base_uri>/area/	http://data.Webfoundation.org/Webindex/area/
<base_uri>/area/region/{name}	http://data.Webfoundation.org/Webindex/area/region/Americas
<base_uri>/area/country/{iso-code-3}	http://data.Webfoundation.org/Webindex/area/country/ARG
<base_uri>/organization/{name}	http://data.Webfoundation.org/Webindex/organization/WESO
<base_uri>/people/{name}	http://data.Webfoundation.org/Webindex/people/Chema
<base_uri>/score/s{id}[1]	http://data.Webfoundation.org/Webindex/score/s38

    b.   URIs for encoding code lists such as observations or countries, in this particular case ID URIs are used because of the URI extension does not allow a human-readable format.

7.   Tasks t_7. t_8. t_9. t_{10} t_{16}. These tasks are in charge of preparing and performing the transformation of raw data to RDF. Once the data model is designed a template for the target RDF resources (task t_7) can be used to ease the creation and validation of the generated RDF resources. In this case, Code Listings in the Results section perfectly explain the output of this task. The transformation of raw data is carried out by task t_8, several tools can be used here to establish mappings between a cell in the MSExcel files and the data coded as RDF. In this case, Google Refine and its extension GRefine (a RDF plug-in) have been

firstly used for the RDF generation and mapping of countries and regions to existing datasets. Although existing tools such as TARQL (Cyganiak, 2012) or the TABELS project (Noriega, Tejo, González-Moriyon et al., 2012) present good features to perform the promotion of data from table-based structures to RDF the whole transformation of observations and indicators has required a the construction of a more powerful tool to deal with data particularities and heterogeneities. That is why a tool called LODIN (Linked Open Data Generator of Index Data) and a custom XML vocabulary have been designed to represent how to transform raw data and perform other tasks such as the enrichment of RDF resources (t_9), the reconciliation of entities (t_{10}) or the addition of meta-information to the generated RDF (t_{16}). Basically, the LODIN XML vocabulary, see Listing 1, is a mapping vocabulary, inspired by (Das, Sundara & Cyganiak, 2012), in which it is possible to configure both how the tuples in the MSExcel files must be processed and which metadata information must be added to finally generate URIs and links to other external RDF resources. These XML files and other extra metadata information such as providers or indicators are read by the LODIN processor (a JAXB and Java based tool) that generates in a single (or several) files the Web Index data coded as RDF. Although this approach implies the creation of a tool from the scratch, the experience of adapting existing tools to specific problems is more time-consuming than the creation of a simple vocabulary for representing data tables. Moreover this processor is completely declarative so this tool can be easily adapted to other domains (on-going work) in which data is coming from structured sources such as CSV, TSV or MSExcel and can be represented as a table (one row is a tuple of data). Finally, the process of reconciling country names in observations has been carried out customizing an existing tool for creating links between products and services, in this case this tool have been parameterized with country names.

Once the process of producing RDF is finished next step includes data publication under the principles the LOD initiative paying special attention to the necessity of delivering data through a SPARQL endpoint accomplishing the requirements of content negotiation among others. To fulfil these requirements the OpenLink Virtuoso server has been selected as RDF repository in which a SPARQL endpoint is automatically deployed. All data have been organized in different named graphs according to its meaning, in this case indexes, components, indicators, observations, countries, regions, etc. has a particular named graph containing their RDF triples thus partial updates of a dataset do not affect to the other ones. Nevertheless to ease the querying of the Web Index all triples have been added to a default named graph (http://data.Webfoundation.org/Webindex) with the objective of avoiding the use

Listing 1. Example of the LODIN XML vocabulary

```
<dataset
xmlns="http://purl.org/weso/lodin"
        id="FHA-Imputed"
        indicator="FHA"
>
<table rowStart="2" rowEnd="62">
    <values     countryCol="A"
                valueCol="B"
                year="2007"
                datatype="number"
    />

    <values     countryCol="A"
                valueCol="C"
                year="2008"
                datatype="number"
    />

    <values     countryCol="A"
                valueCol="D"
                year="2009"
                datatype="number"
    />

    <values     countryCol="A"
                valueCol="E"
                year="2010"
                datatype="number"
    />

    <values     countryCol="A"
                valueCol="F"
                year="2011"
                datatype="number"
    />
</table>
</dataset>
```

of *n* FROM SPARQL clauses in the client queries. At this point it must be highlighted that this approach should be only used when all RDF data is available and consolidated in the endpoint and with the unique objective of easing the writing of SPARQL queries. Moreover an extra step must be carried out in order to ensure the proper dissemination (discovering and browsing) of the published dataset, all RDF resources and datasets must contain adequate metadata to ease the navigation through links applying the pattern "*follow-your-nose*", the use of the VoID vocabulary to describe public datasets and the Dublin Core terms are essential to implement this navigational and discovering pattern. Finally Pubby has been selected as a Linked Data Front-end, see Figure 5, to provide content negotiation and accomplish with the rules of best practices for publishing RDF vocabularies and datasets and a

Figure 4. Simple visualization of some ITU indicators in Spain during the period 2007-2011

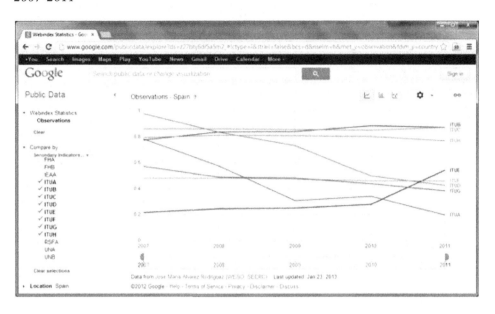

Figure 5. Browsing the web index through the linked data front-end-pubby

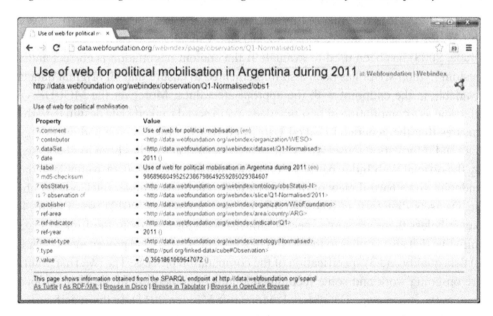

Figure 6. Querying the web index through the SNORQL interface

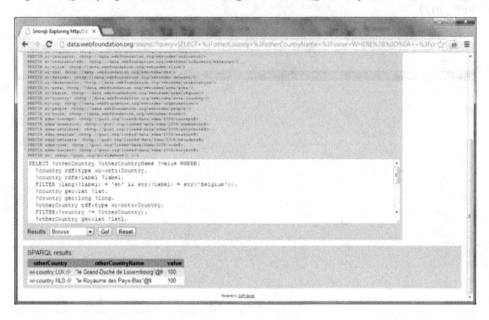

SNORQL interface, see Figure 6, to perform live queries has also been deployed to test SPARQL queries against the endpoint.

On the other hand the validation process seeks for providing a method to assess that the production and publication of Linked Data has been successful in terms of accomplishing the principles of this initiative delivering a 5 start dataset. To achieve this major objective the Vapour-Linked Data Validator (Berrueta, Fernández & Frade, 2008) has been used to evaluate if the content negotiation is correct and a custom Python script has been also implemented to ensure that all original data is available in the endpoint with the appropriate values. Moreover the MOLDEAS lifecycle as a compilation of best practices, recipes and Linked Data design patterns ensures that the generated Linked Data is correct in order to ease and encourage data and information reuse. An example a visualization tool has been implemented by the official Web Index partner Iconomical reusing the metadata available in the endpoint and a partial view of the dataset is also published under the Google Public Datasets directory (Álvarez-Rodríguez & Labra-Gayo, 2012), see Figure 4. Nevertheless there are some specific drawbacks with regards to the Linked Data initiative that also applies to the Web Index project: 1) trust and provenance of data; 2) data quality and 3) specification of the computation process. The two first points are on-going work and some recommendations are emerging in the W3C groups such as the Provenance Data Model (Moreau & Missier, 2011). In the specific case of the Web Index project to partially address the provenance and trust of data, a data property with a hash MD5 of an observation has been added. It is calculated generating the MD5 hash of the indicator, type of dataset, country ISO-code-3, year, value and the string literal "WESO" (all fields separated by #). For instance, given the next string "ITUG#Raw#MLI#2010#WESO", the corresponding MD5 hash is 204884280430351833456528445921380743306.

Thus clients can check if the data provided by the endpoint is really generated by the publisher, man-in-the-middle attaches are avoided. As an important point for reusing information and data in a trustworthy environment all data published in the Web Index is licensed under the Open Data Commons Attribution License (ODC-By) v1.0.

RESULTS AND EXAMPLES

Since the process of producing RDF is finished, data is published under the principles of the LOD initiative and a standard method to query through SPARQL is also provided some typical statistics about the transformation (see Table 4), examples of the main entities as Linked Data and demo queries are provided in order to ease the comprehension of the new public data and information.

Table 4. The web index as linked data statistics

Type of entity	Number of distinct entities	Example
Index	4	See Listing 2
Component	7	See Listing 3
Indicator (primary, secondary, external)	(51, 34, 11)	See Listing 4
RDF Data Cube dataset	215 and 213 definitions	See Table 3
RDF Data Cube slice	636	See Table 3
RDF Data Cube observation	110729	See Listing 5
Region	9	See Listing 6
Country	246	See Listing 7
Organization	12	See Listing 8
People	4	See Table 3
Others: scores, etc.	5368, etc.	See Table 3
Number of generated RDF triples	**1152056** RDF triples containing **81628** distinct subjects and **69824** distinct objects	

Listing 2. Representation and definition of a sub-index in RDF

```
wi-index:Readiness a wi-onto:Index;
      wi-onto:weight 0.2;
      rdfs:comment "This sub-Index assesses the state of the communications and institutional infrastructure
      that is needed to be able to access the Web in a country."@en;
      rdfs:label "Readiness"@en;
      skos:broader wi-index:ds;
      skos:narrower wi-component:CommunicationsInfrastructure,
      wi-component:InstitutionalInfrastructure.
```

Listing 3. Representation and definition of a component in RDF

```
wi-component:CommunicationsInfrastructure a wi-onto:Component;
      rdfs:label "Communications"@en;
      rdfs:comment "This component assesses the state and availability of the physical and communications
      infrastructure that enables access to the Web."@en;
      skos:broader wi-index:Readiness;
      wi-onto:weight "0.3333"^^xsd:double.
```

Listing 4. Representation and definition of an indicator, more specifically a primary one, in RDF

```
wi-indicator:Q1 a wi-onto:PrimaryIndicator ;
      rdfs:label "Q1"@en ;
      rdfs:comment "Use of Web for political mobilisation"@en ;
      wi-onto:ref-source wi-org:WebFoundation ;
      wi-onto:weight "1.0"^^xsd:double ;
      wi-onto:high-low wi-onto:High ;
      skos:notation "Q1" ;
      time:intervalStarts "2007"^^xsd:int ;
      time:intervalFinishes "2011"^^xsd:int ;
      skos:definition "Survey Question: To what extent has the Web been used for political mobilisation in
      your country (e.g. through the use of social networking sites)? [1 = not at all; 10 = extensively]"@en ;
      skos:broader wi-component:Political .
```

Following some SPARQL demo queries are also provided in order to show how to query the endpoint. Assuming there are 5 main variables in each observation: indicator, dataset, country, year, status, next SPARQL query, see Listing 9, is a template for querying the endpoint replacing the names between sharps for those available. The Web Index ranking can be also extracted from the endpoint out using the SPARQL query depicted in Listing 10. Finally a human query exploiting geographical and multilingual characteristics of data such as *"Give me the observations about countries (name in French) close to Belgium (> 200km) with regards to indicator IEAA."* can be rewritten as a SPARQL query as Listing 11 shows.

Listing 5. Representation and definition of an observation, more specifically a primary one, in RDF

```
<http://data.Webfoundation.org/Webindex/observation/Q1-Normalised/obs1>
        a           qb:Observation ;
        rdfs:comment "Use of Web for political mobilisation"@en ;
        rdfs:label "Use of Web for political mobilisation in Argentina during 2011"@en ;
        wi-onto:md5-checksum
"9868968049525238679864925928502938460" ;
        wi-onto:ref-area wi-country:ARG ;
        wi-onto:ref-indicator wi-indicator:Q1 ;
        wi-onto:ref-year "2011"^^xsd:int ;
            wi-onto:sheet-type wi-onto:Normalised ;
          wi-onto:value "-0.3561861069647072"^^xsd:double ;
            dcterms:contributor wi-org:WESO ;
              dcterms:date "2011"^^xsd:int ;
          dcterms:publisher wi-org:WebFoundation ;
            qb:dataSet wi-dataset:Q1-Normalised ;
                sdmx-concept:obsStatus
                wi-onto:obsStatus-N .
```

Listing 6. Representation and definition of a region in RDF

```
wi-region:Americas a wi-onto:Region;
        rdfs:label "Americas"@en;
        wi-onto:ref-dbpedia ;
        wi-onto:has-country wi-country:ARG;
        ...
        wi-onto:has-country wi-country:USA;
        wi-onto:has-country wi-country:VEN.
```

CONCLUSION AND FUTURE WORK

The main advantage of applying Linked Data to the Web Index project lies in the possibility of integrating data statistics coming from different providers (12) according to a common and shared data model (RDF, SKOS, and OWL). Thus the access to more than 96 MSExcel files (1 file per indicator) containing geolocated information (246 countries grouped in 9 regions) from 2007 to 2011 is now unified in only one 5 stars dataset that can be query using a formal language such as SPARQL. Although the core of the Web Index is focused only in 61 countries due to the lack of information of some countries the design and structure of the Web Index enables the addition of new information and data empowering its extensibility in future versions. Nowadays the new emerging data realm is continuously flowing and changing. This situation provides an excellent environment for the construction of new added-value services for both final users and policy makers that seek for the exploitation of this information. Due to the relevance of the Web across the World,

Listing 7. Representation and definition of a country in RDF

```
wi-country:ARG a wi-onto:Country;
            wi-onto:has-iso-alpha2-code "AR";
            wi-onto:has-iso-alpha3-code "ARG";
            wi-onto:ref-dbpedia dbpedia:ISO_3166-1:AR;
                rdfs:label "Argentina"@en;
            geo:lat "-38.416097";
            geo:long "-63.61667199999999";
            skos:altLabel "Argentina"@EN,
                "la Argentina"@ES,
                "l'Argentine"@FR,
                "Аргентина"@RU,
                "@AR,

                "阿根廷共和国"@ZH;

        skos:exactMatch ;

            ...

        skos:prefLabel "la República Argentina"@ES,
            "la République argentine"@FR,
            "the Argentine Republic"@EN,
            "Аргентинская Республика"@RU,
            "الأرجنتين جمهورية"@AR,
            "阿根廷共和国"@ZH.
```

Listing 8. Representation and definition of a provider/organization in RDF

```
wi-org:WebFoundation a org:Organization ;
    rdfs:label "World Wide Web Foundation"@en ;
    rdfs:comment "The World Wide Web Foundation was established in 2009 by Web inventor Sir Tim
    Berners-Lee to tackle the fundamental obstacles to realizing his vision of an open Web available, usable,
    and valuable for everyone."@en ;
    org:identifier "WebFoundation"@en;
    wi-onto:ref-source-data <http://data.Webfoundation.org/Webindex/>;
    foaf:homepage <http://www.Webfoundation.org/>;
    org:hasSite [
    rdfs:label "World Wide Web Foundation"@en ;
    org:siteAddress [
            v:fn "World Wide Web Foundation" ;
            v:org [ v:organisation-name "World Wide Web Foundation"@en ;
                    v:organisation-unit "World Wide Web Foundation-Switzerland"@en ] ;
                    v:adr [ rdf:type v:Work ;
                     v:country-name "Switzerland"@en ;
                     v:locality "Geneva"@en ;
                     v:postal-code "1208" ;
                     v:street-address "c/o Lenz & Staehelin Route de Chêne 30" ] ;
            v :geo [ v:latitude "46.1996244" ;
                     v:longitude "6.167931" ] ;
        v:logo <http://www.Webfoundation.org/wp-content/themes/Webfoundation/assets/img/logo_wf.gif> .
    ]; ]; ]; .
```

Listing 9. SPARQL template for querying observation in the web index endpoint

```
SELECT ?obs ?value ?indicator ?dataset ?country ?year ?status WHERE{
    ?obs rdf:type qb:Observation.
    ?obs wi-onto:ref-indicator ?indicator.
    FILTER(?indicator = wi-indicator:#INDICATOR#).
    ?obs qb:dataSet ?dataset.
    FILTER(?dataset = wi-dataset:#INDICATOR#-#DATASET#).
    ?obs wi-onto:ref-area ?country.
    FILTER(?country = wi-country:#COUNTRY#).
    ?obs wi-onto:ref-year ?year.
    FILTER(?year = #YEAR#).
    ?obs sdmx-concept:obsStatus ?status.
    FILTER(?status = #STATUS#). //It could be removed
    ?obs wi-onto:value ?value.
}
```

Listing 10. SPARQL query to extract the web index 2011 rankings

```
SELECT ?countryName ?value WHERE {
    ?obs rdf:type qb:Observation.
    ?obs wi-onto:sheet-type wi-onto:Score.
    ?obs wi-onto:ref-type wi-index:WebIndex.
    ?obs wi-onto:ref-year ?year.
    FILTER (?year = 2011).
    ?obs wi onto:ref-area ?country.
    ?country rdfs:label ?countryName.
    ?obs wi-onto:ref-value ?value.
} ORDER BY desc(?value)
```

Listing 11. Example of a more advanced SPARQL query

```
SELECT ?otherCountry ?otherCountryName ?value WHERE{
    ?country rdf:type wi-onto:Country.
    ?country rdfs:label ?label.
    FILTER (lang(?label) = 'en' && str(?label) = str('Belgium')).
    ?country geo:lat ?lat.
    ?country geo:long ?long.
    ?otherCountry rdf:type wi-onto:Country.
    FILTER(?country != ?otherCountry).
    ?otherCountry geo:lat ?lat1.
    ?otherCountry geo:long ?long1.
    FILTER(xsd:double(?lat1) - xsd:double(?lat) <= 2 &&
            xsd:double(?lat) - xsd:double(?lat1) <= 2 &&
            xsd:double(?long1) - xsd:double(?long) <= 2 &&
            xsd:double(?long) - xsd:double(?long1) <= 2).
    ?otherCountry skos:prefLabel ?otherCountryName.
    FILTER (lang(?otherCountryName)= 'fr').
    ?obs rdf:type qb:Observation.
    ?obs wi-onto:ref-area ?otherCountry.
    ?obs wi-onto:ref-indicator wi-indicator:IEAA.
    ?obs wi-onto:value ?value
}
```

the Web Index data and information is a key-enabler to detect the necessities of countries from different points of view. That is why the Web Index must be publicly available as Linked Data to enforce the importance of the Web in the Internet era and help in the development of a real digital ecosystem for the new information and knowledge society. This initiative among others also coined by Sir Tim Berners-Lee in conjunction with the Open Data effort can ease the creation of new business opportunities keeping the transparency and the reuse of information and data as a major objective. From a technical point of view the application of a lifecycle helps to manage and control the production, publication, consumption and validation of Linked Data. Nevertheless proper techniques to handle the trust, provenance and quality of data are considered to be the next major step in this research area and in the particular case of the Web Index, these issues must be addressed to demonstrate the necessity and applicability of these methods providing a trustworthy environment for reusing data.

Future actions in the project lay in the full automation of the whole lifecycle and the dynamic addition of new providers, indicators and observations; the inclusion of new serialization formats to encourage data reuse (for instance data should be available to be processed by R) and the specification of the computation process as an ontology. Apart from that new visualization tools must be provided in order to ease the navigability and usability of data and the entire dataset will be added to the Linked Open Data Cloud Diagram in order to boost its reuse by third parties. In conclusion this chapter has presented the experience of promoting raw statistics to the Linked Open Data initiative in the context of the Web Index project with the objective of boosting the standardization, reusing existing information, data and vocabularies, integrating heterogeneous data sources and fulfilling the requirements of the new Web of Data realm.

ACKNOWLEDGMENT

The present work corresponds to the activities carried out by the WESO Research Group in the context of the Web Index project, coordinated by the Web Foundation and developed in conjunction with Global Integrity, Iconomical, Oxford Economics, and Zonda Design. Finally, particular thanks must go to Tim Berners-Lee for leading the initiative, Jose Manuel Alonso Cienfuegos (Web Foundation), and Google for seed funding the development and production of the first Web Index.

REFERENCES

Alexander, K., Cyganiak, R., Hausenblas, M., & Zhao, J. (2011). Describing linked datasets with the VoID vocabulary. *W3C Interest Group Note*. Retrieved from http://www.w3.org/TR/void/

Álvarez-Rodríguez, J. M. (2012). *Methods on linked data for e-procurement applying semantics*. (PhD Dissertation). University of Oviedo, Oviedo, Spain.

Álvarez-Rodríguez, J. M., & Labra-Gayo, J. E. (2012). *The web index statistics*. Retrieved from http://www.google.com/publicdata/explore?ds=z27bhj6dr5a5m2_

Alvarez-Rodríguez, J. M., Labra-Gayo, J. E., Cifuentes-Silva, F., Alor-Hérnandez, G., Sánchez, C., & Guzmán-Luna, J. (2012). Towards a pan-European e-procurement platform to aggregate, publish and search public procurement notices powered by linked open data: The MOLDEAS approach. *Journal of Software Engineering and Knowledge Engineering, 22*(3), 19.

Anicic, D., Fodor, P., Rudolph, S., & Stojanovic, N. (2011). EP-SPARQL: A unified language for event processing and stream reasoning. In *Proceedings of the 20th International Conference on World Wide Web*, (pp. 635-644). IEEE.

Barbieri, D., Braga, D., Ceri, S., Valle, E., & Grossniklaus, M. (2010). Querying RDF streams with C-SPARQL. *SIGMOD Record, 39*(1), 20–26. doi:10.1145/1860702.1860705

Bennett, D., & Harvey, A. (2009). Publishing open government data. *W3C*. Retrieved from http://www.w3.org/TR/gov-data/

Berners-Lee, T. (2006). *Linked data*. Retrieved from http://www.w3.org/DesignIssues/LinkedData.html

Berners-Lee, T. (2008). *Cool URIs don't change*. Retrieved from http://www.w3.org

Berrueta, D., Fernández, S., & Frade, I. (2008). *Cooking HTTP content negotiation with vapour*. Paper presented at the ESWC2008 Workshop on Scripting for the Semantic Web (SFSW2008). Tenerife, Spain.

Berrueta, D., Phipps, J., Miles, A., Baker, T., & Swick, R. (2008). Best practice recipes for publishing RDF vocabularies. *W3C*. Retrieved from http://www.w3.org

Bizer, C., & Cyganiak, R. (2009). Quality-driven information filtering using the WIQA policy framework. *Web Semantics: Science . Services and Agents on the World Wide Web, 7*(1), 1–10. doi:10.1016/j.websem.2008.02.005

Bosch, T., Cyganiak, R., Wackerow, J., & Zapilko, B. (2012). Leveraging the DDI model for linked statistical data in the social, behavioural, and economic sciences. In *Proceedings of the International Conference on Dublin Core and Metadata Applications*. IEEE.

Buil-Aranda, C., Arenas, M., & Corcho, O. (2011). Semantics and optimization of the SPARQL 1.1 federation extension. In *Proceedings of the 8th Extended Semantic Web Conference on The Semantic Web: Research and Applications*. Berlin: Springer-Verlag.

Cyganiak, R. (2012). *Tarql: SPARQL for tables*. Retrieved from https://github.com/cygri/tarql/

Cyganiak, R., & Reynolds, D. (2012). The RDF data cube vocabulary. *W3C*. Retrieved from http://www.w3.org/TR/vocab-data-cube/

Das, S., Sundara, S., & Cyganiak, R. (2012). R2RML: RDB to RDF mapping language. *W3C*. Retrieved from http://www.w3.org/TR/r2rml/

Dodds, L., & Davis, I. (2011). *Linked data patterns: A pattern catalogue for modelling, publishing, and consuming linked data*. Retrieved from http://patterns.dataincubator.org/book/

Farhan, H., & D'Agostino, D. (2012). *Web index key-findings*. Retrieved from http://theWeb Index.org/2012/10/2012-Web-Index-Key-Findings.pdf

Hausenblas, M., Villazón-Terrazas, B., & Hyland, B. (2011). GLD life cycle. *W3C*. Retrieved from http://www.w3.org/2011/gld/wiki/GLD_Life_cycle

Heath, T., & Bizer, C. (2011). *Linked data: Evolving the web into a global data space*. London: Morgan & Claypool. doi:10.2200/S00334ED1V01Y201102WBE001

Hyland, B., Villazón-Terrazas, B., & Capadisli, S. (2011). Cookbook for open government linked data. *W3C*. Retrieved from http://www.w3.org/2011/gld/wiki/Linked_Data_Cookbook

Jing, Y., Jeong, D., & Baik, D. K. (2008). SPARQL graph pattern rewriting for OWL-DL inference query. In *Proceedings of the 2008 Fourth International Conference on Networked Computing and Advanced Information Management* (pp. 675–680). Washington, DC: IEEE Computer Society.

LAPSI Project. (2012). *The European thematic network on legal aspects of public sector information*. Retrieved from http://www.lapsi-project.eu/

LATC Project. (2012). *Linked open data around-the-clock*. Retrieved from http://latc-project.eu/

LOD2 Project. (2013). *Creating knowledge out of interlinked data*. Retrieved from http://lod2.eu/

LOTED Project. (2012). *Linked open tenders electronic daily*. Retrieved from http://loted.eu:8081/LOTED1Rep/

Moreau, L., & Missier, P. (2011). The PROV data model and abstract syntax notation. *W3C*. Retrieved from http://www.w3.org/TR/2011/WD-prov-dm-20111018/

Nally, M., & Speicher, S. (2011). *Toward a basic profile for linked data*. Retrieved from http://www.ibm.com/developerworks/rational/library/basic-profile-linked-data/index.html

Nally, M., Speicher, S., Arwe, J., & Le Hors, A. (2012). Linked data basic profile 1.0. *W3C*. Retrieved from http://www.w3.org/Submission/2012/02/

Noriega, A., Tejo, C., González-Moriyón, G., Mínguez, I., & Polo, L. (2012). *Tabels (tabular cells)*. Retrieved from http://idi.fundacionctic.org/tabels/

Reynolds, D. (2012). An organization ontology. *W3C*. Retrieved from http://www.w3.org/TR/vocab-org/

Rivera-Salas, P. E., Martin, M., Maia Da Mota, F., Auer, S., Breitman, K., & Casanova, M. (2012). Publishing statistical data on the web. In *Proceedings of the 2012 IEEE Sixth International Conference on Semantic Computing (ICSC)*. IEEE.

SCOVO. (2009). *The statistical core vocabulary*. Retrieved from http://sw.joanneum.at/scovo/schema.html

SDMX Initiative. (2005). *Statistical data and metadata exchange information model: UML conceptual design (version 2.0)*. Retrieved from http://sdmx.org/docs/2_0/SDMX_2_0%20SECTION_02_InformationModel.pdf

Spanish Government. (2012). *Proyecto APORTA*. Retrieved from http://www.aporta.es/

UK Government. (2012a). *Opening up government*. Retrieved from http://data.gov.uk/

UK Government. (2012b). *Creating URIs*. Retrieved from http://data.gov.uk/resources/uris

W3C Members. (2011). Best practices discussion summary. *W3C*. Retrieved from http://www.w3.org/2011/gld/ wiki/Best_Practices_Discussion_Summary

White House. (2009). *Open government initiative*. Retrieved from http://www. whitehouse.gov/open

Zapilko, B., & Mathiak, B. (2011). Performing statistical methods on linked data. In *Proceedings of the International Conference on Dublin Core and Metadata Applications*. IEEE.

ENDNOTES

[1]   Scores are supposed to be removed from the SPARQL endpoint due to these values should be generated by clients applying the computation process.

Compilation of References

Agrawal, R., & Srikant, R. (1994) Fast algorithms for mining association rules in large data-bases. In *Proceedings of International Conference on Very Large Data Bases* (pp. 487-499). IEEE.

Agris. (2012). Retrieved May, 2012, from http://agris.fao.org/knowledge-and-information-sharing-through-agris-network

AGROVOC. (2012). *AGROVOC thesaurus.* Retrieved Jan, 2012, from http://aims.fao.org/standards/agrovoc/functionalities/search

AgrovocLOD. (2012). Retrived May, 2012 from http://aims.fao.org/agrovoc/lod

Agune, R. M., Filho, A. S. G., & Bolliger, S. P. (2009). *Governo aberto SP: Disponibilização de bases de dados e informações em formato aberto.* Public Managment Congress, Panel 13/050. Retrieved from http://www.repositorio.seap.pr.go v.br/.../governo_aberto_sp_disponibilizacao_de_bases_de_dados_e_informacoes_em_formato_aberto.pdf

Alexander, K., Cyganiak, R., Hausenblas, M., & Zhao, J. (2011). *Describing linked datasets with the VoID vocabulary.* W3C Interest Group Note. Retrieved from http://www.w3.org/TR/void/

Altschul, S. F., Madden, T. L., Schaffer, A. A., Zhang, J., Zhang, Z., & Miller, W. et al. (1997). Gapped BLAST and PSI-BLAST: A new generation of protein database search programs. *Nucleic Acids Research, 25*(17), 3389–3402. doi:10.1093/nar/25.17.3389 PMID:9254694.

Álvarez-Rodríguez, J. M. (2012). *Methods on linked data for e-procurement applying semantics.* (Unpublished doctoral dissertation). University of Oviedo, Oviedo, Spain.

Álvarez-Rodríguez, J. M., Labra, J. E., Calmeau, R., Marín, A., & Marín, J. L. (2011). Innovative services to ease the access to the public procurement notices using linking open data and advanced methods based on semantics. In *Proceedings of the 5th International Conference on Methodologies and Tools Enabling e-Government.* Camerino, Italy: MeTTeG.

Álvarez-Rodríguez, J. M., Polo, L., Abella, P., Jimenez, W., & Labra, J. E. (2011). Application of the spreading activation technique for recommending concepts of well-known ontologies in medical systems. *In Proceedings of First International Workshop on Semantic Applied Technologies on Biomedical Informatics.* Chicago, IL: ACM-BCB

Álvarez-Rodríguez, J. M., Rubiera, E., & Polo, L. (2008). Promoting government controlled vocabularies for the semantic web: The EUROVOC thesaurus and the CPV product classification system. In *Proceedings of the 1st International Workshop, Semantic Interoperability in the European Digital Library*. Tenerife, Spain: SIEDL.

Bachelard, G. (2006). *The formation of the scientific mind*. Lisboa: Dinalivro. (In Portuguese).

Bachmann, A., Schult, R., Lange, M., & Spiliopoulou, M. (2011). Extracting cross references from life science databases for search result ranking. In *Proceedings of the 20th ACM international conference on Information and Knowledge Management* (pp. 1253-1258). New York: ACM.

Baeza-Yates, R. (2004). Excavating the web. *El Profesional de la Información, 13*(1), 4–10. doi:10.1076/epri.13.1.4.29026.

Baralis, E., Cerquitelli, T., Chiusano, S., & Grand, A. (2010). Array-tree: A persistent data structure to compactly store frequent itemsets. In *Proceedings of IEEE Conference of Intelligent Systems* (pp. 108-113). IEEE.

Bennett, D., & Harvey, A. (2009). *Publishing open government data*. W3C Working Draft. Retrieved from http://www.w3.org/TR/gov-data/

Bergman, M. (2001). The deep web: Surfacing hidden value. *Journal of Electronic Publishing, 7*(1). doi:10.3998/3336451.0007.104.

Berners-Lee, T. (2006). Linked data. *Design Issues*. Retrieved from http://www.w3.org/Desi gnIssues/LinkedData.html

Berners-Lee, T. (2008). *Cool URIs don't change*.

Berners-Lee, T. (2009). Putting government data online. *Design Issues*. Retrieved from http://www.w3.org/DesignIssues/GovData.html

Berrueta, D., Labra, J. E., & Polo, L. (2006). *Searching over public administration legal documents using ontologies*. Paper presented at Conference on Knowledge-Based Software Engineering. Tallinn, Estonia.

Berrueta, D., Phipps, J., Miles, A., Baker, T. & Swick, R. (2008). *Best practice recipes for publishing RDF vocabularies*. W3C.

Bird, S., Klein, E., & Loper, E. (2009). *Natural language processing with Python*. O'Reilly Media.

Bizer, C., & Cyganiak, R. (2007). D2RQ – Lessons learned. *W3C Workshop on RDF Access to Relational Databases*. Retrieved May 2010, from http://www.w3.org/2007/03/RdfRDB/papers/d2rq-positionpaper/

Bizer, C., & Seaborne, A. (2004). *D2RQ - Treating non-RDF databases as virtual RDF graphs*. Poster presented at the 4th International Semantic Web Conference. Retrieved May 2010, from http://sites.wiwiss.fu-berlin.de/suhl/bizer/pub/Bizer-D2RQ-ISWC2004.pdf

Bizer, C., Cyganiak, R., & Heath, T. (2007). *How to publish linked data on the web*. Retrieved from http://sites.wiwiss.fu-berlin.de/suhl/bizer/pub/LinkedDataTutorial/20070727/

Bizer, C., Cyganiak, R., Garbers, J., Maresch, O., & Becker, C. (2009). *The D2RQ Platform v0.7 – Treating non-RDF relational databases as virtual RDF graphs (user manual and language specification)*. Retrieved May 2010, from http://www4.wiwiss.fu-berlin.de/bizer/d2rq/spec/

Bizer, C., et al. (2008). *Linked data on the web*. Paper presented at the 17th International World Wide Web Conference. Beijing, China. Retrieved from http://events.linkeddata.org/ldow2008/papers/00-bizer-heath-ldow2008-intro.pdf

Bizer, C., Heath, T., & Berners-Lee, T. (2009). Linked data - The story so far. *International Journal on Semantic Web and Information Systems*. Retrieved from http://tomheath.com/papers/bizer-heath-berners-lee-ijswis-linked-data.pdf

Bizer, C., & Cyganiak, R. (2009). Quality-driven information filtering using the WIQA policy framework. *Web Semantics: Science. Services and Agents on the World Wide Web*, *7*(1), 1–10. doi:10.1016/j.websem.2008.02.005.

Bizer, C., Lehmann, J., Kobilarov, G., Auer, S., Becker, C., Cyganiak, R., & Hellmann, S. (2009). DBpedia – A crystallization point for the web of data. *Journal of Web Semantics: Science. Services and Agents on the World Wide Web*, *7*, 154–165. doi:10.1016/j.websem.2009.07.002.

Bollacker, K., Evans, C., Paritosh, P., Sturge, T., & Taylor, J. (2008). Freebase: A collaboratively created graph database for structuring human knowledge. In *Proceedings of ACM SIGMOD International Conference on Management of Data* (pp. 1247-1250). ACM.

Bouquet, P., Serafini, L., & Zanobini, S. (2003). Semantic coordination: A new approach and an application. In *Proceedings of the 2nd International Semantic Web Conference (ISWO'03)*. Sanibel Islands, FL: ISWO.

Bourdieu, P., Chamboredon, J.-C., & Passeron, J.-C. (1991). *The craft of sociology: Epistemological preliminaries*. Berlin, Germany: Walter de Gruyter & Co. doi:10.1515/9783110856460.

Brin, S., Motwani, R., & Silverstein, C. (1997) Beyond market baskets: Generalizing association rules to correlations. In *Proceedings of ACM SIGMOD International Conference on Management of Data* (pp. 265–276). ACM.

Bry, F., & Kröger, P. (2003). A computational biology database digest: Data, data analysis, and data management. *Distributed and Parallel Databases*, *13*(1), 7–42. doi:10.1023/A:1021540705916.

Chea, S., & Lou, M. (2008). Post-adoption behaviors of e-service customers: The interplay of cognition and emotion. *International Journal of Electronic Commerce*, *12*(3), 29–56. doi:10.2753/JEC1086-4415120303.

Chellappan, C. (2008). *E-services: The need for higher levels of trust by populace*. Chennai, India: Anna University.

Cifuentes-Silva, F.A., Sifaqui, C\. & Labra, J.E. (2011). *Towards an architecture and adoption process for linked data technologies in open government contexts: A case study for the library of congress of Chile*. I-SEMANTICS.

Clusty. (2012). *MetaSearch engine*. Retrieved March, 2012, from http://clusty.com/

Cockburn, A., & McKenzie, B. (2000). What do web users do? An empirical analysis of web use. *International Journal of Human-Computer Studies*, *54*(6), 903–922. doi:10.1006/ijhc.2001.0459.

Cohen-Boulakia, S., Biton, O., Davidson, S., & Froidevaux, C. (2007). BioGuideSRS: Querying multiple sources with a user-centric perspective. *Bioinformatics (Oxford, England)*, *23*(10), 1301–1303. doi:10.1093/bioinformatics/btm088 PMID:17344233.

Cohen, W. W., Ravikumar, P., & Fienberg, S. E. (2003). *A comparison of string distance metrics for name-matching tasks*. IJCAI.

Collins, A. M., & Loftus, E. F. (1975). A spreading activation theory of semantic processing. *Psychological Review, 82*(6), 407–428. doi:10.1037/0033-295X.82.6.407.

Cuahsi. (2012). Retrieved 5 June, 2012 http://his.cuahsi.org/mastercvdata.html

Cyganiak, R., & Jentzsch, A. (n.d.). *The linking open data cloud diagram*. Retrieved from http://richard.cyganiak.de/2007/10/lod/

D'Ambra, J., & Rice, R. E. (2001). Emerging factors in user evaluation of the world wide web. *Information & Management, 38*, 373–384. doi:10.1016/S0378-7206(00)00077-X.

Daphne, K., & Sahami, M. (1997). Hierarchically classifying documents using very few words. In D. H. Fisher (Ed.), *Proceedings of ICML-97, 14th International Conference on Machine Learning*, (pp. 170–178). Nashville, TN: Morgan Kaufmann Publishers.

David, J., Guillet, F., & Briand, H. (2007). Association rule ontology matching approach. *International Journal on Semantic Web and Information Systems, 3*(2), 27–49. doi:10.4018/jswis.2007040102.

Dědek, J., Eckhardt, A., & Vojtáš, P. (2009). Web semantization - Design and principles. In *Proceedings of the 6th Atlantic Web Intelligence Conference 2009* (pp. 3018). Prague, Czech Republic: Springer Verlag.

Delgado, J., & Davidson, R. (2002). Knowledge bases and user profiling in travel and hospitality recommender systems. In K. Wöber, A. Frew, & M. Hitz (Eds.), *Proceedings of the 9th International Conference Information and Communications Technologies in Tourism* (pp. 1-16). Wien: Springer.

Dell'Erba, M., Fodor, O., Ricci, F., & Werthner, H. (2002). Harmonise: A solution for data interoperability. In J. Monteiro, P. Swatman, & L. Tavares (Eds.), *Proceedings of the 2nd IFIP Conference on E-Commerce, E-Business and E-Government* (pp. 433-445). Dordrecht: Kluwer.

Diniz, V. (n.d.). *Como conseguir dados governamentais abertos*. Public Managment Congress, Panel 13/049. Retrieved from http://www.consad.org.br/sites/1500/150 4/00001870.pdf

Divoli, A., Hearst, M., & Wooldridge, M. A. (2008). Evidence for showing gene/protein name suggestions in bioscience literature search interfaces. In *Pacific Symposium on Biocomputing, 13*, 568–579.

DMOZ. (2012). *Open directory project*. Retrieved Jan, 2012, from http://www.dmoz.org/

Dodds, L., & Davis, I. (2011). *Linked data patterns: A pattern catalogue for modelling, publishing, and consuming linked data*. Retrieved from http://patterns.dataincubator.org/book/

Doms, A., & Schroeder, M. (2005). GoPubMed: Exploring PubMed with the gene ontology. *Nucleic Acids Research, 33*, 783–786. doi:10.1093/nar/gki470 PMID:15980585.

E-Gov IG. (2009). *Melhorando o acesso ao governo com o melhor uso da web*. Comitê Gestor da Internet no Brasil. 1a edição. São Paulo. Retrieved from http://www.w3c.br/divulgacao/pdf/gov-web.pdf

Elmagarmid, K., Panagiotis, G., & Vassilios, S. (2007). *Duplicate record detection: A survey*. Retrieved from http://www.cs.purdue.edu/homes/ake/pub/survey2.pdf

Compilation of References

Errami, M., Wren, J. D., Hicks, J. M., & Garner, H. R. (2007). eTBLAST: A web server to identify expert reviewers, appropriate journals and similar publications. *Nucleic Acids Research*, *35*, W12–W15. doi:10.1093/nar/gkm221 PMID:17452348.

Etzold, T., Ulyanow, A., & Argos, P. (1996). SRS: Information retrieval system for molecular biology data banks. *Methods in Enzymology*, *266*, 114–128. doi:10.1016/S0076-6879(96)66010-8 PMID:8743681.

Euroalert.net. (2012). Retrieved from http://euroalert.net/

European Commission. (2010). *Consultation on the green paper on expanding the use of e-procurement in the EU*. Brussels, Belgium: European Commission. Retrieved from http://ec.europa.eu/internal_market/consultations/docs/2010/e-procurement/green-paper_en.pdf

European Commission. (2010b). *Public procurement indicators 2009*. Retrieved from http://ec.europa.eu/internal_market/publicprocurement/docs/indicators2010_en.pdf

European Commission. (2011a). *Modernising European public procurement to support growth and employment*. Press Release. Brussels, Belgium: European Commission. Retrieved from http://europa.eu/rapid/pressReleasesAction.do?reference=IP/11/1580

European Commission. (2011b). *Digital agenda*: *Turning government data into gold*. Press Release. Brussels, Belgium: European Commission. Retrieved from http://europa.eu/rapid/pressReleasesAction.do?reference=IP/11/1524

EuroWordNet. (2012). Retrieved Jan,2012, from http://www.illc.uva.nl/EuroWordNet/

Euzenate, J., & Shaviko, P. (Eds.). (2007). *Ontology matching*. Berlin: Springer.

EXIS-TI. (2012). Retrieved from http://www.exis-ti.com/

Faatz, T., Kamps, A., & Steinmetz, R. (2000). Background knowledge, indexing and matching interdependencies of document management and ontology maintenance. In *Proceedings of the First Workshop on Ontology Learning* (OL-2000). OL.

Fensel, D., Ding, Y., & Omelayenko, B. (2001). Product data integration in B2B ecommerce (pp. 54-59). IEEE-Intelligent E-Business.

Fielding, R. (2000). Principled design of modern web architecture. In *Proceedings of the 22nd International Conference on Software Engineering* (pp. 407-416). New York: ACM.

Fišer, D. (2011). *Semantic annotation of domain dependent data*. (Master's thesis). Charles University, Prague, Czech Republic. Retrieved from http://semanticweb.projekty.ms.mff.cuni.cz/index/release/

Flickr (2012). Retrieved March,2012, from http://www.flickr.com/

Fox, M. S., Barbuceanu, M., & Gruninger, M. (1995). An organisation ontology for enterprise modelling: Preliminary concepts for linking structure and behaviour. In *Proceedings of the 4th Workshop on Enabling Technologies: Infrastructure for Collaborative Enterprises* (p. 71). Washington, DC: IEEE.

Gale, W., Church, K., & Yarowsky, D. (1992). A method for disambiguating word senses in a large corpus. *Computers and the Humanities*, *26*, 415–439. doi:10.1007/BF00136984.

Galla, T. (2006). Theory of neural information processing systems. *Journal of Physics. A, Mathematical and General, 39*(14), 3849. doi:10.1088/0305-4470/39/14/B01.

Galperin, M. Y., & Fernandez-Suarez, X. M. (2012). The 2012 nucleic acids research database issue and the online molecular biology database collection. *Nucleic Acids Research, 40*(D1), D1–D8. doi:10.1093/nar/gkr1196 PMID:22144685.

Gao, Q., Yan, J., & Liu, M. (2008). A Semantic approach to recommendation system based on user ontology and spreading activation model. In *Proceedings of the 2008 IFIP* (pp. 488–492). Washington, DC: IEEE. doi:10.1109/NPC.2008.74.

Garrote, A., & Moreno García, M. N. (2012). *A JavaScript RDF store and application library for linked data client applications.* Paper presented at W3C 2012 Web Conference. New York, NY.

Gateway Strategic Consultancy Services, S.L. (2012). Retrieved from http://gateway-scs.es/en/

Gelgi, F., Vadrevu, S., & Davulcu, H. (2005). Improving web data annotations with spreading activation. In WISE.

Getoor, L., & Diehl, C. P. (2005). Link mining: A survey. *SIGKDD Explorations, 7*(2), 3–13. doi:10.1145/1117454.1117456.

Giardine, B., Riemer, C., Hardison, R. C., Burhans, R., Elnitski, L., & Shah, P. et al. (2005). Galaxy: A platform for interactive large-scale genome analysis. *Genome Research, 15*(10), 1451–1455. doi:10.1101/gr.4086505 PMID:16169926.

Gilchrist, A., Aitchison, J., & Bawden. (2006). *Thesaurus construction and use: A practical manual* (4th ed). London: Aslib.

Giunchiglia, F., & Shvaiko, P. (2003). Semantic matching. *International Journal of Computer and Artificial Intelligence.*

Giunchiglia, F., Shvaiko, P., & Yatskevich, M. (2004). S-match: An algorithm and an implementation of semantic matching. In *Proceedings of ESWS'04.* ESWS.

Golbreich, C. (2004). Combining rule and ontology reasoners for the semantic web. In G. Antoniou & H. Boley (Eds.), *Proceedings of the Third International Workshop-* (LNCS), (Vol. 3323, pp. 6-22). Berlin, Germany: Springer.

Gouws, S., Van Rooyen, G.-J., & Engelbrecht, H. E. (2010). Measuring conceptual similarity by spreading activation over Wikipedia's hyperlink structure. In *Proceedings of the 2nd Workshop on The People's Web Meets NLP: Collaboratively Constructed Semantic Resources* (pp. 46–54). Beijing, China: IEEE.

Grabisch, M., Marichal, J. L., Mesiar, R., & Pap, E. (2009). *Aggregation functions.* New York: Elsevier. doi:10.1017/CBO9781139644150.

Grimnes, G., Chalmers, S., Edwards, P., & Preece, A. (2003). GraniteNights - A multi-agent visit scheduler utilising semantic web technology. In M. Klusch, S. Ossowski, A. Omicini, & H. Laamanen (Eds.), *Proceedings of the 7th International Workshop on Cooperative Information Agents* (LNCS), (Vol. 2782, pp. 137-151). Berlin, Germany: Springer.

Haas, L. M., Schwarz, P. M., Kodali, P., Kotlar, E., Rice, J. E., & Swope, W. C. (2001). DiscoveryLink: A system for integrated access to life sciences data sources. *IBM Systems Journal, 40*(2), 489–511. doi:10.1147/sj.402.0489.

Han, J., Pei, J., & Yin, Y. (2010). Mining frequent patterns without candidate generation. In*Proceedings of the 2000 ACM SIGMOD International Conference on MANAGEMENT of Data* (pp. 1-12). ACM.

Hanisch, D., Fundel, K., Mevissen, H. T., Zimmer, R., & Fluck, J. (2005). Prominer: Rule-based protein and gene entity recognition. *BMC Bioinformatics*, *6*, S14. doi:10.1186/1471-2105-6-S1-S14 PMID:15960826.

Hausenblas, M., Grossman, R., Harth, A., & Cudré-Mauroux, P. (2012). *Large-scale linked data processing: Cloud computing to the rescue?* Paper presented at 2nd International Conference on Cloud Computing and Services Science. Porto, Portugal.

Hausenblas, M., Villazón-Terrazas, B., & Hyland, B. (2011). *GLD life cycle.* Retrieved from http://www.w3.org/2011/gld/wiki/GLD_Life_cycle

Heath, T. (2009). *An introduction to linked data.* Austin, TX:Talis Information Ltd. Retrieved from http://tomheath.com/slides/2009-02-austin-linkeddata-tutorial.pdf

Heath, T., & Bizer, C. (2011). Linked data: Evolving the web into a global data space. In Synthesis Lectures on the Semantic Web: Theory and Technology. Morgan & Claypool.

Heath, T., et al. (2008). (How to publish linked data on the web. Paper presented at 7th International Semantic Web Conference. Karlsruhe, Germany: SWSA. Retrieved from http://events.linkeddata.org/iswc2 008tutorial/how-to-publish-linked-data-iswc2008-slides.pdf.

Heijden, H. (2000). *Using the technology acceptance model to predict website usage: Extension and empirical test.* Amsterdam, The Netherlands: Vrije Universiteit.

Hepp, M. (2005). eClassOWL: A fully-fledged products and services ontology in OWL. In *Proceedings of the 4th International Semantic Web Conference.* Galway, Ireland: ISWC.

Hepp, M. (2006a). The True complexity of product representacion in the semantic web. In *Proceedings of the 14th European Conference on Information System.* Gothenburg, Sweden: ECIS

Hepp, M. (2006). A methodology for deriving OWL ontologies from products and services categorization standards. *International Journal on Semantic Web and Information Systems*, *2*(1), 72–99. doi:10.4018/jswis.2006010103.

Hepp, M. (2007). Possible Ontologies. *IEEE Internet Computing*, *11*(1), 90–96. doi:10.1109/MIC.2007.20.

Hernández, G. A., Berbís, J. M. G., & González, A. R. et al. (2010). HYDRA: A middleware-oriented integrated architecture for e-procurement in supply chains. *Computational Collective Intelligence*, *1*, 1–20. doi:10.1007/978-3-642-15034-0_1.

Hobbs, J., & Pan, F. (2004). An ontology of time for the semantic web. *ACM Transactions on Asian Language Information Processing*, *3*(1), 66–85. doi:10.1145/1017068.1017073.

Hoffman, D. L., & Novak, T. P. (1995). *Marketing in hypermedia computer-mediated environments: Conceptual foundations.* Working Paper No. 1 (Revised July 11, 1995). Project 2000: Research Program on Marketing in Computer-Mediated Environments: 1-36.

Hogan, A., Harth, A., Umbrich, J., Kinsella, S., Polleres, A., & Decker, S. (2011). Searching and browsing linked data with SWSE: The semantic web search engine. *Journal of Web Semantics.* doi:10.1016/j.websem.2011.06.004 PMID:21918645.

Hu, J., Fang, L., Cao, Y., Zeng, H.-J., Li, H., Yang, Q., & Chen, Z. (2008). Enhancing text clustering by leveraging Wikipedia semantics. In *Proceedings of ACM SIGIR Conference on Research and Development in Information Retrieval* (pp. 179-186). ACM.

Hu, W., & Qu, Y. (2007). Discovering simple mappings between relational database schemas and ontologies. In K. Aberer, K.-S. Choi, N. Noy, D. Allemang, K.-I. Lee, L. Nixon P. Cudré-Mauroux (Eds.), *Proceedings of the 6th International Semantic Web Conference, 2nd Asian Semantic Web Conference* (LNCS), (Vol. 4825, pp. 225-238). Berlin, Germany: Springer.

Huang, C.-Y., Shen, Y.-C., Chiang, I.-P., & Lin, C.-S. (2007). Concentration of web users' online information behaviour. *Information Research, 12*(4). Retrieved from http://InformationR.net/ir/12-4/paper324.html

Hyland, B., Villazón-Terrazas, B., & Capadisli, S. (2011). *Cookbook for open government linked data.* Retrieved from http://www.w3.org/2011/gld/wiki/Linked_Data_Cookbook

Ibekwe-San Juan, F. (2006). *Construction and maintaining knowledge organization tools a symbolic approach.*

Inmon, W. H. (1996). *Building the data warehouse* (2nd ed.). Hoboken, NJ: John Wiley & Sons.

Jaschke, R., Hotho, A., Schmitz, C., Ganter, B., & Stumme, G. (2008). Discovering shared conceptualizations in folksonomies. *Journal of Web Semantics, 6*(1), 38–53. doi:10.1016/j.websem.2007.11.004.

Jérôme, D., Euzenat, J., Scharffe, F., & dos Santos, C. T. (2011). The alignment API 4.0. *Semantic Web Journal, 2*(1), 3–10.

Jian, G. C. I., Hu, W., & Qu, Y. (2005). Falcon-ao: Aligning ontologies with falcon. In *Proceedings of the International and Interdisciplinary Conference on Modeling and Using Context (CONTEXT)*, (pp. 85-91). CONTEXT.

Jiang, T., & Tan, A.-H. (2006). Mining RDF metadata for generalized association rules. *Lecture Notes in Computer Science, 4080*, 223–233. doi:10.1007/11827405_22.

Jing, Y., Jeong, D., & Baik, D. K. (2008). SPARQL graph pattern rewriting for OWL-DL inference query. In *Proceedings of the 2008 4th International Conference on Networked Computing and Advanced Information Management* (pp. 675–680). Washington, DC: IEEE

Joinup and European Commission. (2012). *Share and reuse open source software, semantic assets and other interoperability solutions for public administrations.* Retrieved on http://joinup.ec.europa.eu/

Jones, C., Alani, H., & Tudhope, D. (2001). Geographical information retrieval with ontologies of place. In D. Montello (Ed.), *Proceedings of the International Conference Spatial Information Theory, Foundations of Geographic Information Science (COSIT 2001)* (LNCS), (Vol. 2205, pp. 323-335). Berlin: Springer.

Kanehisa, M., & Goto, S. (2000). KEGG: Kyoto encyclopedia of genes and genomes. *Nucleic Acids Research*, *28*(1), 27–30. doi:10.1093/nar/28.1.27 PMID:10592173.

Karp, P. D. (1995). A strategy for database interoperation. *Journal of Computational Biology*, *2*(4), 573–586. doi:10.1089/cmb.1995.2.573 PMID:8634909.

Klímek, J., Knap, T., Mynarz, J., Nečaský, M., Stárka, J., & Svátek, V. (n.d.). *Public contracts ontology* (Vol. 1). Retrieved from purl.org/procurement/public-contracts

Klyne, G., & Carrol, J. (2004). *Resource description framework (RDF): Concepts and abstract syntax*. W3C. Retrieved from http://www.w3.org/TR/2 004/REC-rdf-concepts-20040210/

Knublauch, H. (2006). Semantic web rules: Tools and languages. *Tutorial Bridging Research and Practice - Making Real-World Application of Ontologies and Rules at the Second International Conference on Rules and Rule Markup Languages for the Semantic Web*. Retrieved May 2010, from http://2006.ruleml.org/slides/tutorial-holger.pdf

Koufaris, M. (2002). Applying the technology acceptance model and flow theory to online consumer behaviour. *Information Systems Research*, *13*(2), 205–223. doi:10.1287/isre.13.2.205.83.

Kuittinen, H., Tuominen, J., & Hyvonen, E. (2008). Extending an ontology by analyzing annotation co-occurrences in a semantic cultural heritage portal. *Workshop on Collective Intelligence*.

Laborda, C., & Conrad, S. (2005). Relational OWL: A data and schema representation format based on OWL. In S. Hartmann & M. Stumptner (Eds.), *Proceedings of the 2nd Asia-Pacific Conference on Conceptual Modelling: Conferences in Research and Practice in Information Technology* (Vol. 43, pp. 89-96). Sydney, Australia: Australian Computer Society.

Laborda, C. (2007). *Incorporating relational data into the semantic web – From databases to RDF using relational.OWL*. Saarbrücken: VDM Verlag.

Labra, J. E., Ordoñez-de Pablos, P., & Cueva, J. M. (2007). Combining collaborative tagging and ontologies in image retrieval systems. In *Proceedings of 2nd International Conference on Metadata and Greece Semantic Web Research*. Corfu Island, Greece: Electronic Library.

Lacroix, Z., & Critchlow, T. (2003). *Bioinformatics: Managing scientific data*. San Francisco, CA: Morgan Kaufmann Publishers.

Lacroix, Z., Parekh, K., Vidal, M.-E., Cardenas, M., Marquez, N., & Raschid, L. (2005). BioNavigation: Using ontologies to express meaningful navigational queries over biological resources. In *CSB Workshops* (pp. 137–138). New York: IEEE. doi:10.1109/CSBW.2005.32.

Lange, M., Himmelbach, A., Schweizer, P., & Scholz, U. (2007). Data linkage graph: Computation, querying and knowledge discovery of life science database networks. *Journal of Integrative Bioinformatics*, *4*(3), e68.

Lange, M., Spies, K., Bargsten, J., Haberhauer, G., Klapperstück, M., & Leps, M. et al. (2010). The LAILAPS search engine: Relevance ranking in life science databases. *Journal of Integrative Bioinformatics*, *7*(2), e110.

Lašek, I., & Vojtáš, P. (2011). News filtering with semantic web entities. In ITAT 2011, Zborník príspevkov prezentovaných na konferencii ITAT. Terchová, Slovakia, ISBN: 978-80-89557-01-1, 2011

Lašek, I. (2011). Model for news filtering with named entities. =. *Lecture Notes in Computer Science*, *7032*, 309–316. doi:10.1007/978-3-642-25093-4_23.

LCA. (2012). *Library congress author list*. Retrieved Feb, 2012 http://www.loc.gov/bookfest/2009/authors/

LCSH. (2012). *The library of congress classification system*. Retrieved from http://www.loc.gov/catdir/cpso/lcco/lcco.html/

Le Grand, B. (2005). *Semantic web methodologies and tools for intra-European sustainable tourism*. Retrieved May 2005, from http://www.mondeca.com/articleJITT-hitouch-legrand.pdf

Leiper, N. (2004). *Tourism management*. Frenchs Forest: Pearson Education Australia.

Leukel, J. (2004). Automating product classification. In *Proceedings of the IADIS International Conference e-Society*. Avila, Spain: IADIS.

Liang, H., Xu, Y., & Nayak, R. (2009). Personalized recommender systems integrating social tags and item taxonomy. In *Proceedings of the 2009 IEEE/WIC/ACM International Conference on Web Intelligence and Intelligent Agent Technology Workshops*. Milano, Italy: IEEE/WIC/ACM.

Lima, S. (2003). *Webware crisis? The new werewolves are also slaughtered*. Viana do Castelo: Escola Superior de Tecnologia e Gestão.

Lima, S., & Moreira, J. (2009). The semantic web in tourism. In Cunha, M., Oliveira, E., Tavares, A., & Ferreira, L. (Eds.), *Handbook of Research on Social Dimensions of Semantic Technologies and Web Services* (pp. 675–703). Hershey, PA: IGI Global. doi:10.4018/978-1-60566-650-1.ch033.

Lin, D. (1998). Dependency-based evaluation of minipar. In *Proceedings of International Conference on Language Resources and Evaluation*. IEEE.

Lin, H. T., Koul, N., & Honavar, V. (2011). Learning relational bayesian classifiers from RDF data. *Lecture Notes in Computer Science*, *7031*, 389–404. doi:10.1007/978-3-642-25073-6_25.

Liu, G., Lu, H., Lou, W., & Xu Yu, J. (2003). On computing, storing and querying frequent patterns. In *Proceedings of the 9th ACM SIGKDD International Conference on Knowledge Discovery and Data Mining* (pp. 607-612). ACM.

Liu, G., Lu, H., & Xu Yu, J. (2007). CFP-tree: A compact disk-based structure for storing and querying frequent itemsets. *Information Systems*, *32*(2), 295–319. doi:10.1016/j.is.2005.11.004.

LOD. (2012). *Linked open data*. Retrieved June, 2012, from http://linkeddata.org/

LOD2 Project. (2012). *Creating knowledge out of interlinked data*. Retrieved from http://lod2.eu/

LOTED Project. (2012). *Linked open tenders electronic daily*. Retrieved from http://loted.eu:8081/LOTED1Rep/

Lu, Z. (2011). PubMed and beyond: A survey of web tools for searching biomedical literature. *Database*. doi:10.1093/database/baq036 PMID:21245076.

Magrane, M., & Consortium, U. (2011). UniProt knowledgebase: A hub of integrated protein data. *Database*. doi:10.1093/database/bar009 PMID:21447597.

Manola, F., & Miller, E. (2004). *Resource description framework (RDF) primer*. W3C. Retrieved from http://www.w3.org/TR/rdf-primer/

Map. (2012). *GoogleMaps*. Retrieved June, 2012, from https://maps.google.com.au/

Ma, X., Wu, C., Carranza, E. J. M., Schetselaar, E. M., van der Meer, F. D., & Liu, G. et al. (2010). Development of a controlled vocabulary for semantic interoperability of mineral exploration geodata for mining projects. *Computers & Geosciences*, *36*(12), 1512–1522. doi:10.1016/j.cageo.2010.05.014.

McCulloch, E. (2005). *Digital direction thesauri: Practical guidance for construction*.

McGuinness, D. L., Shvaiko, P., Giunchiglia, F., & Pinheiro da Silva, P. (2004). Towards explaining semantic matching. In *Proceedings of the International Workshop on Description Logics at KR'04*. KR.

Merabti, T., Soualmia, L. F., Grosjean, J., Joubert, M., & Darmoni, S. J. (2003). Aligning biomedical terminologies in French: Towards semantic interoperability in medical applications. In *Medical Informatics* (pp. 41–68). InTech.

MeSH. (2012). *The national library of medicine's controlled vocabulary thesaurus*. Retrieved April, 2012, from http://www.nlm.nih.gov/mesh/

Miles, A., & Bechhofer, S. (2009). *SKOS simple knowledge organisation systems*. Retrieved from http://www.w3.org/TR/skos-reference/

Miller, G. (1998). *WordNet: An electronic lexical database*. Boston: MIT Press.

Miller, G. A. (1995). WordNet: A lexical database for English. *Communications of the ACM*, *38*(11), 39–41. doi:10.1145/219717.219748.

Moreau, L., & Missier, P. (2011). *The PROV data model and abstract syntax notation*. Retrieved from http://www.w3.org/TR/2011/WD-prov-dm-20111018/

Morris, M. G., & Turner, J. M. (2001). Assessing users' subjective quality of experience with the world wide web: An exploratory examination of temporal changes in technology acceptance. *International Journal of Human-Computer Studies*, *54*, 877–901. doi:10.1006/ijhc.2001.0460.

Morshed, A. (2009). Controlled vocabulary matching in distributed system. In *Proceedings of the 26th British National Conference on Databases*. London, UK: Databases.

Morshed, A., Caracciolo, C., Johannsen, G., & Keizer, J. (2011). Thesaurus alignment for linked data publishing. In *Proceedings of the DCMI International Conference on Dublin Core and Metadata Applications*. DC.

Morshed, A. (2010). *Aligning controlled vocabularies for enabling semantic matching in a distributed knowledge management system. (Unpublished doctoral disseration)*. Trento, Italy: University of Trento.

Mudunuri, U., Che, A., Yi, M., & Stephens, R. M. (2009). Biodbnet: The biological database network. *Bioinformatics (Oxford, England)*, *25*(4), 555–556. doi:10.1093/bioinformatics/btn654 PMID:19129209.

Nally, M., & Speicher, S. (2011). *Toward a basic profile for linked data*. Retrieved from http://www.ibm.com/developerworks/rational/library/basic-profile-linked-data/index.html

Nally, M., Speicher, S., Arwe, J., & Le Hors, A. (2012). *Linked data basic profile 1.0*. Retrieved from http://www.w3.org/Submission/2012/02/

Narasimha, N., Kappara, P., Ichise, R., & Vyas, O. P. (2011). LiDDM: A data mining system for linked data. *Workshop on Linked Data on the Web*.

Nebot, V., & Berlanga, R. (2010). Mining association rules from Semantic Web data. *Lecture Notes in Computer Science, 6097*, 504–513. doi:10.1007/978-3-642-13025-0_52.

Ngomo, A.-C. N. & Auer, S. (2011). LIMES - A time-efficient approach for large-scale link discovery on the Web of data. *Framework, 15*(3).

Nguyen, D. P. T., Matsuo, Y., & Ishizuka, M. (2008). Exploiting syntactic and semantic information for relation extraction from Wikipedia. *Workshop on Text-Mining & Link-Analysis*.

Nie, J.-Y. (2003). Query expansion and query translation as logical inference. *Journal of the American Society for Information Science and Technology, 54*(4), 335–346. doi:10.1002/asi.10214.

Novotny, Vojtas, & Maruscak. (2009). Information extraction from web pages. In *Proceedings of International Joint Conference on Web Intelligence and Intelligent Agent Technology 2009*. Washington, DC: IEEE.

Oinn, T., Addis, M., Ferris, J., Marvin, D., Senger, M., & Greenwood, M. et al. (2004). Taverna: A tool for the composition and enactment of bioinformatics workflows. *Bioinformatics (Oxford, England), 20*(17), 3045–3054. doi:10.1093/bioinformatics/bth361 PMID:15201187.

Oja, E. (1982). A simplified neuron model as a principal component analyzer. *Journal of Mathematical Biology, 15*(3), 267–273. doi:10.1007/BF00275687 PMID:7153672.

Omelayenko, B., & Fensel, D. (2001). An analysis of B2B catalogue integration problems. In *Proceedings of the International Conference on Enterprise Information Systems*. Setubal, Portugal: ICEIS

OpenAgris. (2012). Retrieved May, 2012, from http://agris.fao.org/news/openagris-journals-rdf-visual-reader

Opengovdata.org. (2007). *Open government data principles*. Public.Resource. Retrieved from http://resource.org/8_principles.html

OpenTravel Alliance. (2001). *OpenTravel alliance 2001A specification*. Retrieved April 2010, from http://www.opentravel.org/Specifications/DownloadZip.ashx?spec=2001A

OpenTravel Alliance. (2007). *OpenTravel alliance 2007A specification*. Retrieved April 2010, from http://www.opentravel.org/Specifications/DownloadZip.ashx?spec=2007A

OVP. (2011). *Open video project*. Retrieved December, 2011, from http://www.open-video.org/

Parundekar, R., Knoblock, C. A., & Ambite, J. L. (2010). Linking and building ontologies of linked data. *Lecture Notes in Computer Science, 6496*, 598–614. doi:10.1007/978-3-642-17746-0_38.

Compilation of References

Pei, J., Han, J., Mortazavi-Asl, B., Wang, J., Pinto, H., & Chen, Q. et al. (2004). Mining sequential patterns by pattern-growth: The PrefixSpan approach. *IEEE Transactions on Knowledge and Data Engineering*, *16*(10).

Perry, M., Sheth, A., & Arpinar, I. (2006). Geospatial and temporal semantic analytics. *Large scale distributed information systems (LSDIS) technical report*. Retrieved March 2010, from http://lsdis.cs.uga.edu/library/download/encyclopedia_geoinformatics_uga_tech_report.pdf

Peska, L., Eckhardt, A., & Vojtas, P. (2011). UPComp - A PHP component for recommendation based on user behaviour. In *Proceedings of International Joint Conference on Web Intelligence and Intelligent Agent Technology 2011* (pp. 306-309). Lyon, France: IEEE.

Podlogar, M. (2007). E-procurement success factors: Challenges and opportunities for a small developing country. In Pani, A. K., & Agrahari, A. (Eds.), *E-Procurement in Emerging Economies Theory and Cases*. Loveland, CO: Group Publishing. doi:10.4018/978-1-59904-153-7.ch003.

Preece, S. E. (1981). *A spreading activation network model for information retrieval*. (PhD Dissertation). University of Illinois, Urbana, IL.

Qiu, Y., & Frei, H. P. (1993). Concept-based query expansion. In *Proceedings of the 16th Annual Internation ACM-SIGIR Conference on Research and Development in Information Retrieval* (pp. 160-169). Pittsburgh, PA: ACM.

Ramaswami, S. N., Strader, T. J., & Brett, K. (2000-2001). Determinants of on-line channel use for purchasing financial products. *International Journal of Electronic Commerce*, *5*(2), 95–118.

Reingold, E., & Dershowitz, N. (2001). *Calendrical calculations: The millennium edition*. Cambridge, MA: Cambridge University Press.

Reynolds, D. (2010). *An organization ontology*. Epimorphics Ltd. Retrieved from http://www.epimorphics.com/web/category/category/developers/organization-ontology

Reynolds, D. (2010). *Jena 2 inference support*. Retrieved March 2010, from http://jena.sourceforge.net/inference/

Reynolds, D. (2012). *An organization ontology*. W3C. Retrieved from http://www.w3.org/TR/vocab-org/

Ricci, F., Arslan, B., Mirzadeh, N., & Venturini, A. (2002). ITR: A case-based travel advisory system. In S. Craw & A. Preece (Eds.), *Proceedings of the 6th European Conference Advanced in Case-Based Reasoning* (LNCS),(Vol. 2416, pp. 613-627). Berlin, Germany: Springer.

Rocha, C., Schwabe, D., et al. (2004). A hybrid approach for searching in the semantic Web. In *Proceedings of the 13th International Conference on World Wide Web* (pp. 374–383). New York: ACM.

Roos, D. S. (2001). Computational biology: Bioinformatics–Trying to swim in a sea of data. *Science*, *291*(5507), 1260–1261. doi:10.1126/science.291.5507.1260 PMID:11233452.

Ruiz-Casado, M., Alfonseca, E., & Castells, P. (2005). Automatic extraction of semantic relationships for WordNet by means of pattern learning from Wikipedia. *Lecture Notes in Computer Science*, *3513*, 67–79. doi:10.1007/11428817_7.

Schuler, G. D., Epstein, J., Ohkawa, H., & Kans, J. (1996). Entrez: Molecular biology database and retrieval system. *Methods in Enzymology*, *266*, 141–161. doi:10.1016/S0076-6879(96)66012-1 PMID:8743683.

Schumacher, K., Sintek, M., & Sauermann, L. (2008). Combining metadata and document search with spreading activation for Semantic desktop search. In S. Bechhofer, M. Hauswirth, J. Hoffmann, & M. Koubarakis (Eds.), *Proceedings of 5th European Semantic Web Conference* (pp. 569–583). Berlin, Germany: Springer.

Sebastiani, F. (2002). Machine learning in automated text categorization. *ACM Computing Surveys*, *34*(1), 1–47. doi:10.1145/505282.505283.

Semantic Web Search and Metadata Engine. (2004). *Restaurant ontology*. Retrieved May 2005, from http://www-agentcities.doc.ic.ac.uk/ontology/restaurant.daml

SEMEDA. (2003). *Ontology based semantic integration of biological databases..*

Sheridan, J., & Tennison, J. (2010). *Linking UK government data*. Paper presented at Linked Date on the Web Workshop. Raleigh, NC: LDOW. Retrieved from http://events.linkeddata.org/ldow2010/papers/ldow2010_paper14.pdf

Sheth, A. P., & Larson, J. A. (1990). Federated database systems for managing distributed, heterogeneous, and autonomous databases. *ACM Computing Surveys*, *22*(3), 183–236. doi:10.1145/96602.96604.

Shnarch, E., Barak, L., & Dagan, I. (2009). Extracting lexical reference rules from Wikipedia. In *Proceedings of the Annual Meeting of the ACL*. ACL.

Shvachko, K., Kuang, H., Radia, S., & Chansler, R. (2010). *The Hadoop distributed file system*. Paper presented at IEEE 26th Symposium on Mass Storage Systems and Technologies (MSST). New York, NY.

Shvaiko, P., Giunchiglia, F., & Yatskevich, M. (2006). Discovering missing background knowledge in onology matching. In *Proceedings of the 17th European Conference on Artificial Intelligence (ECAI 2006)*, (vol. 141, pp. 382-386). ECAI.

Siepel, A., Farmer, A., Tolopko, A., Zhuang, M., & Mendes, P., Beavis, Sobral, B. (2001). ISYS: A decentralized, component-based approach to the integration of heterogeneous bioinformatics resources. *Bioinformatics (Oxford, England)*, *17*(1), 83–94. doi:10.1093/bioinformatics/17.1.83 PMID:11222265.

Spanish Government. (2011). *Proyecto APORTA*. Retrieved from http://www.aporta.es/

Srinubabu, G. (2011). *Integration, warehousing, and analysis strategies of omics data, methods in molecular biology*.

Stein, L. D. (2002). Creating a bioinformatics nation. *Nature*, *417*(6885), 119–120. doi:10.1038/417119a PMID:12000935.

Stevens, R., Baker, P., Bechhofer, S., Ng, G., Jacoby, A., & Paton, N. W. et al. (2000). TAMBIS: Transparent access to multible bioinformatics information sources. *Bioinformatics (Oxford, England)*, *16*(4), 184–185. doi:10.1093/bioinformatics/16.2.184 PMID:10842744.

Stevens, R., Goble, C., Baker, P., & Brass, A. (2001). A classification of tasks in bioinformatics. *Bioinformatics (Oxford, England)*, *17*(2), 180–188. doi:10.1093/bioinformatics/17.2.180 PMID:11238075.

Compilation of References

Stoilos, G., Stamou, G., & Kollias, S. (2005). A string metric for ontology alignment. In *Proceedings of the 4th International Semantic Web Conference*, (pp. 624–637). Berlin: Springer-Verlag.

Suchanek, F. M., Kasneci, G., & Weikum, G. (2007). Yago: A core of semantic knowledge. In *Proceedings of the International Conference on World Wide Web* (pp. 697–706). IEEE.

Swoogle. (2012). *Semantic search engine*. Retrieved March, 2012, from http://swoogle.umbc.edu/

Szczuka, M. S., Janusz, A., & Herba, K. (2011). Clustering of rough set related documents with use of knowledge from DBpedia. *Lecture Notes in Computer Science*, *6954*, 394–403. doi:10.1007/978-3-642-24425-4_52.

Taggart, C., & McKinnon, R. (2010). *The open database of the corporate world*. Retrieved on http://opencorporates.com/

Tan, P.-N., Kumar, V., & Srivastava, J. (2002). Selecting the right interestingness measure for association patterns. In *Proceedings of ACM SIGKDD International Conference on Knowledge Discovery and Data Mining* (pp. 32–41). ACM.

Tan, P., Steinbach, M., & Kumar, V. (2006). *Introduction to data mining*. Boston, MA: Addison-Wesley.

Tatusova, T. A., Karsch-Mizrachi, I., & Ostell, J. A. (1999). Complete genomes in WWW Entrez: Data representation and analysis. *Bioinformatics, 15*(7/8), 536–543.

Taylor, S., & Todd, P. A. (1995). Understanding information technology usage: A test of competing models. *Information Systems Research*, *6*(2), 144–176. doi:10.1287/isre.6.2.144.

The DARPA Agent Markup Language. (2003). *DAML time ontology*. Retrieved January 2005, from http://www.cs.rochester.edu/~ferguson/daml/daml-time-20020728.daml

The DARPA Agent Markup Language. (2004). *DAML ontology library*. Retrieved April 2010, from http://www.daml.org/ontologies/

Torra, V., & Narukawa, Y. (2007). *Modeling decisions. Information Fusion and Aggregation Operators*. Berlin, Germany: Springer.

Truong, K., Abowd, G., & Brotherton, J. (2001). Who, what, when, where, how – Design issues of capture & access applications. In G. Abowd, B. Brumitt, & S. Shafer (Eds.), *Proceedings of the International Conference on Ubiquitous Computing* (LNCS), (Vol. 2201, pp. 209-224). Berlin, Germany: Springer.

UK Government. (2011). *Opening up government*. Retrieved from http://data.gov.uk/

United Nations. (2010). *United Nations e-government survey 2010*. New York: UN Publishing Section. Retrieved from http://unpan1.un.org/intradoc/groups/public/documents/un/unpan038851.pdf

Uno, T., Kiyomi, M., & Arimura, H. (2004). LCM ver. 2: Efficient mining algorithms for frequent/closed/maximal itemsets. *Workshop on Frequent Itemset Mining Implementations*.

VacationCoach Inc. (2002). *Using knowledge personalization to sell complex products*. Retrieved May 2010, from http://www.sourceit-travel.com/documents/pdf/vacationcoach_knowle dge_personalisation.pdf van Riel, A. C. R., Liljander, V., & Jurriëns, P. (2001). Exploring consumer evaluations of e-services: A portal site. *International Journal of Service Industry Management, 12*(40), 359–377. doi:10.1108/09564230110405280.

Vivisimo. (2012). *MetaSearch engine*. Retrieved March,2012, from http://vivisimo.com/

VocBench. (2012). Retrieved June, 2012, from http://aims.fao.org/tools/vocbench-2

Vojtas, P., & Eckhardt, A. (2008). Considering data-mining techniques in user preference learning. In *Proceedings of International Joint Conference on Web Intelligence and Intelligent Agent Technology 2008* (pp. 33-36). IEEE/WIC/ACM.

Vojtáš, P., Pokorný, J., Nečasky, M., Skopal, T., Matoušek, K., & Kubalík, J. … Maryška M. (2011). SoSIReČR - IT professional social network. In *Proceedings of International Conference on Computational Aspects of Social Networks 2011* (pp. 108-113). Salamanca, Spain: CASoN.

Volker, J., & Niepert, M. (2011). Statistical schema induction. *Lecture Notes in Computer Science, 6643*, 124–138. doi:10.1007/978-3-642-21034-1_9.

Volz, J., Bizer, C., Gaedke, M., & Kobilarov, G. (2009). *Silk – A link discovery framework for the web of data*. Paper presetned at the 2nd Workshop about Linked Data on the Web (LDOW2009). Madrid, Spain.

W3C (2011a). *Best practices discussion summary*. Retrieved from http://www.w3.org/2011/gld/wiki/Best_Practices_Discussion_Summary

W3C (2011b). *Government linked data working group charter*. Retrieved from http://www.w3.org/2011/gld/charter

W3C Brazilian Office. (2010). *O governo de inovação na copa 2014: Uso de redes sociais e dados abertos*. Paper presented at Seminar on Electronic Government Innovation. Porto Alegre, Brazil. Retrieved from http://www.procergs.rs.gov.br/uploads/1285856001W3C_Seminario_Inovacao_eGov_POA_17092010.pdf

Wang, J., Han, J., & Pei, J. (2003). Closet+: Searching for the best strategies for mining frequent closed itemsets. In *Proceedings of ACM SIGKDD International Conference on Knowledge Discovery and Data Mining* (pp. 236–245). New York: ACM.

Wang, P., Hu, J., Zeng, H. J., & Chen, Z. (2009). Using Wikipedia knowledge to improve text classification. *Knowledge and Information Systems, 19*, 265–281. doi:10.1007/s10115-008-0152-4.

Weber, M. (1987). *Economy and society*. Berkeley, CA: University of California Press.

Webster, J., Trevino, L. K., & Ryan, L. (1993). The dimensionality and correlates of flow in human computer interactions. *Computers in Human Behavior, 9*(4), 411–426. doi:10.1016/0747-5632(93)90032-N.

Werbos, P. (1974). *Beyond regression: New tools for prediction and analysis in the behavioral sciences*. (PhD thesis). Harvard University, Cambridge, MA.

WESO (Oviedo Semantic Web). (2012b). Retrieved from http://www.weso.es/

White House. (2009). *Open government initiative*. Retrieved from http://www.whitehouse.gov/open

Wiederhold, G. (1992). Mediators in the architecture of future information systems. *IEEE Computer*, *25*(3), 38–49. doi:10.1109/2.121508.

Yaobin, L., & Tao, Z. (2007). A research of consumers' initial trust in online stores in China. *Journal of Research and Practice in Information Technology*, *39*(3). Retrieved from http://www.jrpit.acs.org.au/jrpit/JR-PITVolumes/JRPIT39/JRPIT39.3.167.pdf.

YouTube. (2012). Retrieved May, 2012, from http://www.youtube.com/

Yun, J., Jing, L., Yu, J., & Huang, H. (2012). A multi-layer text classification framework based on two-level representation model. *Expert Systems with Applications*, *39*(2), 2035–2046. doi:10.1016/j.eswa.2011.08.027.

Zeithaml, V. A., Parasuraman, A., & Malhotra, A. (2000). *A conceptual framework for understanding e-service quality: Implications for future research and managerial practice.* Marketing Science Institute.

Zhu, H., & Madnick, S. (2006). *A lightweight ontology approach to scalable interoperability.* Working paper CISL. Cambridge, MA: The Massachusetts Institute of Technology.

Zou, Y., Finin, T., Ding, L., Chen, H., & Pan, R. (2003). Using semantic web technology in multi-agent systems: A case Study in the TAGA trading agent environment. In N. Sadeh (Ed.), *Proceedings of the 5th International Conference on Electronic Commerce*: ACM *International Conference Proceeding Séries* (Vol. 50, pp. 95-101). New York: ACM.

Related References

Abed, M. A. (2013). WSMO and WSMX support to the semantic web services technology. In Alkhatib, G. (Ed.), *Network and Communication Technology Innovations for Web and IT Advancement* (pp. 30–47). Hershey, PA: Information Science Reference.

Acuña, C. J., Minoli, M., & Marcos, E. (2012). Integrating web portals with semantic web services: A case study. In Tavana, M. (Ed.), *Enterprise Information Systems and Advancing Business Solutions: Emerging Models* (pp. 326–336). Hershey, PA: Business Science Reference. doi:10.4018/978-1-4666-1761-2.ch019.

Adán-Coello, J. M. (2009). Semantic web services. In Pagani, M. (Ed.), *Encyclopedia of Multimedia Technology and Networking* (2nd ed., pp. 1293–1298). Hershey, PA: Information Science Reference.

Adan-Coello, J. M., Tobar, C. M., Garcia Rosa, J. L., & de Freitas, R. L. (2007). Towards the educational semantic web. In Neto, F., & Brasileiro, F. (Eds.), *Advances in Computer-Supported Learning* (pp. 145–172). Hershey, PA: Information Science Publishing.

Adda, M. (2012). A pattern language for knowledge discovery in a semantic web context. In Alkhatib, G. (Ed.), *Models for Capitalizing on Web Engineering Advancements: Trends and Discoveries* (pp. 59–74). Hershey, PA: Information Science Publishing. doi:10.4018/978-1-4666-0023-2.ch004.

Ahsan, S., & Shah, A. (2009). Quality metrics for evaluating data provenance. In Tiako, P. (Ed.), *Designing Software-Intensive Systems: Methods and Principles* (pp. 455–473). Hershey, PA: Information Science Reference.

Ahtisham Aslam, M., Auer, S., & Fähnrich, K. (2009). Towards semantic business processes: Concepts, methodology, and implementation. In Garcia, R. (Ed.), *Semantic Web for Business: Cases and Applications* (pp. 244–274). Hershey, PA: Information Science Reference.

Akkiraju, R. (2007). Semantic web services. In Cardoso, J. (Ed.), *Semantic Web Services: Theory, Tools and Applications* (pp. 191–216). Hershey, PA: Information Science Reference. doi:10.4018/978-1-59904-045-5.ch009.

Aleman-Meza, B. (2009). Association analytics for network connectivity in a bibliographic and expertise dataset. In Cardoso, J., & Lytras, M. (Eds.), *Semantic Web Engineering in the Knowledge Society* (pp. 188–207). Hershey, PA: Information Science Reference.

Andrés, I. (2010). A new framework for intelligent semantic web services based on GAIVAs. In Alkhatib, G., & Rine, D. (Eds.), *Web Engineering Advancements and Trends: Building New Dimensions of Information Technology* (pp. 38–62). Hershey, PA: Information Science Reference. doi:10.4018/978-1-60566-719-5.ch003.

Association, I. R. (2013). Data mining: Concepts, methodologies, tools, and applications (4 Volumes) (pp. 1-2120). doi: doi:10.4018/978-1-4666-2455-9.

Association, I. R. (2013). Digital literacy: Concepts, methodologies, tools, and applications (3 Volumes) (pp. 1-1907). doi: doi:10.4018/978-1-4666-1852-7.

Auer, S. (2009). RapidOWL: A methodology for enabling social semantic collaboration. In Cardoso, J., & Lytras, M. (Eds.), *Semantic Web Engineering in the Knowledge Society* (pp. 267–289). Hershey, PA: Information Science Reference. doi:10.4018/978-1-60566-984-7. ch043.

Auer, S., & Ives, Z. G. (2008). Enabling social semantic collaboration: bridging the gap between web 2.0 and the semantic web. In Rech, J., Decker, B., & Ras, E. (Eds.), *Emerging Technologies for Semantic Work Environments: Techniques, Methods, and Applications* (pp. 1–15). Hershey, PA: Information Science Reference. doi:10.4018/978-1-59904-877-2.ch001.

Aufaure, M. A., Le Grand, B., Soto, M., & Bennacer, N. (2006). Metadata- and ontology-based semantic web mining. In Taniar, D., & Rahayu, J. (Eds.), *Web Semantics & Ontology* (pp. 259–296). Hershey, PA: Idea Group Publishing. doi:10.4018/978-1-59140-905-2. ch009.

Aufaure, M. A., Le Grand, B., Soto, M., & Bennacer, N. (2008). Metadata- and ontology-based semantic web mining. In Wang, J. (Ed.), *Data Warehousing and Mining: Concepts, Methodologies, Tools, and Applications* (pp. 3531–3556). Hershey, PA: Information Science Reference. doi:10.4018/978-1-59904-951-9.ch222.

Awad, M., Khan, L., & Thuraisingham, B. (2012). Policy enforcement system for inter-organizational data sharing. In Nemati, H. (Ed.), *Optimizing Information Security and Advancing Privacy Assurance: New Technologies* (pp. 197–213). Hershey, PA: Information Science Reference.

Bajaj, A., & Ram, S. (2009). A comprehensive framework towards information sharing between government agencies. In Erickson, J. (Ed.), *Database Technologies: Concepts, Methodologies, Tools, and Applications* (pp. 1723–1740). Hershey, PA: Information Science Reference. doi:10.4018/978-1-60566-058-5.ch104.

Banerjee, P. (2009). Semantic data mining. In Wang, J. (Ed.), *Encyclopedia of Data Warehousing and Mining* (2nd ed., pp. 1765–1770). Hershey, PA: Information Science Reference.

Baousis, V., Spiliopoulos, V., & Zavitsanos, E. (2009). Semantic web services and mobile agents integration for efficient mobile services. In Taniar, D. (Ed.), *Mobile Computing: Concepts, Methodologies, Tools, and Applications* (pp. 2936–2956). Hershey, PA: Information Science Reference.

Baousis, V., Spiliopoulos, V., & Zavitsanos, E. (2010). Semantic web services and mobile agents integration for efficient mobile services. In Lytras, M., & Sheth, A. (Eds.), *Progressive Concepts for Semantic Web Evolution: Applications and Developments* (pp. 25–43). Hershey, PA: Information Science Reference.

Baousis, V., Spiliopoulos, V., Zavitsanos, E., Hadjiefthymiades, S., & Merakos, L. (2008). Semantic web services and mobile agents integration for efficient mobile services. [IJSWIS]. *International Journal on Semantic Web and Information Systems*, *4*(1), 1–19. doi:10.4018/jswis.2008010101.

Related References

Barnaghi, P. M., Wang, W., & Kurian, J. C. (2009). Semantic association analysis in ontology-based information retrieval. In Theng, Y., Foo, S., Goh, D., & Na, J. (Eds.), *Handbook of Research on Digital Libraries: Design, Development, and Impact* (pp. 131–141). Hershey, PA: Information Science Reference. doi:10.4018/978-1-59904-879-6. ch013.

Baruh, L. (2010). Social media marketing: Web X.0 of opportunities. In Dumova, T., & Fiordo, R. (Eds.), *Handbook of Research on Social Interaction Technologies and Collaboration Software: Concepts and Trends* (pp. 33–44). Hershey, PA: Information Science Reference.

Basharat, A., & Spinelli, G. (2010). Enabling distributed cognitive collaborations on the semantic web. In Tatnall, A. (Ed.), *Web Technologies: Concepts, Methodologies, Tools, and Applications* (pp. 517–603). Hershey, PA: Information Science Reference.

Bassiliades, N., Antoniou, G., & Vlahavas, I. (2006). A defeasible logic reasoner for the semantic web. [IJSWIS]. *International Journal on Semantic Web and Information Systems*, 2(1), 1–41. doi:10.4018/jswis.2006010101.

Belhajjame, K., Missier, P., & Goble, C. (2009). Data provenance in scientific workflows. In Cannataro, M. (Ed.), *Handbook of Research on Computational Grid Technologies for Life Sciences, Biomedicine, and Healthcare* (pp. 46–59). Hershey, PA: Medical Information Science Reference. doi:10.4018/978-1-60566-374-6.ch003.

Benlamri, R., Berri, J., & Atif, Y. (2008). Context-aware mobile learning on the semantic web. In Mostefaoui, S., Maamar, Z., & Giaglis, G. (Eds.), *Advances in Ubiquitous Computing: Future Paradigms and Directions* (pp. 23–44). Hershey, PA: IGI Publishing. doi:10.4018/978-1-59904-840-6.ch002.

Bergenti, F., Franchi, E., & Poggi, A. (2012). Enhancing social networks with agent and semantic web technologies. In Brüggemann, S., & d'Amato, C. (Eds.), *Collaboration and the Semantic Web: Social Networks, Knowledge Networks, and Knowledge Resources* (pp. 83–100). Hershey, PA: Information Science Reference. doi:10.4018/978-1-4666-0894-8. ch005.

Berger, O., Vlasceanu, V., Bac, C., Dang, Q. V., & Lauriere, S. (2010). Weaving a semantic web across OSS repositories: Unleashing a new potential for academia and practice. [IJOSSP]. *International Journal of Open Source Software and Processes*, 2(2), 29–40. doi:10.4018/jossp.2010040103.

Berlanga, R., & Nebot, V. (2013). XML mining for semantic web. In Association, I. (Ed.), *Data Mining: Concepts, Methodologies, Tools, and Applications* (pp. 625–649). Hershey, PA: Information Science Reference.

Berlanga, R., Romero, O., Simitsis, A., Nebot, V., Pedersen, T. B., Abelló, A., & Aramburu, M. J. (2012). Semantic web technologies for business intelligence. In Zorrilla, M., Mazón, J., Ferrández, Ó., Garrigós, I., Daniel, F., & Trujillo, J. (Eds.), *Business Intelligence Applications and the Web: Models, Systems and Technologies* (pp. 310–339). Hershey, PA: Business Science Reference.

Bernardi, A., & Decker, S. (2009). The social semantic desktop: A new paradigm towards deploying the semantic web on the desktop. In Cardoso, J., & Lytras, M. (Eds.), *Semantic Web Engineering in the Knowledge Society* (pp. 290–314). Hershey, PA: Information Science Reference.

Bernardi, A., Decker, S., van Elst, L., & Grimnes, G. A. (2010). The social semantic desktop: A new paradigm towards deploying the semantic web on the desktop. In Dasgupta, S. (Ed.), *Social Computing: Concepts, Methodologies, Tools, and Applications* (pp. 2280–2304). Hershey, PA: Information Science Reference.

Berrueta, D., Campos, A., Rubiera, E., Tejo, C., & Labra, J. E. (2011). The web of data and the tourism industry. In Lytras, M., Ordóñez de Pablos, P., Damiani, E., & Diaz, L. (Eds.), *Digital Culture and E-Tourism: Technologies, Applications and Management Approaches* (pp. 75–89). Hershey, PA: Information Science Reference.

Bhat, T. N. (2012). Building chemical ontology for semantic web using substructures created by chem-BLAST. In Sheth, A. (Ed.), *Semantic-Enabled Advancements on the Web: Applications Across Industries* (pp. 1–16). Hershey, PA: Information Science Reference. doi:10.4018/978-1-4666-0185-7.ch001.

Biskup, T., Heyer, N., & Gómez, J. M. (2009). Conceptual model driven software development (CMDSD) as a catalyst methodology for building sound semantic web frameworks. In Tiako, P. (Ed.), *Software Applications: Concepts, Methodologies, Tools, and Applications* (pp. 611–634). Hershey, PA: Information Science Reference. doi:10.4018/978-1-60566-060-8.ch040.

Bitzer, S., Thoroe, L., & Schumann, M. (2010). Folksonomy: Creating metadata through collaborative tagging. In Dumova, T., & Fiordo, R. (Eds.), *Handbook of Research on Social Interaction Technologies and Collaboration Software: Concepts and Trends* (pp. 147–157). Hershey, PA: Information Science Reference.

Bizer, C., & Schultz, A. (2009). The Berlin SPARQL benchmark. [IJSWIS]. *International Journal on Semantic Web and Information Systems*, *5*(2), 1–24. doi:10.4018/jswis.2009040101.

Blanco-Fernández, Y., Pazos-Arias, J. J., & Gil-Solla, A. (2009). Semantic web technologies in the service of personalization tools. In Cruz-Cunha, M., Oliveira, E., Tavares, A., & Ferreira, L. (Eds.), *Handbook of Research on Social Dimensions of Semantic Technologies and Web Services* (pp. 68–87). Hershey, PA: Information Science Reference. doi:10.4018/978-1-60566-650-1.ch004.

Blanco-Fernández, Y., Pazos-Arias, J. J., Gil-Solla, A., Ramos-Cabrer, M., & López-Nores, M. (2007). A hybrid strategy to personalize the digital television by semantic inference. In Lekakos, G., Chorianopoulos, K., & Doukidis, G. (Eds.), *Interactive Digital Television: Technologies and Applications* (pp. 33–51). Hershey, PA: Idea Group Publishing. doi:10.4018/978-1-59904-361-6.ch003.

Bodea, C., Lipai, A., & Dascalu, M. (2013). An ontology-based search tool in the semantic web. In Ordóñez de Pablos, P., Nigro, H., Tennyson, R., & Gonzalez Cisaro, S. (Eds.), *Advancing Information Management through Semantic Web Concepts and Ontologies* (pp. 221–249). Hershey, PA: Information Science Reference.

Bouras, A., Gouvas, P., & Mentzas, G. (2007). A semantic service-oriented architecture for business process fusion. In Salam, A., & Stevens, J. (Eds.), *Semantic Web Technologies and E-Business: Toward the Integrated Virtual Organization and Business Process Automation* (pp. 40–76). Hershey, PA: Idea Group Publishing. doi:10.4018/978-1-59904-192-6.ch002.

Bouras, A., Gouvas, P., & Mentzas, G. (2009). A semantic service-oriented architecture for business process fusion. In Lee, I. (Ed.), *Electronic Business: Concepts, Methodologies, Tools, and Applications* (pp. 504–532). Hershey, PA: Information Science Reference.

Brambilla, M., & Facca, F. M. (2010). Building semantic web portals with a model-driven design approach. In Tatnall, A. (Ed.), *Web Technologies: Concepts, Methodologies, Tools, and Applications* (pp. 541–570). Hershey, PA: Information Science Reference.

Brüggemann, S., & d'Amato, C. (2012). *Collaboration and the semantic web: Social Networks, knowledge networks, and knowledge resources* (pp. 1-387). doi:10.4018/978-1-4666-0894-8

Bruijn, J. (2007). Logics for the semantic web. In Cardoso, J. (Ed.), *Semantic Web Services: Theory, Tools and Applications* (pp. 24–43). Hershey, PA: Information Science Reference. doi:10.4018/978-1-59904-045-5.ch002.

Bruns, R., Dunkel, J., & Ossowski, S. (2006). Applying advisory agents on the semantic web for e-learning. [IJIIT]. *International Journal of Intelligent Information Technologies*, *2*(3), 40–55. doi:10.4018/jiit.2006070103.

Brussee, R. (2007). Reasoning on the semantic web. In Cardoso, J. (Ed.), *Semantic Web Services: Theory, Tools and Applications* (pp. 110–133). Hershey, PA: Information Science Reference. doi:10.4018/978-1-59904-045-5.ch006.

Bry, F., Koch, C., Furche, T., Schaffert, S., & Badea, L. (2007). Querying the web reconsidered: Design principles for versatile web query languages. In Sheth, A., & Lytras, M. (Eds.), *Semantic Web-Based Information Systems: State-of-the-Art Applications* (pp. 190–212). Hershey, PA: CyberTech Publishing.

Bryan, M., & Cousins, J. (2010). Applying semantic web technologies to car repairs. In Tatnall, A. (Ed.), *Web Technologies: Concepts, Methodologies, Tools, and Applications* (pp. 924–942). Hershey, PA: Information Science Reference.

Buffa, M., Erétéo, G., & Gandon, F. (2008). A wiki on the semantic web. In Rech, J., Decker, B., & Ras, E. (Eds.), *Emerging Technologies for Semantic Work Environments: Techniques, Methods, and Applications* (pp. 115–137). Hershey, PA: Information Science Reference. doi:10.4018/978-1-59904-877-2.ch008.

Caliusco, L., Maidana, C., Galli, M. R., & Chiotti, O. (2006). Contextual ontology modeling language to facilitate the use of enabling semantic web technologies. In Taniar, D., & Rahayu, J. (Eds.), *Web Semantics & Ontology* (pp. 68–90). Hershey, PA: Idea Group Publishing. doi:10.4018/978-1-59140-905-2.ch003.

Cannoy, S. D. (2009). Semantic web standards and ontologies in the medical sciences and healthcare. In Tan, J. (Ed.), *Medical Informatics: Concepts, Methodologies, Tools, and Applications* (pp. 65–77). Hershey, PA: Medical Information Science Reference.

Cannoy, S. D., & Iyer, L. (2009). Semantic web standards and ontologies in the medical sciences and healthcare. In Lee, I. (Ed.), *Electronic Business: Concepts, Methodologies, Tools, and Applications* (pp. 2323–2335). Hershey, PA: Information Science Reference.

Carbonaro, A., & Ferrini, R. (2008). Personalized information retrieval in a semantic-based learning environment. In Goh, D., & Foo, S. (Eds.), *Social Information Retrieval Systems: Emerging Technologies and Applications for Searching the Web Effectively* (pp. 270–288). Hershey, PA: Information Science Reference. doi:10.4018/978-1-60566-034-9.ch018.

Cardoso, J. (2007). The syntactic and the semantic web. In Cardoso, J. (Ed.), *Semantic Web Services: Theory, Tools and Applications* (pp. 1–23). Hershey, PA: Information Science Reference. doi:10.4018/978-1-59904-045-5. ch001.

Cardoso, J., & Lytras, M. D. (2009). *Semantic web engineering in the knowledge society* (pp. 1-424). doi:10.4018/978-1-60566-112-4

Catley, C., Frize, M., & Petriu, D. (2008). Semantic web services for healthcare. In Sugumaran, V. (Ed.), *Intelligent Information Technologies: Concepts, Methodologies, Tools, and Applications* (pp. 765–773). Hershey, PA: Information Science Reference.

Chaka, C. (2010). E-learning 2.0: Web 2.0, the semantic web and the power of collective intelligence. In Association, I. (Ed.), *Web-Based Education: Concepts, Methodologies, Tools and Applications* (pp. 1765–1787). Hershey, PA: Information Science Reference.

Chaves, M. S., Trojahn, C., & Pedron, C. D. (2012). A framework for customer knowledge management based on social semantic web: A hotel sector approach. In Colomo-Palacios, R., Varajão, J., & Soto-Acosta, P. (Eds.), *Customer Relationship Management and the Social and Semantic Web: Enabling Cliens Conexus* (pp. 141–157). Hershey, PA: Business Science Reference.

Chebotko, A., Deng, Y., Lu, S., Fotouhi, F., & Aristar, A. (2007). An ontology-based multimedia annotator for the semantic web of language engineering. In Sheth, A., & Lytras, M. (Eds.), *Semantic Web-Based Information Systems: State-of-the-Art Applications* (pp. 140–160). Hershey, PA: CyberTech Publishing.

Chen, L., Shadbolt, N. R., Goble, C., & Tao, F. (2006). Managing semantic metadata for web/grid services. [IJWSR]. *International Journal of Web Services Research*, *3*(4), 73–94. doi:10.4018/jwsr.2006100104.

Chen, Y., & Zhang, Y. (2010). A genetic fuzzy semantic web search agent using granular semantic trees for ambiguous queries. In Yao, J. (Ed.), *Novel Developments in Granular Computing: Applications for Advanced Human Reasoning and Soft Computation* (pp. 426–438). Hershey, PA: Information Science Reference. doi:10.4018/978-1-60566-324-1. ch018.

Chevalier, M., Julien, C., & Soulé-Dupuy, C. (2012). User models for adaptive information retrieval on the web: Towards an interoperable and semantic model. [IJARAS]. *International Journal of Adaptive, Resilient and Autonomic Systems*, *3*(3), 1–19. doi:10.4018/jaras.2012070101.

Chiu, D., Trojer, T., Hu, H., Hu, H., Zhuang, Y., & Hung, P. (2010). Flow-based adaptive information integration. In Wang, M., & Sun, Z. (Eds.), *Handbook of Research on Complex Dynamic Process Management: Techniques for Adaptability in Turbulent Environments* (pp. 209–231). Hershey, PA: Business Science Reference.

Choi, B. (2009). Web mining by automatically organizing web pages into categories. In Sugumaran, V. (Ed.), *Distributed Artificial Intelligence, Agent Technology, and Collaborative Applications* (pp. 214–231). Hershey, PA: Information Science Reference.

Cicurel, L., Bas Uribe, J. L., Gonzalez, S. B., Contreras, J., López-Cobo, J., & Losada, S. (2010). Using semantic web services in e-banking solutions. In Tatnall, A. (Ed.), *Web Technologies: Concepts, Methodologies, Tools, and Applications* (pp. 971–987). Hershey, PA: Information Science Reference. doi:10.4018/978-1-61520-967-5.ch059.

Cicurel, L., Luis Bas Uribe, J., Bellido Gonzalez, S., Contreras, J., López-Cobo, J., & Losada, S. (2010). Using semantic web services in e-banking solutions. In I. Management Association (Ed.), Electronic Services: Concepts, Methodologies, Tools and Applications (pp. 972-988). Hershey, PA: Information Science Reference. doi: doi:10.4018/978-1-61520-967-5.ch059.

Colomo-Palacios, R., Varajão, J., & Soto-Acosta, P. (2012). *Customer relationship management and the social and semantic web: Enabling cliens conexus* (pp. 1-360). doi:10.4018/978-1-61350-044-6

Conger, S. (2009). Personal information privacy: A multi-party endeavor. [JECO]. *Journal of Electronic Commerce in Organizations*, 7(1), 71–82. doi:10.4018/jeco.2009010106.

Corcho, O., Losada, S., & Benjamins, R. (2010). Semantic web-enabled protocol mediation for the logistics domain. In Tatnall, A. (Ed.), *Web Technologies: Concepts, Methodologies, Tools, and Applications* (pp. 1878–1895). Hershey, PA: Information Science Reference.

Costa, P. C., Blackmond Laskey, K., & Lukasiewicz, T. (2009). Uncertainty representation and reasoning in the semantic web. In Cardoso, J., & Lytras, M. (Eds.), *Semantic Web Engineering in the Knowledge Society* (pp. 315–340). Hershey, PA: Information Science Reference. doi:10.4018/978-1-60566-982-3.ch100.

Costa, P. C., Laskey, K. B., & Lukasiewicz, T. (2010). Uncertainty representation and reasoning in the semantic web. In Tatnall, A. (Ed.), *Web Technologies: Concepts, Methodologies, Tools, and Applications* (pp. 1852–1877). Hershey, PA: Information Science Reference.

Crosslin, M. (2012). When the future finally arrives: Web 2.0 becomes web 3.0. In I. Management Association (Ed.), Grid and Cloud Computing: Concepts, Methodologies, Tools and Applications (pp. 1738-1751). Hershey, PA: Information Science Reference. doi: doi:10.4018/978-1-4666-0879-5.ch801.

Cunha Cardoso, R., da Fonseca, F., & Salgado, A. C. (2006). Retrieving specific domain information from the web through ontologies. [IJIIT]. *International Journal of Intelligent Information Technologies*, 2(3), 56–71. doi:10.4018/jiit.2006070104.

Cunha Cardoso, R., da Fonseca de Souza, F., & Salgado, A. C. (2008). Using semantic web concepts to retrieve specific domain information from the web. In Sugumaran, V. (Ed.), *Intelligent Information Technologies and Applications* (pp. 249–270). Hershey, PA: IGI Publishing.

Curran, K., & Gumbleton, G. (2008). The semantic web. In Freire, M., & Pereira, M. (Eds.), *Encyclopedia of Internet Technologies and Applications* (pp. 505–511). Hershey, PA: Information Science Reference.

Curran, K., & McCarthy, S. (2009). Really simple syndication (RSS). In Khosrow-Pour, M. (Ed.), *Encyclopedia of Information Science and Technology* (2nd ed., pp. 3213–3218). Hershey, PA: Information Science Reference.

Cuzzocrea, A. (2009). Modeling and querying XMLBased P2P information systems: A semantics-based approach. In Z. Ma, & H. Wang (Eds.), The Semantic Web for Knowledge and Data Management (pp. 207–242). Hershey, PA: Information Science Reference. doi: doi:10.4018/978-1-60566-028-8.ch009.

D'Aubeterre, F., Singh, R., & Iyer, L. (2007). Semantic knowledge transparency in e-business processes. In Salam, A., & Stevens, J. (Eds.), *Semantic Web Technologies and E-Business: Toward the Integrated Virtual Organization and Business Process Automation* (pp. 255–286). Hershey, PA: Idea Group Publishing. doi:10.4018/978-1-59904-192-6.ch011.

Dag, F., & Erkan, K. (2010). A personalized learning system based on semantic web technologies. In Stankov, S., Glavinic, V., & Rosic, M. (Eds.), *Intelligent Tutoring Systems in E-Learning Environments: Design, Implementation and Evaluation* (pp. 258–284). Hershey, PA: Information Science Reference. doi:10.4018/978-1-61692-008-1.ch013.

Dai, H. (2009). Integrating semantic knowledge with web usage mining for personalization. In Mourlas, C., & Germanakos, P. (Eds.), *Intelligent User Interfaces: Adaptation and Personalization Systems and Technologies* (pp. 205–232). Hershey, PA: Information Science Reference.

Dai, H., & Mobasher, B. (2008). Integrating semantic knowledge with web usage mining for personalization. In Wang, J. (Ed.), *Data Warehousing and Mining: Concepts, Methodologies, Tools, and Applications* (pp. 3557–3585). Hershey, PA: Information Science Reference. doi:10.4018/978-1-59904-951-9.ch223.

Damljanovic, D., & Devedžic, V. (2009). Semantic web and e-tourism. In Khosrow-Pour, M. (Ed.), *Encyclopedia of Information Science and Technology* (2nd ed., pp. 3426–3432). Hershey, PA: Information Science Reference.

Damljanovic, D., & Devedžic, V. (2010). Applying semantic web to e-tourism. In Tatnall, A. (Ed.), *Web Technologies: Concepts, Methodologies, Tools, and Applications* (pp. 1027–1049). Hershey, PA: Information Science Reference.

De Troyer, O. (2009). Audience-drive design approach for web systems. In Khosrow-Pour, M. (Ed.), *Encyclopedia of Information Science and Technology* (2nd ed., pp. 274–278). Hershey, PA: Information Science Reference.

Dieng-Kuntz, R. (2011). Corporate semantic webs. In Schwartz, D., & Te'eni, D. (Eds.), *Encyclopedia of Knowledge Management* (2nd ed., pp. 131–149). Hershey, PA: Information Science Reference.

Dietze, S., Gugliotta, A., & Domingue, J. (2009). Bridging the gap between mobile application contexts and semantic web resources. In Stojanovic, D. (Ed.), *Context-Aware Mobile and Ubiquitous Computing for Enhanced Usability: Adaptive Technologies and Applications* (pp. 217–234). Hershey, PA: Information Science Reference. doi:10.4018/978-1-60566-290-9.ch009.

Dietze, S., Gugliotta, A., & Domingue, J. (2009). Supporting interoperability and context-awareness in e-learning through situation-driven learning processes. [IJDET]. *International Journal of Distance Education Technologies*, 7(2), 20–43. doi:10.4018/jdet.2009040102.

Dietze, S., Gugliotta, A., Domingue, J., & Mrissa, M. (2011). Mediation spaces for similarity-based semantic web services selection. [IJWSR]. *International Journal of Web Services Research*, 8(1), 1–20. doi:10.4018/jwsr.2011010101.

Ding, Q. (2009). Data mining on XML data. In Wang, J. (Ed.), *Encyclopedia of Data Warehousing and Mining* (2nd ed., pp. 506–510). Hershey, PA: Information Science Reference.

do Prado, H. A., Filho, A. H., Sayão, M., & Ferneda, E. (2009). Multiagent systems in the web. In Khosrow-Pour, M. (Ed.), *Encyclopedia of Information Science and Technology* (2nd ed., pp. 2734–2740). Hershey, PA: Information Science Reference.

Du, T. C., & Li, E. Y. (2009). Building dynamic business process in P2P semantic web. In I. Lee (Ed.), Selected Readings on Information Technology and Business Systems Management (pp. 186-201). Hershey, PA: Information Science Reference. doi: doi:10.4018/978-1-60566-086-8.ch010.

Duke, A. (2009). Semantic integration for B2B service assurance. In Garcia, R. (Ed.), *Semantic Web for Business: Cases and Applications* (pp. 50–64). Hershey, PA: Information Science Reference.

Elia, G., Secundo, G., & Taurino, C. (2009). SWELS: A semantic web system supporting e-learning. In Zilli, A., Damiani, E., Ceravolo, P., Corallo, A., & Elia, G. (Eds.), *Semantic Knowledge Management: An Ontology-Based Framework* (pp. 120–145). Hershey, PA: Information Science Reference. doi:10.4018/978-1-60566-982-3.ch044.

Eljinini, M. A. (2013). The medical semantic web: Opportunities and issues. In Alkhatib, G. (Ed.), *Network and Communication Technology Innovations for Web and IT Advancement* (pp. 19–29). Hershey, PA: Information Science Reference.

Ermolayev, V., Keberle, N., Kononenko, O., & Terziyan, V. (2007). Proactively composing web services as tasks by semantic web agents. In Zhang, L. (Ed.), *Modern Technologies in Web Services Research* (pp. 217–246). Hershey, PA: CyberTech Publishing. doi:10.4018/978-1-59904-280-0.ch011.

Farkas, C. (2008). Data confidentiality on the semantic web: Is there an inference problem? In Nemati, H. (Ed.), *Information Security and Ethics: Concepts, Methodologies, Tools, and Applications* (pp. 3309–3320). Hershey, PA: Information Science Reference.

Fernández, S., Berrueta, D., Shi, L., Labra, J. E., & Ordóñez de Pablos, 7. (2009). Mailing lists and social semantic web. In M. Lytras, & P. Ordóñez de Pablos (Eds.), *Social Web Evolution: Integrating Semantic Applications and Web 2.0 Technologies* (pp. 42-56). Hershey, PA: Information Science Reference. doi:10.4018/978-1-60566-272-5.ch004

Fernández, S., Berrueta, D., Shi, L., Labra, J. E., & Ordóñez de Pablos, 1. (2010). Mailing lists and social semantic web. In A. Tatnall (Ed.), *Web Technologies: Concepts, Methodologies, Tools, and Applications* (pp. 1090-1104). Hershey, PA: Information Science Reference. doi:10.4018/978-1-60566-982-3.ch058

Fernández, S., Berrueta, D., Shi, L., Labra, J. E., & Ordóñez de Pablos, 4. (2010). Mailing lists and social semantic web. In S. Dasgupta (Ed.), *Social Computing: Concepts, Methodologies, Tools, and Applications* (pp. 335-349). Hershey, PA: Information Science Reference. doi:10.4018/978-1-60566-984-7.ch025

Ferrara, A., Nikolov, A., & Scharffe, F. (2011). Data linking for the semantic web. [IJSWIS]. *International Journal on Semantic Web and Information Systems*, 7(3), 46–76. doi:10.4018/jswis.2011070103.

Fortier, J., & Kassel, G. (2006). Organizational semantic webs. In Schwartz, D. (Ed.), *Encyclopedia of Knowledge Management* (pp. 741–748). Hershey, PA: Information Science Reference. doi:10.4018/978-1-59140-573-3.ch097.

Fortier, J., & Kassel, G. (2011). Organizational semantic webs. In Schwartz, D., & Te'eni, D. (Eds.), *Encyclopedia of Knowledge Management* (2nd ed., pp. 1298–1307). Hershey, PA: Information Science Reference.

Franz, T., & Sizov, S. (2008). Communication systems for semantic work environments. In Rech, J., Decker, B., & Ras, E. (Eds.), *Emerging Technologies for Semantic Work Environments: Techniques, Methods, and Applications* (pp. 16–32). Hershey, PA: Information Science Reference. doi:10.4018/978-1-59904-877-2.ch002.

Frasincar, F., Borsje, J., & Hogenboom, F. (2011). Personalizing news services using semantic web technologies. In Lee, I. (Ed.), *E-Business Applications for Product Development and Competitive Growth: Emerging Technologies* (pp. 261–289). Hershey, PA: Business Science Reference.

Frasincar, F., Borsje, J., & Levering, L. (2010). A semantic web-based approach for building personalized news services. In Tatnall, A. (Ed.), *Web Technologies: Concepts, Methodologies, Tools, and Applications* (pp. 503–521). Hershey, PA: Information Science Reference.

Fugazza, C., David, S., Montesanto, A., & Rocchi, C. (2009). Approaches to semantics in knowledge management. In Erickson, J. (Ed.), *Database Technologies: Concepts, Methodologies, Tools, and Applications* (pp. 257–281). Hershey, PA: Information Science Reference. doi:10.4018/978-1-60566-058-5.ch019.

Furtado, V., Ayres, L., & Fernandes, G. (2009). A multiagent approach for configuring and explaining workflow of semantic web services. In Alkhatib, G., & Rine, D. (Eds.), *Agent Technologies and Web Engineering: Applications and Systems* (pp. 77–94). Hershey, PA: Information Science Reference.

Gannod, G. C., Timm, J. T., & Brodie, R. J. (2006). Facilitating the specification of semantic web services using model-driven development. [IJWSR]. *International Journal of Web Services Research*, 3(3), 61–81. doi:10.4018/jwsr.2006070103.

Gannod, G. C., Timm, J. T., & Brodie, R. J. (2008). Model-driven semantic web services. In Zhang, L. (Ed.), *Web Services Research and Practices* (pp. 304–338). Hershey, PA: CyberTech Publishing. doi:10.4018/978-1-59904-904-5.ch010.

Related References

Ganzha, M., Gawinecki, M., Paprzycki, M., Gasiorowski, R., Pisarek, S., & Hyska, W. (2009). Utilizing semantic web and software agents in a travel support system. In Zilli, A., Damiani, E., Ceravolo, P., Corallo, A., & Elia, G. (Eds.), *Semantic Knowledge Management: An Ontology-Based Framework* (pp. 341–369). Hershey, PA: Information Science Reference. doi:10.4018/978-1-60566-060-8. ch089.

García, F. J., Berlanga, A. J., & García, J. (2006). A semantic learning objects authoring tool. In Ghaoui, C. (Ed.), *Encyclopedia of Human Computer Interaction* (pp. 504–510). Hershey, PA: Information Science Reference.

Garcia, R. (2009). *Semantic web for business: Cases and applications* (pp. 1-446). doi:10.4018/978-1-60566-066-0

García-Castro, R. (2009). Benchmarking in the semantic web. In Cardoso, J., & Lytras, M. (Eds.), *Semantic Web Engineering in the Knowledge Society* (pp. 341–370). Hershey, PA: Information Science Reference.

García-Crespo, Á., Colomo-Palacios, R., Gómez-Berbís, J. M., & Martín, F. P. (2012). Customer relationship management in social and semantic web environments. In Eid, R. (Ed.), *Successful Customer Relationship Management Programs and Technologies: Issues and Trends* (pp. 83–92). Hershey, PA: Business Science Reference. doi:10.4018/978-1-4666-0288-5.ch006.

García-Crespo, Á., Colomo-Palacios, R., Mencke, M., & Gómez-Berbís, J. M. (2009). CUSENT: Social sentiment analysis using semantics for customer feedback. In Lytras, M., & Ordóñez de Pablos, P. (Eds.), *Social Web Evolution: Integrating Semantic Applications and Web 2.0 Technologies* (pp. 89–101). Hershey, PA: Information Science Reference. doi:10.4018/978-1-60566-272-5.ch007.

Garito, M. (2009). Convergence in mobile internet with service oriented architecture and its value to business. In B. Unhelkar (Ed.), Handbook of Research in Mobile Business, Second Edition: Technical, Methodological and Social Perspectives (pp. 584-594). Hershey, PA: Information Science Reference. doi: doi:10.4018/978-1-60566-156-8.ch054.

Ghorbel, H., Bahri, A., & Bouaziz, R. (2012). Fuzzy ontologies building platform for semantic web: FOB platform. In Jouis, C., Biskri, I., Ganascia, J., & Roux, M. (Eds.), *Next Generation Search Engines: Advanced Models for Information Retrieval* (pp. 92–113). Hershey, PA: Information Science Reference. doi:10.4018/978-1-4666-0330-1.ch005.

Ginsberg, A. (2010). Ontological indeterminacy and the semantic web or why the controversy over same-sex marriage poses a fundamental problem for current semantic web architecture. In Lytras, M., & Sheth, A. (Eds.), *Progressive Concepts for Semantic Web Evolution: Applications and Developments* (pp. 148–185). Hershey, PA: Information Science Reference.

Gómez, J. M., & Duc, T. (2009). A personalized portal on the basis of semantic models and rules. In Lytras, M., & Ordóñez de Pablos, P. (Eds.), *Emerging Topics and Technologies in Information Systems* (pp. 153–164). Hershey, PA: Information Science Reference. doi:10.4018/978-1-60566-222-0.ch008.

Gómez, J. M., & Memari, A. (2009). Semantic web and adaptivity: Towards a new model. In Cruz-Cunha, M., Oliveira, E., Tavares, A., & Ferreira, L. (Eds.), *Handbook of Research on Social Dimensions of Semantic Technologies and Web Services* (pp. 521–540). Hershey, PA: Information Science Reference. doi:10.4018/978-1-60566-650-1.ch027.

Gómez-Pérez, J. M., & Méndez, V. (2012). Towards supporting interoperability in e-invoicing based on semantic web technologies. In Kajan, E., Dorloff, F., & Bedini, I. (Eds.), *Handbook of Research on E-Business Standards and Protocols: Documents, Data and Advanced Web Technologies* (pp. 705–724). Hershey, PA: Business Science Reference. doi:10.4018/978-1-4666-0146-8.ch032.

Gong, Y., Overbeek, S., & Janssen, M. (2013). Integrating semantic web and software agents: Exchanging RIF and BDI rules. In Chiu, D. (Ed.), *Mobile and Web Innovations in Systems and Service-Oriented Engineering* (pp. 102–119). Hershey, PA: Information Science Reference.

Goudos, S. K., Peristeras, V., & Tarabanis, K. (2010). Application of semantic web technology in e-business: Case studies in public domain data knowledge representation. In I. Management Association (Ed.), Business Information Systems: Concepts, Methodologies, Tools and Applications (pp. 1223-1233). Hershey, PA: Business Science Reference. doi: doi:10.4018/978-1-61520-969-9.ch075.

Goy, A., & Magro, D. (2013). How semantic web technologies can support the mediation between supply and demand in the ICT market: The case of customer relationship management. In I. Management Association (Ed.), Supply Chain Management: Concepts, Methodologies, Tools, and Applications (pp. 710-734). Hershey, PA: Business Science Reference. doi: doi:10.4018/978-1-4666-2625-6.ch041.

Gubala, T., Bubak, M., & Sloot, P. (2009). Semantic integration for research environments. In Cannataro, M. (Ed.), *Handbook of Research on Computational Grid Technologies for Life Sciences, Biomedicine, and Healthcare* (pp. 514–530). Hershey, PA: Medical Information Science Reference. doi:10.4018/978-1-60566-374-6.ch026.

Guizzardi, R. S., Ludermir, P. G., & Sona, D. (2008). A recommender agent to support knowledge sharing in virtual enterprises. In Protogeros, N. (Ed.), *Agent and Web Service Technologies in Virtual Enterprises* (pp. 115–134). Hershey, PA: Information Science Reference.

Gunter, D. (2012). The semantic web: History, applications and future possibilities. In Polanka, S. (Ed.), *E-Reference Context and Discoverability in Libraries: Issues and Concepts* (pp. 199–208). Hershey, PA: Information Science Reference.

Haarslev, V., Pai, H., & Shiri, N. (2009). Semantic web uncertainty management. In Khosrow-Pour, M. (Ed.), *Encyclopedia of Information Science and Technology* (2nd ed., pp. 3439–3444). Hershey, PA: Information Science Reference.

Hadrich, T., & Priebe, T. (2009). A context-based approach for supporting knowledge work with semantic portals. In Lytras, M., & Ordóñez de Pablos, P. (Eds.), *Emerging Topics and Technologies in Information Systems* (pp. 231–253). Hershey, PA: Information Science Reference. doi:10.4018/978-1-60566-222-0.ch014.

Hanh, H. H., Tho, M. N., & A., M. T. (2010). A semantic web-based approach for context-aware user query formulation and information retrieval. In G. Alkhatib, & D. Rine (Eds.), *Web Engineering Advancements and Trends: Building New Dimensions of Information Technology* (pp. 1-23). Hershey, PA: Information Science Reference. doi:10.4018/978-1-60566-719-5.ch001

Hellmann, S., Lehmann, J., & Auer, S. (2009). Learning of OWL class descriptions on very large knowledge bases. [IJSWIS]. *International Journal on Semantic Web and Information Systems*, *5*(2), 25–48. doi:10.4018/jswis.2009040102.

Related References

Hermida, J. M., Meliá, S., Montoyo, A., & Gómez, J. (2013). Developing rich internet applications as social sites on the semantic web: A model-driven approach. In Chiu, D. (Ed.), *Mobile and Web Innovations in Systems and Service-Oriented Engineering* (pp. 134–155). Hershey, PA: Information Science Reference.

Herrero Cárcel, G. (2009). Towards the use of networked ontologies for dealing with knowledge-intensive domains: A pharmaceutical case study. In Garcia, R. (Ed.), *Semantic Web for Business: Cases and Applications* (pp. 298–320). Hershey, PA: Information Science Reference.

Hoang, H. H., Nguyen, T. M., & Tjoa, A. M. (2009). A semantic web based approach for context-aware user query formulation and information retrieval. In Chevalier, M., Julien, C., & Soule-Dupuy, C. (Eds.), *Collaborative and Social Information Retrieval and Access: Techniques for Improved User Modeling* (pp. 313–336). Hershey, PA: Information Science Reference. doi:10.4018/978-1-60566-306-7.ch015.

Hogan, A., Harth, A., & Polleres, A. (2009). Scalable authoritative OWL reasoning for the web. [IJSWIS]. *International Journal on Semantic Web and Information Systems, 5*(2), 49–90. doi: doi:10.4018/jswis.2009040103.

Hüsemann, B., & Vossen, G. (2006). OntoMedia— Semantic multimedia metadata integration and organization. [IJSWIS]. *International Journal on Semantic Web and Information Systems, 2*(3), 1–16. doi:10.4018/jswis.2006070101.

Iglesias, A. (2008). A new framework for intelligent semantic web services based on GAIVAs. [IJITWE]. *International Journal of Information Technology and Web Engineering, 3*(4), 30–58. doi:10.4018/jitwe.2008100102.

Ilyas, Q. M. (2013). Developing semantic web applications. In Buragga, K., & Zaman, N. (Eds.), *Software Development Techniques for Constructive Information Systems Design* (pp. 320–331). Hershey, PA: Information Science Reference. doi:10.4018/978-1-4666-3679-8.ch017.

Jabin, S., & Mustafa, K. (2012). A survey of semantic web based architectures for adaptive intelligent tutoring system. In Ali, S., Abbadeni, N., & Batouche, M. (Eds.), *Multidisciplinary Computational Intelligence Techniques: Applications in Business, Engineering, and Medicine* (pp. 239–256). Hershey, PA: Information Science Reference. doi:10.4018/978-1-4666-1830-5.ch015.

Janev, V., Dudukovic, J., & Vraneš, S. (2009). Semantic web based integration of knowledge resources for expertise finding. [IJEIS]. *International Journal of Enterprise Information Systems, 5*(4), 53–70. doi:10.4018/jeis.2009090204.

Janev, V., & Vraneš, S. (2012). Applicability assessment of semantic web technologies in human resources domain. In I. Management Association (Ed.), Human Resources Management: Concepts, Methodologies, Tools, and Applications (pp. 470-485). Hershey, PA: Business Science Reference. doi: doi:10.4018/978-1-4666-1601-1.ch030.

Jiang, J., Huang, X., Wu, Y., & Yang, G. (2013). Campus cloud storage and preservation: From distributed file system to data sharing service. In Yang, X., & Liu, L. (Eds.), *Principles, Methodologies, and Service-Oriented Approaches for Cloud Computing* (pp. 284–301). Hershey, PA: Business Science Reference. doi:10.4018/978-1-4666-2854-0.ch012.

João Viamonte, M. (2009). A semantic web-based information integration approach for an agent-based electronic market. In Garcia, R. (Ed.), *Semantic Web for Business: Cases and Applications* (pp. 150–169). Hershey, PA: Information Science Reference. doi:10.4018/978-1-60566-060-8.ch086.

Joo, J., Lee, S., & Jeong, Y. (2007). Application of semantic web based on the domain-specific ontology for global KM. In Salam, A., & Stevens, J. (Eds.), *Semantic Web Technologies and E-Business: Toward the Integrated Virtual Organization and Business Process Automation* (pp. 287–309). Hershey, PA: Idea Group Publishing. doi:10.4018/978-1-59904-192-6.ch012.

Joo, J., Lee, S. M., & Jeong, Y. (2009). Application of Semantic web based on the domain-specific ontology for global KM. In Lytras, M., & Ordóñez de Pablos, P. (Eds.), *Social Web Evolution: Integrating Semantic Applications and Web 2.0 Technologies* (pp. 160–176). Hershey, PA: Information Science Reference. doi:10.4018/978-1-60566-272-5.ch013.

Kabak, Y., Olduz, M., Laleci, G. B., Namli, T., Bicer, V., & Radic, N. et al. (2010). A semantic web service based middleware for the tourism industry. In Mentzas, G., & Friesen, A. (Eds.), *Semantic Enterprise Application Integration for Business Processes: Service-Oriented Frameworks* (pp. 189–211). Hershey, PA: Business Science Reference.

Kalogeras, A. P., Alexakos, C., & Georgoudakis, M. (2011). The semantic web as a catalyst for enterprise/industrial interoperability. In Kajan, E. (Ed.), *Electronic Business Interoperability: Concepts, Opportunities and Challenges* (pp. 415–436). Hershey, PA: Business Science Reference. doi:10.4018/978-1-60960-485-1.ch017.

Kamthan, P. (2008). Addressing the credibility of web applications. In Freire, M., & Pereira, M. (Eds.), *Encyclopedia of Internet Technologies and Applications* (pp. 23–28). Hershey, PA: Information Science Reference.

Kamthan, P. (2009). Establishing the credibility of social web applications. In Khosrow-Pour, M. (Ed.), *Encyclopedia of Information Science and Technology* (2nd ed., pp. 1432–1437). Hershey, PA: Information Science Reference. doi:10.4018/978-1-60566-984-7.ch009.

Kamthan, P. (2009). Extreme programming for web applications. In Khosrow-Pour, M. (Ed.), *Encyclopedia of Information Science and Technology* (2nd ed., pp. 1510–1515). Hershey, PA: Information Science Reference.

Kamthan, P. (2009). Knowledge representation in semantic mobile applications. In Taniar, D. (Ed.), *Mobile Computing: Concepts, Methodologies, Tools, and Applications* (pp. 796–804). Hershey, PA: Information Science Reference.

Kamthan, P. (2009). Using patterns for engineering high-quality e-commerce applications. In Al-Hakim, L., & Memmola, M. (Eds.), *Business Web Strategy: Design, Alignment, and Application* (pp. 1–25). Hershey, PA: Information Science Reference.

Kanellopoulos, D. (2011). Localising e-learning websites in the semantic web era. In Lazarinis, F., Green, S., & Pearson, E. (Eds.), *Handbook of Research on E-Learning Standards and Interoperability: Frameworks and Issues* (pp. 284–299). Hershey, PA: Information Science Reference.

Karastoyanova, D., van Lessen, T., Leymann, F., Ma, Z., Nitzche, J., & Wetzstein, B. (2009). Semantic business process management: Applying ontologies in BPM. In Cardoso, J., & van der Aalst, W. (Eds.), *Handbook of Research on Business Process Modeling* (pp. 299–317). Hershey, PA: Information Science Reference. doi:10.4018/978-1-60566-288-6.ch014.

Karkaletsis, V., & Stamatakis, K. Karampiperis, Karampiperis, Pythagoras, & Pythagoras, (2009). Management of medical website quality labels via web mining. In P. Berka, J. Rauch, & D. Zighed (Eds.), Data Mining and Medical Knowledge Management: Cases and Applications (pp. 206-226). Hershey, PA: Medical Information Science Reference. doi: doi:10.4018/978-1-60566-218-3.ch010.

Katsiouli, P., Papapanagiotou, P., Tsetsos, V., Anagnostopoulos, C., & Hadjiefthymiades, S. (2009). Matching relational schemata to semantic web ontologies. In Ferraggine, V., Doorn, J., & Rivero, L. (Eds.), *Handbook of Research on Innovations in Database Technologies and Applications: Current and Future Trends* (pp. 434–442). Hershey, PA: Information Science Reference. doi:10.4018/978-1-60566-242-8.ch047.

Kauppinen, T., Paakkarinen, P., Mäkela, E., Kuittinen, H., Väätäinen, J., & Hyvönen, E. (2011). Geospatio-temporal semantic web for cultural heritage. In Lytras, M., Ordóñez de Pablos, P., Damiani, E., & Diaz, L. (Eds.), *Digital Culture and E-Tourism: Technologies, Applications and Management Approaches* (pp. 48–64). Hershey, PA: Information Science Reference.

Keller, U., Lara, R., Lausen, H., & Fensel, D. (2007). Semantic web service discovery in the WSMO framework. In Cardoso, J. (Ed.), *Semantic Web Services: Theory, Tools and Applications* (pp. 281–316). Hershey, PA: Information Science Reference. doi:10.4018/978-1-59904-045-5.ch012.

Kidd, P. T. (2011). On the social shaping of the semantic web. In I. Management Association (Ed.), Virtual Communities: Concepts, Methodologies, Tools and Applications (pp. 936-950). Hershey, PA: Information Science Reference. doi: doi:10.4018/978-1-60960-100-3.ch317.

Kim, H., Breslin, J. G., Decker, S., & Kim, H. (2010). Representing and sharing tagging data using the social semantic cloud of tags. In Dumova, T., & Fiordo, R. (Eds.), *Handbook of Research on Social Interaction Technologies and Collaboration Software: Concepts and Trends* (pp. 519–527). Hershey, PA: Information Science Reference.

Kim, H. M., Sengupta, A., Fox, M. S., & Dalkilic, M. (2009). A measurement ontology generalizable for emerging domain applications on the semantic web. In Erickson, J. (Ed.), *Database Technologies: Concepts, Methodologies, Tools, and Applications* (pp. 2384–2404). Hershey, PA: Information Science Reference. doi:10.4018/978-1-60566-058-5.ch146.

Kimmerle, J., & Cress, U. (2009). Knowledge communication with shared databases. In Erickson, J. (Ed.), *Database Technologies: Concepts, Methodologies, Tools, and Applications* (pp. 1670–1681). Hershey, PA: Information Science Reference. doi:10.4018/978-1-60566-058-5.ch102.

Koffina, I., Serfiotis, G., Christophides, V., & Tannen, V. (2006). Mediating RDF/S queries to relational and XML sources. [IJSWIS]. *International Journal on Semantic Web and Information Systems*, *2*(4), 68–91. doi:10.4018/jswis.2006100103.

Koffina, I., Serfiotis, G., Christophides, V., & Tannen, V. (2009). Mediating RDF/S queries to relational and XML sources. In Erickson, J. (Ed.), *Database Technologies: Concepts, Methodologies, Tools, and Applications* (pp. 596–614). Hershey, PA: Information Science Reference. doi:10.4018/978-1-60566-058-5.ch036.

Kona, S., Bansal, A., Simon, L., Mallya, A., & Gupta, G. (2009). USDL: A service-semantics description language for automatic service discovery and composition. [IJWSR]. *International Journal of Web Services Research*, *6*(1), 20–48. doi:10.4018/jwsr.2009010102.

Koné, M. T., & McIver, W. Jr. (2009). Semantic web in e-government. In Khosrow-Pour, M. (Ed.), *Encyclopedia of Information Science and Technology* (2nd ed., pp. 3433–3438). Hershey, PA: Information Science Reference.

Kontopoulos, E., & Bassiliades, N. (2008). Visual development of defeasible logic rules for the semantic web. In Ferri, F. (Ed.), *Visual Languages for Interactive Computing: Definitions and Formalizations* (pp. 273–301). Hershey, PA: Information Science Reference.

Kontopoulos, E., Bassiliades, N., Governatori, G., & Antoniou, G. (2011). A modal defeasible reasoner of deontic logic for the semantic web. [IJSWIS]. *International Journal on Semantic Web and Information Systems*, *7*(1), 18–43. doi:10.4018/jswis.2011010102.

Kor, A. L. (2007). Semantic web, RDF, and portals. In Tatnall, A. (Ed.), *Encyclopedia of Portal Technologies and Applications* (pp. 905–911). Hershey, PA: Information Science Reference. doi:10.4018/978-1-59140-989-2.ch149.

Kotis, K. (2009). Perspectives and key technologies of semantic web search. In Wang, J. (Ed.), *Encyclopedia of Data Warehousing and Mining* (2nd ed., pp. 1532–1537). Hershey, PA: Information Science Reference.

Krogstie, J., Veres, C., & Sindre, G. (2008). Integrating semantic web technology, web services, and workflow modeling: Achieving system and business interoperability. In Becker, A. (Ed.), *Electronic Commerce: Concepts, Methodologies, Tools, and Applications* (pp. 591–610). Hershey, PA: Information Science Reference.

Krogstie, J., Veres, C., & Sindre, G. (2011). Achieving system and business interoperability by semantic web services. In I. Management Association (Ed.), Enterprise Information Systems: Concepts, Methodologies, Tools and Applications (pp. 731-751). Hershey, PA: Business Science Reference. doi: doi:10.4018/978-1-61692-852-0.ch312.

Kumar, S., & Kumar, K. (2010). A QoS aware, cognitive parameters based model for the selection of semantic web services. In Sugumaran, V. (Ed.), *Methodological Advancements in Intelligent Information Technologies: Evolutionary Trends* (pp. 320–335). Hershey, PA: Information Science Reference.

Kumar, S., Kumar, K., & Jain, A. (2010). An agent-enabled semantic web service composition framework. In Alkhatib, G., & Rine, D. (Eds.), *Web Engineering Advancements and Trends: Building New Dimensions of Information Technology* (pp. 63–82). Hershey, PA: Information Science Reference. doi:10.4018/978-1-60566-719-5.ch004.

Kumar, S., & Mishra, R. (2008). A hybrid model for service selection in semantic web service composition. [IJIIT]. *International Journal of Intelligent Information Technologies*, 4(4), 55–69. doi:10.4018/jiit.2008100104.

Kumar, S., & Mishra, R. B. (2008). A framework towards semantic web service composition based on multi-agent system. [IJITWE]. *International Journal of Information Technology and Web Engineering*, 3(4), 59–81. doi:10.4018/jitwe.2008100103.

Kuster, U., Konig-Ries, B., & Klusch, M. (2010). Evaluating semantic web service technologies: Criteria, approaches and challenges. In Lytras, M., & Sheth, A. (Eds.), *Progressive Concepts for Semantic Web Evolution: Applications and Developments* (pp. 1–24). Hershey, PA: Information Science Reference.

Küster, U., König-Ries, B., Petrie, C., & Klusch, M. (2008). On the evaluation of semantic web service frameworks. [IJSWIS]. *International Journal on Semantic Web and Information Systems*, 4(4), 31–55. doi:10.4018/jswis.2008100102.

Lange, C., & Kohlhase, M. (2008). SWiM: A semantic wiki for mathematical knowledge management. In Rech, J., Decker, B., & Ras, E. (Eds.), *Emerging Technologies for Semantic Work Environments: Techniques, Methods, and Applications* (pp. 47–68). Hershey, PA: Information Science Reference. doi:10.4018/978-1-59904-877-2.ch004.

Le, D. X., Rahayu, J. W., & Taniar, D. (2009). Web data warehousing convergence: From schematic to systematic. In Erickson, J. (Ed.), *Database Technologies: Concepts, Methodologies, Tools, and Applications* (pp. 678–701). Hershey, PA: Information Science Reference. doi:10.4018/978-1-60566-058-5.ch041.

Lee, J., Goodwin, R., & Akkiraju, R. (2006). Ontology management for large-scale enterprise systems. In Taniar, D., & Rahayu, J. (Eds.), *Web Semantics & Ontology* (pp. 91–114). Hershey, PA: Idea Group Publishing. doi:10.4018/978-1-59140-905-2.ch004.

Lee, S. (2007). Developing intelligent semantic web services. In Li, E., & Du, T. (Eds.), *Advances in Electronic Business* (Vol. 2, pp. 74–92). Hershey, PA: Idea Group Publishing.

Lee, S. (2008). Developing intelligent semantic web services. In Becker, A. (Ed.), *Electronic Commerce: Concepts, Methodologies, Tools, and Applications* (pp. 422–438). Hershey, PA: Information Science Reference. doi:10.4018/978-1-60566-056-1.

Léger, A., Heinecke, J., Nixon, L. J., Shvaiko, P., Charlet, J., Hobson, P., & Goasdoué, F. (2010). Semantic web take-off in a european industry perspective. In Tatnall, A. (Ed.), *Web Technologies: Concepts, Methodologies, Tools, and Applications* (pp. 880–908). Hershey, PA: Information Science Reference.

Li, C., & Ling, T. W. (2007). A basis for the semantic web and e-business: Efficient organization of ontology languages and ontologies. In Salam, A., & Stevens, J. (Eds.), *Semantic Web Technologies and E-Business: Toward the Integrated Virtual Organization and Business Process Automation* (pp. 212–235). Hershey, PA: Idea Group Publishing. doi:10.4018/978-1-59904-192-6.ch009.

Li, C., & Ling, T. W. (2009). A basis for the semantic web and e-business: efficient organization of ontology languages and ontologies. In Lytras, M., & Ordóñez de Pablos, P. (Eds.), *Social Web Evolution: Integrating Semantic Applications and Web 2.0 Technologies* (pp. 249–266). Hershey, PA: Information Science Reference. doi:10.4018/978-1-60566-272-5. ch018.

Li, J., & Cheung, W. K. (2012). Access control on semantic web data using query rewriting. In Sasaki, H., Chiu, D., Kapetanios, E., Hung, P., Andres, F., Leung, H., & Chbeir, R. (Eds.), *Intelligent and Knowledge-Based Computing for Business and Organizational Advancements* (pp. 135–156). Hershey, PA: Information Science Reference. doi:10.4018/978-1-4666-1577-9.ch008.

Liberati, D. (2009). A framework for semantic grid in e-science. In Udoh, E., & Wang, F. (Eds.), *Handbook of Research on Grid Technologies and Utility Computing: Concepts for Managing Large-Scale Applications* (pp. 235–240). Hershey, PA: Information Science Reference. doi:10.4018/978-1-60566-184-1. ch023.

Lisi, F. A. (2009). Using prior knowledge in data mining. In Wang, J. (Ed.), *Encyclopedia of Data Warehousing and Mining* (2nd ed., pp. 2019–2023). Hershey, PA: Information Science Reference.

Lisi, F. A. (2011). AL-QuIn: An Ontorelational learning system for semantic web mining. [IJSWIS]. *International Journal on Semantic Web and Information Systems, 7*(3), 1–22. doi:10.4018/jswis.2011070101.

López-Cuadrado, J. L., González-Carrasco, I., García-Crespo, Á., & Ruiz-Mezcua, B. (2012). Exploding web 3.0 and web 2.0 for sales processes definition. In Colomo-Palacios, R., Varajão, J., & Soto-Acosta, P. (Eds.), *Customer Relationship Management and the Social and Semantic Web: Enabling Cliens Conexus* (pp. 212–230). Hershey, PA: Business Science Reference.

Lu, L., & Yeh, C. (2009). Collaborative e-learning using semantic course blog. In Kock, N. (Ed.), *E-Collaboration: Concepts, Methodologies, Tools, and Applications* (pp. 463–472). Hershey, PA: Information Science Reference. doi:10.4018/978-1-60566-652-5. ch038.

Ludwig, L., & O'Sullivan, D. (2012). Deploying decision support systems using semantic web technologies. In Zaraté, P. (Ed.), *Integrated and Strategic Advancements in Decision Making Support Systems* (pp. 51–61). Hershey, PA: Information Science Reference. doi:10.4018/978-1-4666-1746-9.ch004.

Lukasiewicz, T., & Straccia, U. (2008). Tightly coupled fuzzy description logic programs under the answer set semantics for the semantic web. [IJSWIS]. *International Journal on Semantic Web and Information Systems, 4*(3), 68–89. doi:10.4018/jswis.2008070104.

Lukasiewicz, T., & Straccia, U. (2010). Tightly coupled fuzzy description logic programs under the answer set semantics for the semantic web. In Lytras, M., & Sheth, A. (Eds.), *Progressive Concepts for Semantic Web Evolution: Applications and Developments* (pp. 237–256). Hershey, PA: Information Science Reference.

Lytras, M., Ordóñez de Pablos, P., & Damiani, E. (2011). *Semantic web personalization and context awareness: Management of personal identities and social networking* (pp. 1-232). doi:10.4018/978-1-61520-921-7

Lytras, M. D., & Sheth, A. (2010). *Progressive concepts for semantic web evolution: Applications and developments* (pp. 1-410). doi:10.4018/978-1-60566-992-2

Ma, Z., Lv, Y., & Yan, L. (2008). A fuzzy ontology generation framework from fuzzy relational databases. [IJSWIS]. *International Journal on Semantic Web and Information Systems, 4*(3), 1–15. doi:10.4018/jswis.2008070101.

Ma, Z., & Wang, H. (2009). *The semantic web for knowledge and data management* (pp. 1-386). doi:10.4018/978-1-60566-028-8

Maceli, M., & Song, M. (2009). Deep web mining through web services. In Wang, J. (Ed.), *Encyclopedia of Data Warehousing and Mining* (2nd ed., pp. 631–637). Hershey, PA: Information Science Reference.

Management Association. I. (2010). Information resources management: Concepts, methodologies, tools and applications (4 Volumes) (pp. 1-2686). doi: doi:10.4018/978-1-61520-965-1.

Manouselis, N., Kastrantas, K., Sanchez-Alonso, S., Caceres, J., Ebner, H., & Palmer, M. (2009). Architecture of the organic edunet web portal. [IJWP]. *International Journal of Web Portals, 1*(1), 71–91. doi:10.4018/jwp.2009092105.

Marík, V., Vrba, P., & Obitko, M. (2009). The impacts of semantic technologies on industrial systems. In Cruz-Cunha, M., Oliveira, E., Tavares, A., & Ferreira, L. (Eds.), *Handbook of Research on Social Dimensions of Semantic Technologies and Web Services* (pp. 759–779). Hershey, PA: Information Science Reference. doi:10.4018/978-1-60566-650-1.ch037.

Markellos, K., & Markellou, P. (2009). E-learning and semantic technologies. In Rogers, P., Berg, G., Boettcher, J., Howard, C., Justice, L., & Schenk, K. (Eds.), *Encyclopedia of Distance Learning* (2nd ed., pp. 810–816). Hershey, PA: Information Science Reference. doi:10.4018/978-1-60566-198-8.ch115.

Markellos, K., Markellou, P., Panayiotaki, A., & Tsakalidis, A. (2007). Semantic web mining for personalized public services. In Al-Hakim, L. (Ed.), *Global E-Government: Theory, Applications and Benchmarking* (pp. 1–20). Hershey, PA: Idea Group Publishing.

Martínez-Cruz, C., Blanco, I. J., & Vila, M. A. (2009). Looking for information in fuzzy relational databases accessible via web. In Erickson, J. (Ed.), *Database Technologies: Concepts, Methodologies, Tools, and Applications* (pp. 2448–2471). Hershey, PA: Information Science Reference. doi:10.4018/978-1-60566-058-5.ch149.

Maué, P., & Schade, S. (2010). Data integration in the geospatial semantic web. In Kalfoglou, Y. (Ed.), *Cases on Semantic Interoperability for Information Systems Integration: Practices and Applications* (pp. 272–293). Hershey, PA: Information Science Reference.

Maukkanen, M., & Helin, H. (2008). Applying semantic web in competence management. In Tomei, L. (Ed.), *Online and Distance Learning: Concepts, Methodologies, Tools, and Applications* (pp. 1084–1104). Hershey, PA: Information Science Reference.

Mawlood-Yunis, A. (2009). Fault-tolerant emergent semantics in P2P networks. In J. Cardoso, & M. Lytras (Eds.), Semantic Web Engineering in the Knowledge Society (pp. 161-187). Hershey, PA: Information Science Reference. doi: doi:10.4018/978-1-60566-112-4.ch007.

McGuinness, D. L., Furtado, V., da Silva, P. P., Ding, L., Glass, A., & Chang, C. (2010). Explaining semantic web applications. In Tatnall, A. (Ed.), *Web Technologies: Concepts, Methodologies, Tools, and Applications* (pp. 2304–2327). Hershey, PA: Information Science Reference.

McGuinness, D. L., Furtado, V., Pinheiro da Silva, P., & Ding, L. (2009). Explaining semantic web applications. In Cardoso, J., & Lytras, M. (Eds.), *Semantic Web Engineering in the Knowledge Society* (pp. 1–24). Hershey, PA: Information Science Reference.

Mendes, D., & Rodrigues, I. P. (2013). A semantic web pragmatic approach to develop clinical ontologies, and thus semantic interoperability, based in HL7 v2.xml messaging. In Martinho, R., Rijo, R., Cruz-Cunha, M., & Varajão, J. (Eds.), *Information Systems and Technologies for Enhancing Health and Social Care* (pp. 205–214). Hershey, PA: Medical Information Science Reference. doi:10.4018/978-1-4666-3667-5.ch014.

Mey Eap, T., Hatala, M., Gaševic, D., Kaviani, N., & Spasojevic, R. (2009). Open security framework for unleashing semantic web services. In Khan, K. (Ed.), *Managing Web Service Quality: Measuring Outcomes and Effectiveness* (pp. 264–285). Hershey, PA: Information Science Reference.

Mikroyannidis, A., & Theodoulidis, B. (2010). Semantic web adaptation. In Tatnall, A. (Ed.), *Web Technologies: Concepts, Methodologies, Tools, and Applications* (pp. 78–88). Hershey, PA: Information Science Reference.

Miranda Lima, S., & Moreira, J. (2009). The semantic web in tourism. In Cruz-Cunha, M., Oliveira, E., Tavares, A., & Ferreira, L. (Eds.), *Handbook of Research on Social Dimensions of Semantic Technologies and Web Services* (pp. 675–703). Hershey, PA: Information Science Reference. doi:10.4018/978-1-60566-650-1.ch033.

Mohamed, M., Stankosky, M., & Ribière, V. (2012). Adopting the grid computing & semantic web hybrid for global knowledge sharing. In I. Management Association (Ed.), Grid and Cloud Computing: Concepts, Methodologies, Tools and Applications (pp. 1721-1736). Hershey, PA: Information Science Reference. doi: doi:10.4018/978-1-4666-0879-5.ch712.

Mohammadian, M., & Jentzsch, R. (2008). Computational intelligence techniques driven intelligent agents for web data mining and information retrieval. In Wang, J. (Ed.), *Data Warehousing and Mining: Concepts, Methodologies, Tools, and Applications* (pp. 1435–1445). Hershey, PA: Information Science Reference. doi:10.4018/978-1-59904-951-9.ch081.

Morandi, V., & Sgobbi, F. (2013). Semantic web applications to enhance the market opportunities of SMEs: The case of NeP4B. In I. Management Association (Ed.), Small and Medium Enterprises: Concepts, Methodologies, Tools, and Applications (pp. 340-352). Hershey, PA: Business Science Reference. doi: doi:10.4018/978-1-4666-3886-0.ch019.

Moreno-Sanchez, R. (2009). The geospatial semantic web: What are its implications for geospatial information users? In Cruz-Cunha, M., Oliveira, E., Tavares, A., & Ferreira, L. (Eds.), *Handbook of Research on Social Dimensions of Semantic Technologies and Web Services* (pp. 588–609). Hershey, PA: Information Science Reference. doi:10.4018/978-1-60566-650-1.ch030.

Moser, L. E., & Meliar-Smith, P. M. (2006). Web services. In Khosrow-Pour, M. (Ed.), *Encyclopedia of E-Commerce, E-Government, and Mobile Commerce* (pp. 1222–1229). Hershey, PA: Information Science Reference. doi:10.4018/978-1-59140-799-7.ch196.

Muthaiyah, S. (2007). Propagation and delegation of rights in access controls and risk assessment techniques. In Radhamani, G., & Rao, G. (Eds.), *Web Services Security and E-Business* (pp. 328–337). Hershey, PA: Idea Group Publishing. doi:10.4018/978-1-59904-168-1.ch018.

Naeve, A. (2007). The human semantic web: Shifting from knowledge push to knowledge pull. In Sheth, A., & Lytras, M. (Eds.), *Semantic Web-Based Information Systems: State-of-the-Art Applications* (pp. 22–59). Hershey, PA: CyberTech Publishing.

Navas-Delgado, I., & Aldana-Montes, J. F. (2009). Data integration: Introducing semantics. In Ferraggine, V., Doorn, J., & Rivero, L. (Eds.), *Handbook of Research on Innovations in Database Technologies and Applications: Current and Future Trends* (pp. 460–470). Hershey, PA: Information Science Reference. doi:10.4018/978-1-60566-242-8.ch050.

Neaga, E. I. (2007). Semantics enhancing knowledge discovery and ontology engineering using mining techniques: A crossover review. In Zhu, X., & Davidson, I. (Eds.), *Knowledge Discovery and Data Mining: Challenges and Realities* (pp. 163–188). Hershey, PA: Information Science Reference. doi:10.4018/978-1-59904-252-7.ch009.

Ngane, L. D., Goh, A., & Tru, C. H. (2009). A survey of web service discovery systems. In Alkhatib, G., & Rine, D. (Eds.), *Agent Technologies and Web Engineering: Applications and Systems* (pp. 266–281). Hershey, PA: Information Science Reference. doi:10.4018/978-1-60566-222-0.ch015.

O'Connor, M., Musen, M., & Das, A. (2009). Using the semantic web rule language in the development of ontology-driven applications. In Giurca, A., Gasevic, D., & Taveter, K. (Eds.), *Handbook of Research on Emerging Rule-Based Languages and Technologies: Open Solutions and Approaches* (pp. 525–539). Hershey, PA: Information Science Reference. doi:10.4018/978-1-60566-402-6.ch022.

O'Hara, K., Alani, H., Kalfoglou, Y., & Shadbolt, N. (2008). Features for killer apps from a semantic web perspective. In Li, E., & Yuan, S. (Eds.), *Agent Systems in Electronic Business* (pp. 265–288). Hershey, PA: Information Science Reference.

O'Nualláin, C., Westerski, A., & Kruk, S. (2007). Discursive context-aware knowledge and learning management systems. In Lytras, M., & Naeve, A. (Eds.), *Ubiquitous and Pervasive Knowledge and Learning Management: Semantics, Social Networking and New Media to Their Full Potential* (pp. 293–310). Hershey, PA: Idea Group Publishing. doi:10.4018/978-1-59904-483-5.ch011.

Olaniran, B. A. (2012). Challenges facing the semantic web and social software as communication technology agents in e-learning environments. In Thomas, M. (Ed.), *Design, Implementation, and Evaluation of Virtual Learning Environments* (pp. 265–278). Hershey, PA: Information Science Reference. doi:10.4018/978-1-4666-1770-4.ch018.

Olaniran, B. A., Burley, H. E., Chang, M., Kuo, R., & Agnello, M. (2011). Socio-technical challenges of semantic web: A culturally exclusive proposition? In I. Management Association (Ed.), Virtual Communities: Concepts, Methodologies, Tools and Applications (pp. 2332-2344). Hershey, PA: Information Science Reference. doi: doi:10.4018/978-1-60960-100-3.ch713.

Olvera-Lobo, M. (2009). Cross-language information retrieval on the web. In Cruz-Cunha, M., Oliveira, E., Tavares, A., & Ferreira, L. (Eds.), *Handbook of Research on Social Dimensions of Semantic Technologies and Web Services* (pp. 704–719). Hershey, PA: Information Science Reference. doi:10.4018/978-1-60566-650-1.ch034.

Ordóñez de Pablos, P., Nigro, H. O., Tennyson, R., & Gonzalez Cisaro, S. E. (2013). *Advancing information management through semantic web concepts and ontologies* (pp. 1-433). doi:10.4018/978-1-4666-2494-8

Osman, T., Thakker, D., & Al-Dabass, D. (2010). Utilisation of case-based reasoning for semantic web services composition. In Tatnall, A. (Ed.), *Web Technologies: Concepts, Methodologies, Tools, and Applications* (pp. 604–622). Hershey, PA: Information Science Reference.

Osman, T., Thakker, D., & Schaefer, G. (2009). Semantic annotation and retrieval of images in digital libraries. In Theng, Y., Foo, S., Goh, D., & Na, J. (Eds.), *Handbook of Research on Digital Libraries: Design, Development, and Impact* (pp. 261–268). Hershey, PA: Information Science Reference. doi:10.4018/978-1-59904-879-6.ch026.

Owen, K., & Willis, R. (2010). Critical success factors in the development of folksonomy-based knowledge management tools. In Dumova, T., & Fiordo, R. (Eds.), *Handbook of Research on Social Interaction Technologies and Collaboration Software: Concepts and Trends* (pp. 509–518). Hershey, PA: Information Science Reference. doi:10.4018/978-1-61520-965-1.ch203.

Padiya, T., Bhise, M., & Chaudhary, S. (2013). Semantic web data partitioning. In Ordóñez de Pablos, P., Nigro, H., Tennyson, R., & Gonzalez Cisaro, S. (Eds.), *Advancing Information Management through Semantic Web Concepts and Ontologies* (pp. 154–165). Hershey, PA: Information Science Reference.

Paiano, R., & Guido, A. L. (2009). A design tool for business process design and representation. In Lee, I. (Ed.), *Electronic Business: Concepts, Methodologies, Tools, and Applications* (pp. 451–468). Hershey, PA: Information Science Reference.

Paptaxiarhis, V., Tsetsos, V., Karali, I., & Stamotopoulos, P. (2009). Developing rule-based web applications: Methodologies and tools. In Giurca, A., Gasevic, D., & Taveter, K. (Eds.), *Handbook of Research on Emerging Rule-Based Languages and Technologies: Open Solutions and Approaches* (pp. 371–392). Hershey, PA: Information Science Reference. doi:10.4018/978-1-60566-402-6.ch016.

Paquette, G. (2010). *Visual knowledge modeling for semantic web technologies: Models and ontologies* (pp. 1-494). doi:10.4018/978-1-61520-839-5

Paquette, G. (2010). Visual ontology modeling and the semantic web. In Paquette, G. (Ed.), *Visual Knowledge Modeling for Semantic Web Technologies: Models and Ontologies* (pp. 198–223). Hershey, PA: Information Science Reference. doi:10.4018/978-1-61520-839-5.ch010.

Paquette, G., & Marino, O. (2012). A multi-actor ontology-based assistance model: A contribution to the adaptive semantic web. In S. Graf, F. Lin, Kinshuk, & R. McGreal (Eds.), Intelligent and Adaptive Learning Systems: Technology Enhanced Support for Learners and Teachers (pp. 213-228). Hershey, PA: Information Science Reference. doi: doi:10.4018/978-1-60960-842-2.ch014.

Park, H., Rho, S., & Park, J. (2013). A link-based ranking algorithm for semantic web resources: A class-oriented approach independent of link direction. In Siau, K. (Ed.), *Innovations in Database Design, Web Applications, and Information Systems Management* (pp. 1–25). Hershey, PA: Information Science Reference.

Parry, D. (2010). Healthcare information systems and the semantic web. In Rodrigues, J. (Ed.), *Health Information Systems: Concepts, Methodologies, Tools, and Applications* (pp. 178–184). Hershey, PA: Medical Information Science Reference.

Paschke, A., & Boley, H. (2010). Rule markup languages and semantic web rule languages. In Tatnall, A. (Ed.), *Web Technologies: Concepts, Methodologies, Tools, and Applications* (pp. 623–647). Hershey, PA: Information Science Reference.

Passant, A., Kinsella, S., Bojars, U., Breslin, J. G., & Decker, S. (2011). Understanding online communities by using semantic web technologies. In Daniel, B. (Ed.), *Handbook of Research on Methods and Techniques for Studying Virtual Communities: Paradigms and Phenomena* (pp. 429–456). Hershey, PA: Information Science Reference.

Peng, Z., Zhao, T., & Zhang, C. (2011). Geospatial semantic web services: A case for transit trip planning systems. In Zhao, P., & Di, L. (Eds.), *Geospatial Web Services: Advances in Information Interoperability* (pp. 169–188). Hershey, PA: Information Science Reference.

Pennington, C. (2007). Introduction to web services. In Cardoso, J. (Ed.), *Semantic Web Services: Theory, Tools and Applications* (pp. 134–154). Hershey, PA: Information Science Reference. doi:10.4018/978-1-59904-045-5.ch007.

Peraboni, C., & Ripamonti, L. A. (2008). Socio-semantic web for sharing knowledge. In Putnik, G., & Cruz-Cunha, M. (Eds.), *Encyclopedia of Networked and Virtual Organizations* (pp. 1482–1488). Hershey, PA: Information Science Reference. doi:10.4018/978-1-59904-885-7.ch196.

Perdrix, F., Gimeno, J. M., Gil, R., Oliva, M., & García, R. (2010). Semantic web for media convergence: A newspaper case. In Tatnall, A. (Ed.), *Web Technologies: Concepts, Methodologies, Tools, and Applications* (pp. 1003–1026). Hershey, PA: Information Science Reference.

Pereira, R. G., & Freire, M. M. (2009). Classification of semantic web technologies. In Khosrow-Pour, M. (Ed.), *Encyclopedia of Information Science and Technology* (2nd ed., pp. 545–555). Hershey, PA: Information Science Reference.

Perry, M., Sheth, A., Arpinar, I. B., & Hakimpour, F. (2009). Geospatial and temporal semantic analytics. In Karimi, H. (Ed.), *Handbook of Research on Geoinformatics* (pp. 161–170). Hershey, PA: Information Science Reference. doi:10.4018/978-1-59140-995-3.ch021.

Peter, H. (2009). Aligning the warehouse and the web. In Wang, J. (Ed.), *Encyclopedia of Data Warehousing and Mining* (2nd ed., pp. 18–24). Hershey, PA: Information Science Reference.

Peter, H., & Greenidge, C. (2013). An ontology-based extraction framework for a semantic web application. In Wang, J. (Ed.), *Intelligence Methods and Systems Advancements for Knowledge-Based Business* (pp. 231–246). Hershey, PA: Information Science Reference.

Petrucco, C. (2010). The EduOntoWiki project for supporting social, educational, and knowledge construction processes with semantic web paradigm. In Dasgupta, S. (Ed.), *Social Computing: Concepts, Methodologies, Tools, and Applications* (pp. 841–854). Hershey, PA: Information Science Reference.

Piero, G. (2009). Using semantic web tools for ontologies construction. In Ferraggine, V., Doorn, J., & Rivero, L. (Eds.), *Handbook of Research on Innovations in Database Technologies and Applications: Current and Future Trends* (pp. 418–433). Hershey, PA: Information Science Reference. doi:10.4018/978-1-60566-242-8.ch046.

Poggi, A., & Turci, P. (2009). Multi-agent systems for semantic web services composition. In Cruz-Cunha, M., Oliveira, E., Tavares, A., & Ferreira, L. (Eds.), *Handbook of Research on Social Dimensions of Semantic Technologies and Web Services* (pp. 324–339). Hershey, PA: Information Science Reference. doi:10.4018/978-1-60566-650-1.ch016.

Poletti, G. (2006). Semantic web and digital libraries. In Cartelli, A. (Ed.), *Teaching in the Knowledge Society: New Skills and Instruments for Teachers* (pp. 271–285). Hershey, PA: Information Science Publishing. doi:10.4018/978-1-59140-953-3.ch018.

Politis, D. (2009). Data mining of personal information: A taste of the intrusion legacy with a sprinkling of semantic web. In Politis, D., Kozyris, P., & Iglezakis, I. (Eds.), *Socioeconomic and Legal Implications of Electronic Intrusion* (pp. 230–245). Hershey, PA: Information Science Reference. doi:10.4018/978-1-60566-204-6.ch014.

Pollet, Y. (2010). An algebra of ontology properties for service discovery and composition in semantic web. In Gargouri, F., & Jaziri, W. (Eds.), *Ontology Theory, Management and Design: Advanced Tools and Models* (pp. 98–118). Hershey, PA: Information Science Reference. doi:10.4018/978-1-61520-859-3.ch004.

Pomonis, T., Koutsomitropoulos, D. A., Christodoulou, S. P., & Papatheodorou, T. (2011). Combining semantic web and web 2.0 technologies to support cultural applications for web 3.0. In Styliaras, G., Koukopoulos, D., & Lazarinis, F. (Eds.), *Handbook of Research on Technologies and Cultural Heritage: Applications and Environments* (pp. 16–28). Hershey, PA: Information Science Reference.

Predoiu, L. (2009). Probabilistic models for the semantic web: A survey. In Ma, Z., & Wang, H. (Eds.), *The Semantic Web for Knowledge and Data Management* (pp. 74–105). Hershey, PA: Information Science Reference. doi:10.4018/978-1-60566-982-3.ch102.

Predoiu, L., & Stuckenschmidt, H. (2010). Probabilistic models for the semantic web: A survey. In Tatnall, A. (Ed.), *Web Technologies: Concepts, Methodologies, Tools, and Applications* (pp. 1896–1928). Hershey, PA: Information Science Reference.

Predoiu, L., & Zhdanova, A. V. (2008). Semantic web languages and ontologies. In Freire, M., & Pereira, M. (Eds.), *Encyclopedia of Internet Technologies and Applications* (pp. 512–518). Hershey, PA: Information Science Reference.

Qin, L., & Atluri, V. (2006). SemDiff: An approach to detecting semantic changes to ontologies. [IJSWIS]. *International Journal on Semantic Web and Information Systems*, 2(4), 1–32. doi:10.4018/jswis.2006100101.

Rabaey, M., Tromp, H., Vandenborre, K., Vandijck, E., & Timmerman, M. (2007). Semantic web services and BPEL: Semantic service-oriented architecture economical and philosophical issues. In Salam, A., & Stevens, J. (Eds.), *Semantic Web Technologies and E-Business: Toward the Integrated Virtual Organization and Business Process Automation* (pp. 127–153). Hershey, PA: Idea Group Publishing. doi:10.4018/978-1-59904-192-6.ch005.

Raisinghani, M. S., & Sahoo, T. R. (2006). Emergent semantic web. In Khosrow-Pour, M. (Ed.), *Encyclopedia of E-Commerce, E-Government, and Mobile Commerce* (pp. 418–423). Hershey, PA: Information Science Reference. doi:10.4018/978-1-59140-799-7.ch069.

Reeve, L., & Han, H. (2006). A comparison of semantic annotation systems for text-based web documents. In Taniar, D., & Rahayu, J. (Eds.), *Web Semantics & Ontology* (pp. 165–188). Hershey, PA: Idea Group Publishing. doi:10.4018/978-1-59140-905-2.ch006.

Reffay, C., Dyke, G., & Betbeder, M. (2012). Data sharing in CSCR: Towards in-depth long term collaboration. In Juan, A., Daradoumis, T., Roca, M., Grasman, S., & Faulin, J. (Eds.), *Collaborative and Distributed E-Research: Innovations in Technologies, Strategies and Applications* (pp. 111–134). Hershey, PA: Information Science Reference. doi:10.4018/978-1-4666-0125-3.ch006.

Reformat, M., Yager, R., & Li, Z. (2010). Ontology driven document identification in semantic web. In Lytras, M., & Sheth, A. (Eds.), *Progressive Concepts for Semantic Web Evolution: Applications and Developments* (pp. 186–220). Hershey, PA: Information Science Reference.

Rege, M., Dong, M., & Fotouhi, F. (2007). Enhancing e-business on the semantic web through automatic multimedia representation. In Salam, A., & Stevens, J. (Eds.), *Semantic Web Technologies and E-Business: Toward the Integrated Virtual Organization and Business Process Automation* (pp. 154–168). Hershey, PA: Idea Group Publishing. doi:10.4018/978-1-59904-192-6.ch006.

Rege, M., Dong, M., & Fotouhi, F. (2009). Enhancing e-business on the semantic web through automatic multimedia representation. In Zilli, A., Damiani, E., Ceravolo, P., Corallo, A., & Elia, G. (Eds.), *Semantic Knowledge Management: An Ontology-Based Framework* (pp. 329–340). Hershey, PA: Information Science Reference.

Remli, M. A., & Deris, S. (2013). An approach for biological data integration and knowledge retrieval based on ontology, semantic web services composition, and AI planning. In Nazir Ahmad, M., Colomb, R., & Abdullah, M. (Eds.), *Ontology-Based Applications for Enterprise Systems and Knowledge Management* (pp. 324–342). Hershey, PA: Information Science Reference.

Rezgui, A., Rouguettaya, A., & Malik, Z. (2008). Enforcing privacy on the semantic web. In Nemati, H. (Ed.), *Information Security and Ethics: Concepts, Methodologies, Tools, and Applications* (pp. 3713–3727). Hershey, PA: Information Science Reference.

Roa-Valverde, A. J., Navas-Delgado, I., & Aldana-Montes, J. F. (2009). Semantic web services: Towards an appropriate solution to application integration. In Cruz-Cunha, M., Oliveira, E., Tavares, A., & Ferreira, L. (Eds.), *Handbook of Research on Social Dimensions of Semantic Technologies and Web Services* (pp. 259–280). Hershey, PA: Information Science Reference. doi:10.4018/978-1-60566-650-1.ch013.

Rodríguez-González, A., García-Crespo, Á., Colomo-Palacios, R., Labra-Gayo, J. E., & Berbís, J. M. (2011). Locating doctors using social and semantic web technologies: The MedFinder approach. In Lytras, M., Ordóñez de Pablos, P., & Damiani, E. (Eds.), *Semantic Web Personalization and Context Awareness: Management of Personal Identities and Social Networking* (pp. 94–106). Hershey, PA: Information Science Reference. doi:10.4018/978-1-61520-921-7.ch009.

Rodriguez-Herola, V. (2009). Industrial use of semantics: NNEC semantic interoperability. In Cardoso, J., & Lytras, M. (Eds.), *Semantic Web Engineering in the Knowledge Society* (pp. 25–51). Hershey, PA: Information Science Reference.

Roman, D., Toma, I., & Fensel, D. (2008). Semantic web services: A technology for service-oriented computing. In Freire, M., & Pereira, M. (Eds.), *Encyclopedia of Internet Technologies and Applications* (pp. 519–524). Hershey, PA: Information Science Reference.

Sánchez, D. M., Acuña, C. J., Cavero, J. M., & Marcos, E. (2012). Toward UML-compliant semantic web services development. In Tavana, M. (Ed.), *Enterprise Information Systems and Advancing Business Solutions: Emerging Models* (pp. 313–325). Hershey, PA: Business Science Reference. doi:10.4018/978-1-4666-1761-2.ch018.

Santos, N., Campos, F. C., & Braga Villela, R. M. (2009). Digital libraries and ontology. In Theng, Y., Foo, S., Goh, D., & Na, J. (Eds.), *Handbook of Research on Digital Libraries: Design, Development, and Impact* (pp. 206–215). Hershey, PA: Information Science Reference. doi:10.4018/978-1-59904-879-6.ch020.

Sarker, B. K., Descottes, J., Sohail, M., & Kosaraju, R. K. (2012). Smart rooms: A framework for inferencing using semantic web technology in ambient intelligent network. In Prakash Vidyarthi, D. (Ed.), *Technologies and Protocols for the Future of Internet Design: Reinventing the Web* (pp. 289–303). Hershey, PA: Information Science Reference. doi:10.4018/978-1-4666-0203-8.ch016.

Schaffert, S. (2008). Semantic social software: Semantically enabled social software or socially enabled semantic web? In Rech, J., Decker, B., & Ras, E. (Eds.), *Emerging Technologies for Semantic Work Environments: Techniques, Methods, and Applications* (pp. 33–46). Hershey, PA: Information Science Reference. doi:10.4018/978-1-59904-877-2.ch003.

Scheir, P., Lindstaedt, S. N., & Ghidini, C. (2008). A network model approach to retrieval in the semantic web. [IJSWIS]. *International Journal on Semantic Web and Information Systems*, 4(4), 56–84. doi:10.4018/jswis.2008100103.

Scheir, P., Prettenhofer, P., Lindstaedt, S. N., & Ghidini, C. (2010). An associative and adaptive network model for information retrieval in the semantic web. In Lytras, M., & Sheth, A. (Eds.), *Progressive Concepts for Semantic Web Evolution: Applications and Developments* (pp. 309–344). Hershey, PA: Information Science Reference.

Sfakianakis, S. (2010). Social semantic web and semantic web services. In Dasgupta, S. (Ed.), *Social Computing: Concepts, Methodologies, Tools, and Applications* (pp. 350–368). Hershey, PA: Information Science Reference.

Shabo, A. S., & Hughes, K. S. (2007). Family history information exchange services using HL7 clinical genomics standard specifications. In Sheth, A., & Lytras, M. (Eds.), *Semantic Web-Based Information Systems: State-of-the-Art Applications* (pp. 254–278). Hershey, PA: CyberTech Publishing.

Sheth, A. (2005). [IJSWIS]. *International Journal on Semantic Web and Information Systems*. doi: doi:10.4018/IJSWIS.

Sheth, A. (2013). *Semantic web: Ontology and knowledge base enabled tools, services, and applications* (pp. 1-360). doi:10.4018/978-1-4666-3610-1

Sheth, A., Ramakrishnan, C., & Thomas, C. (2007). Semantics for the semantic web: The implicit, the formal, and the powerful. In Sheth, A., & Lytras, M. (Eds.), *Semantic Web-Based Information Systems: State-of-the-Art Applications* (pp. 1–21). Hershey, PA: CyberTech Publishing. doi:10.4018/978-1-59904-935-9.ch068.

Sheth, A., Ramakrishnan, C., & Thomas, C. (2008). Semantics for the semantic web: The implicit, the formal and the powerful. In Tomei, L. (Ed.), *Online and Distance Learning: Concepts, Methodologies, Tools, and Applications* (pp. 776–788). Hershey, PA: Information Science Reference.

Silva Souza, V. E., de Almeida Falbo, R., & Guizzardi, G. (2009). Designing web information systems for a framework-based construction. In Halpin, T., Krogstie, J., & Proper, E. (Eds.), *Innovations in Information Systems Modeling: Methods and Best Practices* (pp. 204–238). Hershey, PA: Information Science Reference. doi:10.4018/978-1-60566-278-7.ch011.

Singh, R., Iyer, L., & Salam, A. (2009). Semantic e-business. In Lee, I. (Ed.), *Electronic Business: Concepts, Methodologies, Tools, and Applications* (pp. 44–58). Hershey, PA: Information Science Reference.

Siqueira, S. W., Braz, M. H., & Melo, R. N. (2008). Accessibility, digital libraries and semantic web standards in an e-learning architecture. In Pahl, C. (Ed.), *Architecture Solutions for E-Learning Systems* (pp. 137–153). Hershey, PA: Information Science Reference.

Smart, P. D., Abdelmoty, A., & El-Geresy, B. A. (2009). Semantic web rule languages for geospatial ontologies. In Giurca, A., Gasevic, D., & Taveter, K. (Eds.), *Handbook of Research on Emerging Rule-Based Languages and Technologies: Open Solutions and Approaches* (pp. 149–169). Hershey, PA: Information Science Reference. doi:10.4018/978-1-60566-402-6.ch007.

Smart, P. D., Abdelmoty, A. I., El-Geresy, B. A., & Jones, C. B. (2010). Semantic web rule languages for geospatial ontologies. In Tatnall, A. (Ed.), *Web Technologies: Concepts, Methodologies, Tools, and Applications* (pp. 648–669). Hershey, PA: Information Science Reference.

Srinivasa, K. G., Venugopal, K. R., & Patnaik, L. M. (2009). Soft computing for XML data mining. In Wang, J. (Ed.), *Encyclopedia of Data Warehousing and Mining* (2nd ed., pp. 1806–1809). Hershey, PA: Information Science Reference.

Tang, J., Zhang, D., Yao, L., & Li, Y. (2009). Automatic semantic annotation using machine learning. In Ma, Z., & Wang, H. (Eds.), *The Semantic Web for Knowledge and Data Management* (pp. 106–150). Hershey, PA: Information Science Reference.

Tara, M. (2010). Semantic web architecture to provide e-health content and services. In Mohammed, S., & Fiaidhi, J. (Eds.), *Ubiquitous Health and Medical Informatics: The Ubiquity 2.0 Trend and Beyond* (pp. 233–257). Hershey, PA: Medical Information Science Reference. doi:10.4018/978-1-61520-777-0.ch012.

Taylor, S. J. E., Bell, D., Mustafee, N., de Cesare, S., Lycett, M., & Fishwick, P. (2010). Semantic web services for simulation component reuse and interoperability: An ontology approach. In Gunasekaran, A., & Shea, T. (Eds.), *Organizational Advancements through Enterprise Information Systems: Emerging Applications and Developments* (pp. 336–352). Hershey, PA: Business Science Reference.

Tektonidis, D., & Bokma, A. (2011). The utilization of semantic web for integrating enterprise systems. In I. Management Association (Ed.), Enterprise Information Systems: Concepts, Methodologies, Tools and Applications (pp. 550–564). Hershey, PA: Business Science Reference. doi: doi:10.4018/978-1-61692-852-0.ch215.

Terziyan, V. (2009). Semantic web services for smart devices based on mobile agents. In Taniar, D. (Ed.), *Mobile Computing: Concepts, Methodologies, Tools, and Applications* (pp. 630–641). Hershey, PA: Information Science Reference.

Thakker, D., Osman, T., & Al-Dabass, D. (2011). Semantic web services composition with case based reasoning. In Sugumaran, V. (Ed.), *Intelligent, Adaptive and Reasoning Technologies: New Developments and Applications* (pp. 36–63). Hershey, PA: Information Science Reference. doi:10.4018/978-1-60960-595-7.ch003.

Tho, Q. T., Cheung, H. S., & Fong, A. C. (2008). Semantic web support for customer services. In Becker, A. (Ed.), *Electronic Commerce: Concepts, Methodologies, Tools, and Applications* (pp. 571–590). Hershey, PA: Information Science Reference.

Thuraisingham, B., & Khan, L. (2008). Secure semantic grids. In Nemati, H. (Ed.), *Information Security and Ethics: Concepts, Methodologies, Tools, and Applications* (pp. 1145–1157). Hershey, PA: Information Science Reference.

Thuraisingham, B., Tsybulnik, N., & Alam, A. (2009). Administering the semantic web: Confidentiality, privacy and trust management. In Nemati, H. (Ed.), *Techniques and Applications for Advanced Information Privacy and Security: Emerging Organizational, Ethical, and Human Issues* (pp. 262–277). Hershey, PA: Information Science Reference. doi:10.4018/978-1-60566-210-7.ch017.

Toma, I., De Paoli, F., & Fensel, D. (2012). On modelling non-functional properties of semantic web services. In Reiff-Marganiec, S., & Tilly, M. (Eds.), *Handbook of Research on Service-Oriented Systems and Non-Functional Properties: Future Directions* (pp. 61–85). Hershey, PA: Information Science Reference.

Tsetsos, V. (2007). Semantic web service discovery: Methods, algorithms, and tools. In Cardoso, J. (Ed.), *Semantic Web Services: Theory, Tools and Applications* (pp. 240–280). Hershey, PA: Information Science Reference. doi:10.4018/978-1-59904-045-5.ch011.

Tsetsos, V. (2009). Personalization based on semantic web technologies. In Cardoso, J., & Lytras, M. (Eds.), *Semantic Web Engineering in the Knowledge Society* (pp. 52–75). Hershey, PA: Information Science Reference.

Udoh, E. (2009). Database integration in the grid infrastructure. In Khosrow-Pour, M. (Ed.), *Encyclopedia of Information Science and Technology* (2nd ed., pp. 955–960). Hershey, PA: Information Science Reference.

Ungrangsi, R., Anutariya, C., & Wuwongse, V. (2012). Enhancing folksonomy-based content retrieval with semantic web technology. In Sheth, A. (Ed.), *Semantic-Enabled Advancements on the Web: Applications Across Industries* (pp. 173–193). Hershey, PA: Information Science Reference. doi:10.4018/978-1-4666-0185-7.ch008.

Vargas-Vera, M., Nagy, M., Zyskowski, D., Haniewicz, K., & Abramowicz, W. (2011). Challenges on semantic web services. In I. Management Association (Ed.), *Virtual Communities: Concepts, Methodologies, Tools and Applications* (pp. 2134-2157). Hershey, PA: Information Science Reference. doi: doi:10.4018/978-1-60960-100-3.ch702.

Vat, K. H. (2011). The generative potential of appreciative inquiry as an essential social dimension of the semantic web. In I. Management Association (Ed.), *Virtual Communities: Concepts, Methodologies, Tools and Applications* (pp. 605-628). Hershey, PA: Information Science Reference. doi: doi:10.4018/978-1-60960-100-3.ch215.

Viamonte, M. J., & Silva, N. (2009). A semantic web-based information integration approach for an agent-based electronic market. In Tiako, P. (Ed.), *Software Applications: Concepts, Methodologies, Tools, and Applications* (pp. 1458–1477). Hershey, PA: Information Science Reference. doi:10.4018/978-1-60566-060-8.ch086.

Viroli, M., Zambonelli, F., Stevenson, G., & Dobson, S. (2013). From SOA to pervasive service ecosystems: An approach based on semantic web technologies. In Ortiz, G., & Cubo, J. (Eds.), *Adaptive Web Services for Modular and Reusable Software Development: Tactics and Solutions* (pp. 207–237). Hershey, PA: Information Science Reference.

Vrakas, D., & Hatzi, O. (2008). A visual programming tool for designing planning problems for semantic web service composition. In Ferri, F. (Ed.), *Visual Languages for Interactive Computing: Definitions and Formalizations* (pp. 302–326). Hershey, PA: Information Science Reference.

Wagner, C. Cheung, K. S. K., Ip, R. K. F., & Bottcher, S. (2011). Building semantic webs for e-government with wiki technology. In A. Al Ajeeli & Y. Al-Bastaki (Eds.), Handbook of Research on E-Services in the Public Sector: E-Government Strategies and Advancements (pp. 389-405). Hershey, PA: Information Science Reference. doi: doi:10.4018/978-1-61520-789-3.ch029.

Wahl, T., & Sindre, G. (2011). A survey of development methods for semantic web service systems. In Wang, J. (Ed.), *Information Systems and New Applications in the Service Sector: Models and Methods* (pp. 117–132). Hershey, PA: Business Science Reference.

Wang, H. (2009). A review of fuzzy models for the semantic web. In Ma, Z., & Wang, H. (Eds.), *The Semantic Web for Knowledge and Data Management* (pp. 23–37). Hershey, PA: Information Science Reference. doi:10.4018/978-1-60566-982-3.ch005.

Wang, H., Ma, Z., Yan, L., & Cheng, J. (2010). A review of fuzzy models for the semantic web. In Tatnall, A. (Ed.), *Web Technologies: Concepts, Methodologies, Tools, and Applications* (pp. 63–77). Hershey, PA: Information Science Reference.

Wang, H. H., Gibbins, N., Dong, J. S., Li, Y. F., Sun, J., Pan, J., & Payne, T. R. (2008). An integrated formal approach to semantic work environments design. In Rech, J., Decker, B., & Ras, E. (Eds.), *Emerging Technologies for Semantic Work Environments: Techniques, Methods, and Applications* (pp. 262–280). Hershey, PA: Information Science Reference. doi:10.4018/978-1-59904-877-2.ch015.

Wang, S., & Wang, H. (2007). Semantic web portals. In Tatnall, A. (Ed.), *Encyclopedia of Portal Technologies and Applications* (pp. 901–904). Hershey, PA: Information Science Reference. doi:10.4018/978-1-59140-989-2.ch148.

Wecel, K., Abramowicz, W., & Kalczynski, P. J. (2008). Enhanced knowledge warehouse. In Jennex, M. (Ed.), *Knowledge Management: Concepts, Methodologies, Tools, and Applications* (pp. 1029–1034). Hershey, PA: Information Science Reference.

Widén-Wulff, G., & Tötterman, A. (2010). A social capital perspective on collaboration and web 2.0. In Dumova, T., & Fiordo, R. (Eds.), *Handbook of Research on Social Interaction Technologies and Collaboration Software: Concepts and Trends* (pp. 101–109). Hershey, PA: Information Science Reference. doi:10.4018/978-1-60960-100-3.ch607.

Wimmer, H., Yoon, V., & Rada, R. (2012). Applying semantic web technologies to ontology alignment. [IJIIT]. *International Journal of Intelligent Information Technologies, 8*(1), 1–9. doi:10.4018/jiit.2012010101.

Wood, J., Tung, H., Marshall-Bradley, T., Sofge, D. A., Grayson, J. M., Bergman, M., & Lawless, W. F. (2010). Applying an organizational uncertainty principle: Semantic web-based metrics. In Tatnall, A. (Ed.), *Web Technologies: Concepts, Methodologies, Tools, and Applications* (pp. 1814–1833). Hershey, PA: Information Science Reference.

Woods, S., Poteet, S. R., Kao, A., & Quach, L. (2006). Dissemination in portals. In Schwartz, D. (Ed.), *Encyclopedia of Knowledge Management* (pp. 115–121). Hershey, PA: Information Science Reference. doi:10.4018/978-1-59140-573-3.ch015.

Wouters, C., Rajagopalapillai, R., Dillon, T. S., & Rahayu, W. (2006). Ontology extraction using views for semantic web. In Taniar, D., & Rahayu, J. (Eds.), *Web Semantics & Ontology* (pp. 1–40). Hershey, PA: Idea Group Publishing. doi:10.4018/978-1-59140-905-2.ch001.

Wrembel, R. (2009). A survey of managing the evolution of data warehouses. [IJDWM]. *International Journal of Data Warehousing and Mining, 5*(2), 24–56. doi:10.4018/jdwm.2009040102.

Yang, S. Q., & Xu, A. (2012). Applying semantic web technologies to meet the relevant challenge of customer relationship management for the U.S. academic libraries in the 21st century using 121 e-agent framework. In Colomo-Palacios, R., Varajão, J., & Soto-Acosta, P. (Eds.), *Customer Relationship Management and the Social and Semantic Web: Enabling Cliens Conexus* (pp. 284–311). Hershey, PA: Business Science Reference.

Yau, S. S. (2006). Trustworthy data sharing in collaborative pervasive computing environments. In Ferrari, E., & Thuraisingham, B. (Eds.), *Web and Information Security* (pp. 265–281). Hershey, PA: IRM Press. doi:10.4018/978-1-59140-588-7.ch013.

Yearwood, J., & Stranieri, A. (2012). Ontologies and the Semantic Web. In Approaches for Community Decision Making and Collective Reasoning: Knowledge Technology Support (pp. 179-195). Hershey, PA: Information Science Reference. doi: doi:10.4018/978-1-4666-1818-3.ch007.

Yessad, A., Faron-Zucker, C., Sander, P., & Laskri, M. T. (2010). OrPAF: An environment for adaptive hypermedia courses in the semantic web context. In Karacapilidis, N. (Ed.), *Novel Developments in Web-Based Learning Technologies: Tools for Modern Teaching* (pp. 159–173). Hershey, PA: Information Science Reference. doi:10.4018/978-1-60566-938-0.ch009.

Youn, S., & McLeod, D. (2006). Ontology development tools for ontology-based knowledge management. In Khosrow-Pour, M. (Ed.), *Encyclopedia of E-Commerce, E-Government, and Mobile Commerce* (pp. 858–864). Hershey, PA: Information Science Reference. doi:10.4018/978-1-59140-799-7.ch138.

Yue, P., Di, L., Yang, W., Yu, G., & Zhao, P. (2009). Towards automatic composition of geospatial web services. In Karimi, H. (Ed.), *Handbook of Research on Geoinformatics* (pp. 205–212). Hershey, PA: Information Science Reference. doi:10.4018/978-1-59140-995-3.ch026.

Yue, P., He, L., & Di, L. (2011). Semantic web enabled intelligent geoprocessing service chaining. In Zhao, P., & Di, L. (Eds.), *Geospatial Web Services: Advances in Information Interoperability* (pp. 310–331). Hershey, PA: Information Science Reference.

Zander, S., & Schandl, B. (2012). Semantic web-enhanced context-aware computing in mobile systems: Principles and application. In Kumar, A., & Rahman, H. (Eds.), *Mobile Computing Techniques in Emerging Markets: Systems, Applications and Services* (pp. 47–96). Hershey, PA: Information Science Reference. doi:10.4018/978-1-4666-0080-5.ch003.

Zarri, G. P. (2006). RDF and OWL. In Schwartz, D. (Ed.), *Encyclopedia of Knowledge Management* (pp. 769–779). Hershey, PA: Information Science Reference. doi:10.4018/978-1-59140-573-3.ch101.

Zhao, P., Di, L., Yang, W., Yu, G., & Yue, P. (2009). Geospatial semantic web: Critical issues. In Karimi, H. (Ed.), *Handbook of Research on Geoinformatics* (pp. 178–187). Hershey, PA: Information Science Reference. doi:10.4018/978-1-59140-995-3.ch023.

Zhao, Y., & Halang, W. A. (2009). Mapping ontologies by utilising their semantic structure. In Rabuñal Dopico, J., Dorado, J., & Pazos, A. (Eds.), *Encyclopedia of Artificial Intelligence* (pp. 1049–1055). Hershey, PA: Information Science Reference.

Zhao, Y., Wang, X., & Halang, W. A. (2009). Security in semantic interoperation. In Cruz-Cunha, M., Oliveira, E., Tavares, A., & Ferreira, L. (Eds.), *Handbook of Research on Social Dimensions of Semantic Technologies and Web Services* (pp. 489–504). Hershey, PA: Information Science Reference. doi:10.4018/978-1-60566-650-1.ch025.

Zhdanova, A. V., Li, N., & Moessner, K. (2010). Semantic web in ubiquitous mobile communications. In Tatnall, A. (Ed.), *Web Technologies: Concepts, Methodologies, Tools, and Applications* (pp. 41–62). Hershey, PA: Information Science Reference.

About the Contributors

Patricia Ordóñez de Pablos is a professor in the Department of Business Administration in the Faculty of Economics and Business of the University of Oviedo, Spain. Her teaching and research interests focus on the areas of strategic management, knowledge management, intellectual capital measuring and reporting, organizational learning, human resources management and IT. She serves as Executive Editor of the International Journal of Learning and Intellectual Capital and the International Journal of Strategic Change Management. She also serves as Associate Editor of Behaviour and Information Technology.

Miltiadis D. Lytras is lecturer at the American College of Greece. His research focuses on Semantic Web, knowledge management and e-learning, with many publications in these areas. He has co-edited 25 special issues in International Journals (e.g., IEEE Transaction on Knowledge and Data Engineering, IEEE Internet Computing, IEEE Transactions on Education, Computers in Human Behavior, Interactive Learning Environments, Journal of Knowledge Management, Journal of Computer Assisted Learning, etc.).

Jose Emilio Labra Gayo obtained his PhD in Computer Science Engineering in 2001 at the University of Oviedo with distinction. Since 2004, he is the Dean of the School of Computer Science Engineering at the University of Oviedo and he is also the main researcher of the Semantic Web research group WESO. The group collaborates is focused on practical applications of semantic web and linked open data and has been involved in several projects with industrial partners and public administrations. Apart from teaching at the University of Oviedo, He has been regularly invited to teach in several doctorate or postgraduate courses in the Universidad Técnica Federico Santa María, in Chile, or the Universidad Pontificia de Salamanca, in Madrid, Spain. His research interests are Semantic Web technologies and Programming Languages and Web Engineering, where he has published a number of papers in selected conferences and journals. He participates in several committees, such asthe European Semantic Web Conference, the International Conference on Web Engineering, and the International Workshop on Social Data on the Web.

* * *

Jose María Alvarez received a Master's Degree in Computer Science (2007) and aBachelor's Degree in Computer Science (2005) from the University of Oviedo. In June 2008, he was rewarded with the "Best Final Degree Project in Computer Science" by the Official Association of Computer Engineers of Asturias (Spain) thanks to his project "Activation of concepts in ontologies through the Spreading ActivationTechnique". From 2005 to 2010, he worked at the R&D Department in the Semantic Technologies area within CTIC Foundation; more specifically, he worked in projects related to Semantic Web services, rule based systems, search systems, linked data, and others. During this stage, he participated in several research projects in different research programmes: PRAVIA project-PCTI Asturias cod. IE05-172 (Regional scope), PRIMA-Plan Avanza-cod. TSI-020302-2008-32 (National scope) and ONTORULE-FP7 cod. 231875 (European scope). He now holds a position as Assistant Professor at the Department of Computer Science within the University of Oviedo and he is also senior researcher at WESO Research Group (University of Oviedo). He has defended his PhD dissertation (2012) about e-procurement and Linked Data supervised by Dr. José Emilio Labra Gayo.

Lucas de Ramos Araújo holds a degree in Computer Science from the Federal University of the Juiz de Fora (UFJF) in Brazil, and now works with commercial semantic web applications.

Elena Baralis has been a full professor at the Dipartimento di Automatica e Informatica of the Politecnico di Torino since January 2005. She holds a Master's Degree in Electrical Engineering and a PhD in Computer Engineering, both from Politecnico di Torino. Her current research interests are in the field of database systems and data mining; more specifically on mining algorithms for very large databases and sensor/stream data analysis. She has published over 80 papers in international journals and conference proceedings. She has served on the program committees or as area chair of several international conferences and workshops, including VLDB, IEEE ICDM, ACM SAC, DaWak, ACM CIKM, and PKDD.

Giulia Bruno holds a Master's Degree and a PhD in Computer Engineering from Politecnico di Torino, Italy. She is currently working in the field of database and data mining. Her activity is focused on anomaly detection in temporal and medical databases and on geographical information system development. She is also investigating data mining techniques for clinical analysis, particularly the extraction of medical pathways from electronic patients' records and classification of physiological signals to detect unsafe events in patients' monitoring, and microarray data analysis to select genes relevant for tumor classification.

Tania Cerquitelli has been an assistant professor at the Dipartimento di Automatica e Informatica of the Politecnico di Torino since October 2011. She received a Master's Degree in Computer Engineering and a PhD from the Politecnico di Torino in Italy, and a Master's Degree in Computer Science from the Universidad De Las Américas Puebla. Her research interests include the design of innovative algorithms to efficiently perform large-scale data mining, novel and efficient data mining techniques for sensor readings, and innovative algorithms to extract high level abstraction of the mined knowledge (e.g., generalized association rules). She has been a teaching assistant in different databases and data mining courses at the Politecnico di Torino since 2004-2005.

Silvia Chiusano has been an assistant professor at the Dipartimento di Automatica e Informatica of the Politecnico di Torino since January 2004. She holds a Master's Degree and a PhD in Computer Engineering, both from Politecnico di Torino. Her current research interests are in the areas of data mining and database systems, in particular integration of data mining techniques into relational DBMSs, and classification of structured and sequential data.

Alessandro Fiori received a European PhD from Politecnico di Torino, Italy. He has been a project manager at the Institute for Cancer Research and Treatment (IRCC) of Candiolo, Italy since January 2012. His research interests are in the field of data mining, in particular bioinformatics and text mining. His activity is focused on the development of information systems and analysis frameworks oriented to the management and integration of biological and molecular data. His research activities are also devoted to text summarization and social network analysis.

Dominik Fiser is a former student in the Department of Software Engineering, Charles University, Prague. In his master's thesis, he designed framework for assisted annotation of websites. His interests include searching with Semantic information, web resource annotations, and web development.

María N. Moreno García is Associate Professor at the University of Salamanca in Spain. She is the head of the Data Mining Research Group of the University of Salamanca . She has published more than 100 papers in international journals and conference proceedings. She is co-author of several book chapters and has co-edited national and international books. She is a reviewer of journals indexed by ISI Journal citation reports and she has been member of the scientific committee of numerous international conferences. Her research interests are in the areas of Web Mining, Semantic Web and software engineering.

Alberto Grand has been a PhD student at the Dipartimento di Automatica e Informatica of the Politecnico di Torino since January 2010. He holds a Master's Degree in Computer Engineering from Politecnico di Torino and a Master's Degree in Computer and Electrical Engineering from the University of Illinois, Chicago. His current research interests are in the field of data mining, with particular emphasis on large-scale data mining. He is also currently involved in the development of information systems and analysis frameworks oriented to the management and integration of biological and molecular data at the Institute for Cancer Research and Treatment (IRCC) of Candiolo, Italy.

Antonio Garrote Hernández is a PhD student at the Universidad de Salamanca. His main research area is linked data APIs, trying to combine the architectural principles of RESTful architectures and the core concepts of linked data and Semantic Web technologies. He has also been involved in the design and implementation of open source libraries like RDFStore-JS, making it possible for developers to apply linked data technologies in their own web projects. He has presented different papers at linked data and REST design conferences and workshops, such as W3C's Web Conference or the First International Workshop on RESTful Design.

José Emilio Labra has been the Associate Professor in the Department of Computer Science at the University of Oviedo. since 1992. In 2001, he obtained a PhD in Philosophy in Information and Computer Science with the dissertation "Developing Modular Language Processors through Reusable Semantic Specifications." This researchwas awarded with the Extraordinary Doctorate Award. Since 2004, he has been the Dean of the Computer Engineering School at the University of Oviedo. From a research point view, he is focused on (but not restricted to) the application and development of innovative solutions with Semantic technologies. In this context he is the main researcher of the WESO Research Group at the Department of Computer Science and he is involved in several research projects at different scopes: regional, national and European. Finally, he is the author of more than 50 scientific publications and member, reviewer, and part of the program committee of the main conferences and journals in his research area like the International Conference on Web Engineering, Social Data on The Web, Workshop on Web Services or ACM. He is currently editor of different special issues of the IGI Global journal.

Matthias Lange studied computer science at the Otto-von-Guericke University in Magdeburg, Germany. In 1999, he received a Master's Degree. In 2006 he received aPh.D. in Computer Science from the Otto-von-Guericke University in Magdeburg. Between 1999 and 2001 he worked as scientific assistant at the University Magdeburg in the Institute of Technical Information Systems in Bioinformtics research projects with focus to database integration. Between 2002 and 2006 he worked at Leibniz Institute of Plant Genetics and Crop Plant Research Gatersleben (IPK), Germany, as Bioinformatician in research projects with focus to information systems and data networks. Since 2007 he has worked as postdoc in the research group Bioinformatics and Information Technology at the same institute. His research focus isinformation retrieval, search engine technology, and primary data management. Furthermore, he coordinates the central lab information systems in the IPK, is responsible for IPK datacenter activities in the frame of the DataCite consortium, and works in the EU research project to build up a trans-national data infrastructure for plant genomics data.

Ivo Lasek is a PhD student at the Department of Software Engineering, Charles University, Prague, and Faculty of Information Technology, Czech Technical University, Prague. He is a member of SWING Research Group. His research interests include Semantic Web and Linked Data and Information Filtering (particularly news filtering). He is a co-founder of a popular Czech Web price comparison portal.

Salvador Lima received his PhD in Computer Science from the Universidade Portucalense Infante D. Henrique do Porto (Portugal) in 2011 and earned his M.S. in Computer Science from the Universidade Nova de Lisboa (Portugal) in 1995. He is a Professor Adjunto in the Escola Superior de Tecnologia e Gestão of the Instituto Politécnico de Viana do Castelo, having taught several disciplines in the area of software engineering, namely algorithms, data structure, programming languages, and modeling. His interest areas lie in software engineering, Web engineering, Semantic Web, ontological engineering, Semantic technologies in tourism and social sciences in the context of new technologies.

Hendrik Mehlhorn studied bioinformatics at the Martin Luther University in Halle-Wittenberg, Germany, and is currently a PhD candidate there. His main research interests aim at pattern recognition, sequence analysis, and the integration of biological networks. Currently, he is working as a research associate at the Leibniz Institute of Plant Genetics and Crop Plant Research Gatersleben (IPK Gatersleben), Germany.

Rubens Nascimento Melo is a Senior Professor and Researcher in the field of Databases at the Computer Science Department of the Pontifical Catholic University of Rio de Janeiro, PUC-Rio. He holds a B.S. in Electronic Engineering (1968), a

M.S. (1971), and a PhD (1976) in Computer Science from the Air Force Institute of Technology (ITA) in Sao Paulo. Currently, he is Associate Professor at PUC-Rio, where he leads the Database Research Lab (TecBD). One of his current interests is the application of Database Technology to distance learning. In this field he has also served as Director of the Centre of Distance Education under the Vice-Rectory for Academic Affairs of PUC-Rio.

José Moreira received his PhD in Computer Science and Networks from the École Nationale Supérieure des Télécommunications de Paris (France) and the Faculdade de Engenharia da Universidade do Porto (Portugal) in 2001. He is currently an Assistant Professor at the Department of Electronics, Telecommunications and Informatics of the Universidade de Aveiro and a researcher at IEETA, a non-profit R&D institute affiliated with the same university. His background includes programming languages, data structures, and databases. His main research interests cover spatiotemporal database systems and geographical information systems. He is also interested in Web Semantics and spatiotemporal data mining.

Ahsan Morshed is an Information Management Specialist in the Knowledge and Capacity for Development (OEKC) Group at the Food and Agriculture Organization of UN (FAO). Before joining FAO, Mr. Morshed was a PhD student at the University of Trento in Italy, a Research Developer at ECTRL Solutions **in** Trento, Italy, as well as an Assistant Programmer at the Bangladesh Open University, in Gazipur, Bangladesh. During his career, Mr. Morshed has focused on semantic web technology, ontologies, taxonomies, thesauri, information retrieval, and text classification, especially as it affects digital libraries and Linked Open Data. He is the author of several scientific papers. His current work addresses the question of "KOS mapping" within the agricultural related information domain, in particularly at FAO addressing the AGROVOC thesaurus and the AGROVOC Concept Server. Mr. Morshed has won numerous awards, including the Graduate Scholarship from the University of Trento, Italy, as well as the Summer School Scholarship from the Free University of Bozen-Bolzano in Italy, and also the Junior Scholarship from the Ministry of Primary Education in Bangladesh. He is a member of the Institute of Engineers in Bangladesh, an associate member of the Bangladesh Computer Society, as well as a member of the program committee DESWeb2010 STAKE 2011, MTSR2011, SerSy2012. Mr. Morshed earned a B.S. in Computer Science and Engineering from the Ahsanullah University of Science and Technology in Bangladesh and a M.S. in Engineering and Information Management System (EMIS) from the Royal Institute of Technology in Sweden.

Martin Necasky is an assistant professor at the Department of Software Engineering, Charles University, in Prague. He is a member of the SemWeX and XRG research group. His research interests include conceptual modeling, integrity constraints, data semantics and similarity, data integration, data evolution, and adaptability and service-oriented architectures.

Ladislav Peska is a PhD student in Software Engineeringat Charles University,in Prague. His research interests include recommender systems–design, algorithms, usage, testing,, user preferences and implicit user feedback, social networking, and the process of Web semantization.

Luis Polo has been the coordinator of the Semantic Technologies Unit in CTIC since 2007. His activity involves the management of CTIC participation in research projects at a national and European level (especially FP7 calls), and the analysis and design of Semantic-oriented solutions for business needs based on W3C standards. He has also participated in the Rule Interchange Format W3C Working Group. Furthermore, he is very active in dissemination activities with 20 publications focused on the application of Semantic technologies to problems in the industry.

Alejandro Rodríguez-González, PhD, is a Post-Doctoral Researcher of Bioinformatics Group at the Centre for Plant Biotechnology and Genomics (UPM-INIA), Polytechnic University of Madrid. His main research interests are the Semantic Web, artificial intelligence, and biomedical informatics field, with a particular interest in the creation of medical diagnosis systems. He has a degree in Computer Science, a M.S. in Computer Science and Technology in the Specialty of Artificial Intelligence, a M.S in Engineering Decision Systems and a PhD in Computer Science. He has published several papers in international journals and edited various special issues in high quality journals. He also has participated in the organization of several workshops in top international conferences such as the International Semantic Web Conference, the Extended Semantic Web Conference, and others.

Emilio Rubiera is a philologist at the Semantic Technologies Unit within CTIC Foundation. Since 2005 he has worked on projects related to Semantic Web technologies, documental databases, rule based systems, search systems, linked data, and others. He is also author of several publications in the Semantic Web area, including conferences, journals, and books. Currently, he is developing his PhD about lexical resources and linked data.

Kamaljeet Sandhu is a Senior Lecturer of Accounting and Information Systems at the School of Business, Economics and Public Policy of the University of New England. He earned his PhD in Information Systems from Deakin University in Melbourne. His teaching and research expertise are in electronic services and services management at universities, corporate governance, accounting information systems, management accounting, asset management, and e-learning.

Uwe Scholz studied Computer Science in Köthen/Anhalt and Magdeburg, Germany. In 1995 he got his Master's Degree in Computer Science from the Otto-von-Guericke-University in Magdeburg, Germany. In 2002 he earned a PhD in Computer Science from the Otto-von-Guericke-University in Magdeburg. Between 1995 and 1996 he worked as part of the scientific staff in a third-party funded project of the Country Saxony-Anhalt "New Production Systems - Experimental Factory", Institute of Technical and Business Information Systems at Otto-von-Guericke-University. From 1996 to 2001, he was employed as part of the scientific staff at the research group in Bioinformatics/Medical Informatics, at the Institute of Technical and Business Information Systems.. Between 2001 and 2003 he worked as Bioinformatician at Leibniz Institute of Plant Genetics and Crop Plant Research in Gatersleben, Germany. Since 2003 he has been the head of the research group Bioinformatics and Information Technology at the same institute. In his research he worked on the development of molecular biological databases and data integration of different data domains (e.g., sequence, marker, transcript, metabolic, or phenotypic information). The sequence analysis is an additional research interest of his. He worked in the assembly of next-generation sequencing data of crop plant genomes and transcript based sequences.

Falk Schreiber obtained a PhD (2001, Dr. rer. nat.) and a habilitation in Computer Science (2006) from the University of Passau in Germany. –From 2001 to 2002 he worked as a Research Fellow and Lecturer at the University of Sydney in Australia. Since 2003, he has been head of a research group at the Leibniz Institute of Plant Genetics and Crop Plant Research (IPK) in Gatersleben, Germany. In 2007, he was appointed Professor of Bioinformatics at the Martin Luther University in Halle-Wittenberg, Germany and Bioinformatics Coordinator at the IPK. Falk Schreiber's research focuses on the modeling, analysis, and visualization of biological networks in their spatial and temporal embedding as well as the visual analytics of multimodal and multidimensional biological data.

Sean Wolfgand Matsui Siqueira is an Assistant Professor of Applied Informatics at theFederal University of the State of Rio de Janeiro (UNIRIO) in Brazil, where he teaches courses in databases, information systems, and Semantic Web.

He holds a M.S. (1999) and a PhD (2005) in Computer Science, both from the Pontifical Catholic University of Rio de Janeiro (PUC-Rio) in Brazil. His research interests include knowledge representation, semantic web, ontologies, information integration;,semantic models, user models, e-learning, social web, and music information systems. He has experience in the computer science area, with focus on information systems and technology-enhanced Learning. He has participated in some international research projects and has published more than 70 papers for conferences, journals, and books.

Jairo Francisco de Souza is an Assistant Professor at of Computer Science at theFederal University of the Juiz de Fora (UFJF) inBrazil, where he teaches courses in Software Engineering and Semantic Web. He holds a M.S. (2007) from Federal University of Rio de Janeiro (UFRJ) and he is a PhD candidate in the Pontifical Catholic University of Rio de Janeiro (PUC-Rio), Brazil, both in the computer science area. His research interests include knowledge representation, Semantic Web, ontologies, information integration, and semantic models.

Peter Vojtas is a Computer Science professor in the Department of Software Engineering atCharles University.. He also has a M.S. Suma Cum Laude in Theoretical Cybernetics and aa PhD in Mathematical Logic from Charles University. He got Professor Titulaire in Mathematical Informatics from the President of Slovak Republic and Doctor of Science from Czech Academy of Science. His research interests include computational intelligence, connecting Web to the user, process of the Web semantization, modeling, learning, querying user preferences uncertainty and preferences in databases and indexes, among others. He was advisor of more than 10 PhD students who successfully defended their theses.

Index

A

Academic Institution Internal Structure Ontology (AIISO) 111
Ambiguous Tokens 75
Apache Stanbol 195
Association Rule Mining 35, 156, 159-161, 171, 174-175
automated support 151

B

bag-of-word (BOW) 163
bioinformatics 58-59, 61, 63, 77-80, 92
bioinformatics domain 92
biomedical literature 59, 79

C

cellular pathways 59
Collaborative Semantic Services 2, 107, 200
Common Procurement Vocabulary (CPV) 9
Comprehensive Knowledge Archive Network (CKAN) 5, 202
consumer behaviour 183, 190
Context Match (CTXmatch) 98
controlled vocabulary (CV) 84-85
Czech Republic 28, 31-33, 37

D

D2RQ maps 142, 144-146, 148, 151
data collection 182

Data Exchange 35, 92, 197
Data Linkage Graphs (DLG) 62
data mining 157-160, 163, 173-174, 176, 178-179
data pre-processing 158, 160, 163-166
data sources 22, 32-34, 43-48, 53-54, 60, 78, 92, 98, 101, 132-133, 140-141, 144-146, 150, 158, 192-193, 195, 209, 222
data warehouses 60-61, 64
DBpedia Spotlight 35, 54
DNA sequences 58-59

E

e-commerce 6, 8, 14, 28, 34-35, 152
e-government 3, 6, 39-41, 53, 55, 107, 129, 152, 200-202
e-health 3, 6, 106-107, 200-202
Electronic Government 40-41, 54-55
e-procurement 1, 3-6, 9, 14, 21, 24-26, 106-109, 114, 118, 120, 128-129, 200, 223
e-services system
    confidence 183, 188-189
    finding information 183
    interacting awareness 183, 187
    movement within 183, 185-186, 189
    understanding 184
European Commission (EC) 4, 108
European Regional Development Fund (EFDR) 3, 107
Extensible Markup Language (XML) 134

F

Facebook 31
Flickr 93, 102
Foundation for Intelligent Physical Agents
    (FIPA) 135
frequent itemsets 159, 161, 166-169, 171-
    172, 175-176, 178

G

gene sequence 59
genome 59, 62, 78
Google Maps 93

H

Hadoop Distributed File System (HDFS)
    193
harmonisation space 134
Hierarchical relationships 5, 9
HTML 24, 26, 32-33, 41, 43-51, 53-55, 57,
    62, 80, 101-102, 121-122, 129, 131,
    158, 174, 176, 190, 195, 223, 225
HTML Representation 49-51, 53
human annotation 30, 38
hyper-media information 91

I

IDPredictor 60, 73, 75-77, 81
infoboxes 30, 158
Information Society Technologies Program
    (IST Program) 134
integration 4, 22, 25-26, 34, 37, 41, 52, 59-
    61, 64, 76, 80, 92, 101, 104, 108, 119,
    132-133, 136-137, 140, 144-146, 150,
    158, 176, 192, 202
interactive information 92
international students 181-189
item filtering 172
itemset length 172
itemset mining 161, 166, 171, 174, 179
itemset support 166, 172

J

Java framework 195

K

knowledge filtering 158, 161, 171-172
knowledge organization systems (KOS) 5

L

LAPSI project 204, 224
Library of Congress Subject Headings
    (LCSH) 98
life science databases 59-60, 62, 64, 77, 79
Linked Data 5, 14, 23, 119, 202-203, 205,
    216
Linked Data practices 39, 52
LinkedIn 31
Linking Open Data (LOD) 3, 107, 202
loosely coupled components 195

M

Methods on Linked Data for E-Procure-
    ment Applying Semantics (MOLD-
    EAS) 9, 114
Mondeca's Intelligent Topic Manager
    (Mondeca's ITM) 135
multilingual 5, 10, 13-14, 23, 86, 119, 128,
    218
multimedia data 92
MySQL 47

N

neural network 65-66, 69-71, 76
Non Governmental Organization (NGO)
    46

O

Ontological layers 147
ontological schemes 134
OpenCalais 35, 38, 122
Open Corporates 120-121
Open Data 1-3, 6-7, 11, 21, 23, 33, 44, 52-
    53, 55, 84, 93-94, 98, 100, 103, 105,
    107-108, 117, 119, 128-129, 199-200,
    203-206, 213, 217, 222-223, 225
Open Government Data (OGD) 5, 108, 203
OpenTravel Alliance 134, 136, 153

P

part-of-speech (POS) 164, 167, 180
persistent structure 156, 180
Product Ontology (PO) 14
Product Scheme Classification (PSC) 1, 6, 8-10, 12, 14-23, 117
protein 58-59, 62-64, 74, 76-79
psycholinguistic research 86
public procurement 1-6, 9-10, 16, 18-19, 21, 23, 32-34, 105, 107, 109, 114, 116-118, 120, 122, 124-129, 203, 223

Q

quasi-ontology 140-142
query operators 60-61

R

Raw Data Tokens 76
RDF Query Language (SPARQL) 142
Resource Description Framework (RDF) 55, 132, 178, 202
rule based systems (RBS) 3, 107

S

search engines 29, 44, 61, 77, 87, 110, 126, 158
search queries 87
Semantic Annotator 30-31, 36
semantic architectures 2, 107, 200
Semantic Matcher (S-match) 98
Semantic Model for Tourism (SeMoT) 132, 137, 150
semantic technologies 2-3, 106-108, 114, 119, 150, 153, 198, 200
Semantic Web Rule Language (SWRL) 142
social network 28-29, 31, 36-37, 93
spatial domain 136-137
spatial information 132, 152
Spreading Activation (SA) 3, 10, 107, 110
SQL format 89
Standard International Trade Classification (SITC) 9

Statistical Data and Metadata Exchange Vocabulary (SDMX) 204
Subject Specific Controlled Vocabulary (SSCV) 87
Suboptimal Tokenization 75
sub-websites 185

T

tagging 86, 93, 130, 164, 180
Telecommunication Union (ITU) 203
temporal domain 136-137
temporal information 132
term frequency 161, 180
thematic domain 136, 139
third party annotation 29-30, 36
third-party systems 40
tourism 3, 107, 132-140, 150, 152-154
touristic information 132-133, 136, 140, 144, 146, 150
traditional vocabulary 89

U

Uniform Resource Identifier (URI) 12-13, 15-16, 23-24, 35, 42-43, 45, 48, 50-51, 89, 98, 117, 122, 142, 193, 195-196, 202, 205-206, 211-213, 223, 225
Uniform Resource Locator (URL) 7, 47, 63, 80, 89, 110, 173, 204, 209
user software agent 30

V

Very Short Tokens 76

W

web application 194, 196
web content annotation 38
Web'ifying 88
web information extraction 28-30, 34, 36, 38
web intelligence 37, 93, 103
web semantization 29, 36-37
Webware 141-142, 153-155
WESO 2, 19-20, 27, 106, 123, 131, 200, 217, 222

Wikipedia 29-30, 36, 80, 98, 130, 156-159,
    162-163, 166, 171-172, 174-175,
    177-179
World Tourism Organization (WTO)
    thesaurus 135
World Wide Web Consortium (W3C) 135

Y

YouTube 91, 104

Z

Zemanta 35, 38